D1522660

HOW
WAR BEGAN

KEITH F.
OTTERBEIN

Texas A&M
University Press
COLLEGE
STATION

Library of Congress Cataloging-in-Publication Data

Otterbein, Keith F.
  How war began / Keith F. Otterbein. — 1st ed.
    p. cm. — (Texas A&M University anthropology series ; no. 10)
  Includes bibliographical references and index.
  ISBN 1-58544-329-8 (cloth : alk. paper) — ISBN 1-58544-330-1 (pbk. : alk. paper)
  1. War.   2. Warfare, Prehistoric.   3. War, Causes of.   4. War and society.
  I. Title.   II. Series.
  GN497.078   2004
  303.6'6 — dc22
                                                    2004003679

How War Began

For my wife
ON THE
FORTIETH YEAR
OF OUR
COLLABORATION

Contents

Figures

Preface

Much of my knowledge of warfare came from books that I read before I was fifteen years old. A favorite book of mine from childhood, which I still have, is *The Book of Indians* by Holling C. Holling. I read about the lives of Indian children in four regions. I learned that the warfare of the Indians of the Northeast, the Great Plains, the Northwest Coast, and the Southwest of the North American continent was serious. These Native Americans attacked each other's villages and inflicted heavy casualties when they could. For example, a girl in the Northeast alerts her village to an advancing enemy war party. In the ensuing battle the enemy raiders are annihilated, with high casualties to both sides. Or, a boy in the Southwest spots enemy raiders climbing the mesa on which his village is located. By prying a boulder loose and rolling it down upon the attackers, he nearly wipes out the enemy.[1] Plains Indian warfare was a staple of my youth. As a third grader I organized an expedition to a wooded area to get the poles to build a tepee to use in a class play. A classmate had a genuine Plains Indian war bonnet, which I wore.[2]

I learned that the Roman legion and the Macedonian phalanx were awesome military forces. In junior high and high school I took Latin. In second-year Latin the class read *Caesar's Gallic War*. A year later I read Harold Lamb's *Alexander of Macedon*. I remember the end of World War II and the Korean War—an era of deadly warfare.

Much of what I have read about warfare since I was fifteen I now know to be incorrect. War has been reformulated. For example, the warfare of native peoples has been renamed "ritual war."[3] Guerrilla warfare—once deemed a deadly form of combat that had brought to power Mao Tse-tung in China, Fidel Castro in Cuba, and Ho Chi Minh in Vietnam—has become "low intensity conflict" (LIC). War itself has been defined by members of the Department of Defense to exclude killing—by defining war as the pursuit of national interests. If civilians are killed, that is called "collateral damage."

Warfare is serious. It is armed combat. Combatants and noncombatants alike are killed. Warfare occurred in prehistory, in history, and it occurs at the present. Using euphemisms such as ritual war, LIC, or collateral damage does not alter the lethality of war. When someone is killed, whether it be by club, missile, or explosive, a family or kinship

Keith F. Otterbein at age 6.

group experiences a loss. Fancy terms do not alter this reality. And if the focus is upon the individual, that person's death is real—as is the probable agony that accompanied it—regardless of how war is defined.[4]

How War Began attempts to resolve a dispute between those who argue that war existed in early human history and those who say that it arose only when states developed. The former group sees early hunters engaging in warfare, warfare which continued to develop. It achieved full form after the first states appeared. The latter group denies that hunters and early agriculturalists had war and instead sees war slowly arising as steps toward statehood took place. In the synthesis set forth in this book, both groups win. The former group, which I call hawks, gets to keep its hunting hypothesis, and the latter group, which I call doves, gets to keep its peaceful early villages. I am in both the hawk and the dove camps. My argument for sporadic early warfare and intense warfare in the late Upper Paleolithic places me with the hawks. My argument for long periods of peace among settled gatherers and early agriculturalists places me with the doves. I argue that early hunter warfare declined in many regions and did not reemerge until after the first states formed. Some hawks may dispute the decline in hunter warfare after the extinction of large animals, and some doves may dispute the notion that early hunters ever had war. True believers among the hawks will think I am wrong about the peaceful cultivators; true believers among the doves will think I am wrong about the existence of early warfare. I would like these members of each group to withhold judgment. I believe that my synthesis takes the essence of each approach and combines the two into a satisfying theory. I hope to appeal to the nonideologues in both camps.

Books by military writers fall into at least three categories: descriptions of great battles or wars written by participants, generals, or historians; principles of war written by generals and strategists; and analytic studies of war written by historians and social scientists. *How War Began* falls into the third category. It is an attempt to understand the origins of war. It is written for those who are interested in warfare, whether they be military buffs or individuals who seek to understand the past and the present. Many pieces of data germane to the subject were not known in the 1950s and 1960s but are available today. Even now its writing may be precipitate. I believe, though, that the data are sufficient to support the interpretation presented in *How War Began*. In this book, I have presented a new interpretation; hence, the book is also for my fellow anthropologists, social scientists, and historians as well. And the book is for my students, both past and future.

How did war begin? Answering the question has forced me to focus upon several other perennial questions. To preview, I would like to note that the following questions, usually considered of great significance in anthropology and the other social sciences, may be answered by this book. How did the Neanderthals become extinct? How did plants become domesticated? How did the state arise? Indeed, the spread of *Homo sapiens,* the origin of war, the origin of agriculture, and the origin of the state are inextricably intertwined. Answering any of the questions required answering them all. All four questions have been answered, I believe, by *How War Began.*

Recently anthropologist Robert Carneiro, at the end of a book summarizing the history of evolutionism in cultural anthropology, makes the following assertion: "After all, the most salient feature in human history is the fact that, beginning as small, simple Paleolithic bands, human societies were eventually transformed into the large, powerful, and complex states of today. And tracing the course of this transformation—this *evolution*—and laying bare the factors and forces that brought it about, remains the most challenging and rewarding task any anthropologist can undertake."[5] *How War Began* deals with the factors and forces that underlay this transformation.

Readers have a right to know who I am. When I pick up a book, the first thing I try to find out is who the author is. Dust jackets often provide that information; university libraries typically throw them out. Acknowledgments often give clues as to the author's identity by telling us where he or she studied and who assisted with the project. I now provide a brief autobiographical sketch that focuses on my longtime interest in warfare.

My father had a rifle range in the basement. In northwestern Pennsylvania, where I grew up, hunting was and still is a way of life for many. I shot my BB gun indoors in the winter and rifles and shotguns outdoors on my father's farm in the summer. As a child during World War II, I became aware that warfare was an omnipresent feature of life. In third grade, I became fascinated with American Indian warfare. By high school I became interested in military history. At Pennsylvania State University I veered away from military history and into archaeology, one of the major subfields of anthropology.[6] In graduate school, first at the University of Pennsylvania, then the University of Pittsburgh, I focused on cultural anthropology. In August, 1961, after my second field trip to the Bahama Islands, where I studied family organization, I read an article on warfare written by an anthropologist. I realized that my interest in military history could be combined with my interest in cultural anthropology.[7] I received the Ph.D. in 1963.[8] For my next field site I chose the Mandara Mountains of northeastern Nigeria, where I focused on the tribal group known as the Higi.[9] That was 1965; I was a faculty member at the University of Kansas. In 1966, I moved to the University at Buffalo, where I have been ever since, conducting research on the Bahama Islands and on warfare. Thirty-three times I have taught a course on warfare to University at Buffalo undergraduates.

For years my style manual has been *The Elements of Style* by Strunk and White (1959). To add interest—I hope—I have included in this book some personal anecdotal material and the occasional ironic remark. These asides have largely been confined to notes. If you, the reader, do not like these, skip the notes.

How War Began originated in an article published in *Critical Review* in 1997. The editor, Jeffrey Friedman, at the suggestion of Brian Ferguson, solicited a review of Lawrence Keeley's *War before Civilization*. My review became a summary of the origin and early evolution of warfare. *How War Began,* however, is not an expansion of that article, which offered a single origin of war. It is an entirely new work that proposes two separate origins for war. It draws upon that article, in particular the identification of the hawk and dove camps, and many other books and articles that I have written. *How War Began* presents both a new thesis—new to my work and new to the social sciences—and a synthesis of much of my writing on feuding and warfare.

Numerous individuals have helped in various ways in the development of this book. First and foremost is my wife, Charlotte Swanson Otterbein, my lifelong collaborator and companion. Conrad Kottak helped at an early stage in the selection of the title. Rob Williams helped in delineating the scope of the book. Bob Dentan, Bill Engelbrecht, Andrew Shryock, Ted Steegmann, Sherm Milisauskas, Mike Alvard, Charlaine Coburn, and Claudio Cioffi-Revilla provided sources and discussions. Alan LaFlamme read the first draft of the manuscript. Beth Judge, Elka Kazmierczak, and Peter Storkerson have given help with illustrative materials. Carina Iezzi drew the atlatl and maps. Bruce Dickson directed me to his university's press. Gentry Steele and an anonymous reviewer provided sources in the final stage. Texas A&M University Press staff guided the manuscript through the many stages of the publication process, and Maureen Creamer Bemko performed careful copyediting. The index was prepared by University at Buffalo librarian Charles D'Aniello.

Brief sections of the manuscript have been presented in seminars held at the annual meetings of the Human Relations Area Files in New Haven, presided over by Mel Ember and Carol Ember.

I read a book backward. Why? Authors, like mystery writers, sneak up on their conclusion. I want the conclusion first. Thus, I have placed the conclusion—the thesis—in the first chapter, in the section titled "The Thesis." Reading and rereading this section should help keep the overall picture in front of the reader. Internal summaries that inform the reader where we are now and where we have been I largely avoid, although I repeat central points where appropriate.

How War Began

I
Introduction

How did war begin? In this book I argue for two separate origins. My conclusion stems from the identification of two types of military organization, one of which, I believe, can be found two million years ago, at the dawn of humankind, and the other five thousand years ago. It is the thesis of this book that early warfare arose first among hunting peoples, who sometimes had lethal encounters with other hunting peoples, and later among peaceful agricultural peoples, whose societies first achieved statehood and then proceeded to embark upon military conquests. The situation that gave rise to the first origin occurred all over the earth— wherever early humans hunted in groups near other groups of hunters; the second occurred independently at different times in four regions, regions in which the first states arose. These two types of military organizations differ in personnel and in the type of armed combat in which they engaged.

Both of these types of military organizations engaged in modes of combat that were equally deadly forms of warfare. From the time of their separate origins, the combatants in each type of military organization tried to kill their opponents, and often did. They engaged in serious warfare. Although it may be difficult for some readers to comprehend, there are "schools" in the social sciences that view the warfare of many nonliterate peoples as nonserious. *How War Began* challenges these views. To the first school belong military historians who focus on warrior traditions. The warrior is seen as an honorable person, and combat is viewed as being bound by rules. The warrior fights for glory and honor; killing the opponent is of secondary importance. The focus of research, however, should be on military organizations, not on warriors or their traditions (see the section titled "Warrior Traditions" in this chapter). To the second school belong the doves, scholars who are usually pacifists, who deny the existence of both early warfare and warfare among nonliterate peoples. This view of reality is incorrect (see the section title "Hawks and Doves" in chapter 2). The third school is composed of scholars, mostly military historians, who erroneously believe that the warfare of nonliterate peoples (which they term "primitive warfare") is so surrounded by ritual that casualties are infrequent and fatalities rare (see the section "Ritual Warfare—An Illusion" in chapter 2).

3

Military Organizations

Warfare consists of the activities of military organizations, groups of men—under the direction of leaders—who engage in armed combat. From the earliest times, these three components of military organizations can be identified: leaders, groups of men, and armed combat. Occasionally women are formed into military units; it occurred in the African kingdom of Dahomey in the eighteenth and nineteenth centuries.[1] Further, the social and political organization of a people— whether it be a modern industrial nation, one of the first states five thousand years ago, or a hunting-gathering band in prehistory or in recent centuries—spawns and maintains the military organization of that people.

Military organizations engage in armed combat in order to obtain certain goals. These goals include subjugation and tribute, land, plunder, trophies and honors, defense, and revenge. Military organizations differ from other social organizations in that the goals or objectives they pursue can be achieved only at the expense of other independent political entities, technically referred to as political communities, by means of armed force—warfare.[2] Thus, the activities of military organizations are usually directed at the military organizations of other political communities. When two military organizations engage in an armed combat, the outcome—victory for one, defeat for the other—will depend upon the efficiency of their respective military practices. A victorious military organization makes a political community militarily successful and increases its likelihood of survival in interpolitical community conflicts. The political community with a successful military organization will almost undoubtedly expand its territory.

Basic Types of Military Organizations

Military organizations are typically either nonprofessional, composed of part-time personnel, or professional, composed of full-time personnel. In small-scale societies nearly every able-bodied man is, at one time in his life, a member of an active military organization, but that military organization may be involved in war only a few days out of the year and perhaps not every year. Thus, for much of the time these nonprofessional military personnel are engaged not in military activities but in the subsistence activities of their societies, such as hunting, gathering, fishing, or farming. On the other hand, in large-scale societies the military organizations are composed of professional, full-time personnel. Professionals, in contrast to nonprofessionals, devote substantial time during early adulthood to intensive training, which may involve not only practice in the use of weapons but also practice in performing maneuvers. They may be members of groups comprising all males of a given age, of military societies, or of standing armies, or they may serve as mercenaries employed for a specific purpose.[3]

The vast majority of small-scale societies have military organizations composed only of nonprofessionals. These military organizations are likely to be fraternal interest groups—localized groups of related males who can resort to aggressive measures when the interests of their members are threatened. Fraternal interest groups constitute the vengeance parties that engage in feuding in small-scale societies as well as in modern polities, and in small-scale societies they form the backbone of military organizations. As a cause of war, fraternal interest groups play an important role in all societies except those with an advanced level of sociopolitical complexity—the state. In bands, tribes, and chiefdoms, fraternal interest groups provide the membership core of most military organizations. The leader of a fraternal interest group is a senior member; he often accompanies the group on raids. The ambush and the line form the basic pattern of tactics for these military organizations.

At the state level of sociopolitical complexity, professional military organizations play an important role in producing interstate violence. They are led by officers, who are typically members of the upper class. Officers, particularly the senior officers, may well be members of the aristocracy. Indeed, the leader of the state may be the supreme commander. The common soldiers are usually drawn from the lower class and are likely to have been conscripted; they have had to become members of the military organization whether they wanted to or not. These conscripts are usually placed in units of massed infantry. The troops march and drill as units under the direction of officers. On the battlefield the units are positioned side by side. A coercive command structure forces soldiers to fight even when outnumbered. Corporal and capital punishment can be used to enforce discipline.[4] Battles and sieges are the two major tactics of warfare employed by professional military organizations.

Warrior Traditions

The approach set forth above—that military organizations are the key to understanding warfare—contrasts with a recently developed approach that emphasizes the warrior and the warrior tradition, rather than the military organization in which the warrior operates. By stressing the individual combatant, both writer and reader can lose sight of the central role that military organizations play in their societies. Scholars who focus on the warrior have produced books with such titles as *The Antique Drums of War, Women Warriors, Demonic Males,* and *Blood Rites.* In *A History of Warfare* John Keegan also focuses on the warrior, identifying three military traditions linked to the individual.[5]

Andrew Sanders's discussion of the anthropology of warriors admirably sets forth the underlying premises of the approach: "Warriors are persons whose vocation is warfare, and who engage in the actual physical activity of fighting. In contrast to soldiers, and in particular to conscripts, they fight for personal glory." They fight as individuals, rather than as members of disciplined military formations. Warfare is a way of life to warriors, and its values underlie much of their behavior. Warriors supply their own weapons. Further, according to Sanders, the warrior is central in the military organization of some societies.[6] Warrior societies place a strong positive value upon warfare and warlike achievements; outstanding fighting men receive honor and prestige. Warfare is strongly integrated with religious and social values, and from childhood a male is socialized into warrior ideals and trained in military activities. War achievements are ranked, and the highest ranked achievement typically stresses the bravery involved in the exploit. By performing the higher ranked deeds, warriors achieve prestige and become war leaders. Competition between warriors for glory drives the successful warrior to seek greater achievements, forcing him to become an individual who invites death. In aristocratic states warriorhood was an occupation closely associated with the ruling class; it involved a strong hereditary aspect. Only members of the aristocracy possessed specialized armaments and could develop skill in their use; thus a warrior ethic was a part of the aristocratic way of life.

Warriors often engage in duels. In a study of dueling, I identified four characteristics of the duel: armed combat—fighting with matched weapons that are lethal; agreed-upon conditions, such as time, place, weapons, and those who should be present; duelists from the same social class, often a military aristocracy; and motives ranging from preserving honor, to revenge, to the killing of a rival. I discovered a sequence of stages. In hunting and gathering bands, dueling is nonexistent or rare. In some tribal to state-level societies, duels occur between elite warriors from two political communities, each representing his military organization. A warrior will step forward from the group to take on a challenger. These are the warriors Sanders describes in detail. With intense warfare a new stage arises: Duels occur between military personnel who are members of the same military organization. Finally, in recent centuries in Western civilization, duels take place between civilians within a political community.[7]

Although warriors, considered as a whole, have much in common, it is possible, as John Keegan has done, to distinguish different warrior traditions: "All civilizations owe their origins to the warrior." Although "there are three distinct warrior traditions . . . there is only one warrior culture. Its evolution and transformation over time and place from man's beginnings to his arrival in the contemporary world, is the history of warfare."[8] I believe, however, that the history of warfare should not be restricted to the study of "warrior culture." The sociopolitical organization of a people must be studied because it generates and nurtures the military organization of that people.

"Primitive warfare" is Keegan's first tradition. For Keegan its study is instructive because it shows that "warmaking man" has the capacity to limit the nature and effects of his action. The most important device for limiting this conflict is "ritual, which defines the nature of the combat itself and requires that, once defined rituals have been performed, the contestants shall recognize the fact of their satisfaction and have recourse to conciliation, arbitration, and peacemaking."[9] Note the similarity between Keegan's description of "primitive warfare" and the characteristics of the duel. The view that "primitive war" is "ritual war" is an incorrect interpretation.[10]

Asian warmaking (which includes that of Islam), based on the steppe nomad and the horse warrior, is Keegan's second tradition. In this "oriental" tradition evasion, delay, and indirectness lead to a concept of military restraint.[11] This view is seldom accepted by military historians; for example, Robert O'Connell argues that the most lethal warfare stemmed from attacks by mounted warriors on agricultural villages.[12]

Keegan's third tradition is the "Western Way of War," which comprises three elements. The first element appeared, Keegan writes, when the Greeks "in the fifth century BC cut loose from the constraints of the primitive style, with its respect above all for ritual in war, and adopted the practice of the face-to-face battle to the death." The second element is the ethic of the holy war, while the third element is the perfection of the gunpowder revolution in the eighteenth century.[13] Keegan's identification of this third tradition is taken from Victor Davis Hanson's study of Greek hoplite warfare, with its emphasis upon the decisive battle. Recently Hanson has expanded his idea; he relates Western military powers to the democratic and constitutional governments of Western nations from Greece to the present.[14]

Keegan's incorrect interpretation of both the warfare of nonliterate peoples and the warfare of the Middle East and Asia leads him to an optimistic conclusion: "Future peacekeepers and peacemakers have much to learn from alternative military cultures, not only that of the Orient but of the primitive world also. There is a wisdom in the intellectual restraint and even of symbolic ritual that needs to be rediscovered."[15] A correct interpretation of the two alternative military cultures would, I believe, have led him to a pessimistic conclusion.

Although the bulk of the writing on the warrior and warrior traditions considers the combatants to be honorable men and the traditions to include restraint, at least one military writer, Ralph Peters, treats warriors with disdain. They are, he writes, dishonorable men who kill and like to kill, even women and children. Peters describes "warriors" as "erratic primitives of shifting allegiance, habituated to violence, with no stake in civil order. Unlike soldiers, warriors do not play by our rules, do not respect treaties, and do not obey orders they do not like." Peters describes "five social pools" from which most warriors emerge: the underclass, young males deprived of education, entrepreneurs of conflict, patriots, and failed military men. The entrepreneurs and the patriots, he believes, pose the greatest danger to our social order; the others are swept along by the tide.[16]

The warriors that Peters describes are a product of the modern world. They are not the nonprofessional and professional military personnel I described earlier. For Peters it is the professional soldier who is honorable, not the warrior. Peters does not discuss Keegan's warrior traditions but would probably find them irrelevant for understanding warfare in the twenty-first century. Peters envisions a future in which soldiers and warriors will engage in mortal combat. It is already taking place. The terrorists who hijacked and crashed commercial airliners into the World Trade Center towers and the Pentagon on September 11, 2001, are an example of Peters's "warriors."

The combatants that Peters describes are not new to the late twentieth century. One distinct group, the "borderers" (or Scots-Irish), people from the borderlands between northern England and southern Scotland, emigrated from that region to the American colonies in the eighteenth century. They settled in the mountains extending from what was to become southwestern Pennsylvania to Tennessee and Georgia. There an Old World cultural pattern of self-reliance, based on violent retaliation, raiding of livestock, and feuding among clans, persisted into the twentieth century. These warriors became marksmen with their so-called Kentucky flintlock rifles made by Germans in Pennsylvania, Virginia, and North Carolina. They shot both wild game and each other, usually from ambush. Recently I have described how the borderers served as snipers in the American Revolution and the wars that followed.[17] When infantry tactics changed in 1875, from massed infantry to skirmish lines, the ideal soldier became a rifleman who could stand alone. The borderer was such a combatant. However, these mountain marksmen at this time were engaged in feuds in the states of West Virginia, Kentucky, and Tennessee. Their behavior clearly conformed to that of Peters's warriors. The governor of Kentucky numerous times sent the militia to eastern Kentucky to stop the feuding. But once conscripted for World War I the borderers became excellent solders.[18]

To focus on warriors, whether gentle and kind or mean and nasty, is to miss the target. We should put our sights on military organizations. My aim in *How War Began* is to examine groups of men, the armed combat in which they engage, and their leaders. I will be describing nonprofessional and professional military organizations, not warriors per se or their traditions. The latter approach tends to glorify war, which I have no intention of doing.

War Defined

To begin our inquiry we must first gain some understanding of what war is. Definitions abound. Some are restricted in that they seemingly pertain only to modern polities; for example, "War . . . is the application of state violence in the name of policy. It involves killing and wounding people and destroying property until the survivors abandon their military resistance or the belligerents come to a negotiated agreement."[19] I prefer, however, a broad definition that is so inclusive that an armed combat (fighting with weapons) between two men may be considered war if the men are from independent political entities. Terrorist acts, I believe, can also be considered war if the attackers are from another polity. Is an ancient rock painting of two men shooting arrows at each other war? It could be, by my definition, if they are from separate kinship groups. But what if there is intermarriage between the groups? I would still consider it war if the groups are politically independent, each with its own headman. However, if the groups are units within a single political entity, I would not. But perhaps my definition of war is still not broad enough. Intuitively, I want to call what I see painted on the rocks war, yet I realize it could be other things: a game—they are trying to hit but not hurt each other; a representation of other peoples or perhaps deities; a duel to resolve a dispute. Even if what is pictured represents an actual event, I do not know why they are shooting arrows at each other—are they trying to kill each other? And I do not know what kind of groups they belong to.

I do not, however, like definitions that are so broad that almost any aggression leading to potentially lethal violence is considered war. My definition of war—armed combat between political communities—focuses on the use of weapons, not on aggression. If one's definition focuses on aggression, then one will seek the cause of war in psychological dispositions. Since I focus on armed combat, which I define as fighting with weapons, I put the emphasis on learning to use weapons. Learning is socialization. Thus, learning to use weapons is socialization for armed combat. Once the weapons are used in lethal combat between members of two political entities, war has occurred.

In our search for how war began, however, we need to set aside to some extent definitions of war because of the difficulty of identifying war in the archaeological record. Elsewhere I have distinguished six forms of killing: homicide, political assassination, feuding, warfare, capital punishment, and human sacrifice.[20] Dueling can be added to the list. While these seven forms of killing can be differentiated from each other in ethnographic descriptions with the help of definitions, they cannot be differentiated in the archaeological record. When a human pelvis is found with an arrow point lodged in it, no conclusion can be reached as to which form of killing occurred. Indeed, it could even have been a hunting accident.

I will try, where possible, to differentiate the forms of killing from each other, but we cannot unequivocally speak of war until we have clearly defined political entities. I have numerous times defined war as armed combat between political communities.[21] I now have more and more trouble applying the definition. If a band of warriors attacks a camp or settlement occupied only by unarmed women, children, and old men and kills them, where is the armed combat? Raids of this kind are common among nonliterate peoples and occur widely today, carried out by "modern" armies.[22] We call this practice genocide and condemn it. Terrorist attacks against noncombatants also do not involve armed combat. In spite of difficulties in applying my definition, I think that it is the most straightforward definition available and hence the easiest to apply.

The definition of war, as well as when war first occurred, may depend upon the theory employed by the scholar. For example, sociobiologists or evolutionary psychologists believe that the acquisition of mates is critical to the survival of the group. Men, as members of groups, fight over women. The groups may be fraternal interest groups, that is, localized groups of related males. Defense and revenge go hand-in-hand with fighting over women — defense of the group's women and revenge for women lost to another group. Since mating obviously occurs early in human evolution, war may have occurred early, as soon as weapons were used for hunting. Materialists, on the other hand, use a model that employs an assessment of resource availability; they also use a decision-making (rational) approach—a political science cost-benefit analysis. With this model it is hard to "see" war in early times when populations were small and resources presumably abundant. Thus, various definitions of war, as well as theories of war, influence when war is thought to have begun.

My approach does not have theories built into it. Warfare is armed combat between political communities. I look for evidence of armed combat, and I find it in prehistoric times.

The Thesis

Warfare developed along two separate paths. The hunting of large game animals was critical to the development of the first path. Early hunters working as a group in pursuit of game sometimes engaged in attacks upon members of competing groups of hunters; they devised a mode of warfare based upon ambushes and lines. At the origin of the second path were foragers who did little hunting but depended largely upon gathering for subsistence, became sedentary, and then domesticated plants. Intergroup aggression was absent among these early agricultur-

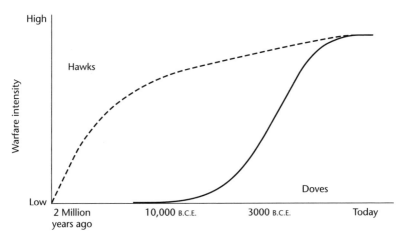

Figure 1.1. **Increase in Warfare Intensity over Time—Two Views**

alists. The first states developed only in these regions, but once city-states arose, a mode of warfare based upon battles and siege operations sprang forth. The two paths at times intertwined when state-level societies and bands of hunter-gatherers came in contact. *How War Began* describes how each path arose and what the consequences were.

Scholars who study war are at war with each other. One faction, which I have called hawks, believes that warfare arose millions of years ago and has characterized humankind in all places ever since; the other faction, which I have called doves, believes that warfare arose only about five thousand years ago, when the first states developed, and then spread to peaceful hunter-gatherers and agriculturalists. The positions of the hawks and the doves are shown in Figure 1.1, a diagram that relates warfare intensity to time. The two curves are far apart since the hawks see war as early and intense, while the doves see war as late and becoming intense only after 3000 B.C.E.

Scholars who look at big game hunters see warfare, while scholars who look at early agriculturalists see peace. Big game hunters, both in antiquity and in descriptions of native peoples, do indeed appear to engage in intergroup aggression that involves the killing of other hunters. However, a region in which warfare occurs is a region in which agriculture cannot develop; a peaceful, settled life for perhaps two thousand years is a prerequisite for the development of agriculture. Anthropologists Julian Steward and Elman Service both note that the first states arose in regions where warfare was not prevalent.[23] The first state in a region is known as a primary or pristine state. Primary states arose in four regions: Mesoamerica, Peru, Mesopotamia, and northern China. Warfare arose in these regions just as statehood was achieved. The origin of the state and the origin of war are inextricably linked. If warfare

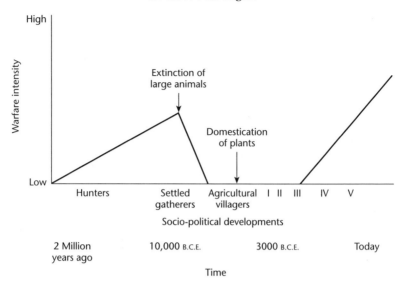

Figure 1.2. The Two Paths Warfare Has Taken

had occurred in one of these areas before statehood, statehood would not have emerged.

The thesis of *How War Began* is diagrammed in Figure 1.2. The two paths for the development of warfare are far apart in a totally different sense. They began at different times and in different locations. Warfare intensity increased early, then rapidly declined in both the New and the Old World with the extinction of large animals. In those areas where there was little warfare, settled gatherers began the domestication of plants and became agricultural villagers. Once the villages became organized into larger units, political centralization was well under way; warfare developed. The Roman numerals in Figure 1.2 represent five stages of increasing political complexity: I, minimal chiefdom; II, typical chiefdom; III, maximal chiefdom/inchoate early state; IV, typical early state; and V, transitional early state, transitional to a mature state. Warfare is shown originating near the end of stage III. Whereas the theories of the hawks and the doves are oriented to time and do not focus on geographic differences, the theory presented in this book focuses on the changes over time in a particular region of the world. This theory acknowledges that, beginning with the first real extinction of large game animals, the intensity of war was not the same for all geographic areas and, furthermore, that the nature of war in a geographic area was not the same across time. Indeed, the four case studies describing the warfare of pristine states begin at different dates.

Two key features of the theory underlying the thesis are illustrated in Figure 1.2. First, as early hunters increased in number and hunting ability, large game species declined in number due to both the hunting and the changing climatic conditions related to the receding of the last glacier; this theory holds true for both the Old World and the New. (However, in the Old World the continent of Africa retained many of its large animals.) Warfare increased at the same time. Hunting and warfare went hand-in-hand. More people were competing for the game with better weapons and hunting tactics. Once the extinction of many large animals began, the early hunters turned to small game procurement (a form of hunting that had begun earlier) and developed a greater reliance upon gathering wild plant food. The frequency of warfare declined, and I believe it did so rapidly. Weapons and tactics used to hunt large game fell into disuse and populations became more stationary. For an area to have little or no warfare, big game hunting must no longer be significant. For agriculture and permanent settlements to arise, there must be no warfare. It was settled gatherers who domesticated plants and developed agriculture. It took hundreds of years of domestication —perhaps two thousand years—for the major crop species to evolve from their wild ancestry, longer in Mesoamerica, sooner in the Fertile Crescent. If warfare occurred in a region of emerging domesticated plants, the domestication process would stop because people would be forced to leave their fertile agricultural lands and move to locations suitable for defense but not optimal for growing plants. Where hunting remained strong and warfare continued, plants were not domesticated. Those societies that did not domesticate plants because warfare continued or was reintroduced nevertheless could, at a later time, accept domesticated crops and animals from peoples who had developed them. But the first people to domesticate plants did not have war, and they did not have war because they had ceased to be hunters of large game.

Second, as the early hunter-gatherers spread over the earth, they developed different cultures with different tool traditions and different ways of life. Some remained hunters, while others became gatherers. Gatherers who settled and domesticated plants became agricultural villagers. Since warfare did not disrupt their lives—through battle casualties, crop destruction, and the burning of houses and settlements— populations grew in size and settlements developed into villages. The different groupings of villages constituted people of differing cultures. Within villages, wealth differences arose between individuals and between kinship groups. Social stratification emerged, with the dominant wealthier class providing the leaders. Competition and conflict between leaders led to internal power struggles. When the leaders who emerged from these struggles consolidated their power, they were able to form chiefdoms. Multiple chiefdoms arose within each culture. Despotism followed. States emerged. The culture—its people and their resources—produced the state in the sense that chiefdoms within each culture became states. Specifically, an ideology that the winners should

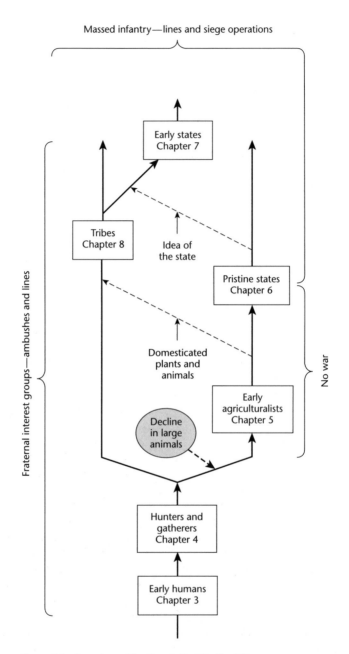

Figure 1.3. Overview—The Two Paths War Has Taken

rule the losers developed. A ruling class emerged. The *idea* of the state crystallized as political leaders gained power over their constituent populations. Warfare arose. The first state-level battles took place between elite fighters who were drawn from the ruling class. Coercion of the population eventually led to the creation of military units that could engage in battle with similar units from other states. The first people to develop states did not have war until they had centralized political systems. Thus, warfare cannot be the cause of pristine state formation.

A schematic overview (Figure 1.3) shows the relationships of the key features of the theory to the origins and development of military organizations and tactics. Specifically, it shows the two paths of warfare through time. Furthermore, it suggests how the chapters of this book relate to each other. Early humans (chapter 3) and hunters and gatherers (chapter 4) lie at the base of the first path. The first path—the path that originated in a hunting and gathering way of life—persisted into the twentieth century in those regions where large animals continued to be hunted. Examples include nineteenth-century Indian hunters of the American bison, herders of eastern Africa who hunt lions, and Australian aborigines who hunted the kangaroo into the twentieth century. The same weapons used in the hunt were used in war. Early agriculturalists (chapter 5) lie at the base of the second path. As pointed out above, the decline in large animals moves us from the first path to the second. Early agriculturalists became villagers, then members of chiefdoms and the first states (chapter 6). Pristine states in their initial stages are early states. The diffusion of the idea of the state to nonstate peoples created other early states (chapter 7). Domesticated plants and animals spread from path two to path one and created tribes (chapter 8). Some hunting and gathering peoples, after agriculture and the state had developed in a few regions, acquired plants and crop technology from their more advanced neighbors. They became tribes, with their way of life based on hunting and gathering as well as agriculture. The spread of warfare eventually encompassed nearly all peoples except some isolated hunter-gatherers. There are a few agricultural tribal peoples who, in the nineteenth and twentieth centuries, gave up warfare.

Methodology

The methodology I use in this book consists of inferential techniques that permit the interpretation of archaeological data. My approach is eclectic; it employs techniques used by archaeologists, physical anthropologists, historians, and cross-cultural researchers.

Analogy

Interpretation in archaeology consists of what Joyce Marcus and Kent Flannery have called "bridging arguments"—the connection between archaeological data and the theoretical framework used.[24] These arguments can range from simple ethnographic analogy to complex inferential methods. I identify four arguments: implicit ethnographic analogy, the "direct historical approach," explicit ethnographic analogy, and "Murdock's method of ethnology." All of these methods make use of ethnographic data—descriptions of peoples living in the last two hundred years or so, often at the time or just after they were first contacted by members of a European culture.

Implicit ethnographic analogy finds the archaeologist making a common-sense evaluation; for example, a burial is uncovered, and the body is laid out with breastplate, shield, sword, and spear. The researcher deduces that the body is that of a man who must have been a warrior and the culture he is from must have had war. (We will later see, in "How the State Arose" in chapter 5, an example of this reasoning from a 5800 B.C.E. tomb at Catal Huyuk in present-day southern Turkey.)

The "direct historical approach" utilizes ethnographic and historical data from the area in which the excavations are under way in order to provide meaning and interpretation to what is found. The method assumes that there is a direct link from the ethnographic case to the archaeological culture being interpreted.[25] In other words, what peoples of a given region were doing in the nineteenth and twentieth centuries is probably what inhabitants of that region were doing several hundred years earlier.

Explicit ethnographic analogy draws upon a worldwide ethnographic data base. Anthropologists have grouped societies into categories such as hunting-gathering band, autonomous village society, and chiefdom. Since societies within a category have many characteristics or traits in common, the archaeologist determines the appropriate category for the people under investigation and infers that they probably were doing what peoples in that category were doing in the past two hundred years. Thus, a hunter-gatherer group found by archaeological excavation is assumed to be similar to hunter-gatherers in recent ethnographic description. Although ethnographic analogy is much used, there are two major difficulties in its application. First, the matching—how does the archaeologist know, for example, that the people at a site being excavated are a chiefdom? By the presence of elite burials, platform complexes, or various-sized settlements in the immediate area? The criteria have been widely discussed by archaeologists in the past few decades. Without agreement on criteria, matching has been difficult. Second, the way nonliterate peoples lived in the past two centuries may not be the way hunter-gatherers and agricultural villagers lived thousands of years ago. The archaeologist must be cautious in inferring early life ways from recent practice. Two examples germane to *How War Began* show the difficulty. Hunter-gatherers living today, or described in ethnographies, are sometimes peaceful. Can it then be inferred that hunter-gatherers, say, ten thousand years ago, were also? This book argues "no." Nearly all state-level societies engage in warfare. Can it be inferred that pristine states in their earlier stages had war? This book argues "no."

The fourth mode of ethnographic analogy has been called "Murdock's method of ethnology." [26] George Peter Murdock pioneered the cross-cultural method, a research technique from cultural anthropology that utilizes a probability sample of societies drawn from a large sampling universe of primarily nonliterate societies. The purpose of this research is to test theories and the relational hypotheses drawn from the theories. If the research finds a strong association in a worldwide sample of societies, the hypothesis is deemed supported and one assumes that the association reflects human behavior in general. [27] The generalization should hold for prehistoric societies as well. Sometimes the research is explicitly designed to help the archaeologist. [28] Furthermore, cross-cultural studies provide frequencies of culture traits and correlations between traits for peoples at the same level of sociopolitical complexity as archaeologically known peoples. The cautions discussed for using explicit ethnographic analogy must be followed; however, there are circumstances when probabilities can be assigned with some assurance. Numerous empirically supported generalizations, derived from cross-cultural research, are utilized throughout *How War Began* to interpret archaeological data in support of the central thesis.

The results of cross-cultural research studies are not used as a substitute for a lack of archaeological data. Rather, the studies are used to interpret those data. For example—and this is a key argument of this book—there are substantial data to support the notion that homicide and warfare were prevalent in the late Upper Paleolithic and that there is a lack of data to support the notion that homicide and warfare occurred in the early Neolithic. Why? The cross-cultural research that shows that hunting (the primary mode of subsistence in the Upper Paleolithic) and frequent warfare are linked and that gathering (a major activity of early agricultural villages) and infrequent warfare are linked helps us interpret why the archaeological data appear as they do.

Physical anthropologists, especially paleontologists and primatologists, also use bridging arguments to interpret the fossil record. Using methods akin to explicit ethnographic analogy, experts on fossil humans use conclusions from studies of hunter-gatherers to infer what the behavior of early humans might have been like. Primatologists, on the other hand, use the behavior of primates, commonly chimpanzees, to make inferences about the behavior of early humans, particularly the predecessors of *Homo sapiens*. Sometimes a single local population, such as the chimpanzees of Gombe made famous by Jane Goodall, is used to make the inferences; sometimes multiple populations—up to nine in one study—are used to establish chimpanzee behavior before deriving implications for human evolution.[29] The nine-group study, as well as a more recent comparative study of six chimpanzee populations that focused upon cultural differences between the groups, employs a research procedure nearly identical to Murdock's method of ethnology.[30]

Results of cross-cultural studies that play a key role in support of the thesis of *How War Began* include the findings enumerated below. I think of these generalizations as "bricks" or building blocks; each stands alone, but placed together they produce a structure that is greater than the parts. The bricks are presented below in the approximate order in which they make their appearance in this book.

1. A two-component warfare pattern of ambushes and lines is associated with uncentralized political systems (bands and tribes), while a two-component pattern of battles and sieges is associated with centralized political systems (chiefdoms and states).
2. Military organizations vary in efficiency, thus permitting the construction of a military sophistication scale. For a society, the higher the level of political centralization, the more likely the society is to have a high military sophistication scale score.
3. The tool use of wild chimpanzees includes both "missile-throw" and "stick-club," which constitute antipredatory patterns of weapons use.
4. Spears with stone tips are used in big game hunting and warfare.
5. Hunter-gatherer bands are not internally peaceful. Homicide rates are high, and frequent executions of killers and witches occur.
6. Hunters have a greater frequency of warfare than gatherers.
7. Fraternal interest groups are associated with feuding and internal war.
8. Tribes with fraternal interest groups and despotic states kill captured enemies; despotic states also kill their own members.
9. Centralized political systems at war suppress feuding.
10. Centralized political systems are likely to have fortified villages.
11. Village fortifications predict warfare; the opposite is not true—war does not predict village fortifications.
12. Centralized political systems at war with neighboring societies are likely to have siege operations.
13. Societies with high military sophistication scale scores have high battlefield casualties.
14. Uncentralized political systems with councils of elders may have human sacrifice. Centralized political systems, particularly despotic states, have human sacrifice and slavery.
15. War is nearly universal in human society. Societies without war are usually physically isolated. For nonisolated societies an efficient

military organization—one that has a high score on the military sophistication scale—is needed for survival. A high score on the scale is associated with offensive external war.

Scientific and Historical Explanation

How War Began focuses on what happened long ago. It presents an interpretation of what is known. Archaeological data are interpreted, sometimes with the assistance of ethnographic analogy; these data are organized to support an overarching interpretation. The interpretation argues that war arose first among hunter-gatherers and then arose a second time once agriculture was firmly established. This interpretation is based on both scientific and historical explanations.

Scientific and historical explanations go hand-in-hand. They are not alternative modes of explanation, nor are they incompatible. There are two components to science: description and explanation. Objective reporting of observations, whether the descriptions are ethnographic or historical, is science. Explanation, however, goes beyond description. It is an attempt to answer the "why" question: Why does something occur? Scientific explanation consists of "laws," that is, empirically verified generalizations, each of which would be the statement of a relationship between or among two or more variables.[31] The results of cross-cultural studies are verified generalizations. They are scientific laws, and because they presumably hold for all times and places, they can be used to explain events in the past.

Historical explanation, on the other hand, deals with the determination of a unique event. While historians have used the notion of causality in at least five senses, most seem to have settled on a paradigm that employs two levels: particular causes (actions of individuals and the reasons they had for acting) and profound or underlying causes. Military historians are likely to use this two-level paradigm, which I believe is the equivalent of Aristotle's material and efficient causes. With this paradigm events are seen as inevitable. Historians may focus on one or the other level. Historian Allan Millet, who seems to focus on the first level, has noted that the traditional focus of academic military historians is on the three "C's"—the causes, conduct, and consequences of warfare.[32]

Historical explanation uses a narrative style, a style that is employed today by some evolutionists in the biological sciences. Paleontologist Stephen Jay Gould has described the style: "Narrative explanations . . . require a knowledge and reconstruction of actual sequences of antecedent events, for outcomes are contingent upon a previous chain of occurrences." Such explanations may be as detailed, as decisive, and as satisfying as those developed via the experimental method. Gould concludes that "the nature of history's complex and singular unfolding enjoins this style of explanation as the only adequate approach for achieving the detail of understanding that we seek."[33] *How War Began* uses a narrative style of presentation; it also seeks to be vigorously scientific.

Unique historical events can be explained by the simultaneous application of both the narrative style and scientific laws. The two modes of explanation are both ways of trying to explain why something occurs. *How War Began* not only attempts to describe the first occurrence of war, meaning when and where, but also attempts to explain why it occurred. As noted in "The Thesis" section above, war had multiple origins. Insofar as possible, sequences of the type that military historians employ will be constructed and they will be interpreted through the use of scientific generalizations that have often been derived from cross-cultural studies, the bricks that I have listed above.

Recent scholarship in the social sciences has brought the individual back into explanatory paradigms. Talk of agency abounds. In part it seems to be an attempt to avoid dehumanizing the people studied—a charge that has been leveled against cultural anthropologists in particular. It is also a shift in emphasis from material to efficient causes. One example is cultural anthropologist Andrew Vayda's 1989 "recantation." Vayda, a pioneer of ecological theories of warfare, now argues that it is important to focus on the "context-relatedness of purposeful human behavior," in other words, efficient causes.[34] Earlier he argued that such reasons, which he called proximate causes, were of less importance than material causes.[35] Archaeologists have also tried to bring the individual back into their analyses. Action theory, as described by Joyce Marcus and Kent Flattery, is an explicit attempt to do so: "By putting the actors back into the scheme, action theory also responds to complaints that most evolutionary theory makes humans little more than cogs in a machine." Marcus and Flattery further tell us that "action theory is appropriate for studying the evolutionary history of a single group." They go on to note that "action theory is less useful for comparing all civilizations."[36] For comparative studies they revert to identifying stages in an evolutionary sequence. Another archaeologist who is an action theorist is Elizabeth Brumfiel. As the coeditor of a volume on factional competition and political development in the New World, she argues for the necessity of "a theory that integrates agent-centered and system-centered analyses into a single framework."[37] This view is not new to those who have studied sociopolitical evolution. In 1962 anthropologist Fred Gearing, in his study of the evolution of Cherokee political institutions, stated, "The Cherokees in these pages (though they are usually invisible as particular men) are sentient beings, creators as much as creatures of culture, and social structure is here something in the awareness of actors, under continuing, conscious, purposeful modification."[38]

Although I agree that humans are important, I nevertheless believe that their decisions are determined. I have long noted that the more information available about an event and what led up to it, the more inevitable the event seems. It is a waste of time asking the "what if" question, although it may be a lot of fun to do so: What if a particular leader had thought and done differently? A battle would have been won, not lost, and the course of history would have changed. (Answering this question is a favorite pastime of military writers and readers, and in particular military buffs who play war games with miniature soldiers.[39]) But that leader did not think and do differently. Multiple factors led to the decision. A different decision could not have been made unless the factors had been different. And they were not.

2

Perspectives on How War Originated

Scholars have many views of the origin of war. Their perspectives on early warfare vary in terms of theories, starting points, and characterizations.

History of Research on Warfare

All social scientists draw many of their ideas from ancestors, that is, the scholars who have preceded them, often by a century or more. I am no exception. I have drawn ideas from two pairs of theories. The first pair of theories—killer ape theory and the hunting hypothesis—derive largely from the research of physical anthropologists, while the second pair—developmental theory and world systems theory—derive from the research of cultural anthropologists. The killer ape and the hunting hypothesis theories are directly linked historically, as are the developmental and world systems theories. The first origin of war path, described in chapter 1, grows directly from the hunting hypothesis; the second origin of war path, also described in that chapter, is indebted to several features of the developmental and world systems theories.

Killer Ape Theory

Killer ape theory views humankind as a direct descendant of an ape who had sharp canine teeth and hunted animals, including other apes. This aggressiveness toward other living beings has a genetic basis. For killer ape theorists aggression is innate. This innate aggression is considered the ultimate cause of war.

Physical anthropologist Matt Cartmill has admirably traced the history of the killer ape theory from its Darwinian origins in the late nineteenth century, through its decline after 1920, to its reemergence as the hunting hypothesis during the 1960s, and then its more recent demise.[1] By the 1980s "Man the Killer" had given way to "Man the Scavenger." Cartmill, however, failed to realize that many of his fellow physical anthropologists held a fondness for the hunting hypothesis. Since the publication of his book, which was subtitled *Hunting and Nature through History,* the killer ape–hunting hypothesis theory has reemerged in books titled *Demonic Males* and *The Hunting Apes.*[2]

The killer ape theories developed during the early twentieth century subscribe to evolutionary notions. According to Cartmill, three authors put forward early versions of the killer ape story, but their ideas quickly sank into oblivion.[3] Charles Morris argued that a change in body proportions enabled our tree-dwelling ancestors to chase and capture prey on the ground. Harry Campbell believed that hunting and warfare spurred the development of intelligence and hence were the engines of human progress, progress which he later questioned. Carveth Read went a step further—cooperative hunting in a pack increased the supply of food; indeed, the band itself was a hunting adaptation. Aggressive cruelty and cannibalism were the outcomes. These killer ape theories have in common the notion that warfare occurred well before the emergence of *Homo sapiens,* indeed, that war antedated the emergence of any *Homo* species.

Cartmill attributes the neglect and rejection of the ideas of Morris, Campbell, and Read to the rejection by 1920 of Darwin's theory of natural selection. Not until after World War II did Darwinism become the theoretical cornerstone of biology, and the killer ape theory had reemerged as the hunting hypothesis by the 1960s.[4] In order to present the origin of war theories in chronological order, further discussion of the hunting hypothesis needs to wait, while the developmental theory, which emerged full-blown in anthropology's classical period (1920–60), is described.

Developmental Theory

The salient characteristic of the forty-year classical period was the myth of the peaceful savage—the assertion that people who occupied the lower sociopolitical levels of developmental sequences were people with no war or with only ritual war. This position was a direct outgrowth of evolutionary thought that had become firmly rooted in the late nineteenth century. Numerous scholars subscribed to the notion that long ago there was no war and that there then followed stages of progressively more violent types of warfare. The number of stages varied; at the end of the sequence was modern, imperialistic war. Several examples follow.

Anthropologist Bronislaw Malinowski, in 1941, argued that warfare only slowly evolved as a mechanism of organized force for the pursuit of national policies. He described six types of armed contest: fighting between group members (the prototype of criminal behavior), fighting as a juridical mechanism for the adjustment of differences, armed raids for sport, warfare as a political expression of early nationalism, military expeditions of organized pillage, and war as an instrument of national policy. Each type was an entirely different "cultural phase" in the development of organized fighting.[5]

International relations expert Quincy Wright, writing in 1942, indicated that there were four stages, or causes of war as he called them: defense, social, economic, and political. Social war was defined as "mild warfare" where "no indication was found of fighting for definite economic or political purposes."[6]

Anthropologist Leslie White argued in 1949 that as humankind's cultural heritage increased, economic and political goals became the causes of war. According to White, "Warfare is virtually non-existent among many primitive tribes." Before warfare can emerge, he argued, cultures must progress to the point where fighting over hunting or fishing grounds, grazing lands, or fertile valleys, becomes worth the trouble.[7] W. W. Newcomb, in 1960, building upon White's analysis, delineated four types of warfare, corresponding closely to Wright's types. Type 1 warfare consisted of brief skirmishes between hunting and gathering bands. Type 2 warfare was designated as primitive warfare (Wright's "social war"). Newcomb informed us that primitive war consisted of "crude, sportive, brief, generally unorganized conflicts" and that "small bands of warriors can be spared from time to time for a few days or weeks, to engage in the sport of war." Type 3 warfare was "true" warfare, involving economic causes. And finally, Type 4 warfare constituted world wars based upon the industrial revolution.[8]

Ralph Beals and Harry Hoijer, the authors of a widely used anthropology textbook first published in 1953, presented a three-stage sequence for the development of war that focused on political organization rather than war. Their first stage of social development—a "provisional" category—occurred when there was no true political organization; in that stage, there would be no organized warfare. The other two stages of development took place when people were "politically organized as bands, tribes, or confederacies" and then as "conquest states."[9]

These developmental theories have in common the notion that early hunter-gatherers and then tribal peoples had little or no warfare; later, more advanced societies, such as states, had serious warfare. Thus, warfare comes late in humankind's history. Since 1960 evolutionary sequences have focused on sociopolitical types as stages, as did Beals and Hoijer. The best-known perhaps is Elman Service's sequence, published in 1962: band, tribe, chiefdom, state, and empire.[10] Also from the 1960s is Morton Fried's evolutionary sequence: egalitarian, rank, and stratified society, followed by states.[11] Service's sequence, however, has been most used by anthropologists and others. Recently Robert Carneiro has described why, in his opinion, Service's typology prevailed over Fried's. First, Fried's "stratified society" was an "anomaly," a stratified society that lacked the political institutions of a state. Second, "egalitarian society" was defined in a "peculiar and awkward way." Service's types, in spite of his later "emendation," which was ignored, were relatively easy to apply to both ethnographically known societies and to those in the archeological record, Carneiro contends.[12] I disagree with this; it is difficult to apply Service's typology to either set of data.

More than thirty years ago I conducted a cross-cultural study of war, with the objective of devising and testing a series of hypotheses about both the causes of war and the conditions under which wars occur. The hypotheses that I tested were primarily concerned with the influence of ecological, economic, and sociopolitical factors on warfare.[13] Sociopolitical factors, that is, types of political systems (bands, tribes, chiefdoms, and states), yielded the strongest relationships with various aspects of warfare. Since I used the typology of political systems outlined by Elman Service, it required little effort to cast my study in a similar evolutionary framework. My 1970 book's title, *The Evolution of War,* reflects this framework. However, as I pointed out in the preface to the second edition of that book, "No discussion of the possible warfare practices of early man is included, nor is a discussion of the origin of the state included."[14] For three pages I gave my thoughts on these subjects. The cross-cultural procedure I followed led me to the following two conclusions: First, increasing political centralization goes hand-in-hand with increasing military efficiency, and second, high military efficiency leads to territorial expansion. I now reject Service's evolutionary sequence. Rarely does one of the four types evolve or change into one of the other types.

In a recent study that focuses on the origins and development of ancient warfare, political scientist Claudio Cioffi-Revilla delineates four stages. Stage 0, Protowarfare, consisted of coordinated killing by human groups applying homicidal and hunting skills. Stage I, Chiefly Warfare, involved chiefs organizing raids of spontaneous warriors. Cioffi-Revilla describes stage I as emerging "from the background of homicidal and hunting skills, boosted by chiefly political complexity (centralization of power, social ranks, weak territorial control, simple two- to three-tier settlement hierarchy)." Stage II, Interstate ("stately") Warfare, was based on political motives (territorial conquests), warrior classes, specialized weapons, and basic military engineering. Such warfare "was produced by the earlier chiefly patterns, boosted by state-level conditions of political complexity (hereditary rulership, internal bureaucratic specialization, writing system, multi-tier settlement hierarchy)." Stage III, Imperial Warfare, consisted of all previous features of state warfare, plus long-distance logistics and multiethnic composition of troops and leadership.[15] Unlike the developmental theories from the classical period, Cioffi-Revilla's stages are based upon a detailed examination of archaeological reports from both New World and Old World locations. Nevertheless, his stages are remarkably similar to those constructed decades ago, as well as appearing to be strongly influenced by Service's sequence.

A recent theory of the origin of warfare focuses upon the Upper Paleolithic and identifies four stages that lethal violence traversed: capital punishment, shoot-on-sight, feud, and war. In the "coevolution of war and society," anthropologist Raymond Kelly links the first two stages to "unsegmented societies" and the latter two stages to "segmented societies." A segmented society has distinct kinship or political groups that are often deadly rivals. In the first stage there is no warfare, only executions of unwanted community members, such as murderers and witches. In the second stage a chance encounter leads to shoot-on-sight tactics (ambushes): "The principal objective of the parties to these spontaneous conflicts is to secure subsistence resources without sharing them with others."[16] In the third stage "social substitution" results in the killing of a relative or group member of the malefactor *if* the malefactor cannot be found. When the concept of social substitution is fully developed, the fourth stage, warfare between segmented societies, arises.[17] (Kelly's theory is more fully described in chapter 4, in the section "Warfare.") Kelly's theory does not deal with the period before twenty thousand years ago, nor does it deal with the periods after the Upper Paleolithic. It covers, thus, a shorter span of time than the other developmental theories.

Hunting Hypothesis

The hunting hypothesis flourished in the 1960s, but an opposition camp arose to counter the theory's adherents.

First among the advocates was anatomist Raymond Dart, who discovered *Australopithecus africanus* (the African southern ape) in 1924; he named and described these ancient fossils. The ape walked upright and was a human ancestor. He also hunted.[18] I believe that Dart's description was influenced by authors writing in the late 1800s. By the 1950s, scientists were embracing Dart's views. Kenneth Oakley described early humans as meat eaters. G. A. Bartholomew and J. B. Birdsell portrayed the australopithecines as big game hunters, and William Etkin argued that male specialization as a hunter had shaped the family as we know it, with males bringing home game while females stayed home to care for young that take many years to mature. By the 1960s the theory was fully developed: "Hunting demanded weapons. Weapons encouraged bipedalism. Bipedalism made it possible to carry things—not only weapons and helpless babies but also meat."[19] Among the most respected advocates of the theory was physical anthropologist Sherwood Washburn, who edited the 1961 volume *The Social Life of Early Man* and contributed to the well-known 1966 symposium "Man the Hunter," attended by some seventy-five scholars from around the world; the symposium resulted in the publication of a book with the same title, edited by Richard Lee and Irven DeVore. A few years later playwright Robert Ardrey coined the expression "hunting hypothesis."[20]

Beginning in the mid-1960s the hypothesis took a new form. Innate aggression—that is, an instinct for aggression—was posited as the cause of both hunting and warfare. Nobel laureate Konrad Lorenz gave

the theory its scientific credentials, while Robert Ardrey further popu-
larized it.[21] While the theory that early hominids were hunters persisted, anthropologists were quick to level devastating attacks upon
Lorenz and Ardrey. I briefly reviewed innate aggression theories in 1973
and concluded, as had others, that the theories were simplistic to the
point of being tautological, that fighting between two men is not warfare, and that there is no physiological evidence that humans possess an
aggressive instinct.[22] One voice supporting the innate aggression hypothesis was anthropologist Lionel Tiger, who argued that humankind
is a hunting species that directs violence and aggression toward other
animals as well as other humans.[23]

The hunting hypothesis as formulated by Dart and the physical anthropologists came under attack, became discredited, and was eventually abandoned. Cartmill gives the reasons: *Australopithecus* did not
make tools or weapons; its descendant *Homo erectus* was a scavenger, not
a hunter, so *Australopithecus* also must have been a scavenger; and *Australopithecus* was in turn prey for large carnivores. Perhaps just as important as the scientific evidence has been the changing political climate.[24]
Cartmill states, "Since the early 1970s, anthropologists (who tend to be
left-wing, pacifist, and feminist) have accordingly tended to dismiss the
hunting model as a myth that serves reactionary interests."[25]

Since Cartmill's discussion of its dismissal, however, primatologists
have again focused on the hunting model. Primatologist Richard
Wrangham, in collaboration with scientific writer Dale Peterson, has
been able to ignore the political climate and resurrect the killer ape theory. His argument begins with recent observations of bands of chimpanzees attacking and killing members of other chimpanzee bands. Because the chimpanzee has changed little in five million years, argues
Wrangham, he finds it permissible to infer that behavior patterns observed in contemporary bands of chimpanzees must be characteristic of
the behavior of the common ancestor of both early humans and the
chimpanzee. Presumably there is a genetic basis for the behavior patterns.[26] In response to Wrangham, Robert Sussman has contested the
notion that the chimpanzees have evolved less than *Homo sapiens* since
the time of the common ancestor; furthermore, he questions the evidence that chimpanzee bands attacked and killed members of other
bands. Sussman concludes, "Since data supporting these theories are
extremely weak, and yet the stories continue to repeat themselves, I am
forced to believe that 'Man the Hunter' is a myth."[27]

Another primatologist, Craig Stanford, has developed a theory that
has much in common with the killer ape theory. Since meat is a highly
concentrated source of protein, meat is craved by primates, including
humans. This craving has given meat genuine power—the power to
cause males to form hunting parties and organize entire cultures around
hunting. And it has given men the power to manipulate and control

women in these cultures. Man the Hunter becomes Man the Manipulator with meat. Stanford argues that the skills developed and required for strategic hunting and especially the sharing of meat spurred the rapid growth of human brain size over the past 200,000 years.[28] Furthermore, Stanford has recently argued that Man the Hunter is a myth, a theory that he says developed in the late 1960s to explain how hunting big game led men "to communicate and coordinate their actions, and to do this they needed to be smart, hence big-brained." Yet Stanford has replaced this theory with his own version of the hunting hypothesis, a theory that is remarkably similar to the theory he sets aside. He enumerates three differences between how chimpanzees hunt and how human hunter-gatherers forage for meat. First, while people search for prey, chimpanzees generally do not search—they are opportunistic meat eaters; second, people use weapons when hunting, while chimpanzees do not; third, people kill large animals using weapons to bring them down and other tools to carve them up, but chimpanzees lack this sophisticated technology.[29]

World Systems Theory

Diffusion and acculturation theories from the classical period have given rise in recent years to a composite theory that takes the best from the earlier theories. Diffusion refers to the spread of material and non-material culture traits from one society to another, while acculturation refers to the changes that occur within the recipient society. This diffusion-acculturation theory is usually applied to situations involving contact between centralized and uncentralized political systems. In brief, a centralized political system expands at the expense of its less centralized neighbors, bringing material items, new ideas, disease germs, and often unwanted foreigners to peoples with uncentralized political systems. When the centralized political systems are Western nations taking over the lands of nonliterate peoples, the theory is a world systems approach. Eric Wolf's anthropological classic, *Europe and the People Without History* (1982), describes the expansion of European peoples to the far corners of the earth and the havoc that they wrought upon the native peoples they encountered. Anthropologists from the 1920s through the 1950s often focused upon the changes that a particular nonliterate people underwent when they experienced Western contact.[30] Two variants of the world systems theory deal largely with warfare. One focuses on tribes, the other on states. Both have in common the idea that serious warfare is a feature of centralized political systems, while uncentralized political systems (i.e., tribes) have either no warfare, or if they do it is of a nonserious nature (i.e., ritual warfare).

Deriving from the world systems approach is one that I have referred to as "tribal zone theory."[31] The expression is taken from the title of a book edited by anthropologists Brian Ferguson and Neil Whitehead,

War in the Tribal Zone: Expanding States and Indigenous Warfare (1992). The "tribal zone" is an "area continuously affected by the proximity of a state, but not under state administration." The main effect of state intrusion into a region occupied by native peoples is to increase "armed collective violence." Three factors that can precede contact and destabilize the tribal zone are disease introduction, transformation of ecosystems by alien animals and plants, and technological change produced by trade in manufactured goods. It is important to recognize that these factors can change indigenous societies even before "first contact" has occurred.[32] Death, habitat destruction, and the demise of native institutions often preceded the arrival of European explorers.

State expansion can result in the emergence of a variety of political forms in the tribal zone, including tribes, states, alliances, autonomous villages, bandit groups, and so on. War and, to a lesser degree, trade are responsible for the changes that affect indigenous groups. Ferguson and Whitehead do not see these groups as passive political units that are easily defeated and swept from the tribal zone. Their leaders are instead viewed as active parties who have three basic options: resistance, cooperation, or flight.[33]

Three categories of war can occur in the tribal zone. First, wars of resistance and rebellion: The intruding states have the advantage of being able to amass force against a target, while indigenous peoples have the advantage of mobility. By the nineteenth century, however, the advantage had shifted to the European power, with its modern firearms and improved transportation and communication. Second, ethnic soldiering: Indigenous people fight the war under the control or influence of state agents. It pits native against native. Third, internecine warfare: War is fought between indigenous peoples protecting what they believe to be their own interests. These wars encompass conflict over Western goods, in particular trade in weapons, as well as native peoples raiding to capture slaves for Europeans. Population displacement as a result of war in turn leads to even more conflicts.[34]

Ferguson and Whitehead emphasize that the major part of our information about nonstate warfare is post contact; the warfare observed and described by explorers, missionaries, and ethnographers is not pristine warfare. They conclude, "The result of state impingement is to generate warfare and transform its conduct and purpose."[35]

The idea of statehood—the notion that it is appropriate for some individuals to rule others—can also spread or diffuse from a state to an uncentralized political system. If an economic surplus of material goods is present, that society may be able to transform itself into a state. The economic surplus makes possible the development of a professional military organization, a full-time military organization that is state supported. A newly formed or early state has an efficient military organization.[36] A comparative study of early states by anthropologists Henri

Claessen and Peter Skalnik has revealed two factors that appear to be necessary conditions for state formation: an ideology and a surplus. Four other factors are sometimes present: borrowed ideas, population pressure, war, and conquest. The ideology factor—the idea of state-hood—can arise within an uncentralized political system and thereby propel a society toward statehood, provided the economic surplus is available to support the development. The study found that most early states had standing armies, the sovereign was the supreme commander, and there were military specialists.[37] The two conditions for statehood can be viewed as contributing to the development of a large, efficient military organization. The idea of statehood carries with it the notion of sovereignty (a situation that can be maintained only if an efficient military organization is present), and a surplus permits a concentration of people and a channeling of resources into weapons and subsistence for full-time, professional, military personnel.

The Four Theories: An Overview

Each of the four theories reviewed above implicitly posits an approximate starting point for war. For killer ape theory, the starting point is extremely early in prehistory, before tools were first made; for developmental theories the origin of war is early, but those conflicts are non-serious; for the hunting hypothesis war is early and serious; and for world systems theories it is late, after states have arisen. A time-line (Figure 2.1) shows the approximate point when each theory suggests that war began. Ironically, as more information has become available, the starting point for war has been slowly brought closer and closer to the present. One would think that as more and more archaeological sites are discovered and excavated, the starting point for war would be pushed back in time. That has not happened. New sites often do not yield evidence for war. But they could and sometimes do. I, like many others, watch the news and science magazines for announcements of early human finds; I look in particular for evidence of war. Sometimes I find that evidence.

Figure 2.1. Approximate Time at Which War Began, According to the Four Theories

Theory	[1]		[2]	[3]		[4]
Time	2,000,000 B.C.E.		10,000 B.C.E.			3000 B.C.E.

[1] = Killer Ape Theory   [3] = Hunting Hypothesis
[2] = Developmental Theory [4] = World Systems Theory

Hawks and Doves

The world systems approach and its variants are in direct conflict with the recent versions of the hunting hypothesis. For world systems theo-

rists, military organizations and serious warfare are cardinal characteristics of states. Nonstate societies lack military organizations and serious warfare. For hunting hypothesis theorists, early humans, hunter-
gatherers, and nonliterate peoples not at the state level of sociopolitical
complexity had military organizations and serious warfare. One of the
tasks of *How War Began* is to resolve this dispute. I have labeled the rival
camps as hawks and doves, adopting terms used in the U.S. political
arena.[38] Hawks are likely to be pro-gun and advocates of a strong military, while doves are likely to be anti-gun and advocates of disarming.
The doves lead the peace movement. These terms have been used by
British military historian Michael Howard to describe the rival camps
both in the United States and in Europe. Howard calls both groups "un-
realistic."[39] He also seems to connect hawks with conservatives and
doves with liberals.[40] When hawks and doves focus on early warfare
rather than contemporary politics, they also see things differently.
Being pro-gun, hawks are weapons conscious; they see the missiles and
clubs of chimpanzees as projectile and shock weapons. Doves, with
their anti-gun, antimilitary stance, are less prone to see weapons and
war among pre-state peoples. To put it bluntly, the ideological stance of
some scholars, particularly anthropologists, drives their research pro-
grams. For example, those who are openly peace advocates have been
the strongest critics of the hunting hypothesis, and they have advanced
the notion that native peoples either had no war or adopted war after
contact with European explorers.[41]

This distinction between hawks and doves has been made by anthropologists. Sixty years ago, Bronislaw Malinowski recognized two
camps: One group believed in the "primeval pacifism of man" and the
other group believed "that war was an essential heritage of man." Malinowski says these positions are held by some anthropologists, and he
names individuals, including his colleague Ralph Linton, who at the
time was one of the world's leading anthropologists. He assigns Linton
to the latter group.[42] Recently cultural anthropologist Walter Goldschmidt related the hawk/dove distinction to changing interpretations
of primate studies: "In the early days of chimpanzee studies, no lethal
fighting among them had been seen, and *doves* happily announced that
our ancestry was peaceful by nature, but when the Gombe Reserve
chimps split into two bands and had a war of annihilation between
them, the *hawks* had their day to announce that war is a natural part of
our heritage."[43]

There is no consensus about the origins of war or about how armed
combat developed over time. Indeed, these topics are highly controversial. On the one hand there are hawks, who believe that warfare arose
more than two million years ago and has characterized mankind in all
places ever since. On the other hand, the doves believe that warfare
arose only about five thousand years ago, when the first states devel-

oped, and that war then spread to peaceful hunter-gatherers and agriculturalists. These definitions describe ideal types, of course; nonetheless, many scholars fall into one or the other category. Generally, those scholars who subscribe to the killer ape and the hunting hypothesis theories fall into the hawk camp, while scholars who advocate either a developmental or a world systems approach fall into the dove camp. There are many warfare scholars from anthropology, history, political science, and elsewhere who fall into one or the other of the two camps. I will survey the membership of each camp, though my lists are obviously not exhaustive.

An early hawk is anthropologist Robert Carneiro, who for several decades has argued that chiefdoms and states came into existence through conquest: When a village conquered another village, a chiefdom was produced, and when a chiefdom conquered another chiefdom, a state was created.[44] Military writer Arther Ferrill thinks "prehistoric warfare . . . was as independently important in early society as the discovery of agriculture. . . . In a few places it may actually have been war rather than agriculture that led to the earliest Neolithic settlements." Not surprisingly Ferrill interprets the walls of pre-biblical Jericho—built ten thousand years ago—as fortifications.[45] Jericho is significant in prehistory because it is the first town, a community of perhaps two thousand persons who grew crops. A wall surrounded the settlement and its fields. Military historian John Keegan likewise interprets the walls as fortifications.[46] And so does political scientist Claudio Cioffi-Revilla, who also describes war as a "cross-cultural universal" that reached back thirty thousand years to the "conquest" of the Neanderthals by *Homo sapiens*.[47] Historian James McRandle argues "that the origins of warfare are to be found in the earliest history of mankind." After reviewing my 1970 data on the warfare practices of hunter-gatherers, McRandle concludes, "The continuity of military weapons from the hunting background does offer some reason for suspecting that war may be an institution of some antiquity. The stone spearheads discovered in prehistoric sites, as well as some of the other implements could have served the purposes of combat as well as the hunt."[48] Military historian Robert O'Connell accepts the massive stoneworks at Jericho as fortifications and concludes that "war, true war, began somewhere between seven and nine thousand years ago." More recently he has pushed warfare back to the Upper Paleolithic: Hunters "were already professional killers. . . . It was mandatory to hunt in groups. This was critical, for in these groups were the seeds of armies—or at least platoons."[49] Richard Wrangham and Dale Peterson argue that early humans engaged in lethal raiding and that the combat of simpler peoples, such as the Yanomami, a South American native people, grew directly out of a five-million-year-old past. Evidence of "real war" is to be found at Jericho, which was "designed as a fortress."[50] Writer Barbara Ehrenreich rejects the "conventional account of human origins" (i.e., the killer ape theory) and supplants it with the theory that humans were the prey. Eventually humans became the hunters who hunted to extinction or near-extinction many large animal species. "Underemployed" hunters became warriors.[51] A decade earlier historian Clifton Kroeber and anthropologist Bernard Fontana developed a theory of the origin of war that is similar to that of Ehrenreich: Hunters with no more game to hunt turned to warfare as something to do to occupy their spare time.[52] A recent hawk is archaeologist Lawrence Keeley, who argues that prehistoric as well as most more recent nonliterate people were extremely warlike. His book *War before Civilization,* published in 1996, is a polemic that bashes many anthropologists and historians for erroneously subscribing to "the myth of the peaceful savage." Keeley describes three ways in which the past has been pacified: "by definition, by special pleading interpretation or reinterpretation, and by ignorance."[53] Physical anthropologist Phillip Walker has signed on with the hawks in a review of the forensic evidence for early violence and warfare. Following Keeley's lead, he develops a section titled "Assaulting the Myth of Our Pacifistic Past."[54] Recently an archaeology colleague of Keeley's, Steven LeBlanc, has joined the charge upon unnamed believers in the myth of the peaceful savage. Indeed, LeBlanc gave his book the subtitle *The Myth of the Peaceful, Noble Savage.* He concludes that "essentially every social group on the globe has experienced conflict in practically every time period."[55]

Nearly all these scholars consider the walls of ancient Jericho to have been fortifications, thus giving us an archaeological record of ancient "true" or "real" warfare.[56] Indeed, the walls of pre-biblical Jericho are almost a litmus test indicating whether a scholar is a hawk or a dove. If the scholar interprets the walls as fortifications, he or she is probably a hawk; otherwise he or she is probably a dove. Two notable exceptions are archaeologists Ofer Bar-Yosef, who believes the walls of Jericho are for flood control, and Lawrence Keeley, who accepts Bar-Yosef's interpretation (see chapter 7, under the heading "Walls and Fortifications").[57]

An early dove, contemporaneous with Carneiro, is anthropologist Elman Service, who argued in 1962 that chiefdoms arose when a political leader assumed the role of resource redistributor; he later argued that states crystallize when support for the chief turns him into a political leader with both formal authority and power—the social contract theory.[58] Anthropologist C. R. Hallpike, writing in 1987, saw primitive warfare as neither functional nor adaptive; it occurred in "situations of low competition" and does not result in losers. He titled a chapter of his book "The Survival of the Mediocre."[59] Political scientist Richard Gabriel sees warfare as unimportant until roughly 4000 B.C.E. In the Upper Paleolithic, he contends, there is no evidence that the spear was used against human beings. Tribal warfare in the next period, the Neolithic, was "highly ritualized," and Neolithic town walls, as at Jericho, were to keep out animals.[60] Two cultural anthropologists, Leslie Sponsel and Thomas Gregor, have deliberately chosen to focus on peace and not war.[61] In an article titled "The Natural History of Peace," Sponsel points out that human prehistory is relatively free of systematic evidence of organized violence. In commenting on fossil evidence, he states that "nonviolence and peace were likely the norm throughout most of human prehistory" and "intrahuman killing was probably rare." The walls of Jericho are accepted as fortifications, but, following Gabriel, Sponsel concludes that "the existence of weapons and/or fortifications does not indicate how wide-spread and frequent warfare might have been." He states, "Many analyses of the ethnographic record indicate that, in general, nonviolence and peace prevail in hunter-gatherer societies."[62] Gregor echoes the same belief: "A good number of societies, especially at the simplest socioeconomic level, appear to have successfully avoided organized violence, that is, war."[63]

Archaeologist Jonathan Haas contends, "Archaeologically, there is negligible evidence for any kind of warfare anywhere in the world before about 10,000 years ago." Drawing from his knowledge of prehistoric peoples, Haas concludes that "endemic warfare was much more the exception than the rule until the first appearance of state level societies between 4000 and 2000 B.C.E. in the centers of world 'civilization.'"[64] Recently Haas has reiterated his position in a commentary titled "The Archaeology of War" in the *Anthropology News*.[65] I challenge his position because it underestimates the amount of warfare before 10,000 B.C.E. and exaggerates the amount of warfare in the Early Neolithic. *How War Began* provides the data that support my alternative view.

Ritual Warfare—An Illusion

Historians, and political scientists as well, accept the notion that the warfare of nonliterate peoples is "ritual warfare." This stance places them with the developmental theorists, for ritual warfare is believed to be a stage preceding true warfare. The same argument is made by political scientist Cioffi-Revilla, who distinguishes between protowar and qualifying war (post–3000 B.C.E.).[66] Ritual warfare is thought to be nonserious, involving few casualties, to be rule bound, and to be viewed by the participants as a game. It is a variant of the "myth of the peaceful savage." Ritual warfare, according to Keeley, is "pacification by definition."[67] According to the inventors of ritual war, combat in nonliterate societies consists of two lines of warriors facing each other and throwing spears or shooting arrows. Projectiles fly until someone is wounded. With that injury, the fighting stops. Such a battle is like a boys' snowball fight that ends when one boy is hit in the face.

The origin of the notion of ritual war lies in research done by anthropologists in the classical period—1920 to 1960. It appears directly drawn from scholars who constructed developmental theories. The earliest statement I can find is from Eliot Chapple and Carleton Coon. They assert that when war occurred among tribal-level societies it was ritualistic, game-like in nature; with the first wounding the battle would stop. The argument is based in part upon the belief that warfare between tribal peoples is often arranged mutually—a requirement if war is a game—in the same manner that sporting events, such as lacrosse games (an Eastern Woodlands Indian game), are arranged.[68] In my book *The Evolution of War* I tested the notion that warfare between tribal peoples is often arranged mutually and found it lacked support. In that cross-cultural study I found that only four out of twenty-eight uncentralized political systems initiated war by either announcement or mutual arrangement; the other twenty-four initiated war by surprise attacks.[69] Clearly, when only 14 percent of uncentralized political systems engage in mutually arranged battles, the cross-cultural evidence does not support the notion that the warfare of tribal peoples is ritual war. In that same study I also tested the validity of Quincy Wright's developmental sequence. I found, contrary to Wright, that economic causes of war underlay social causes, rather than the reverse. The study showed that there can be economic causes without social causes, but that social causes do not stand alone.[70] Economic causes are the subfloor, social causes the observable designer carpet lying on top.

Perhaps the most succinct statement of ritual war comes from anthropologist Raoul Naroll, a historian who became a cross-cultural anthropologist. Notice that in the following passage Naroll says "some," not most or all, primitive tribes prearranged their battles (a statement that, to my knowledge, has not been used by historians as a description of ritual war): "Surprise is not a universally applied military tactic. Some primitive tribes simply line up at extreme missile range and work up from hurling insults to hurling rocks at each other; this tournament-like war usually ends when the first enemy is killed. This kind of combat is a prearranged tryst, like duels under the European *code duello*."[71]

The source most likely to be used by historians to support the notion that "primitive warfare" is indeed ritual warfare is anthropologist William Divale's warfare bibliography, the introduction to which contains a generalized description of the warfare of nonliterate peoples. One passage has been taken out of context and used until the present by historians as an accurate description of what they are still calling primitive warfare.[72] For example,

> The pitched battle . . . involved anywhere from two hundred to two thousand warriors and was held in a pre-defined area . . . along the borders of the warring groups. . . . Even though large numbers of

warriors were involved, there was little or no military effort; instead, dozens of individual duels were engaged in. Each warrior shouted insults at his opponent and hurled spears or fired arrows. . . . Regularly occurring pitched battles were generally found among advanced tribal people in fairly dense populations. . . . In spite of the huge array of warriors involved in these pitched battles, little killing took place. . . . In the event that someone was badly wounded or slain, the battle would usually cease for that day.[73]

Divale's passage, however, continues, and a totally different view of the warfare of tribal peoples emerges:

Groups that fought in pitched battles also conducted raids or ambushes, and it was here that most of the killing occurred. In the past, many anthropologists viewed these pitched battles and, noting the small number of casualties, concluded that much or all of primitive warfare was a ritual or game. However, this perspective is now questioned, and it is suggested that such warfare was extremely effective, perhaps even over effective, in the sense that many cultural controls existed whose primary aim was the regulation and limitation of warfare.[74]

Chapple and Coon and Naroll can be criticized for helping to create the notion of ritual warfare, but Divale certainly should not be subject to that criticism.

By the mid-1970s primitive war as ritual war had taken a firm hold upon scholars. An article attacking Edward O. Wilson's *Sociobiology: The New Synthesis* by the Sociobiology Study Group of Science for the People states, "'Primitive' warfare is rarely lethal to more than one or at most a few individuals in an episode of warfare, virtually without significance genetically or demographically (Livingstone 1968). Genocide was virtually unknown until state-organized societies appeared in history (as far as can be made out from the archaeological and documentary records)."[75] At the time of the composition of the article there were thirty-five members of the organization that contributed it for publication; they are identified in a note by one initial preceding the surname, so it is not possible to ascertain whether the group includes anthropologists or historians.[76] The Livingstone article cited does not support but indeed contradicts the description of "primitive" war provided in the article; in statement after statement Frank Livingstone describes high casualty rates for the warfare of prehistoric and nonliterate peoples.[77]

In 1990 Richard Gabriel, author of many books on military organizations and warfare, stated,

Stone Age cultures that have survived into modern times provide a glimpse of what tribal warfare might have been like in the Neolithic period. It appears from these cultures that, for the most part, combat would have been highly ritualized. Extant Stone Age cultures show a remarkable ability to limit carnage in war by the simple tricks either of not using the most deadly available weapons at all or, in other cases, of disabling these weapons to reduce their effectiveness. One tribe in New Guinea, experts with the bow and arrow, remove the stabilizing feathers from the arrows during war, thus making it almost impossible to hit anything.

Gabriel gives the following footnote at the end of the passage: "Dyer [1985], 9. This example of the New Guinea Tribe has been used so often by so many people in so many books and articles that it deserves to be regarded as in the public domain and not require footnoting!"[78] I think it does. I do not know of what tribe Gabriel is writing. Indeed, one New Guinea expert has stated that "no New Guinea Highland arrows are fletched," a statement that undermines Gabriel's assertion that one New Guinea tribe removes the feathers from their arrows during war.[79] The following year Richard Gabriel and Karen Metz stated, "In less than 2,000 years [following the dawn of the fourth millennium], man went from a condition in which warfare was relatively rare and mostly ritualistic to one in which death and destruction were achieved on a modern scale."[80]

In 1993, as noted above, military historian John Keegan quoted William Divale out of context and thus created a statement of ritual warfare that Divale never intended. Keegan, as we saw in chapter 1, used the notion of ritual warfare to create one of his three warrior traditions.

Another example of the metastasis of the ritual war notion can be found in a massive compendium of classic writings on warfare, introduced by the editor, historian Gerard Chaliand, with a "loose typology of wars." The "wars of primitive societies" were excluded because they "were determined by subsistence and demography and were probably not very costly in lives." First on the list are "Ritualized Wars. These usually occur within a given society or neighboring societies in conflicts that are not wars to the death. Generally they are the mark of societies that are still archaic or traditional."[81]

More recently military historian Doyne Dawson has presented an account of "primitive warfare" that focuses on ritualization. In referring to "small decentralized societies" he states,

> Their wars seem as devoid of strategy and tactics as they are of policy; because they are conducted according to such rigid conventions, they resemble some elaborate game, sport, magic, or other ritual more than the rational political operations described as wars by people describing themselves as civilized. Most readers of this book probably have sufficient acquaintance with anthropology to appreciate the importance of ritual in primitive cultures and to understand how difficult it is to separate ritual from the culture itself.

Primitive warfare is a ritual practiced for its own sake; "civilized" warfare is an adaptation of that pattern to serve as a political instrument. . . . But at the start, something must be said about the primitive ritual out of which such wars of policy arose.[82]

A very recent definition of ritual warfare by political communication expert David D. Perlmutter expresses the concept well: "Within the anthropological literature, 'ritual war' is described as low-level, low-intensity combat, in which the object is generally to display bravery to a traditional enemy and to one's own group. Such 'showing off' in warlike displays, which do not necessarily lead to war, or mock battles with low casualties, is a behavior of many uncivilized peoples." No "anthropological literature" is cited, yet Perlmutter reviews at length what he calls the "grisly proof of authentic interhuman warfare before the contact period," which he uses to refute tribal zone theory.[83]

I hope that *How War Began* will change the views embedded in the notion of ritual warfare. I see the warfare of nonliterate peoples as no more ritualized than historic or modern warfare. I see it as rational and policy driven; even a hunting-gathering band has a leader. I see it as deadly to both combatants and noncombatants.

3
Early Humans

Early humans attacked other animals, and animals attacked humans. And sometimes early humans attacked each other. In my discussion of early humans, I explore the reasons that I believe that early hominids were highly successful in their evolution. I also describe their migration out of Africa and their spread into Europe, across Asia, and into the Americas. In conclusion, I speculate about early warfare.

Man the Cooperator

Early humans were cooperators. Among early hominids (australopithecines and early members of the genus *Homo*) cooperation was the key to survival. It permitted them to attack other animals and as well as to repel attacks by them. Group cooperation led to fraternal interest groups, the first military organizations.

Origin of Cooperation

Cooperation has both a genetic and a cultural component. As early humans adapted to the harsh African environment, both individual and group selection for cooperation took place. "Man the Scavenger" is our starting point. Since the 1970s the prevailing view has been that early humans were scavengers. They were prey, not predators. The view that they were prey suggests three capacities that were essential for the survival of early humans. First, they needed an ability to experience fear and to flee from danger. Barbara Ehrenreich argues that a passion for war developed in the trauma of being hunted by animal predators. The terror inspired by the devouring beast led to our human habit of sacralizing violence, to blood rites, and to war.[1] Although I do not accept her theory in its completed form, I do recognize that being able to flee and hide is a prerequisite to survival. Second, in order to survive, early humans needed an ability to climb to hard-to-reach places where predators could not climb and an ability to sleep at night once in a secure location. Individual animals who could not successfully flee from predators and animals who traveled at night would be eaten by roaming carnivores with good night vision. Avoiding this fate may have selected for individuals who desire sanctuaries; there may even be a genetic ba-

39

sis for building defensible space and fortifications.[2] Third, early humans needed the ability to cooperate in repulsing a predator. Cooperation is accomplished by ganging up on the predator. Film footage exists of wild chimpanzees attacking, with sticks, an animated stuffed leopard.[3] Here may lie the roots of cooperative hunting. At some point in human history this cooperation had to occur, possibly 400,000 years ago in Kenya, where a giant baboon, now extinct, appears to have been hunted by a party of late *Homo erectus*.[4] Cooperative hunting certainly occurred in central Europe by that time; archaic *Homo sapiens* used spears in hunting wild horses.[5]

My view is that early hominids cooperated with others of their kind, using rudimentary language to communicate. Cooperation would be useful not only for defending against predators, whether they be carnivores or other early hominids, but also for hunting other animals or one's own kind. Both zoologist Robert Bigelow and cultural anthropologist Bruce Knauft have argued that group selection is as important as individual selection, if not more so, in human evolution, since groups that developed affiliative behavior and communication would have tended to survive. Meanwhile, within a group, aggressively self-interested individuals—noncooperators—might be killed.[6]

In the past, I have argued that the political community with the more efficient military organization would survive and expand territorially at the expense of neighboring political communities.[7] The most cooperative groups of early hominids, because of their efficiency and, hence, success in both defense and hunting, would have been the ones to survive. Robert Carneiro concurs: "As societies compete, the less well adapted tend to fall by the wayside, leaving outstanding those best able to withstand the competition."[8] The argument for what has come to be called cultural group selection pertains to all societies, regardless of size.[9]

Studies of hunters and gatherers point to the conclusion that if the members of a band interpret an act as threatening to the survival of their group, perpetrators of that act will be eliminated—subjected to capital punishment. Offensive acts that endanger the group are incest, sacrilegious acts (such as sorcery, witchcraft, and violations of taboos), and homicide.[10] If a male cannot suppress his aggressive behavior and bond with fellow group members for the good of the group, he may be killed execution style by members of the group. Eliminating the offender both creates safety for group members and ensures a cohesive military/hunting organization. Group survival is also enhanced by the execution of a group member who disrupts the group by directly killing fellow members, appearing to do so through sorcery or witchcraft, or evoking the wrath of supernatural beings. To use the language of sociobiology, the removal of the individual who threatens other members of the group enhances the fitness of those who can suppress aggressive behavior. They are no longer in personal danger, and the group can operate more effectively in combat and in hunting. Capital punishment could be a selection mechanism that, by removing antisocial individuals from the group, removes from the gene pool genes that could have promoted their undesirable behavior.[11]

Recently evolutionary biologist Paul Bingham has offered a theory of both how cooperation arose and how "cheaters" were punished. More than two million years ago the first members of the *Homo* line acquired the capacity to kill or injure fellow adults from a distance. Bingham states that "this capacity resulted from their evolution of unique human virtuosity in throwing and clubbing." The first distance weapon Bingham posits is a "water-polished cobble." By outnumbering a wrong-doer, these "remote-killing individuals"—Bingham uses a 10-to-1 ratio—were able to enforce cooperation, "coalitional enforcement."[12] Weaponry innovations, thus, led to increased levels of social organization and communication. Although I believe that cooperation arose out of a need to repulse predators, as well as to hunt jointly, Bingham's theory is consistent with my view that dangerous individuals or noncooperators might be executed. The victim was probably not surrounded and stoned but rather killed in an ambush with clubs or killed while sleeping. To accomplish this execution did not require a "remote-killing" weapon. Without using weapons, chimpanzees are able to ambush and kill lone individuals from other bands.

Over the years group selection theory has been attacked on the grounds that groups change membership over time. A recent challenge comes from Craig Palmer and Scott Wright, who believe that group selection theory fails for this reason. They argue for individual selection alone.[13] Of course, a group's membership does change over time: Children are born and young and old die. For my theory of cultural group selection, movement of people into and out of the group is not important, whether it is by birth or death, or by voluntarily joining or departing. Departure can also be involuntary, as described above. What is important is whether the group survives. Survival of the group enhances survival of the individual members. And cooperation of group members increases the likelihood that it will survive.

Origin of Fraternal Interest Groups

Defense and attack depend on cooperation.[14] The ability to cooperate to repulse an attacking predator as well as to gang up on a likely predator is the key element in the origin of fraternal interest groups and, hence, the origin of war. The common ancestor of early humans and the chimpanzees probably had these abilities. The two existing species of chimpanzees (*Pan troglodytes* and *Pan paniscus*) have seemingly changed less in the last five million years than the *Homo* line has; with caution, we can use them to show how the early ancestor of humankind probably acted in situations of defense and attack. In the mid-1980s I made a comparison between human and chimpanzee fighting and drew a conclusion about its evolutionary implications. I noted four shared features: localized groups of related males; a leader with limited prerogatives, for example, greater access to females and choice food; bands that may segment with boundaries between them emerging; and raids on other bands, resulting in males, females, and children being attacked and killed.[15] Localized groups of related males are fraternal interest groups, and fraternal interest groups were the first military organizations. If this equation is correct, the roots of war do not lie 100,000 years in the past, but five million years ago. Furthermore, if this theory is correct, early humans engaged in warfare and so have hunter-gatherer peoples through all time.

Chimpanzees (*Pan troglodytes*) and pygmy chimpanzees (*Pan paniscus*), better known as bonobos, are considered by primatologists to be separate species. Bonobos were officially recognized in 1929, based on physical differences between the bonobos and chimpanzees; bonobos have a more gracile form and a rounded skull.[16] Although physically very similar to chimpanzees, bonobo behavior in the wild is fundamentally different. First, chimpanzees have fraternal interest groups, but bonobos do not — they have networks of female kin. Primatologists have described both chimpanzees and bonobos as "male-philopatric — that is, males stay in their natal groups whereas females disperse to neighboring groups."[17] Although bonobo males remain in their natal groups, they do not bond. Female bonobos leave their natal groups before they become sexually active. They visit neighboring communities, eventually joining one. Once they become sexually active, they bond with unrelated females. Second, chimpanzees attack other chimpanzees, while bonobos engage in frequent sexual behavior. Bonobos are known as the nice chimpanzee: They "make love, not war."[18] Third, chimpanzees are keen hunters, but bonobos do not hunt. In my studies of feuding and warfare I have distinguished two different categories or types of societies: Type 1 societies with fraternal interest groups have much conflict, rape, feuding, internal war, and intraclan executions, whereas Type 2 societies without fraternal interest groups have little conflict, no rape, no feuding, no internal war, and politywide executions.[19] These two categories of societies have their counterpart in the primate kingdom — the chimpanzees and the bonobos.

Can the differences in behavior between the chimpanzees and the bonobos be attributed solely to genetic differences? I do not think so. Chimpanzees live in areas inhabited by other primates and by predators. The bonobos live in a region of central Africa where there are no other primates to compete with them for food, so there is ample food for the bonobos. Concentrations of fruits, many of a large size, permit the formation of large bonobo groups. Bonobos also live in a region of far fewer predators. They live in larger groups that are controlled by fe-

Figure 3.1. Comparison of Chimpanzees and Bonobos in Terms of
Environment, Social Organization, and Hunting/Fighting Activities

	Environment	Social Organization	Hunting/Fighting
Chimpanzees	Predators; males defend	Fraternal interest groups	Hunting, raids
Bonobos	No predators; females gather	Female networks	No hunting, no raids

males; there are more females and they form networks; within the female networks there is a strict dominance hierarchy.[20] These differences in social organization can possibly be related to the environment: ample food, no other primate competitors, absence of predators, and females playing a major role in food gathering. Fraternal interest groups are not needed for defense from attacks of predators, so females can gather food alone, and since the food supply is ample, males do not need to hunt. I know I am going out on a limb when I say this, but I believe that if bonobos, who are male philopatric, lived in an environment where food was scarce and there were other primate competitors, as well as predators, the large female food-gathering networks would not develop and bonobos would develop fraternal interest groups. Figure 3.1 displays these relationships. This paradigmatic analysis suggests one way that fraternal interest groups can come into being. They are a response to a hostile environment, as well as an efficient way to organize for hunting. A consequence of this situation is that fraternal interest groups defend, hunt, and raid.

The existence of two genetically related species that are socially and behaviorally different has created a conundrum for researchers who are interested in finding the "best model of the last common ancestor."[21] Who does one pick—the nasty ape or the nice ape? Two strategies have been employed—to treat the bonobos as a specialized anomaly or to minimize the differences.[22] I believe that my treatment of the social and behavioral differences (see Figure 3.1) solves this conundrum. One does not need to choose. The chimpanzees/bonobos, the common ancestor, and the hominid line are genetically similar. The ability to learn is a paramount similarity. Many of the differences observed are a result of being in different environments.

Studies of different chimpanzee groups have shown that each group has a different culture.[23] This situation is also true for the bonobos. Two field sites have been reported upon: Wamba and Lomako, both situated in the Democratic Republic of Congo.[24] Chimpanzee sites lie both west and east of the bonobos: to the west of the bonobos in the Tai Forest in Ivory Coast and in the Bassou Forest in Guinea and to the east of the bonobos at Gombe and at Mahale in Tanzania, and at Kibale in Uganda. The same is also true for modern *Homo sapiens*. Some societies are violence prone and others are not—my Type 1 and Type 2 societies. I believe that this division also existed during prehistoric times. Indeed, cooperating groups of related males probably existed prior to the time that the ancestor of both the bonobos and the chimpanzees branched from the line that led to humankind. Cooperating groups of related females could also have existed. The *ability* to form cooperating groups is, thus, the heritage of both chimpanzees and humankind. Groups may form—either of males or of females—or they may not form. It is the environment, understood in the broadest terms, that seems to determine group formation.

Individuals, whether anthropoids or human beings, respond to a hostile environment in the same manner as do fraternal interest groups. A team comprising a psychologist and geneticists have put forth a paradigm that is frequently observed in mammal groups: "Challenge elicits aggressive response." The challenge is typically to either or both the individual male's status within a group or to his access to females or other important resources, or both.[25] Attacks by predators, such as leopards, are, of course, also a challenge. This paradigm can be related back to the classic statement of frustration-aggression theory, formulated by John Dollard and colleagues in 1939. They assume "that *aggression is always a consequence of frustration.* More specifically the proposition is that the occurrence of aggressive behavior always presupposes the existence of frustration and, contrariwise, that the existence of frustration always leads to some form of aggression."[26] A challenge is a frustration, whether directed toward an individual or a group. On an individual level the challenge elicits a response that is an attempt to reassert status within the group, to gain access to females, or to obtain resources, most likely food and shelter. Indeed, sustenance, a dwelling place, and females seem to be the three basic reasons for war.[27] Another variety of human aggression, according to the team of psychologist and geneticists, is predation. Primates hunt other mammals for food, animals that prey upon them, and major competitors for prey.[28] Chimpanzees hunt monkeys and attack leopards. Hunting major competitors for prey appears to occur only much later in the evolution of humankind, probably not until the emergence of *Homo sapiens* and perhaps not until modern *Homo sapiens* entered Eurasia about forty thousand years ago, equipped with throwing spears that could be launched with a spear thrower.

What constitutes a challenge is subjective; it is an interpretation of the behavior of another person or animal.[29] When an individual encounters another person or animal, he or she makes a judgment about the intent of that person or animal. If they are judged as friendly, their behavior is not interpreted as a challenge; if they are judged as threatening, their behavior is perceived as a challenge. A hypothetical example: If a man is hunting and sees another hunter approaching, the man must judge whether the second hunter intends to attack him *or* whether he wishes to join the first man in his hunting pursuits. The second hunter, rather than planning to steal the first hunter's mate, may be eager to propose a sister exchange. Experiences of an individual, particularly early experiences, may condition one individual to interpret behavior of another as a challenge, while different experiences may condition another individual to view the same behavior as nonthreatening.

Marc Howard Ross, a psychology-oriented political scientist, has shown through cross-cultural research that three child-rearing practices create a disposition to interpret situations as ripe with conflict, making an individual likely to respond with an attack. Ross argues that "*dispositional* patterns build on *cultural* constructions of the world and human relationships." They are culturally learned and approved methods for dealing with others. "What is striking to the outsider," Ross notes, "is the number of times when the same supposedly provocative action occurs and is not followed by aggressive action. This point is crucial. It means that the origins of conflict reside in *interpretations* of such situations, not the objective situations themselves." Ross identified the three child-rearing practices, or "dimensions of socialization," that create the dispositional patterns found in a society: "When early socialization is harsh, when it is low in affection and warmth, and when male gender identity conflict is high, the levels of both internal and external violence are high." Internal violence includes feuding and internal war; external violence refers to external war—war between culturally different peoples. Ross's research also shows that internal violence is related to the presence of fraternal interest groups, while external violence is related to the degree of social and political complexity. Ross observes that "since there is no authority exerted beyond the local level in uncentralized societies, the organization of fraternal interest groups, exogamous [intergroup] marriage, and cross-cutting ties among local communities of the same society are all important in shaping the level and targets of violence in these societies."[30]

In a society with fraternal interest groups, whether that society is a chimpanzee band, a hunting-gathering band, or an agricultural village, the fraternal interest groups, which are based upon the cooperation of kinsmen, are the key elements in situations of conflict. If one individual challenges another, and if kinsmen of the challenged person are in the vicinity, they will come to his aid. If the challenger's kin are also in the vicinity, they in turn will come to his aid. Conflict has escalated, and now it is not two individuals but two fraternal interest groups confronting each other. The explanation for what has occurred is known as fraternal interest group theory, initially developed by anthropologists H. U. E. Thoden van Velzen and W. van Wetering to explain why the local groups of some cultures are internally peaceful, while others are rife with internal dissension. They argued that a fraternal interest group, which is a power group of related males, resorts to aggression when there is a threat to the interests of one of its members; in societies with power groups, any act of violence will be followed by another act of violence, thereby eliciting a chain reaction. In the ethnographic record, a custom known as patrilocal marital residence, which results in wives living in their husbands' local groups, results in related males residing near each other. This situation is the genesis of fraternal interest groups. The individual who is a member of a fraternal interest group acts with the assurance that his group of kinsmen is ready to support him and his interests through thick and thin. Thus, any individual act of violence can lead to conflict between fraternal interest groups, and much aggression within the society can be attributed to the power groups and their struggles for power.

In contrast, in societies without fraternal interest groups there is no such struggle, and differences in power consist primarily in differences in muscular strength and personality. A custom that results in husbands living in their wives' local groups, matrilocal marital residence, scatters related males across the local groups of a culture. Without the presence of fraternal interest groups, potential combatants lack psychological and social support for their acts of aggression; bystanders, instead of supporting and participating in violence, may try to avert it.[31]

Conflict and cooperation are the opposite sides of the same coin: When there is conflict between groups, there is cooperation within the groups in conflict. This theory is known as the conflict-cohesion hypothesis, which was elaborated upon by sociologist Lewis Coser. Several propositions derived from the hypothesis are germane to fraternal interest group theory. Indeed, fraternal interest group theory can be subsumed under the conflict-cohesion theory. Conflict with other groups increases internal cohesion. Conflict, either intense or mild, with another group defines group structure in terms of size and degree of involvement of members. Groups may even search for real or fictional or imagined enemies without or within, with the deliberate or the unintentional result of maintaining unity and internal cohesion. Conflict reaffirms dormant norms of the group while at the same time it creates new norms of the group and modifies old ones. Conflict makes possible a reassessment of relative power and thus serves as a balancing mechanism that helps to maintain and consolidate societies.[32]

Males are challenging and aggressive toward other males; why, then, do males—particularly related males—bond and thus create fraternal interest groups? Two possible answers are suggested: First, as described above in the discussion of the origin of cooperation, males bond for defensive reasons—to repel attacks by predators, as well as attacks by same-species males. Indeed, defense—of females, sustenance, and habitation site—is the underlying reason for war. Fraternal interest groups provide protection from attackers. If the fraternal interest group is threatened, it responds by becoming the attacker; it may remove the threat to its members by killing competitors. If females are captured as a result of the attack, they may become mates; in terms used in socio-biology, this intergroup mating would enhance fitness. Second, certain hunting strategies and technologies, such as drives and surrounds, require more than one person. Group hunting provides improved hunting yield—more food for the hunters, their mates, and their offspring. Without these reasons, there would be no bonding, no fraternal interest groups.

Male aggression and fighting, for most mammalian species, is related to competition over females. In sociobiological terms, the winner enhances his genetic fitness; specifically, he increases personal survival, increases personal reproduction, and enhances survival and reproduction of close relatives who share the same genes by common descent.[33] If local males do not fight each other, whether kinsmen or nonkin males who reside near each other, their fitness is enhanced. Anthropologist Johan van der Dennen has elaborated this perspective further in his search for the origin of war. He argues that war is a male-coalitional reproductive strategy; group territoriality, intelligence that permits scheming, and belief in the superiority of one's own group combine to generate coalitions and lethal male raiding.[34]

Origin of Weapons

Ability to use weapons is biologically based—early humans, chimpanzees, and their common ancestor could throw projectiles and hit with sticks or clubs. Weapons use by early man probably occurred for defensive reasons: to defend the group when attacked by felids, canids, or other predators, for example. If a predator was nearly within arm's reach, early humans grasped a stick to serve as a club, fending off the attacker with blows. If the predator was at a greater distance, early humans grasped and threw stones or other objects, hurling them in the direction of the predator; this action might have frightened and sent scurrying, injured, or even killed these unwelcome visitors. With early humans these abilities to pick up objects in the environment and to hit with them and throw them developed into the making of weapons by modification of these objects. Weapons using and weapons making became part of the cultural system. Probably first developed for defense, this learned behavior could be applied to the hunt and to intergroup conflict.

Observational evidence shows that chimpanzees use weapons in defense—they throw objects and strike with sticks. Darwin provides examples, and he concludes by noting, "As I have repeatedly seen, a chimpanzee will throw any object at hand at a person who offends him."[35] Throwing objects and striking with sticks have been labeled "missile-throw" and "stick-club" by primatologists. I refer to objects used in this fashion as weapons because a target is present. Sticks and stones alone are not weapons, but when they are aimed at and directed toward a target they are. However, there are anatomical limitations to tool using and tool making by chimpanzees. Chimpanzee hands have long fingers and a short thumb; this combination creates a "power grip" suitable for grasping branches and swinging through the trees. On the other hand, members of the genus *Homo* have hands with a "precision grip" that gives them an enhanced ability to grasp objects between the tip of the thumb and the tips of the other fingers. The "precision grip" is not only more precise but also stronger than the "power grip."[36] This ability to hold in one hand an object, such as a stone or a club, made it possible for early humans to use weapons, and to use them effectively. Even before weapons were manufactured, an early *Homo* could have thrown a stone with greater accuracy than could a chimpanzee. This early *Homo* could also deliver with great force a vertical blow with a club.[37] Furthermore, a thrown missile is a projectile weapon and a stick used as a club is a shock weapon. The division of weapons into shock or projectile is the classic distinction used by military historians such as Charles Oman: "We find that there are only two ways in which an enemy can be met and defeated. Either the shock or the missile must be employed against him." To achieve success with shock weapons, the victor wins in a hand-to-hand struggle by his numbers, his weight, the superiority of his arms, or the greater strength and skill with which he uses them. With projectile missiles, the victor wins the day by keeping up a rain of missiles, destroying his enemy and driving him back before he can come to close quarters.[38]

The manner in which the weapons are used by chimpanzees implies tactics. The two tactics that compose the basic military pattern of hunting-gathering societies are the ambush and the line. When chimpanzees are more or less side by side throwing missiles, a nascent line formation occurs, and when chimpanzees encircle a lone predator and attack with clubs, a type of ambush has taken place. (The other type of ambush involves lying in wait.) Thus, in the attacks of chimpanzees upon predators we can see both the basic military pattern and the two types of weapons characteristic of many military organizations.

Primatologist Jane Goodall has reported that the chimpanzees of Gombe patrol their territories and attack any lone aliens they discover. Goodall also reports chimpanzee precursors of the other main hunter-gatherer tactic: the line. Chimpanzee patrols that encounter each other shout and throw sticks and stones. Eventually they draw apart. Like groups of human warriors who sometimes confront each other in demonstrative line formations, a test of strength is occurring. This evidence seems to me to undermine Goodall's own conclusion that "until our remote ancestors acquired *language* they would not have been able to engage in the kind of planned intergroup conflicts that could develop into warfare—into organized, armed combat."[39] How much planning is needed for an ambush or a line encounter? Very little, I think.

There are, however, two major ways in which chimpanzee behavior differs significantly from that of hunter-gatherers today, and probably also from early human behavior: First, the chimpanzee does not make weapons. The chimpanzee may make rudimentary tools, such as wands for ant dipping, but they do not manufacture tools that are used to confront predators, to attack other chimpanzees, or to use in hunting.[40] Second, although chimpanzees hunt in groups, they do not use weapons or tools as they hunt. Even chimpanzees in the Tai Forest of Ivory Coast, who hunt more than any other known chimpanzee group, do not employ tools or weapons, not even those manufactured and made available to them by others. Large canine teeth serve as their weapons, and red colobus monkeys are their favorite prey. Another chimpanzee group at Ngogo in Uganda's Kibale National Park also extensively hunts the red colobus monkey. Since the community is large, large hunting parties form, a factor in hunting success. Hunting is both opportunistic and planned; the hunts are organized patrols.[41] Furthermore, tools are not used to smash skulls or crush bones, although chimpanzees have the ability to use hammer-stones, something they have learned to do in zoos. In the wild chimpanzees use stones to crack oil-palm nuts placed on wooden anvils. As they pound, small pieces break off the stones, creating "refuse accumulation and site formation."[42] These sites in the Tai Forest, in Ivory Coast, and the "tools" created bear a superficial resemblance to the Oldowan tools produced by *Homo habilis* 2.5 million years ago (see next section). Elsewhere in west Africa, in the forest of Bosson, Guinea, chimpanzees have been observed placing nuts on stone platforms and pounding them with smaller stones. Finally, unlike humans, chimpanzees do not make containers, do not store food, and do not build fires.[43]

A study of the tool use of nine wild chimpanzee populations found that four groups had both "missile-throw" and "stick-club" as "antipredatory patterns of weapons use (flail-club-missile)."[44] A recent comparative study of six chimpanzee populations that focused upon cultural differences among the groups found that four populations had missile-throw and three had stick-club.[45] The implication of these studies is that even in chimpanzee populations, the two basic types of weapon use are learned behavior. Some populations have developed their biological potential to throw missiles and others have not; the same is true for the use of the club. Those chimpanzees that have learned to use weapons have used them against predators and possibly against fellow chimpanzees. However, chimpanzees have not been observed to hunt with weapons. Learning to use weapons probably arose through imitative behavior: A single chimpanzee either threw a missile or struck with a club, and the behavior was copied by other members of the group.[46]

The club was probably the first weapon that early humans used. Although stones could have been the first weapons, the presumed lack of bags or nets to carry multiple missiles makes it more likely that the club was the weapon of choice. As will be argued below in the section "The Evolution of Humankind," *Homo erectus* probably left Africa 1.7 million years ago carrying a club. None has been found by archaeologists. However, by 400,000 years ago in Europe, wooden spears with hardened tips were produced and used to hunt large animals, primarily horses.[47] With the development of bands and the hunting of large game animals established as a cultural practice, early humankind could direct an attack upon a lone individual or group of hunters who threatened the subsistence of the hunting and gathering band by venturing into the region it already occupied. "Shoot-on-sight" tactics developed. Indeed, anthropologist Raymond Kelly argues that war had its genesis in "shoot-on-sight" tactics.[48]

Although a lone individual might use a weapon, perhaps in hunting small game, it is more likely that weapons were used by men in groups hunting large game. The nature of band organization of the common ancestor of early humans and the chimpanzee probably consisted of related males with their mates and offspring. These localized groups of males—fraternal interest groups—occur in many hunting and gathering bands described in the ethnographic record. They defend the interests of the band, often in confrontations with other groups. Use of weapons by such groups against each other fits the minimal definition of warfare, provided the bands are considered to be political communities. Such groups of males are, then, military organizations.

Out of Africa Theory

Early humans evolved in Africa. From this heartland, *Homo erectus* migrated into Eurasia more than 1.5 million years ago. In the last forty thousand years, modern *Homo sapiens,* the African descendant of *Homo erectus,* migrated into not only Eurasia but also North and South America.

The Evolution of Humankind

The three most important events in the history of humankind are the emergence and development of the three major *Homo* species: *habilis, erectus,* and *sapiens.*[49] Since the 1960s the evolutionary sequence described below has been accepted by most paleontologists. Starting about 10 million years ago the earth became cooler and drier. Grasses replaced tropical forests. The scene is Africa and a tree-dwelling hominid called *Australopithecus* begins to exploit the grasslands. *Australopithecus* and chimpanzees had a common ancestor. At least seven species of *Australopithecus* have been identified, some walking on the ground and some agile tree climbers, but all bipedal. Cranial capacity was roughly 400 to 500 cubic centimeters. From 10 to 3 million years ago the tree cover continued to shrink, and Africa become cooler and more arid. One hominid spent more time on the ground and over several million years of evolution became fully bipedal.[50] Because it was hotter on the grassy savanna than in the forest, the hominid became thinner, had a less hairy body, and developed an external nose. This australopithecine did not make tools. Out of this ape ancestry emerged, by 2.5 million years ago, *Homo habilis*. Characteristic of this first *Homo* species is a brain expanded to about 630 cubic centimeters, increased tool use (and, soon, tool manufacture), and increased meat eating. Tool use probably included the accurate throwing of rocks at game and the use of a club to kill crippled animals. *Homo habilis* also made tools of a type known as Oldowan, which date from 2.5 to 1.7 million years ago (see Figure 3.2).

Homo erectus evolved rapidly from *Homo habilis* at or before 1.8 million years ago. This hominid had a bigger body and a bigger brain (about 1000 cubic centimeters), and over time brain size increased. Sometime after the appearance of *Homo erectus* a new tool tradition appears, the Acheulean, the hallmark of which is a large biface chopping tool. This tool is believed to have been used to butcher animals. Although from time to time it has been suggested that this tool might have been a projectile weapon, thrown like a discus, this claim cannot be supported.[51] Before the Acheulean tool tradition was established, *Homo erectus* swept out of Africa—the first "out of Africa" migration. An early form of *Homo erectus* has recently been discovered at Dmanisi, in the Republic of Georgia at the eastern end of the Black Sea. The discovery has stunned paleontologists because the finds are confidently dated to 1.7 million years ago and the accompanying tools are Oldowan. They are stone flakes, scrapers, and various chopping tools.[52] Researchers have just begun to speculate on why this rapid exodus from Africa occurred. My guess is that this large, fully bipedal, big-brained hominid was able to enter Eurasia unopposed.[53] Other animals already in the area had seen nothing like this creature before. They were probably unafraid and thus easily brought down by a large club and powerfully pitched stone. The increasing energy requirements of the larger body and brain size of the migrating *Homo erectus* were perhaps met by exploitation of animal protein—and thus, hunting.[54] There is no evidence for clubs, but given the ease with which chimpanzees will pick up sticks and attack a predator, I cannot imagine *Homo erectus* without a club. This dynamic hominid migrated into eastern Asia and fanned out into what is today Java and China. *Homo erectus* finds in Java have been dated to 1.6 million years ago. Oldowan-like tools, rather than Acheulean hand axes (which are

TIME (Years Ago)	AFRICA Hominids	AFRICA Tool Tradition	EUROPE Hominids	EUROPE Tool Tradition	ASIA Hominids	ASIA Tool Tradition
20,000			*Homo sapiens*	Magdalenian	*Homo sapiens*	—
				Solutrean		
				Aurignacian		
40,000		Aterian				
			Homo neanderthalensis	Mousterian		
200,000	*Homo sapiens*					
		Acheulean				
1.8 M	*Homo erectus*		*Homo erectus*	Oldowan	*Homo erectus*	Oldowan
2.5 M	*Homo habilis*	Oldowan				
5 M	*Australopithicus africanus*					

Figure 3.2. Early Humans and Their Tools

also absent from Europe), are found in eastern Asia. The first presence of *Homo erectus* in western Europe seems to be, surprisingly, nearly a million years later. Ice age glaciers perhaps blocked the advance of *Homo erectus* into western Europe for hundreds of thousands of years.

While some *Homo erectus* migrated to Eurasia, many remained in Africa, where they developed the Acheulean tool tradition. Here the australopithecines and *Homo habilis* hunted animals that had learned to flee from primates. Better tools meant that those animals killed were more efficiently processed for food. Clubs would have been used in the hunt. Clubs were probably used 400,000 years ago to kill the giant baboon found in Kenya. Wooden spears, either thrusting or throwing spears, might have been developed, but there is no evidence. Yet reputable books on primate evolution, such as *Lucy: The Beginnings of Humankind,* depict *Homo erectus* carrying a spear.[55] (The first known throwing spears, found in Europe, are only 400,000 years old.) These African *Homo erectus* became the first hominids to invade arid, highly seasonal environments. Perhaps the environmental challenge selected for larger brains. Meat eating may have kept the process going. *Homo erectus* in Africa evolved slowly—over a period of 1 million years—into *Homo sapiens.* By 600,000 years ago there are "archaic *sapiens,*" which appear to have evolved from early *Homo erectus.*[56] The brain in these hominids is larger (about 1230 cubic centimeters) and the cranium less robust. Skeletons of the body retained their overall ruggedness: the *Homo sapiens* head with the *Homo erectus* body. There appears to have been a migration of early archaic *sapiens* out of Africa, a migration that took them into both Europe and Asia.

I have chosen to present the evolution of humankind as essentially linear: a hominid, perhaps an *Australopithecus; Homo habilis;* the Dmanisi *Homo erectus; Homo erectus;* archaic *sapiens;* and *Homo sapiens.* Branching was minimal. One branch arose in Europe: Archaic *sapiens* evolved into *Homo neanderthalensis.* This view of *Homo* taxonomy is taken by the so-called lumpers, in contrast to the splitters, those researchers who, when they view the fossil record, see numerous species of hominids occupying the Old World at the same period. In recent years the splitters have been ascendant. They believe, according to one of their number, that "our family tree is no longer a linear series of species but a dense bush with many dead branches."[57] However, the fossil finds uncovered at Dmanisi show great variability in size. Here, apparently within a single species, are found a huge jawbone and a small skull. In the same layers of rock, parts of as many as six individuals have been found.[58] A splitter would probably distinguish at least two species, if not more. The Dmanisi fossils, however, were found together and thus present a strong argument for a single species and give credence to a linear approach.

A half million years ago there were at least three evolving human lineages: *Homo sapiens* in Africa, *Homo neanderthalensis* in Europe, and *Homo erectus* in Asia. In Europe the archaic *sapiens* did not develop into *Homo sapiens,* but into *Homo neanderthalensis.* Their descendants were excellent hunters—400,000 years ago they hunted wild horses, driving them to an ambush site and killing them with javelins.[59] For the next 300,000 years the European archaic *sapiens* evolved into the classic Neanderthals. The brains of *Homo neanderthalensis* grew larger, as did those of African *Homo sapiens* (to more than 1500 cubic centimeters), and the cranium became robust. The earliest injury to a human being that can conclusively be identified as inflicted by a weapon was that caused by a wooden javelin blow to the femur of one of the Neanderthals from perhaps 50,000 years ago, found at Mugharet es-Skhul.[60] A new tool technology known as the Mousterian developed. Stone spear points are part of the assemblage. In eastern Asia the Java *Homo erectus* evolved little, while the Chinese *Homo erectus* began to approach *Homo sapiens* in braincase size and form. Asian tools changed little.

The early African *Homo sapiens* continued to evolve. Their brains grew larger and their bodies less robust. By about 250,000 years ago biface tools were no longer made and more elaborate tool assemblages appeared. Methods for mounting stone flakes on wooden or bone handles were probably invented at this time. By 200,000 years ago, or soon after, with many dates converging on about 130,000 years ago, the ancestor of all present-day humans was living in Africa, where his or her descendants remained until about 40,000 years ago.[61] Then a distinct rupture occurred: The Middle Stone Age in Africa and the Middle Paleolithic in Europe gave way to the Later Stone Age and the Upper Paleolithic. A late Middle Stone Age tradition of innovative stone tool making, known as the Aterian, spreads widely across the Sahara of northern Africa.[62] Rainfall was probably ample and game animals plentiful.[63] A major advance in weaponry, the "dart-thrower—dart complex," first appeared 40,000 years ago, providing a way to hunt animals more efficiently.[64] According to Donald Johanson and Blake Edgar, "Aterian points are notable for the squared-off tang protruding from the base that must have been used to haft this tool to the end of a wooden shaft as a spear point." These small points measure approximately two inches by one inch, and the tangs are about one-half inch across.[65] They were clearly affixed to light-weight shafts; they were too small to be used with thrusting or throwing spears. Archaeologist Malcolm Farmer states that the "dart-thrower—dart complex" appears about 40,000 years ago in the Aterian culture.[66] Knowledge of how the dart- or spear-throwing tool—the atlatl—was made and used could have easily spread eastward to peoples who were living in the Nile corridor. The Upper Paleolithic ushered in a new tool assemblage that consisted of a large variety of forms, including spear points and spear throwers, known as Aurignacian; the modern *Homo sapiens* who made them are called Cro-Magnon.

Artistically shaped and carved spear throwers have been found in Solutrean and Magdalenian assemblages at 20,000 years ago. These tools are the Upper Paleolithic equivalent of modern engraved knives and firearms. Shortly after 40,000 years ago modern *Homo sapiens* migrated out of Africa, eventually displacing the Neanderthals in Europe and, by 10,000 years ago, the *Homo erectus* of Asia.[67] What delayed *Homo sapiens's* departure from the Nile corridor? I suggest that Neanderthals in the area of the Levant blocked the way. Not until *Homo sapiens* had perfected an assemblage of weapons could they force their way through.[68] Archaeologist John Shea has recently argued that there was intense "competition between Neanderthals and early modern humans for the same ecological niche in the Levant." Shea speaks of projectile points and projectile weaponry aiding the early modern humans but does not inform us as to what the weapon was. Malcolm Farmer's analysis of the dart-thrower—dart complex makes it clear that the weapon must have been the spear thrower.[69]

This migration of *Homo sapiens* from their homeland has been called the "out of Africa hypothesis." In recent years paleontologists have begun to include the much earlier migration of *Homo erectus* out of Africa under the same hypothesis. A summary article in *Time* depicts, on a map labeled "'Out of Africa' Theory," both the spread of *Homo erectus* and the *Homo sapiens* expansion across Eurasia.[70] Since these are two totally different migrations, Richard Kline has suggested that the *Homo erectus* migration of 1.75 million years ago be labeled "Out of Africa 1," while the *Homo sapiens* migration of 40,000 years ago be labeled "Out of Africa 2."[71] I also believe, as I suggested above, that there was an "Out of Africa" migration of archaic *sapiens* that occurred about 600,000 years ago.

Migrations

The migration of *Homo erectus* out of Africa probably took place over a half million years and may well have continued for much longer. These hominids faced no competition from similar primates. Other animals —potential game—at first did not fear *Homo erectus*. Animals' lack of fear of new settlers has been observed in relatively modern times; it is used to explain the rapid extinction of animals on the island of Madagascar and on the islands of Polynesia.[72] As they migrated into new territory, *Homo erectus* could approach close enough to small- to medium-size game to easily kill them with stones and clubs. The first settlers need not have moved far, but each succeeding generation took *Homo erectus* farther into Eurasia. Bands would have been well spread out, perhaps twenty miles apart, hunting over a territory perhaps as large as five hundred square miles.[73] The bands may well have developed fraternal interest groups for defense and hunting. The hunting fraternal interest groups from different bands might from time to time have encountered each other. But since in some areas the environment probably did not hold dangerous predators that could challenge *Homo erectus,* some bands may not have developed fraternal interest groups. Because uninhabited lands rich with game lay before them, conflict over food and dwelling sites would have been infrequent. Fighting over females could have arisen, but peaceful mate exchange was probably more likely. Indeed, anthropologists Douglas MacDonald and Barry Hewlett have reasoned that hunting-gathering bands often range over a larger territory than required by their sustenance needs in order to find other bands with whom they can exchange mates.[74] The widespread distribution of similar skeletal remains shows a pattern of sufficient continuity to suggest enough gene flow across Eurasia and back into Africa to maintain a single species.[75]

For the migration of *Homo sapiens* out of Africa the situation was entirely different. In the Levant and Europe *Homo sapiens* met *Homo neanderthalensis*—a similar species whose males were physically stronger. Evidence is accumulating that in the Levant there were indeed two populations, probably noninterbreeding, and that the "replacement" model of modern human origins, sometimes called the Out of Africa 2 model, is correct.[76] The thicker bones and greater muscularity of *Homo neanderthalensis* would have made for a formidable opponent in hand-to-hand combat, with or without weapons. The thinner boned *Homo sapiens* would not have been nearly as strong. The Neanderthals had weapons—wooden throwing spears and spears hafted with stone points. They also had behind them at least a 400,000-year-old tradition of hunting with spears. They could use spears as both projectile and shock weapons. Indeed, they had killed one of their own with a wooden javelin strike. *Homo sapiens* also had throwing spears and, about 40,000 years ago, invented the dart and spear thrower, or atlatl (see Figure 3.3). A "spear and spear thrower" can be referred to as a "weapons system"; this combination constitutes the first efficient long-range hunting weapon that can also be used in war. It is described by archaeologist Malcolm Farmer: "By the beginning of the Upper Paleolithic, thus by about 40,000 years ago, there seems to have been an innovation of the throwing spear, the dart thrower—a length of wood with a finger hold at the proximal end and a spur at the distal end to engage the butt end of a missile shaft. There were also improved projectile points."[77] The dart thrower or atlatl shown in Figure 3.3 does not illustrate a specific atlatl. It is shown with finger hold, distal spur, and a weight or bannerstone, which is believed by some to add balance and stability to the weapon.[78] Although much practice with the atlatl is required to obtain accuracy, the leverage gained when the arm is brought forward propels the spear much farther than it could be thrown without the assistance of the spear thrower. Pierre Cattelain describes its usefulness: "The purpose of spear thrower use is either accuracy and forceful impact over a

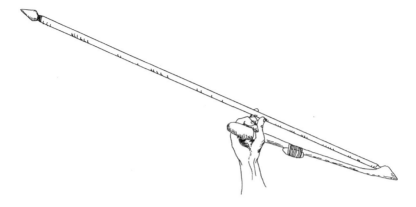

Figure 3.3. Illustration of an Atlatl

short distance (using a relatively long and heavy projectile for hunting and fishing) or a long distance shot (using a light projectile during warfare, for example)."[79]

Thus, *Homo sapiens* had a weapon that was superior to the weapons of *Homo neanderthalensis. Homo sapiens* did not have to engage in hand-to-hand combat or in a close-range spear-throwing battle; the atlatl provided "firepower" that could have been used to drive *Homo neanderthalensis* from the field of battle. (By the time the bow and arrow was invented about fifteen thousand years ago, *Homo neanderthalensis* had vanished from the scene.) I doubt, however, whether *Homo sapiens* and *Homo neanderthalensis* had formal line battles. Peter A. Corning, who attributes the expansion of *Homo sapiens* from their heartland to a "culturally driven process," suggests that two new weapons were the difference that made the difference: "There are two strong candidates for what provided the 'competitive edge' in terms of military technology (though there may have been others that left no archaeological traces): (1) spear throwers, which greatly increased the range and accuracy of their possessors, and (2) hafted stone axes with sophisticated obsidian blades and bitumen mountings. The immense advantages of these weapons over simple wooden clubs or primitive hand-axes in hand-to-hand combat should be obvious."[80] I believe that the spear thrower was far more important than the stone ax; I think it was highly unlikely that the more intelligent *Homo sapiens* would have engaged the stronger *Homo neanderthalensis* in hand-to-hand combat. The weapon superiority of *Homo sapiens* caused the Neanderthals to retreat from their most desirable lands. With a restricted food supply their reproductive rate fell and mortality increased.[81]

In the hypothesized contact described above, no mate exchange or gene flow has been assumed. Indeed, if any Neanderthal females had been captured or had willingly joined the *Homo sapiens,* Neanderthal demise would have occurred faster. But there is no evidence of any interbreeding between *Homo sapiens* and *Homo neanderthalensis.*[82] Although the Neanderthals seem to quickly disappear from the areas where *Homo sapiens* came in contact with them, the total process took nearly fifteen thousand years. Ian Tattersall writes that "at individual [archaeological] sites, the shift between Mousterian [*Homo neanderthalensis*] and Aurignacian [*Homo sapiens*] appears to be abrupt. This pattern starts right at the beginning. . . . What's more the artifact assemblages show no evidence of cultural intermixing."[83] Beginning about forty thousand years ago, in eastern Europe, the existing Neanderthal populations disappeared and were replaced by modern humans, the final replacement taking place in the far west by about twenty-seven thousand years ago, in southern Spain.[84]

With the way cleared, other groups of modern *Homo sapiens* were able to migrate eastward. One branch probably turned southeastward into Java, where *Homo erectus* may have still been living, and then into uninhabited Australia. Watercraft were necessary for the journey. On the Australian continent *Homo sapiens* encountered a megafauna that they hunted to extinction.[85] Another branch probably took a more northerly route, which brought *Homo sapiens* into northeastern Europe, a cold region uninhabited by *Homo neanderthalensis.* Here, *Homo sapiens* used their hunting skills to kill medium-sized to large game. These *Homo sapiens* developed tailored clothing and dwellings, made of the hides of game animals, which permitted them to penetrate into colder climates and to survive there. In China *Homo sapiens* may have encountered *Homo erectus,* and, if so, the Asian *Homo erectus* probably met the same fate as the Neanderthals. The spear thrower that had propelled *Homo sapiens* into ascendance over the Neanderthals was equally effective against any surviving populations of *Homo erectus. Homo sapiens* did not reach northeastern Asia until after thirty-five thousand years ago. From there, entry into the New World was probably blocked by an ice sheet that extended more or less continuously across Canada, although some scholars believe that *Homo sapiens* may have gotten through before the closing phases of the last glaciation fourteen thousand years ago. The theory that hunters and their families followed large herd animals into the New World has been rejected.[86]

Humans present in Siberia 30,000 years ago were positioned to migrate into North America. During the Wisconsin glacial period the sea level dropped and a land bridge connecting the continents opened about 20,000 years ago. It is unlikely, however, that the people could have found their way through a narrow, ice-free strip between two major glaciers. More likely, if they arrived in North America before the glaciers dramatically began to recede, 14,000 years ago, they took a coastal route. Watercraft would have been required for this journey as well. One

site in North America and three sites in South America have been assigned dates earlier than 14,000 years ago. The people inhabiting these
sites were not hunters of large game but subsisted instead on small animals, gathering, and river foraging.[87] Once the glaciers receded, Siber-
ian hunters of large game migrated into North America. These ancestors
of American Indians were efficient hunters who tipped their spears with
fluted projectile points, called Clovis points, after the site where they
were first discovered and described. Most Clovis sites date between
11,200 and 10,800 years ago.[88] At sites where animal bones are pre-
served, some usually come from extinct species, including mammoth,
camel, and horse. The two-migration theory fits with the long-noted
observation that big game hunters were in the Great Plains and eastern
forests, while collectors of wild plants and small game were west of the
Rocky Mountains.[89] By 10,500 years ago, the New World, especially
South America, had great cultural variation. The earliest peoples made a
range of regionally diverse projectile points.[90] Archaeologist Thomas
Dillehay has argued this position; he describes numerous sites that date
to about 10,500 years ago.[91]

Probably because of both the skill of the hunters and climatic change
a large number of New World species disappeared. As in the migration
of *Homo erectus* into Eurasia, the animals had not developed fear of
primates. Hunters, probably organized into fraternal interest groups,
drove animals off cliffs or surrounded them. Throwing spears and atlatl darts dispatched the animals, including woolly mammoths. Wild
horses were also among the animals that became extinct. Because no
horses were left to be domesticated, no indigenous cavalry developed in
the New World—an obvious point, but an event of great significance
for the understanding of military history. During the period of animal
extinction there was probably competition between groups of hunters
who had to range more and more widely to find large game animals.
Kennewick Man, who may have been a descendant of members of the
first migration, lived about eighty-five hundred years ago (after Clovis)
in what is today the state of Washington. Since his pelvis has the tip of
a projectile point healed into it, we can presume that he was a hunter of
large game animals as well as a combatant (see the section "Projectile
Points in Bone," chapter 4).[92]

Two other migrations of early humans to North America took place.
First, the Na Dene speakers, ancestors of the Athabascans in Canada and
the Navaho and Apache in the American Southwest, arrived by eight
thousand years ago, and, second, the Eskimo-Aleuts appeared in Alaska
forty-five hundred years ago.[93]

These migrations and the other two before them led to regional patterns of prehistoric violence in North America. On the west coast, what
is today California, the collectors of wild plants and small game became
relatively sedentary. Once the bow and arrow became available after

A.D. 500, fishes and aquatic animals could be more efficiently procured. Territory became worth defending, and evidence of raids in the form of projectile injuries increased. Farther north along the coast of western Canada the same pattern of warfare arose.[94]

The peoples who had long occupied the Great Plains and the eastern forests, in spite of the decline of the megafauna, still had available to them the American bison and the white-tailed deer. The bow and arrow appeared three hundred years later in the central and eastern parts of North America than it had on the west coast. Its arrival led to intensified hunting and warfare. Large-scale wars and massacres followed by mutilation are found at such sites as Crow Creek in South Dakota (A.D. 1325). To the south, on the western part of the Gulf Coastal Plain, the hunters and gatherers apparently engaged in raids and shoot-on-sight tactics. Here mutilation of enemy dead was uncommon. Two other regions, whose warfare patterns might have been influenced by central American states, present evidence of serious warfare. In the Southeast chiefdoms arose and with them, military fortifications and "armies." In the Southwest chiefdoms likewise developed, and there is evidence of dismemberment and cannibalism.[95] The arrival of the Na Dene speakers— hunters and gatherers—in the Southwest after A.D. 1000 further intensified warfare by pitting the sedentary pueblo peoples against the nomadic intruders.[96]

Speculations about Early Warfare

What is known about the stone tool technologies of early humans, as well as what is known about chimpanzee behavior, makes it possible to conjecture what early warfare was like (see Figure 3.4).

Homo habilis made a variety of chopping tools, tools designed to cut flesh from bones and to break up bones. Since chimpanzees can both throw stones and strike with clubs (although they do not do so in hunting or intergroup conflict), it seems reasonable to assume that *Homo habilis* had the same ability. Indeed, the structure of the hand of *Homo habilis,* a precision grip rather than the chimpanzee's power grip, made it easier for the former to throw stones accurately and to deliver a powerful blow with a club. Although *Homo habilis* were to some extent scavengers, when the opportunity arose they probably killed small game with stones and clubs, implements perhaps saved for this purpose. Social organization would have consisted of a cooperating group of hunter-gatherers. Both males and females subsisted primarily on foraging. Confrontations between bands may have been similar to chimpanzee encounters, where lone individuals were ambushed and groups of males made threat displays to each other. If stones and clubs were used in the ambush or in the group challenges, my minimal definition of war applies—there was armed combat between independent groups.

Figure 3.4. Speculations about Early Warfare

Early Man	Tools	Social Organization	Armed Combat
Modern Homo sapiens	Aurignacian and other tool traditions Numerous tools, clubs, spears, and spear throwers	Hunting-gathering band Semi-sedentary band	Ambushes, raids, lines
Homo neander- thalensis	Mousterian Numerous tools, clubs, spears	Hunting-gathering band Semi-sedentary band	Ambushes, raids
Archaic Homo sapiens	Numerous tools, clubs, throwing spears	Hunting-gathering band Fraternal interest groups	Ambush and line
Homo erectus	Acheulean Hand axes, clubs, spears (?)	Hunting-gathering band Fraternal interest groups	Ambush and line
Homo habilis	Oldowan Chopping tools, clubs (?)	Cooperating group of hunter-gatherers	Possibly like chimpanzees (ambushes and lines)

The basic pattern was ambushes and lines. Thus, war could have begun with *Homo habilis.*

Our next hominid, *Homo erectus,* initially had the same tools as *Homo habilis.* When entering Eurasia from Africa, these hominids almost undoubtedly carried clubs that they used to kill animals. While certainly still scavenging, they were also hunters. There probably was within most hunting-gathering bands at least one fraternal interest group. The abundant wildlife and the availability of uninhabited lands probably made intergroup contacts rare, and when contacts did occur, mate exchange, rather than armed combat, was likely to take place. But the possibility of violent confrontations between fraternal interest groups was an ever-present possibility. Late in their existence, the African *Homo erectus* developed better tools, including a large hand ax and a cleaver made from a single large stone flake. Being heavy and sharp, they were excellent tools for cutting up carcasses of medium-sized animals, either scavenged or killed. No stone points are found in the Acheulean tool tradition, but *Homo erectus* possibly developed a spear with a wooden point. With a club and a spear and membership in a fraternal interest group, later *Homo erectus* groups may have engaged in combat with other groups. Ambushes and lines would both have occurred.

Archaic *Homo sapiens* did have spears, and hunting with the spears was well planned. Social organization consisted of hunting-gathering bands composed of fraternal interest groups. Having throwing spears and the ability to set ambushes for wild animals, such as horses, made it possible to set ambushes for the purpose of killing a person from another band. Even line battles consisting of spear-throwing males could have occurred. Fighting could have been over hunting territories, dwelling sites, and females.

Homo neanderthalensis, a descendant of an early archaic *Homo sapiens* in Europe, made many more tools than the precursor species. The Mousterian tool tradition, which is associated with Neanderthals, includes stone points that could have been hafted to the killing end of a spear. With inhabited land surrounding them, except for the impassable glacier-covered region to the north, the bands lived a semisedentary life. Ambushes, as well as raids upon relatively permanent dwelling sites, could have occurred. There is still no evidence, however, that these ambushes and raids occurred, except for the Neanderthal killed by the javelin blow to the femur.

Modern *Homo sapiens* elaborated upon the tools of the ancestor, an early African *Homo sapiens.* In addition to spears, spear throwers were invented. This weapon, depending upon the weight of the missile, could be used for hunting large game or in battle with Neanderthals or other *Homo sapiens.* The rapid demise of the Neanderthals in the absence of evidence for interbreeding, is, I believe, indirect evidence for warfare. But the Neanderthals were probably more likely to retreat than fight. Physical anthropologist Ian Tattersall suggests "a scenario of well-equipped and cunning *Homo sapiens* descending on Neanderthal groups, killing the males—through strategy and guile, certainly not through strength."[97] I doubt that *Homo sapiens* would risk hand-to-hand combat with Neanderthals. (Direct evidence—paintings on rock walls—for line battles in which spear throwers were used will be presented in chapter 4.) Projectile points in human pelvis bones complete the proof that early modern *Homo sapiens* sometimes targeted each other.

The basic pattern of warfare consisting of ambushes and lines, in which shock and projectile weapons are used, may go back as early as *Homo habilis,* two million years ago. While warfare was probably rare until about forty thousand years ago, it did occur on occasion. Fraternal interest groups, weapons, and hunting form a complex—given its ancient origin it can be called the eternal triangle. Male mammals, including the chimpanzees and the hominids, have the propensity to both give and respond aggressively to challenges. If the complex of fraternal interest group, weapons, and hunting is coupled with the propensity of males to give and respond aggressively to challenges, the result is likely to be armed combat that can lead to deaths.

4
Hunters and Gatherers

Hunter-gatherers in prehistory and in recent times have frequently engaged in warfare. Evidence for this warfare is abundant: rock art, stone points in bone, and ethnographic accounts. A major conclusion of *How War Began* is that warfare and hunting increased in the late Upper Paleolithic, then declined as many large animals became extinct. Supporting this conclusion is the finding that societies that rely heavily on hunting engage in warfare more frequently than do societies that rely heavily on gathering.

Big Game Hunters

Early humans developed excellent hunting weapons, such as the spear thrower. As large game animals were hunted to extinction, the subsistence base expanded to include small game and many wild seeds, and life became more sedentary.

Weapons Development

The key to successful hunting is to have a good weapon. By 250,000 years ago, early humans had probably invented methods for hafting stone points on wooden shafts. The practice of mounting a bone point onto a shaft may also have been developed at this time. By the late Middle Stone Age in Africa and the late Middle Paleolithic in the eastern Mediterranean, there is evidence of points being attached to shafts. North African Aterian tanged points have modifications to accommodate attachment—for example, notches on both sides of the base of the spear point. Such a point can fit into a groove in the end of the shaft. The notches facilitate lashing the point to the shaft. These small points probably tipped short, lightweight shafts that could be launched with a spear thrower.[1] Archaeologists and paleontologists view the development of spear technology as important in the development of humankind for two reasons: First, it indicates that people at this time were obtaining an increasing proportion of their animal protein and fat from hunting; second, it is coterminous with the development of modern *Homo sapiens* and late *Homo neanderthalensis*. Thus, it is possible that these weapons derive from increasing human intelligence. From my point of view, these projectile weapons increase not only hunting efficiency but also the military capability of those who possess them. The spear thrower, or atlatl, as it is known in the New World, probably entered the New World with the first migration of humans, although the earliest evidence for its use is 8,500 years ago. Archaeologist Bruce Dickson notes that Clovis points could have served as effective spear tips for spears launched with atlatls.[2]

Ethnographic observations and experiments have shown that a spear can be thrown about twenty-five meters with the bare hand and about one hundred meters with the spear thrower — three to four times as far. At twenty-five meters the atlatl is an accurate weapon.[3] Pierre Cattelain has described the accuracy of the weapons: In hunting, the effective distance of projectiles shot with a spear thrower seems to be limited to a maximum of forty-five meters, but in general a precise shot does not exceed twenty to thirty meters.[4] If two groups of hunters meet, one armed with thrusting and throwing spears and the other with atlatls, the group with the atlatls would be able to "open fire" long before the other group could reach a suitable throwing distance; at that distance, the hunters armed with atlatls would be able to target their enemies with accuracy.

The next major advance in weapons technology was the bow and arrow, which may have been invented more than twenty thousand years ago. Its origin is unclear. Small, well-fashioned stone points that could have been hafted on arrow shafts are found in various parts of Eurasia and Africa. The bow and arrow spread rapidly in both Africa and Eurasia. A sharp increase in the abundance of tiny, backed bladelets indicates their spread. The first conclusive evidence is from twelve thousand years ago: Fragmentary wooden bows and arrows are found in late Magdalenian sites in France and in Germany, where fragments of bows and arrows, made of pine heartwood, have been discovered in a peat bog.[5] The bow and arrow appeared in the New World much later. It reached the Canadian Arctic by 2500 B.C.E., the Great Plains by A.D. 200, California by A.D. 500, and the Southwest by A.D. 700.[6] As the bow and arrow spread across North America, it gave both a hunting and a military advantage to those groups of hunters who first acquired the new weapon.[7] Just as the spear thrower gave a combat advantage to *Homo sapiens* migrating out of Africa and into Eurasia, the bow and arrow probably permitted the more efficiently armed hunters to defeat and drive away those hunters equipped with the atlatl. A further consequence of adopting the bow and arrow on the North American continent was an escalation in warfare. Archaeologist John Blitz describes what happened: "Archaeological evidence for increased intergroup conflict indicated by small projectile points lodged in human bone, group burials of such individuals, and the appearance of fortified communities or placement of sites into defensive positions, closely correlates with or follows soon after bow introduction into many areas of North America."[8]

The bow and arrow has technological advantages over the atlatl, which may explain why it rapidly replaced the earlier weapon. The first and most obvious advantage is greater range. Both Old World and New World simple bows can send an arrow about 150 meters. Old World composite bows can send an arrow more than 200 meters—twice as far as a spear thrower in the Old World and 50 percent farther than one in the New World.[9] Second, the bow and arrow can be shot from the cover of an ambush or game blind. The intended victim—either an animal or a person—does not see the archer even if the victim is wounded by an arrow or sees the arrow go by. A hunter with a spear thrower needs to operate in the open. Third, more ammunition can be carried, since arrows are lighter and shorter than atlatl darts.[10] Some peoples, however, retained the atlatl for special purposes, such as hunting aquatic animals from watercraft or set-piece battles involving massed infantry where a heavier missile was desired. In Mesoamerica and Peru the first armies used the atlatl before the bow and arrow had diffused to those regions; even later armies, such as those of the Aztec and Inca, retained the atlatl. Fourth, it is easier to learn to shoot the bow and arrow accurately.[11] Cattelain points out that "all evidence indicates that the bow is notably more precise than the spearthrower, and its technique seems to be easier to learn. . . . Stated in other terms, shots can be better concentrated on a precise point of the target with a bow than with a spearthrower." There are, however, drawbacks to using the bow and arrow over a spear thrower: First, bow manufacture itself is more complex and bowstrings must be made, either of vegetable fibers (e.g., flax, nettle, or linden) or animal fibers (sinew or gut).[12] Second, if a wild animal or human adversary is able to close with the archer, the bow or arrow alone is a nearly useless weapon. A spear or heavy atlatl dart can be held in the hand and used in self-defense (see Figure 4.1 for a graphic comparison of the weapons used by early humans).

A cross-cultural study of the use of stone projectile tips by anthropologist Christopher Ellis shows that stone points were used in hunting large game and in war, while nonstone organic points were used in hunting small game, including birds. The sample for the study was composed of 123 groups of native peoples of the New World. Stone-tipped projectiles were used almost exclusively on large game (defined as weighing more than forty kilograms). Stone arrow points intended for warfare could differ in size and shape. In another sample, this time of 53 groups, Ellis found that nearly all spears, whether stone tipped or not, were used on large game or in warfare. Ellis draws the following conclusion: "It is clear that the main advantage of the use of stone projectile tips is that they are more lethal and effective than points made of most of the materials that would be readily available in many geographic ar-

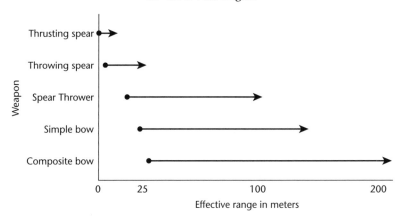

Figure 4.1. Effective Range of Weapons

eas." Moreover, stone points are almost exclusively associated with large game in the ethnographic record. "In fact," Ellis states, "this pattern is so strong that in prehistoric cases one can almost always assume that stone points were used in large animal hunting." [13] Large animal hunting encompasses warfare in the sense that human beings are large animals. From this cross-cultural study I derive three implications: First, if stone points and large game are in an area, there is hunting and possibly war; second, if stone points and *no* large game, there is war; and third, if there are no stone points, there is no war unless organic-tipped thrusting spears are present.

Extinction of Large Animals

Until the last few thousand years, the earth was inhabited by megafauna, perhaps the best known being the woolly mammoth (*Mammuthus primigenius*). Huge animals lived on every continent except Antarctica. They were largely cold-adapted or cold-resistant species that made their appearance in the past one million years in a response to glacial periods that became progressively colder. *Homo erectus* was evolving into *Homo sapiens* and *Homo neanderthalensis* during this time. When *Homo erectus* bands left Africa, hunting small game, gathering, and scavenging sustained them. Large animals that had misfortunes—injury, natural death, or death by carnivores predators—would have been eagerly sought. By 400,000 years ago large animals were being actively hunted—giant baboon and wild horses are the first known examples. Clubs and throwing spears were used by groups of males—probably fraternal interest groups—to drive and encircle these animals and probably other animals as well. Intercept strategies, based on knowledge of animal migration routes, were probably also employed. The focus would have been upon large herbivores rather than carnivores, and herd animals such as horses, reindeer, and red deer—animals that would flee, not attack their pursuers—were preferred.

Beginning about fifty thousand years ago, tool technology began to improve rapidly. The development of accurate long-range weapons—the spear thrower and the bow and arrow—greatly enhanced the hunting ability of the *Homo sapiens* who made them. The new weapons permitted the hunter to be farther from the animal, with accuracy and force probably remaining the same or even increasing. Early *Homo sapiens* increased their food supply—in terms of both quantity and nutritional quality—and thus their numbers increased. As *Homo sapiens* increased in number, more animals were killed. *Homo neanderthalensis* and *Homo erectus* could not match this new hunting ability; consequently, they decreased in number and withdrew from the advancing *Homo sapiens*.

Homo sapiens, with their new weaponry, probably attacked the megafauna. Neanderthals, despite frequent illustrations of them attacking woolly mammoths, probably did not hunt these huge, dangerous animals. Mammoth bones found at Neanderthal sites were probably scavenged for building materials. *Homo sapiens* may have been a factor in the extinction of the megafauna. Certainly, climatic change was a factor; when the last major glacier receded, the large animals failed to reproduce in sufficient numbers.

The advancing *Homo sapiens* migrated ever northward into northern Europe, Siberia, and eventually the New World. Using watercraft after the glacier receded and the ocean level rose, the *Homo sapiens* who migrated southeastward were able to enter the lands that were to become the islands of Australia and New Guinea.

By the time of this southeastward migration, the Eurasian animals had been hunted and probably had developed fear of *Homo neanderthalensis* and *Homo sapiens*. In the New World and in Australia and New Guinea, *Homo sapiens* encountered animals that had never been hunted—animals that did not have a fear of humans. A combination of rapidly receding glaciers and hunters with "high-tech" weaponry—atlatls with Clovis stone-point-tipped spears in North America—who could get close to their prey led to the extinction of many animals in a short period of time. Approximately 70 percent of all large mammals in the Americas (thirty-three species) became extinct.[14] In Australia and New Guinea, and later in Polynesia, most large land animals and birds rapidly became extinct from overhunting.

Probably the most important series of events in the last forty thousand years was the development of long-range weapons, *Homo sapiens'* migration out of Africa, the increase in their number, the extinction of *Homo neanderthalensis* and *Homo erectus*, and the demise of many large animals. These events set the stage for our story, namely that warfare arose hand-in-hand with the hunting of large game animals, then declined as many large animals became extinct (see chapter 1, Figure 1.2). Before warfare declined, it had to increase. As *Homo sapiens* multiplied in number, the pressure on animal populations increased. Even though large animal extinction may have been caused largely by climatic changes, the increase in hunting with long-range weapons must have hastened the species' demise. Warfare increased during this period—a period in which well-armed people came to inhabit the earth. As animal populations began to decline, hunters covered greater territory and were more likely to encounter other hunters. With increasing contact between groups of hunters, the likelihood of challenges between individual male hunters and between fraternal interest groups of hunters increased. Armed with spears that could be propelled with spear throwers and arrows that could be shot with a bow, these challenges could become lethal, and probably sometimes did. Killing and warfare increased. When the numbers of game declined, the process reversed. With many large animals extinct and many herd animals diminished in numbers, many groups of people developed a gathering way of life that included hunting and trapping small animals. These hunter-gatherers, who no longer retained their sophisticated hunting weapons, led peaceful lives.

Hunters Become Gatherers

As large game animals became extinct or were harder to obtain by hunting, a shift occurred toward the hunting of small game, including birds, which could be shot with the bow and arrow or trapped. Eventually even the taking of small game declined in some areas. The gathering of wild plants increased as the supply of small game shrank. In areas where wild plants were plentiful and species numerous, domestication of plants began. Once plant domestication was firmly established, people no longer needed to rely on wild game or wild plants for their sustenance. In areas where there were species of wild animals that could be tamed and bred in captivity, domestication of animals occurred. A graph developed to illustrate the shift from hunting to gathering to agriculture has been generalized to fit both Old World and New World situations (see Figure 4.2).[15]

Archaeologist Kent Flannery has called the first step in that shift the "broad-spectrum revolution"; he is referring to the increase in dietary breadth that occurred in the late Upper Paleolithic. Adding new species to the diet raised the carrying capacity of an increasingly constrained environment, and population size and density increased. Small game hunting seems to precede the development of weapons for large game hunting.[16] Later, increasing reliance upon small game followed the decline in large game hunting. Flannery has recently pointed out that the broad-spectrum revolution in the Mediterranean and the Near East had

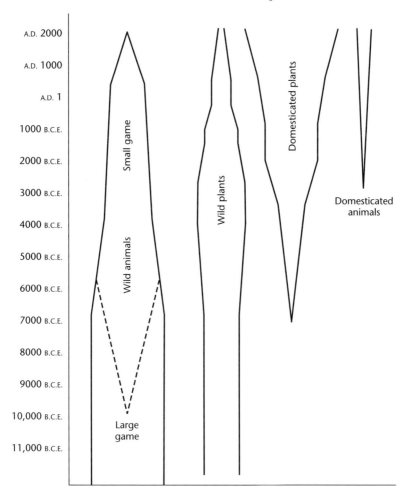

Figure 4.2. The Shift from Hunting to Gathering to Agriculture

two axes: "One axis was time-related: diet breadth increased as the Paleolithic gave way to the Epipaleolithic [about 12,000 to 8500 B.C.E.] and to the prepottery Neolithic. The other axis was geographic: the dietary shift apparently began in the western Mediterranean and moved slowly east to the Zagros Mountains [a chain of mountains running southeastward through Iraq and Iran]."[17] This pattern is consistent with a decline in the availability of large game animals and an increase in the utilization of small game. Population size increased during the late Upper Paleolithic, thanks in part to what has been described as "small-scale storage of consolidated animal tissues and/or seeds and nuts."[18] Population increase may have pushed the development of new technologies for obtaining small game; small game procurement means that children get a more even supply of protein than that supplied by hunting large game and hence are more likely to survive.

The second step in the process involved a shift from the taking of small game to an increase in the gathering of wild plants. Gatherers settled in areas where there were numerous plants that produced large seeds. These were also lands where the soil was fertile. The most important of these areas was the famed Fertile Crescent of the Near East, an arch of land that stretches from the Levant to Mesopotamia. Other important areas were China and Mesoamerica. Three factors seem to account for the shift from hunting to gathering: first, a decline in the availability of wild animals, large and small; second, an increase in the availability of wild cereals due to climatic changes—the habitat for these plants greatly expanded in the Fertile Crescent; and third, technologies developed for collecting, processing, and storing wild foods.[19]

The third step in the process involved the domestication of wild plants: emmer wheat in the Fertile Crescent, millet and rice in China, corn in Mesoamerica, and the potato in Peru. What resulted was a major transformation in the way of life of early peoples: They were no longer nomadic hunters and gatherers, but settled farmers. A number of such settlements, dating to about 9000 B.C.E., have been found across the Fertile Crescent, the best known of which is Jericho. Even earlier (9500 B.C.E.) is the settlement of Abu Hureyra. At later dates settlements appear in China (8000 B.C.E.) and Mesoamerica (4000 B.C.E.). A settled way of life became firmly established.

Thus far I have recounted briefly the well-known story of the domestication of plants. However, the accounts of plant domestication omit mention of something of extreme importance: that a decline in warfare preceded domestication.[20] And since the accounts of domestication do not discuss the decline of warfare, there is of course no discussion of why it declined or why the decline was important in the process of domestication. The decline occurred because of the shifts from the hunting of large game to the procurement of small game through hunting or trapping, and then to the gathering of wild plants. A change in the relative importance of various technologies occurred in response to changing conditions; instead of relying primarily on the spear thrower and bow and arrow to provide game for sustenance, people developed technologies for collecting, processing, and storing wild foods that became more important to survival. Artifactual evidence supports this conclusion; later assemblages do not contain large stone points. There is evidence (to be reviewed in the next section) that spears and arrows had been used to kill people in the late Upper Paleolithic; the evidence consists of rock paintings and projectile points in remains of human pelvis bones. The cross-cultural study of stone projectile tips showed that stone points are used in hunting and in war. Thus, if there are no stone points, there is no war unless organic-tipped thrusting spears are produced. In this period of shifts there is no evidence for organic-tipped thrusting spears. Furthermore, as a settled way of life developed, people were less likely to come in contact with each other and there was less likelihood of challenges between groups. There was no need for hunting weapons to be retained or for specialized weapons of war to be developed. There is no evidence of warfare at early Jericho (before 7000 B.C.E.) or at Abu Hureyra (9500–5000 B.C.E.).

The decline in warfare is extremely important to an understanding of how the domestication of plants took place. If groups were warring, they would be displacing each other. There would be killing, burning of settlements, and looting of stored foods or their destruction. This situation would have made it impossible for domestication to proceed. For domestication to occur the more desirable wild seeds needed to be planted, harvested, and planted again and so on. Many generations of seed replanting and many generations of people in the same location were required for domestication to occur. In Mesoamerica it took two thousand years for the wild seed ancestor of corn to evolve into large corncobs. (The origin of agriculture will be discussed further in chapter 5.) If warfare had continued, or arisen anew in these areas, domestication of plants would never have started.

Direct Evidence for *Homo sapiens* Killing *Homo sapiens*

Direct evidence for intraspecies killing among *Homo sapiens* occurs for the late Upper Paleolithic in the Old World and for the Archaic in the New World. It consists of both rock paintings in western Europe and northern Australia and projectile points from darts or arrows lodged in bone. Taken together, the art and the bones provide evidence that *Homo sapiens* killed other *Homo sapiens* in the Upper Paleolithic and the Archaic. We can dispute whether it was war that led to the killing but not that the killing occurred. My interpretation is that the killings come at the peak of the hunting/warfare curve or pyramid (see Figure 1.2). Future archaeological finds should provide more support.

Rock Art Evidence

Rock paintings from western Europe and northern Australia depict what may be warfare. The "art" falls into three categories. First, figures with shafts protruding from the bodies have been found on several cave walls. At Pech Merle in France the cave wall shows one apparently wounded human being. Seven arrows or darts stick out from the trunk of a standing figure. The drawing is ascribed to the Aurignacian-Perigordian period of the Upper Paleolithic. At Cougnac are separate drawings of human beings pierced with arrows or darts; each is standing. One figure has three shafts protruding from the back and buttock;

a second figure may have seven missiles protruding from the body. The cave drawings at Cougnac are dated to the Early Magdalenian period.[21] Since the Cougnac figures are superimposed over animals, in the first case a stag and in the second case a mammoth, anthropologist Raymond Kelly has offered the following interpretation: "In both paintings one gets a sense of a sequence of events in which the game animal has moved into the foreground of an area that the observers have taken possession of by expelling or slaying a trespasser." He further argues that the two paintings "memorialize spontaneous confrontations over game resources in which the social group of the painters prevailed."[22] However, the human pin cushions are not shown with weapons in hand. The individual depicted, if he had been carrying a weapon, might have dropped his weapon when first struck. Other interpretations of the apparent killings are possible. Accident can be ruled out, given the large number of projectiles sticking in one person, but we cannot rule out human sacrifice, capital punishment, homicide, assassination, or the killing in warfare of an unarmed combatant or noncombatant.[23] There are even other possibilities: The drawings could be a warning to a band member or a trespasser, or they could be sympathetic magic, in which someone in another band is symbolically killed. Ethnographic analogy, however, suggests an execution. Anthropologist Richard Lee describes for the !Kung Bushmen an execution of a recidivist killer in which both men and women participated. Men shot poisoned arrows. Once the man was dead, women and men stabbed him with spears. These cave paintings at Pech Merle and Cougnac may be the earliest evidence for capital punishment. I have argued that capital punishment originated early, probably in several world regions, because it is a universal or near universal feature of society.[24]

Paintings become more complete and explicit several thousand years later. Cave art dated to about 3000 B.C.E. at Morella la Vella in Spain depicts both executions and battle scenes. In the execution scene ten archers are shown with bows raised while a victim lies dead or dying, pierced with ten arrows. Military historian Arther Ferrill believes that the archers were organized into a firing line and presumably firing on command, while Raymond Kelly sees an act committed not only in unison but also with "jubilation."[25] Another painting depicts a battle between two opposing groups of archers, four on one side, three on the other. Arther Ferrill sees "the 'army of four' . . . attempting to direct flanking fire against the 'army of three' in what may be the earliest evidence of 'envelopment' in battle."[26] Another military historian, Robert O'Connell, questions the double envelopment interpretation, even though the photograph he presents shows an "army of five." O'Connell interprets the scene as follows: This, "the earliest surviving image of combat, . . . depicts men fighting with bows." O'Connell states that "it is difficult to see the action as anything but confused and fleeting. The participants appear to be on the run, perhaps hoping to rip off a few quick shots before retreating. Indeed, the scene captures in a single visual metaphor the essence of primitive combat. But is this warfare?"[27] My interpretation is that we are looking at the first representation of a line battle, and that it is warfare.

This development in "Western military art" seems to follow three phases: First, a lone individual has been ambushed and/or executed by a group of shooters; surprise could have been used or the person could have been captured and shot later. The reasons are obscure. Second, both the shooters and the individual shot are in the same scene; since the archers are in a close line, they appear to form a firing squad. We seem to be witnessing an execution, not an ambush. Third, open lines of archers are engaged in combat. I see no indication of retreat or of a planned retreat. We are viewing line tactics.

Rock art in Arnhem Land, in northern Australia, shows the development of armed combat over a six-thousand-year period (ten thousand to four thousand years ago). Archaeologists Paul Tacon and Christopher Chippendale describe three phases: First, figures confronting each other use boomerangs as both throwing and shock weapons, and they carry barbed spears. Spears are shown plunged into fallen figures. Only one skirmish is depicted. Second, figures carry hooked sticks (dart throwers?) and three-pronged barbed spears as well as boomerangs and barbed spears. Large numbers of figures are shown in opposing groups with boomerangs and spears flying overhead, and there are fallen dead and wounded. Third, battle scenes are common and the figures (let's call them warriors now) are energetically engaged in armed combat. Tacon and Chippendale relate the shift from individual combat to large-scale battles to the development of complex social organization, and they further argue that increased military organization led to military success and helped to establish territories and boundaries.[28]

Projectile Points in Bone

The most compelling evidence that *Homo sapiens* killed each other with weapons is the presence of projectile points found in bones, usually the pelvis, ribs, or vertebrae. Anthropologist Brian Ferguson has asserted that "the best evidence for interpersonal violence is a bone-embedded point from a lance, dart, or arrow. The possibility of this being accidental is remote."[29] The presence of points in bones, I believe, confirms that the rock art does indeed represent actual killings, whether they be executions, ambushes, or battles. Human bones pierced by stone artifacts have been found in seven sites—four in Europe, two in Sudan, one in India.[30] One of the Sudan sites, at Wadi Kubbaniya, dates to twenty thousand years ago. Although scholars have been able to describe and classify the stone flakes and points, some as spear or arrow tips, they cannot ascertain the type of shaft or the type of weapon that propelled the stone points.[31]

The most remarkable of the sites is a fourteen thousand- to twelve thousand-year-old cemetery near Jebel Sahaba in Sudanese Nubia, excavated by archaeologist Fred Wendorf. The cemetery is situated atop a knoll less than a mile from the Nile River. It contains remains of fifty-nine individuals of whom twenty-four (40.7 percent) show evidence of being killed with weapons: stone projectile points and barbs embedded in the skeletons or resting within them (110 stone artifacts in all). Most victims showed evidence of multiple wounds. Men, women, and children were killed. Wendorf states, "The startling conclusion is that almost half of the population probably died violently, and the true percentage may have been even higher."[32] The men were likely to be buried alone (five of ten cases), suggesting they were killed away from camp and their bodies brought to the cemetery, or they were executed within the camp, a less likely event. Women and children were likely to be buried together (seven of nine women and three of four children), an indication there might have been raids upon the camp. Raymond Kelly, after a review of the description of the burials, concludes that there is "clear evidence of raids upon encampments (determinable from the age/sex distribution of multiple burials), of collective responsibility for vengeance (indicated by 'pincushioning'), and of group liability (indicated by the killing of children)." Kelly, furthermore, believes that it is possible "to distinguish archaeologically between homicide, capital punishment, and war. Homicide and capital punishment both result in one death at a time, so that multiple burials would be absent."[33]

Finding extensive raiding and warfare along the Nile River before 10,000 B.C.E. has immense implications for the thesis of *How War Began.* A part of my thesis is that warfare prevented the domestication of plants. Both the Nile River region and the Fertile Crescent had early established human populations before the emergence of plant domestication; a comparison of the two areas in terms of the domestication of plants and the occurrence of warfare gives strong support to the thesis. Domestication of plants first emerged in the area where warfare had not occurred—near the central part of the Fertile Crescent—at about 8500 B.C.E. Plants did not become domesticated along the Nile—the area in which Wendorf found evidence of warfare.

Several hundred miles downstream from Jebel Sahaba is a twenty thousand-year-old burial of a young man with two spear points embedded in his pelvic bones. Fred Wendorf, who excavated this site as well, believes that "the most logical explanation is that enemies speared this man from behind." In a *National Geographic Magazine* article, Wendorf is quoted as saying that the victim had "been in three scrapes, separated by at least several months. The last one got him."[34] The evidence for the two previous episodes of armed combat consists of broken forearm bones, probably from warding off a blow, and a spear point chip surrounded by partly healed bone embedded in the left elbow. This man had been in battles with adversaries equipped with clubs and spears, weapons that he himself probably carried. Raymond Kelly believes that "he most probably prevailed in the earlier fight (or he would not, in all likelihood have survived). In other words, he may well have been the perpetrator of an earlier homicide who was slain in retribution." [35] Wendorf thinks "the Jebel Sahaba and Wadi Kubbaniya skeletons indicate that there was a lot of competition for resources in the Nile Valley during the Hyper Arid Period of the last Glacial." [36] I believe that warfare prevailed along the Nile River for thousands of years. I further suspect the tactics were ambushes and lines. I also believe that this warfare is why agriculture did not first arise along the Nile River.

Since the victims at the seven known sites were probably not intentionally buried, with the exception of those of the cemetery at Jebel Sahaba and the burial at Wadi Kubbaniya, I find it remarkable that so many sites have been discovered. This number suggests that more pierced human bones will be found and probably that there are many more that never will be. It would, moreover, be terribly exciting to find a Neanderthal skeleton with an Aurignacian point embedded in the pelvis—evidence that *Homo sapiens* killed *Homo neanderthalensis*. What has been found suggests widespread killing in the Upper Paleolithic.

Not all wounds by weapons would result in embedded lithic materials or even damaged bones; wounds that led to death by soft-tissue injury or loss of blood would leave no such tell-tale forensic evidence. [37] And, of course, people killed by other means would not present such evidence. Individuals strangled to death, drowned, or purposely abandoned to starve would not leave evidence that can be interpreted as homicide. Fractured left arm bones suggest that the individual was trying to block the blows of a club, but this injury alone does not prove fighting and homicide. [38] Skull fractures, likewise, do not prove combat, but they might result from blows with a club. Since we can be fairly certain that killing with projectile weapons did occur twenty thousand years ago, it seems likely that some of the victims of fracture wounds were probably killed by fellow *Homo sapiens*.

Projectile point in bone evidence for violence by one *Homo sapiens* against another has also been found in North America, and the individual did not die directly from the wound. It healed. Two college students found the skeletal remains now known as Kennewick Man, or K-Man, on July 28, 1996, along the Columbia River in the state of Washington. Archaeologist James Chatters first inspected K-Man and gave interviews to the media. He emphasized that K-Man had lived a violent life. Chatters later produced a scientific report on the find, which was dated to 8410 ± 60 B.P. The projectile point, shaped like a willow leaf, is classified as "early Cascade," and it is healed into the pelvis (right ilium). An infection followed, which might have been the cause of death. Only the tip of the point is embedded in K-Man: "When complete, it would have been at least 70 mm [approximately three inches] long." Chatters concludes that "this point was almost certainly the tip of an atlatl-propelled dart."[39] Other injuries included a dislocated shoulder, a healed fracture of the left elbow, thoracic trauma (ribs were broken and had healed), and an "acute infection in the left side of his head," where an indentation had healed.[40] Since K-Man survived a spear attack, it appears he was not the victim of an execution squad but might have been seriously wounded in a line battle where he had kinsmen who could carry him to safety. His other injuries and wounds suggest that he had been in several fights or battles in which clubs were used.

The find became controversial when local Native Americans wanted reburial while other groups claimed K-Man as their own since his features are unlike those of present-day Native Americans but instead resemble those of Caucasoids.[41] He resembles the Ainu of northern Japan, a people that are descended from an early northeast Asian population. A series of legal actions resulted in the Department of the Interior undertaking the scientific evaluation. In September, 2000, Interior Secretary Bruce Babbitt made the decision to return the bones of K-Man to five American Indian tribes for reburial. As of this writing, the decision is being contested in the courts. To date others likewise have reported that K-Man is eighty-five hundred years old and that the lithic object in his pelvis has bone growth around it, confirming Chatters's report.[42]

From the same period, but perhaps a thousand years earlier, is a male in his late teens from the Grimes Burial Shelter in Nevada who was killed by a knife wound to his upper thorax. Researchers Douglas Owsley and Richard Jantz report that "the second rib on his left side has two cuts in it, one of which still retains embedded fragments of obsidian that broke off when the blade was thrust into his chest."[43]

More recent evidence for North American hunter-gatherer warfare comes from western Tennessee. More than six hundred individuals from seven sites have been examined from the Archaic period (specifically, 6000 to 1000/500 B.C.E.) Here six skeletons were found with embedded projectile points.[44] Although the site report is silent on the weapon that might have propelled these points, it was presumably the atlatl since the bow and arrow had not reached the Southeast before 500 B.C.E. Other evidence of "warfare-related violent trauma" on four additional skeletons included scalping (three examples), stab wounds (two examples), and dismemberment (one example). No examples of "blunt trauma" were found, leading physical anthropologist Maria O. Smith to conclude that "it is possible, though highly speculative, that the arsenal of Archaic period warriors did not include clubs or cudgels."[45] I conjecture further that if the hunter/warrior is carrying a spear thrower and several darts, one of which is quite heavy, then his hands are full. A heavy dart can be used as a lance as well as thrown, thus negating the need for a club. The warrior is carrying a weapon system that can fire projectiles as well as serve as a shock weapon in hand-to-hand combat. Line battles and ambushes are consistent with such a weapon system.

Just as many injuries to long bones, ribs, and crania could be accidental and hence not evidence of killing or warfare, the presence of cannibalism at a prehistoric site is not evidence for deliberate killing or warfare either. In situations of near starvation, modern *Homo sapiens* have engaged in cannibalism, either eating those who have died or killing individuals and then eating them. This might well have happened in the Paleolithic, or even much earlier. In the ethnographic record, it is middle-level societies, such as tribes and chiefdoms, that go to war to get captives to be eaten. Such wars usually occur in areas where food, particularly protein, is scarce, such as Polynesia; the islands of Easter, Fiji, and the Marquesas are examples. However, hunter-gatherers are seldom cannibals. I suspect that hunter-gatherers in the Paleolithic were likewise seldom cannibals. But cannibalism did occur. It was reported in *Science* in October, 1999, that Neanderthals were cannibals. Human bones from six individuals were mixed in with animal bones, but there is no evidence of how the six individuals died.[46] The eating of human flesh has been suspected in several other cases, four of which date from the Paleolithic and one from the Neolithic. If those eaten were war captives or individuals killed in ambushes, the evidence for war no longer exists—the evidence of war had been destroyed by the crushing of long bones and skulls.[47]

Hunting and Gathering Bands

The sociopolitical organization of a hunting and gathering band is basically a leader with followers and often one or more fraternal interest groups. Bands are not egalitarian internally; if they are large, with two or more fraternal interest groups, they may be rife with conflict, a situation that can lead to fissioning. Bands that arose after conflict and fissioning are likely to engage in warfare with other bands. The majority of hunting and gathering bands have warfare; those with the greatest reliance upon hunting engage in warfare more frequently than those that are primarily gatherers. This pattern probably also holds for the Upper Paleolithic.

The Myth of the Egalitarian Band

Since the mid-1960s many scholars have asserted that bands are egalitarian and have referred to them as egalitarian societies. Egalitarian, in this context, means that all members are socially and politically equal. Equality is based upon subsistence contributions—men, women, and even children are seen as making important contributions to the commissariat, to use anthropologist Bronislaw Malinowski's term for the cultural response that satisfies basic metabolic needs.[48] In band society the division of labor by age and sex results in complementarity: The men hunt and the women gather, assisted by the children. Egalitarian societies are maintained by the presence of "leveling mechanisms." If anyone—meaning a male—attempts to rise above and dominate his fellows, he is brought down by "leveling mechanisms."

An early discussion of egalitarian societies and leveling mechanisms is to be found in anthropologist Morton Fried's *The Evolution of Political Society.*[49] He emphasized external factors that inhibited social hierarchy, such as a nomadic life in which a cooperating band was unable to accumulate material wealth. People possessed no more than they could carry. Property was communally owned and thus there was no private property. For Fried, leveling mechanisms "prevent the appearance of overly wide gaps in ability among members."[50] His hypothetical example points out that many societies give multiple credit to the hunters who bring down a game animal. More recently anthropologist Christopher Boehm has employed eight sanctions or leveling mechanisms in a "world survey of egalitarian sanctioning": public opinion, criticism, ridicule, disobedience, deposition, desertion, exile, and execution. The first four are mild negative sanctions; the second four are what Boehm refers to as "extreme sanctions." I would change the order by placing desertion before deposition; only the last three sanctions are extreme. Deposition means deposing the leader; exile, sending him away; and execution, killing him. Of the forty-eight societies in Boehm's sample, each had one or more of these leveling mechanisms. Only the Iban of Borneo had four. Many of the egalitarian societies examined by Boehm are tribes, not bands. These leveling mechanisms prevent leaders or would-be leaders from dominating their followers or fellow band members. According to Boehm, as long as band members can apply these leveling mechanisms, a "reverse dominance hierarchy" is maintained, meaning that followers dominate leaders.[51]

Hunting and gathering societies are not egalitarian—it is a myth that they are.[52] Bands have leaders, leaders make decisions. Leveling mechanisms do not bring leaders down to the level of their followers. Only the last sanction—execution—truly disposes of leaders; only ten of the forty-eight societies in Boehm's survey used execution in this fashion. My own study of capital punishment, which included six hunting and gathering bands, showed that bands use executions to rid societies of witches and recidivist criminals, not political leaders.[53] Political leaders carry out executions; they are not the executed. Political leaders are far more in danger of being singled out by an enemy raiding party and killed than they are in danger of being killed by a fellow band member. I suspect that if any follower harbored thoughts of executing the leader and the leader became suspicious, the follower would be executed. But I know of no examples.

Ironically, the existence of negative sanctions proves that bands are not egalitarian; sanctions would not have come into existence if bands had been egalitarian. There would have been no need for them. Bands are hierarchical in the sense that there are leaders and followers, and the presence of mild negative sanctions does not obliterate this distinction. In fact, the presence of sanctions that can be aimed at leaders serves the latent function of pointing out that there are leaders in societies and then identifying these individuals. On the other hand, sanctions can be aimed at followers. Theories of egalitarian society fail to describe the sanctions that leaders can use to maintain their position. These sanctions include several said to be available to followers who wish to hold the leader in check. They range from criticism to execution. Sanctions help create the hierarchy, not destroy it.

Discussions of equality and inequality in anthropology have not abated. The comparative study undertaken by Christopher Boehm included "little centralized societies." I have chosen to focus on bands. And recently a controversy has flared concerning the issue of whether pastoralists are egalitarian. A group—called "revisionists" by anthropologist Philip Carl Salzman—has identified inequalities in herding societies and called egalitarianism in these societies a "pastoral myth." Salzman is critical of the revisionists; he contends that contrasting "equality" with "inequality" is overly simplistic.[54] I also believe that Boehm's contrast between societies with and without an "egalitarian ethos" is overly simplistic.

I have argued that in the political realm leaders are not powerless figures—the same sanctions that can be used against them, they can use against others, often more effectively. My reason for contending that there is a "myth of the egalitarian band" is to refute the notion that coercive leadership is absent from hunting and gathering society. Underlying leadership and coercion is the formation of coalitions, which are often fraternal interest groups.

Missing from the various theories of the egalitarian society are discussions of fraternal interest groups. Scholars who write about egalitarian societies see cooperating individuals—every male seems to be a brother to every other male. This situation, however, would actually occur only in those circumstances where band size was small. It would be far more likely to find several groupings of male kinsmen in bands—fraternal interest groups. A leader in a large band has the support of his fraternal interest group. It is unlikely that a man could become a leader without the backing of kinsmen. Although confrontations and challenges could arise between two men wishing to be the leader of the band, it is more likely that the confrontation will be between rival fraternal interest groups, each of which has its own leader—the aspiring leader of the band. As pointed out in the section "Origin of Fraternal Interest Groups" in chapter 3, some early hominid bands had fraternal interest groups while others did not. Two types of societies were identified: fraternal interest group societies with conflict and non-fraternal interest group societies without conflict. The two types are found among hunting-gathering bands. To recognize that some bands have fraternal interest groups is to realize that some bands have a social organization fundamentally different from that hypothesized by the egalitarian society theorists.

Leaders, generally, have characteristics that set them apart from others. They are likely to be strong and healthy, to be excellent hunters, to be knowledgeable about the territory, and to be intelligent. Leaders, whether or not they are supported by fraternal interest groups, have privileges—there are rewards for being a leader. The rewards may include multiple mates, access to more and better food, and the privilege of selecting areas to occupy—dwelling sites and hunting territories. In bands, leaders receive deference—they are not targets of criticism or assassination. Followers, in turn, receive a value, particularly if they are members of the leader's fraternal interest group. Since their abilities may fall short of those of the leader, they may receive more game and other sustenance by following the more skilled leader.[55]

If two men desire to be the leader of the band and each has the support of his fraternal interest group, intense political rivalry can arise. Non-kin may be forced to take sides. Factions develop. Factionalism can lead to fissioning. The band is likely to split rather than engage in combat and have one group defeating the other—which could nearly wipe out the male population of the band. If the band splits, two bands are created. Non-kin are likely to join the band that they supported. If the split has not been violent, the two new bands may see themselves as parts of a larger entity. They may meet from time to time when resources are plentiful in a local area. However, if the split was violent, two bands hostile to each other are formed. Each has a military organization that is a fraternal interest group. The possibility of ambushes and line battles now exists. Thus, factionalism and fissioning play key roles in the development of warfare.

The above analysis permits the construction of a likely developmental sequence: First, rival leaders within a band gather supporters; the band is now composed of factions. Second, the band splits, but the two new bands are within a larger unit, the former band. Third, the two new bands become separate political communities, with fraternal interest groups that are the bases of military organizations; warfare may occur between the bands. Such fissioning results in an increase in the number of hunting and gathering bands and their spread, with one or both bands moving into a new area. This process probably occurred again and again during the history of the hominids. First *Homo erectus,* then

Homo sapiens expanded into Eurasia in this fashion—the two "Out of Africa" migrations.

The migration and spread of hunting and gathering bands into un-inhabited lands result in a fanning out. In time bands will encounter bands of which they had no knowledge. When two bands come in contact, each is faced with the "sovereignty problem" (my term): whether to become incorporated into the other group, to flee, or to attack each other. In other words, there can be loss of sovereignty for one of the bands; co-leadership could occur, but it is more likely that one leader would become subordinate to the other. If they flee from each other, the fanning out continues. They might, however, remain in contact and cooperate with each other. They may cooperate in hunting and they may meet from time to time to exchange mates. While it is probably the young females who are exchanged, it also would be possible for males to shift residence to the other band. If males shift bands, their fraternal interest groups break up. Such bands are less likely to engage in warfare. The core membership of such a band may well be a cooperating group of related females who gather plants. Band social organization, thus, may resemble that of the bonobos. A shortage of males in another band could be the reason a man leaves his natal band. Friction with other males within a band could be another reason. If the bands continue to cooperate, they can be considered microbands, that is, parts of a macroband.

Warfare

Of all the varieties of human societies, the least likely to engage in warfare are the hunting and gathering bands. This assertion, of course, does not mean that they do not have war. Other types of societies, all socially and politically more complex than bands, almost invariably have warfare. It is rare to find a tribe, chiefdom, or state that has not engaged in war within its recent history. In a cross-cultural study of warfare I found only two such societies in my randomly chosen sample of fifty societies.[56] The Toda, described in 1906 by William H. R. Rivers, live on a plateau in southern India in a symbiotic relationship with two neighboring tribal groups, the Kota and Badaga. They apparently have lived for several centuries on this plateau, which is surrounded by a tropical forest infested with malaria-bearing mosquitoes. In the past, the Toda apparently had a military organization, for both shock and projectile weapons are used in ceremonies.[57] The second group are the Tikopia, a Polynesian people who live on a small, isolated island in Melanesia; they were described by Raymond Firth in 1936. Their only neighbors, with whom they intermarry, live on Anuta, a smaller island about seventy miles away. Although Firth describes conflicts in which the losers are forced to flee and heads this discussion "War," there was no evidence of a military organization at the time of Firth's study.[58] Both the Toda and the Tikopia, thus, engaged in warfare in the distant past.[59] Two other societies in the sample of fifty also did not have war—the Copper Eskimo and the Dorobo—both hunting and gathering bands. The Copper Eskimo, described first by Vilhjálmur Stefánsson, live in small, isolated communities along the northern coast of North America. They were occasionally attacked by Indian groups from the south, and although they would fight to defend themselves on an individual basis, there is no evidence that they formed military organizations.[60] The Dorobo live in a forest on a mountaintop in eastern Africa; they were described by ethnographer George Huntingford. They apparently once lived on the plains below, but they were driven into their forest retreat by such warlike peoples as the Nandi. Non-Dorobo who enter their forest are killed.[61] All four societies—Toda, Tikopia, Copper Eskimo, and Dorobo—have in common an absence of military organizations, and they are isolated from other societies. I concluded, "There are indications that the members of all four of these societies were driven from other areas and forced to seek refuge in isolated locations, such as islands, Arctic wastelands, or mountain tops. Protected by their isolation, they have found it unnecessary to maintain military organizations."[62]

Although numerous hunting and gathering bands do not have warfare, due in large part to their isolation and lack of military organizations (no fraternal interest groups), the great majority of bands on occasion engage in warfare. Several cross-cultural studies have consistently documented this. In an early study, Leonard Hobhouse, Gerald Wheeler, and Morris Ginsberg showed that out of 56 hunting societies, 49, or 88 percent, practiced war. Later, Quincy Wright, in an even larger sample incorporating the previous study, showed that of 216 hunting societies, 198, or 92 percent, had wars. In my cross-cultural study of war, I found that of 9 band-level societies, 7, or 78 percent, had warfare. In a cross-cultural study that focused only upon hunter-gatherers, Carol Ember found that of 31 foragers, 20, or 65 percent, saw combat between communities or larger entities at least once every two years, while only 3 societies experienced warfare rarely or never; thus, 28 out of 31, or 90 percent, engaged in warfare. In a cross-cultural study of the killing of combatants and noncombatants, using a probability sample of 60 societies, I found that out of 8 hunter-gatherer societies, 6, or 75 percent, experienced war. Raymond Kelly, working with a sample of 25 foraging societies, found that 22 hunting-gathering societies, or 88 percent, had some form of warfare.[63] Another way to look at the data is to note that peaceful hunter-gatherers in these studies account for only 8 to 25 percent of the samples.

These cross-cultural studies, of course, concern only hunter-gatherer bands observed over the past two centuries. (Interestingly, the earlier studies show a slightly higher percentage of bands engaging in warfare, perhaps because the later studies include recently "pacified" societies.)

The above figures are probably too high for the Paleolithic, yet they show that people organized into hunter-gatherer bands are quite capable of warfare. Nonetheless, and contrary to what many anthropologists would lead us to believe, there is great variability among recently observed hunter-gatherers in terms of the frequency of war, homicide, and capital punishment.[64] This same great variability should also hold for the past.

Those hunting and gathering bands with warfare employ a basic pattern of tactics that consists of ambushes and lines. The Tiwi of northern Australia, studied by ethnographers C. W. M. Hart and Arnold Pilling, illustrate this basic pattern. The Tiwi engaged in arranged spear battles that resulted in low casualties and sneak attacks/night raids that resulted in heavy casualties.[65] Although the arranged battles were the primary mode of combat after the coming of the British, in pre-contact times they may have been a test of strength. If a group appeared weak, it might be raided. The Tiwi entered the anthropological world as a society with "ritual warfare." *The Tiwi of North Australia* contains a well-known account of spear battles in a section titled "Warfare." The example given is from 1928. It is a classic "ritual battle" that I believe helped perpetuate the myth of the peaceful savage. Hart, the senior ethnographer, wrote the section. However, in another section written by Pilling, we are informed that "Tiwi treatment of outsiders prior to 1900 had been to rob them, spear them, kill them."[66] To avoid problems with authorities, starting about 1925, the Tiwi switched from spears to throwing sticks.[67] The implication is that spear battles were aboriginal. This whole picture of Tiwi warfare is, however, a very inaccurate one. Pilling, in comments at the "Man the Hunter" symposium, informs us that night raids occurred until 1912: "In one decade (1893–1903), at least sixteen males in the 25-to-45 age group were killed in feuding; either during sneak attacks or in arranged pitch battles. Those killed represent over 10 percent of all males in that age category."[68] Thus, we learned that the Tiwi warfare pattern was based on both ambushes and lines. A fieldwork edition of Hart and Pilling's ethnography appeared in 1979; no new data on warfare were provided. A third edition, appearing in 1988, contains a new section by Pilling titled "Sneak Attacks." Here he notes that his cases listed fifty-four deaths and nineteen injuries from sneak attacks.[69]

The variation among hunting and gathering bands in warfare and any other type of armed violence can be summarized (see Figure 4.3). The two rows in the figure describe bands with and without fraternal interest groups.

Raymond Kelly's book *Peaceful Societies and the Origin of War* describes the difference between bands with and without warfare. His descriptions parallel the categories in Figure 4.3. His theory, succinctly stated, is that bands without warfare but rife with internal conflict

Figure 4.3. Hunter-Gatherer Armed Combat

Socio-Political Organization	Type of Armed Combat	Military Organization	Tactic	Reasons for Armed Combat
Hunting-Gathering Band	Homicide	None	Fight with weapons	Individual dispute
	Capital punishment		Ambush by group	Eliminate wrongdoer
Hunting-Gathering Band with Fraternal Interest Groups	Shoot-on-sight	Hunters	Attack lone individual, opportunistic ambush	Trespass or being trespassed upon
	Encounter battles		Lines	Test of strength

preceded bands with warfare. Two concepts play central roles: unsegmented societies and social substitution. Unsegmented societies are found in the ethnographic record; they are the bands shown in the first row of Figure 4.3. They do not have fraternal interest groups. If they did, they would be segmented societies. Unsegmented societies seldom engage in violent conflict with neighbors, but they have high rates of homicide and/or capital punishment. Competition over scarce resources may lead to shoot-on-sight attacks if unsegmented societies compete for resources. Here Kelly is using a well-known theory referred to by many anthropologists as CSR theory. Deaths are likely to lead to a desire to kill the killer—revenge. When the desire for revenge can be satisfied by killing any member of the killer's group, all members of an enemy band become equivalent to all other members; thus, social substitution has occurred. For Kelly, the "origination" of war lies in unsegmented societies that use shoot-on-sight tactics and become segmented societies. Segmented societies now arise, and so does war. Buttressing his argument, Kelly states that "the archaeological record supports the conclusion that this transition occurred after 10,000 B.P. [8000 B.C.E.] everywhere except the Nile Valley." Segmented societies are described in the second row of Figure 4.3. Kelly interprets cave paintings of figures with missiles protruding as victims of shoot-on-sight tactics, while burials of men, women, and children, as at Jebel Sahaba in Sudanese Nubia, are interpreted as examples of social substitution and war (see the section "Projectile Points in Bone," above).[70]

There is a fundamental difference between Kelly's approach to the origin of war and the approach presented in this book. I have argued that fraternal interest groups may be found as early as the common ancestor of chimpanzees and humans and that where fraternal interest groups are present, intergroup conflict may occur. If the conflict between bands turns violent and weapons are used, whether in ambushes or line battles, war has occurred. Kelly places the origin of war at twenty thousand years ago in Sudan; I place it many thousands of years earlier (see the section "Speculations about Early Warfare" in chapter 3). Kelly does not consider the possibility that fraternal interest groups could have appeared hundreds of thousands of years ago. His theory does not allow this possibility, since bands with fraternal interest groups are segmented societies and segmented societies have feuding and warfare. Certainly by the Upper Paleolithic, the hunting-gathering bands had grown large and their sociopolitical organizations had become complex, probably due to a rich resource base.[71] I believe the bands were segmented and engaged in armed combat that can be considered warfare.

The approach I have taken in this book shows, through an extended narrative, how hunting led to warfare. The lengthy discussion of hunting in *How War Began* suggests four possible reasons why hunting and warfare are related: Hunters have weapons that are likely to be suitable for use in warfare; hunting itself involves searching for and killing prey; if seeking prey involves the coordinated activities of hunters, a quasi-military organization has been created; and hunters, particularly hunters of large herd animals, may range over a vast region and come in contact with other peoples who also range over a part of the territory and do not wish to share it. The first three reasons stem directly from my earlier research on the evolution of war, where I focused on weapons, tactics, and military organizations.[72]

First, the weapons used by hunters to kill animals can be used to kill human beings. I have described the reason hunting is related to warfare in two previous sections. Military historian Tom Wintringham, more than half a century ago, stated, "The weapons of the first soldiers were of course the weapons with which men had hunted wild beasts for thousands of years."[73] A list of hunting weapons is also a list of military weapons. Listed in the approximate order in which they were invented and developed, they are the club, the knife, the spear, the spear and spear thrower, the bow and arrow, and the sling. All these weapons except for the knife are used to kill animals, either at close or long range; the knife is used to butcher and skin game. The only basic military weapons that are not equally useful in hunting are the dagger and the sword. Another military historian, Arther Ferrill, points out that from fourteen thousand to ten thousand years ago "four staggeringly powerful new weapons make their first appearance (along with the Palaeolithic spear) . . . the bow, the sling, the dagger (or the short, short sword), and the mace." Robert Ardrey has suggested that "it was the idea of the long-distance weapon, whether bow and arrow or sling or throwing spear, inflicting maximum damage with minimum risk, that made possible organized warfare." Wintringham further informs us that bows and flint-tipped arrows "were still employed by 'native levies' that formed part of the Persian army invading Greece in 480 B.C.E. Other troops in this army had wooden javelins with fire-hardened points. Others carried slings." The soldiers were from tribal regions "conquered by the Persians," Wintringham continues, "but their weapons show what all weapons must have been like in the far past before there was any written history."[74] In a cross-cultural study of warfare, I have pointed out that "projectile weapons [i.e., spear and spear thrower, bow and arrows] are often all-purpose implements, used in hunting as well as in war," and, further, that "the tools can be used to strike other men as easily as they can be used to kill animals." And anthropologist James Woodburn has stated, "Hunting weapons are lethal not just for game animals but also for people."[75]

Second, the act of hunting involves searching for and killing animals, both large and small. This activity requires the same skills used in war. Specifically, game can be taken by surrounding the animals or by remaining in hiding and allowing the prey to approach within firing distance. These two basic hunting methods are reflected in the two types of ambush employed in warfare. In a discussion of tactical systems, I distinguished the two types of ambush: surrounding enemy and laying trap. In the first type of ambushing, the warriors quietly surround the enemy village or campsite; at a given signal, they attack from all sides. In the second type of ambushing, the warriors hide along a trail and permit the enemy to walk into the trap.[76] It seems reasonable to conclude, given the striking parallels between the coordinated activities of hunters and the two types of ambushes used by military organizations, that some tactics used in hunting are the same tactics used in war.[77]

Third, if more than one hunter is involved in the hunt, then an organized group must be created—one that can coordinate its activities in silence. Such a group is a nascent military organization. Wintringham pointed out, "In the hunting of wild beasts, for food or safety or sport, men learned to cooperate in groups; and these groups, when men were hunting men, became the first armies or units of armies." Lionel Tiger has argued "that male bonding patterns reflect and arise out of man's history as hunter." Desmond Morris restates this position: "Organized assault forces cannot operate on a personal basis. . . . They grew originally out of the co-operative male hunting group, where survival depended on allegiance to the 'club,' and then, as civilizations grew and flourished and technology advanced, they were increasingly exploited in the new military context." The argument has been well stated by Christian Feest: "Frequently there is a strong association between hunting and war whenever hunting is the primary male economic activity. . . . The principles of male cooperation are to be found in both communal hunts and the organization of war parties." More recently Ferrill has stated that "it is generally assumed [no references provided], probably correctly, that strategy and tactics in human warfare emerged out of the complex hunting patterns of Palaeolithic man."[78]

Fourth, hunting bands may range over a large region and come in contact with other hunters and gatherers, and in later times settled peoples. In the former case, violent conflict over hunting territories may result.[79] The pursuit of large migratory herd animals is likely to produce nomadic hunting bands. The rapid expansion of *Homo sapiens* out of Africa, across Eurasia, and into North America set the stage for the possibility of violent conflict between hunting and gathering bands. K-Man's death may represent such an event.

From this discussion of the relationships between hunting and warfare, we can derive two hypotheses and test them using the cross-cultural method with a sample of hunting-gathering societies. The first hypothesis is that the greater a society's dependence upon hunting for its subsistence, the greater the frequency with which that society goes to war; the greater a society's dependence upon plant gathering for its subsistence, the lower the frequency with which that society goes to war. The subsistence variable can be measured, first, by the percentage of a society's subsistence that depends upon hunting, and, second, by the percentage that depends upon plant gathering. George Peter Murdock examined the subsistence of a large number of societies and published codes for these measures.[80] Carol Ember examined the warfare frequency variable for a group of hunter-gatherers; it describes how often war occurs, as stated in the ethnographic record.[81] Thirty-one hunting and gathering bands examined by both Ember and Murdock make up the sample for the study. The relationship between hunting and warfare is shown in a multicell chart, with each band represented by a point describing its dependence on hunting and its frequency of warfare, as shown in Figure 4.4. The frequency with which a band engages in war-

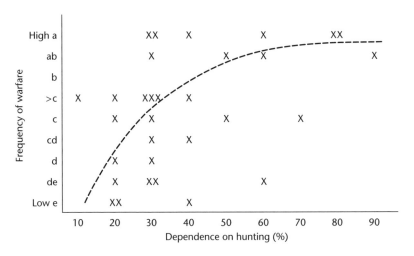

Figure 4.4. Relationship between Dependence on Hunting and
Frequency of Warfare in Bands

fare is shown on the left, with frequency increasing from low at the bottom to high at the top. The importance of hunting in the subsistence of the band is shown across the bottom of the table, with low (10 percent dependence on hunting) at the left and high (90 percent) at the right. The distribution of points, representing bands, in Figure 4.4 shows that indeed the greater the dependence of a band upon hunting, the more likely that it frequently engages in warfare.[82] In the lower right corner of Figure 4.4 is a society that does not fit—it can be considered a deviant case. This society, the Dorobo, has 60 percent dependence upon hunting and yet has warfare "occasionally, rarely, or never." They are one of the four isolated societies in my cross-cultural study of war; I consider the Dorobo not to have military organizations.[83] Their isolation explains their lack of military organizations and absence of warfare even though they are a hunting society.

The relationship between gathering and warfare is shown in the same manner in Figure 4.5. The frequency of warfare is again on the left side of the table. Across the bottom of the table is shown the importance of gathering and small land fauna in the subsistence of the band, again with the low (10 percent dependence on gathering) at the left and high (90 percent) at the right. The distribution of points, representing bands, is opposite that shown in Figure 4.4; the greater the dependence of a band upon plant gathering for its subsistence, the lower the likelihood that it frequently engages in warfare.[84]

Both parts of the hypothesis are supported.[85] We can conclude that bands that depend upon hunting for subsistence have more warfare than those with little hunting and also that bands that have great de-

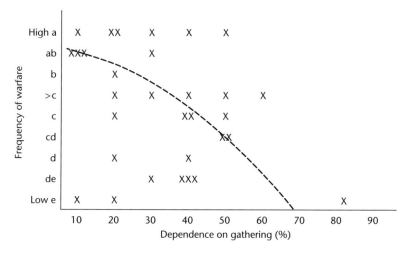

Figure 4.5. Relationship between Dependence on Gathering and Frequency of Warfare in Bands

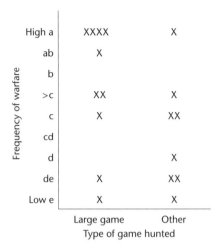

Frequency of warfare	Large game	Other
High a	XXXX	X
ab	X	
b		
>c	XX	X
c	X	XX
cd		
d		X
de	X	XX
Low e	X	X

Type of game hunted

Figure 4.6. Relationship between Hunting
for Large Animals and Frequency of Warfare
in Bands

pendence upon gathering have less warfare than those that get only a small part of their subsistence from gathering.

Because the discussions of hunting and warfare stress the importance of not just hunting, but the hunting of large animals, we can examine a second hypothesis: If large animals are hunted, frequent warfare is likely. Murdock and coauthor D. O. Morrow published a variable that describes the hunting practices of a sample of societies; eighteen of these societies are in the Ember sample.[86] The hypothesis can be tested by comparing the frequency of warfare for bands that hunt large game with those that engage in all other types of hunting; Figure 4.6 shows the relationship—the bands that practice the hunting of large animals are more likely to engage in warfare frequently.[87]

The use of the cross-cultural method with this sample of bands demonstrated that, indeed, the importance of hunting in the subsistence economy is directly related to the frequency of warfare. We can conclude that in bands, hunting, particularly the hunting of large animals, is related to the frequency of warfare. In the ethnographic record, it is hunters, rather than gatherers, who frequently go to war.

The results of this cross-cultural study are based upon synchronic data—for each band in the sample the data have come from one point in time. If these results have implications for historical processes, they can be used as a model to describe the increase, then decrease, in warfare as hunting by early humankind increased, decreased, and then was replaced by gathering. To do this utilizes Murdock's "Method of Ethnology": The results presented in Figures 4.4 and 4.5 are transported back

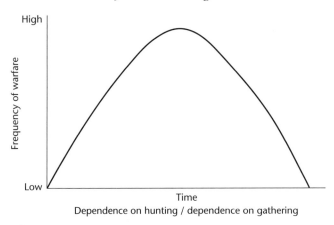

Figure 4.7. **Hunting and Gathering Warfare Curve for Upper Paleolithic**

to the Paleolithic. Three steps need to be followed: First, lines (or curves) are fitted to the data shown in the figures to describe the relationship between frequency of warfare and dependence upon hunting and upon gathering.[88] If this is done on Figure 4.4, a line runs from lower left to upper right. If a line is fitted to Figure 4.5, it runs from upper left to lower right. Second, if these two figures are placed side by side, a single curve is created. Figure 4.7 shows warfare increasing as dependence upon hunting increases and then decreasing as dependence upon gathering increases. What is depicted is the hunting/warfare curve described for the Upper Paleolithic. Third, this curve can be superimposed upon the time-line set forth in chapter 1 (see Figure 1.2) that shows the rise and fall of warfare that accompanied, first, increasing dependence upon hunting, and, second, increasing dependence upon gathering as large game animals became extinct.

The methodology I have employed follows procedures described in chapter 1. A sequence of the type that historians like to employ has been constructed. It is then interpreted through the use of scientific generalizations derived from a cross-cultural study. Two modes of explanation, therefore, have been brought to bear upon a unique historical event— the emergence of warfare. Both historical and scientific explanations propose when, where, and why war first developed. As I stated in the first chapter, "Warfare intensity increased early, then rapidly declined in both the New and the Old World with the extinction of large animals. A period of little warfare followed in which settled gatherers began the domestication of plants and became agricultural villagers."

5

Early Agriculturalists

Agriculture and village life are inextricably linked—one cannot exist without the other.[1] In their earliest development they went hand-in-hand; village life produced crops and crops produced village life. Warfare had to be absent for both to occur; ambushes, raids, and battles would have disrupted the settled way of life necessary for the origin of agriculture and the later development of the state.

Although individual hunter-gatherers differed in individual abilities, even the most skilled female gatherer or male hunter in a band would not have been able to accumulate a surplus of food or objects. Once a settled way of life became established, such differences in abilities between individuals became apparent; some individuals and their families accumulated not only surplus crops but also material goods with lasting value. Rivalry between families and kinship groups of hunters and gatherers probably existed in the Paleolithic, but until village life was well established the rivalry could not express itself materially. Although people in the earliest settlements had kinship groups, the fraternal interest groups that were so prominent in some bands of hunters probably did not exist in settlements where there was no longer need for cooperative hunting. Nevertheless, long-term rivalries between settled kinship groups eventually led to internal conflicts—conflicts within the village. Fraternal interest groups emerged not for hunting, but to protect kin in conflicts. The kinship group that came to dominate in these conflicts became both the governing body of the village and the village's "upper class." The village and its inhabitants were now on the road to statehood.

This road from village to mature state led the inhabitants through a series of stages: minimal chiefdom, typical chiefdom, maximal chiefdom/inchoate early state, typical early state, and transitional early state. The village leader became a headman, then a chief, and finally a despot at the maximal chiefdom stage. The inchoate early state was born. Coercion resulted in the loss of freedom for the "lower class." War began. At first the "army" consisted of the military-leader chief, his followers, and members of the upper class. This arrangement eventually gave way to a military organization composed of upper-class officers and commoners pressed into military service as massed infantry.

91

Origin of Agriculture

Various conditions have been proposed as necessary prerequisites for the rise of agriculture: climatic change, population increase, and improving technology. Climatic change is important because it contributed to the extinction of many large animals, and, more important for the origin of domestication, with the change in climate wild plants with seeds proliferated. As the ice age came to an end, wild cereals spread into lowland areas. As warming increased, according to Donald Henry, "warmth loving, thermophilous plants . . . colonized higher elevations and thus achieved their modern distributions."[2] Population increase and improving technology—the other two conditions for agriculture —were concomitant with the environmental changes.[3]

Archaeological evidence from Eurasia suggests another important condition, namely, that as early as thirty thousand years ago people were beginning to settle for at least part of the year. In central Russia semipermanent dwellings have been excavated. By fifteen thousand years ago settlements of foragers, with as many as fifty people in the community, had facilities for storing what they had gathered—and wealth differences are detectable. In the region of the Fertile Crescent grinding stones have been found that date to eighteen thousand years ago. Thus, people who gathered seeds possessed the necessary technology for storing and processing seeds before the domestication of plants occurred. By 10,000 B.C.E. sedentary communities existed along the Fertile Crescent. One of these communities, in present-day Syria, is the village of Abu Hureyra, which was established by hunter-gatherers along the Euphrates about 9500 B.C.E. (Map 1). The inhabitants occupied the settlement year round. By 8500 B.C.E. it was a large farming community. Excavation revealed that the early inhabitants, the hunter-gatherers, lived in circular dwellings, while their descendants, the farmers, lived in rectangular houses built directly upon the earlier structures.[4] The settlement was occupied for more than forty-five hundred years; during this time the settlement increased in size from a few hundred individuals to nearly six thousand. Moreover, there was a lack of nearby competing contemporary settlements.[5] The self-sufficiency of the settlements along the middle course of the Euphrates seemingly explains the lack of warfare. Crops were grown within two miles of the site. Neighboring settlements were smaller than Abu Hureyra and situated many miles away. There was little regular contact and no competition over scarce resources. Increasing aridity apparently forced the abandonment of the village in about 5000 B.C.E.[6]

The conclusion that the people of Abu Hureyra did not engage in warfare is derived from an examination of all aspects of the culture as well as numerous human skeletal remains.[7] The only piece of evidence that could conceivably be linked to warfare is the skeleton of a young

Map 1. Near East

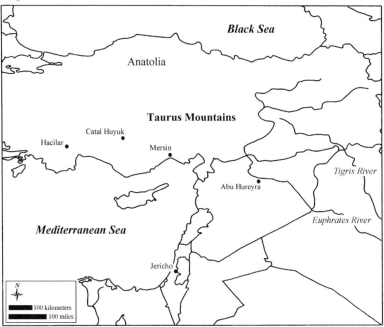

man in a flexed position lying on his side. Embedded in his chest cavity just beneath the ribs was a tanged arrowhead with its tip pointing down toward the pelvis. The archaeologists inferred that the arrowhead killed him. According to Andrew Moore, Gordon Hillman, and Anthony Legge, "This is the only evidence that we have found for death by violence among the people of Abu Hureyra. The injury may have been caused accidentally, during a hunt, for example, or with the intention of inflicting a mortal wound." The downward trajectory of the arrow suggests that the man was shot from a distance or from above, perhaps from a rooftop or the high ground surrounding a pole and pitfall animal trap.[8] In either case, the death was probably accidental. If his death had been a homicide or an execution, I would expect to find multiple wounds, perhaps even the presence of several arrowheads.

Domestication of plants took place gradually. Some archaeologists and biologists use a selectionist explanation: "Incidental domestication" occurred as the product of the dispersal and protection of wild plants. Eventually the human-plant relationship selected for changes in the plants, and plants became more important as food. As they gathered food plants, people selected consciously for size, bitterness, fleshiness, and oiliness; as domestication began, people selected unconsciously for invisible features such as dispersal mechanisms, germination inhibition, and reproductive biology. "Specialized domestication" occurred when people began to selectively destroy unwanted plants and to keep and protect those they wanted because of desirable features. In the final phase practices such as weeding, irrigation, and fertilization (probably unintentional at first) created new opportunities for plant evolution.[9] In the Fertile Crescent the earliest attested date of domestication is 8500 B.C.E. The date for China is one thousand years later, while in the New World, for both Mesoamerica and Peru, the dates are about 3500 B.C.E.[10] Although the manner in which plants were domesticated probably was the same in all four regions, there are major differences among the regions. For one thing, completely different crops were domesticated: wheat, millet, rice, corn or maize, and potatoes. And the rate at which wild plants became domesticated varied greatly—a few hundred years for wheat and about two thousand for corn.

The conditions that I see as important prerequisites for the rise of agriculture are the following: Most large game animals are gone, and seed gatherers with the technology for storing and grinding seed settle in a region, on fertile land along rivers, where no war occurs—thus, gatherers remain in one place for a long period. Of course, seeds that could be domesticated had to be available. Those who continued to hunt and migrate encountered other groups and occasionally engaged in armed combat; those who gathered seeds settled in fertile river valleys and did not attack neighbors. The settlement of Abu Hureyra did not experience warfare throughout its forty-five hundred years of occupation. The groups of migrating hunters were likely to be Type 1 societies, with groups of males formed into fraternal interest groups engaging in hunting; the settled groups were likely to be Type 2 societies, without hunting and without fraternal interest groups. Some archaeologists have argued that a minor degree of social complexity occurred *before* plants were domesticated and that conflicts between individuals needed to be resolved as a prerequisite for a sedentary agricultural system.[11] This argument is consistent with my contention that the Type 2 societies without fraternal interest groups, hunting, or warfare were relatively free of conflict. Peaceful gatherers established villages, plants became domesticated over a period of five hundred to two thousand years, and population grew larger. If serious intervillage fighting occurred, or if villages were attacked by intruders to the region, the population—if it survived—was forced to migrate, and the process of domestication was interrupted if not halted. This scenario apparently was played out in ancient Egypt. Warfare along the Nile River before 10,000 B.C.E. prevented the process of domestication from starting in that region.

Domestication of animals and domestication of plants are fundamentally different, although domestication of plants and animals proceeded simultaneously along a section of the Fertile Crescent known as the Levantine corridor, an alluvial band that runs from the Jordan River to the Euphrates Valley. A domesticated animal is defined as an animal selectively bred in captivity and thereby modified from its wild ancestors for use by humans, who control the animal's breeding and food supply. In the Old World, there are only five large, major domesticated animals: the goat, sheep, pig, cow, and horse. The first four were domesticated in the Fertile Crescent and the fifth in Ukraine. (Large, minor domesticated animals include reindeer and yak.) The New World had only the llama; other suitable candidates, such as the wild horse, had become extinct due to overhunting and climatic changes.[12]

Those who domesticate animals are likely to be those who hunt them. The domestication of animals began with the capture of young animals; those species that could be kept in captivity and bred were domesticated. In the Fertile Crescent, where both plant and animal domestication developed early, the people were both seed gatherers and hunters. The primary animal hunted in the area was the gazelle, a small game animal that lived in migrating herds and was not a suitable candidate for breeding in captivity. However, four other species, noted above, were domesticated early in the Fertile Crescent: the goat, sheep, pig, and cow.

As hunters began to domesticate animals, they were less dependent on hunting for subsistence. The reverse was equally possible: If hunting declined, perhaps because of overhunting (as did indeed happen in the Fertile Crescent in the case of the gazelle), pressure to raise the young of wild animals increased. Thus, the domestication of animals and a decline in hunting went hand-in-hand and contributed to a more settled way of life. Gazelle hunting waned during the period in which plants were domesticated. Herd size declined, hunters had to go a longer distance to find the gazelle, and in some areas the migratory gazelle could be hunted at only one time of the year by sedentary hunter-gatherers, for example in May at Abu Hureyra at about 9500 B.C.E.[13] At Jericho, about 8300 B.C.E., gazelle remains as a percentage of animal remains had decreased to 20 percent and continued to drop as the hunting of gazelle declined.[14]

A decline in hunting meant a decline in war. With little or no war, the process of domesticating plants and animals could continue and accelerate. Once species were domesticated, both plants and animals could spread or diffuse to other groups along the Fertile Crescent or to other areas, perhaps through trade or perhaps by being taken by a man or woman who married into another group. They could also be carried by a group of people migrating along the Fertile Crescent or into new regions. For example, the people at Jericho were hunters of gazelles who received plants, not animals, from peoples to the northeast and grew them at their oasis site. They established a large settlement about 8300 B.C.E. (perhaps as many as two thousand people on ten acres) and built walls to protect their fields from floods and mud flows.[15] There is no evidence for war in this region at this time. The first evidence for warfare at Jericho is the destruction of the town about 7000 B.C.E. The new occupants built square houses whereas the previous occupants had built round houses. By 5700 B.C.E., domesticated plants had spread to Mesopotamia—the lower Tigris and Euphrates Rivers area—the region where the first states evolved.

Plants were domesticated in as many as nine regions; the first states—pristine states—numbered four (the argument for four will be made later in this chapter).[16] All of these first four states arose in regions where plants were domesticated (Mesoamerica, Peru, Fertile Crescent, and northern China), but five of the nine regions where plants were first domesticated did not spawn a pristine state. One of the regions where gatherers domesticated plants is the Fertile Crescent, which produced a pristine state only at its farthest eastern extremity. There is some variance of opinion when it comes to defining the boundaries of the Fertile Crescent, however. Maps in recent books show a Fertile Crescent that does not include Egypt or southern Iraq/Iran near the Persian Gulf, where the first state arose.[17] However, in its original definition by James H. Breasted, the Fertile Crescent did include southern Mesopotamia all the way to the Persian Gulf. The Persian Gulf, it should be pointed out, extended farther northward six thousand years ago.[18] Another region where crops were domesticated was tropical west Africa, where the African yam was domesticated by 3000 B.C.E. States did not arise there. Soon after that date Bantu-speaking peoples from the area began an expansion southeastward across central Africa, displacing the original inhabitants, such as the Mbuti Pygmies and Khoisan hunter-gatherers. What occurred was probably similar to the expansion of *Homo sapiens* into Eurasia. Unlike the Neanderthals, some Pygmy and Khoisan peoples have survived. Warfare probably characterized the relationship between the Bantu groups as well. Bantu states later did develop, probably due to the influence of Egypt.[19] The Bantu states are secondary, not pristine, states.

How the State Arose

The absence of warfare is a prerequisite for both domestication of plants and, later, for the development of centralized political systems. If warfare occurs where plants have been domesticated, then centralized political systems do not emerge. Whether the people are at the village or chiefdom level, the emergence or arrival of warfare in a region of peaceful agriculturalists prevents the development of the state, just as a west-to-east-blowing El Niño wind rips off the top of a developing hurricane and prevents the storm from reaching the most powerful level for a hurricane, category 5 status. Plants can diffuse or be transported from the site of domestication to new regions, where, if there is no war, domestication can continue and centralized political systems can de-velop. When early agriculturalists occupied the regions where the first complex societies developed, these regions did not have warfare. Much later they did. This statement is empirically correct, as will be shown in chapter 6. If the regions had had warfare, social complexity would not have developed for two reasons: First, villages would have been forced to pull away from each other and to situate in defensible parts of the region; second, war would have destroyed villages, created buffer zones or no-man's-land, and reduced population through fatalities, thus pre-venting the population from growing. The first states arose in regions where plants were grown and there was no war.

I reached the above conclusion through a reasoning process that in-volved a series of statements, each one flowing from the previous state-ment: No evidence has been found for warfare in the early stages of the development of the first states; warfare was *not* present in the regions where the first states developed; absence of warfare in a region is essen-tial if a state is to develop; a state will not develop if warfare is present in a region; warfare cannot be the impetus for statehood. The above line of reasoning leads to the rejection of the notion that states arose through the conquest of one group by another—the conquest theory of the state —and any similar theory that falls under the rubric of external conflict theories.[20] The mantra that "war makes states and states make war" is also rejected, although the second half of the statement will later be shown to be correct.[21]

If war is absent from a potentially rich agricultural region, villages can peacefully fission, producing a system of two-tier settlement hierar-chies, generally considered chiefdoms. However, if fissioning results from internal conflict, so that the two segments war with each other, each segment remains an independent political entity; thus, a two-tier settlement hierarchy is not produced. If war remains absent from the region and some of the villages of a two-tier settlement hierarchy fission, a three-tier settlement hierarchy is produced. Another set of fissionings produces a four-tier settlement hierarchy. Political entities with both three- and four-tier settlement hierarchies have been consid-ered states.[22] For a state to arise, two-tier settlement hierarchies, or chief-doms, must not war with each other (see the section "Chiefdoms and States" later in this chapter).

Ethnographic analogy supports the above argument. Tribal peoples do not conquer each other, and minimal and typical chiefdoms do not conquer each other. (See "Tribes Do Not Become States" in chapter 8.) For example, if war occurs among agriculturalists such as the Dani of highland New Guinea, as it did until the 1960s, they do not evolve beyond the village/tribal level. Casualties, buffer zones, and routing of villages keep the population small and dispersed, at least smaller and more dispersed than it otherwise would have been. Under these circumstances no leader can dominate a large area.[23] The same goes for warring herding peoples, such as the Nuer of southern Sudan, who expanded territorially but did not conquer the Dinka and become a state (see the section "Nuer versus Dinka" in chapter 8). For an example of warring chiefdoms not conquering each other, one needs only to look at the early inhabitants of my state of residence—New York State. The Iroquois in the early 1600s waged war against many neighboring chiefdoms, including the Huron who lived in what is today the province of Ontario, Canada. The Iroquois attacked Huron villages; killed and captured the men, women, and children; and burned the longhouses, their homes. Some captives were brought back to Iroquoia and adopted, while others were tortured to death.[24] No increase in political centralization occurred beyond the formation of the initial confederacies (see the section "Iroquois versus Huron" in chapter 8).

The development of warfare along the Fertile Crescent and in adjacent regions after 7000 B.C.E., at such sites as Catal Huyuk (about 5800 B.C.E.) and the fortified town of Hacilar (about 5300 B.C.E.) in south-central Anatolia or Turkey, meant that states did not arise in the heartland where the first plants and animals were domesticated.[25] The large settlement of Abu Hureyra did not develop into a state, in spite of the fact that there was no warfare in the region, because it was abandoned about 5000 B.C.E. The "honor" of creating the first state went to the settlers of southern Mesopotamia. Archaeologists, and military historians as well, have consistently interpreted the settlement pattern and house form of Catal Huyuk as evidence for warfare.[26] The houses were densely packed together without exterior entrances, except roof openings. Portable ladders provided access to the roofs. Some men, who probably were warriors, were buried at Catal Huyuk with mace heads, flint daggers, and obsidian projectile points.

Why did warfare arise by 7000 B.C.E. in the Fertile Crescent? I suggest that it arose as towns tried to control trade routes, in particular the obsidian trade. By 7000 B.C.E. obsidian—an important resource used in making sharp tools and decorative objects—was being widely traded. It was also used in the manufacture of weapons—projectile points and daggers. The sources of obsidian were a volcano in east-central Anatolia and other sites farther to the east. Obsidian from the volcano site, however, has been found in the Levant, to the west, at much earlier dates (between 12,000 and 8800 B.C.E.) and from the more eastern sites after 9000 B.C.E.[27] Catal Huyuk, nestled against the first ranges of the Taurus Mountains, controlled access to the obsidian resources at the volcano.[28] The town was defensible, as noted above, with its architecture providing no easy access to its residents, and the men, or at least some of the men, were warriors. The fortified town of Hacilar lay to the west. To the southeast, on the coast, a thousand years later, was the fortress of Mersin. The first appearance of a professional military organization

Figure 5.1. Theories of How States Arose

	Internal	External
Conflict	Internal Conflict	Conquest
Cooperation	Consensual	Confederation

seems to be at Mersin (about 4300 B.C.E.) in southern Anatolia, where a garrison with soldiers' quarters was destroyed by an attack. Narrow apertures indicate that at least some of the soldiers were archers; a pile of clay sling pellets was also discovered. Control of trade routes is believed to be the cause of wars in this area.[29] The disruption of trade routes across Eurasia as a cause of invasions at a much later period was argued by historian Frederick Teggart. He contended that wars in particular locations disrupted trade routes that were supplying peoples beyond the periphery of the civilized world. When these peoples no longer received the goods to which they had become accustomed, they invaded the great civilizations in order to obtain them.[30]

Many theories of how the state arose have been proposed over the years, indeed over the centuries. I agree with anthropologist Herbert Lewis's statement that the "major reason for disagreement . . . is because we have so many different perspectives" rather than "that we do not have enough material about the origins of most of the pristine states."[31] Since Lewis wrote this statement in 1981, much more material has become available on some of the pristine states, particularly those in the New World. While I have no intention of reviewing most of these theories, I will point out that nearly all theories appear to me to fall into one of four categories. A four-cell typology can be constructed from two dimensions: Conflict vs. Cooperation and Internal (within a polity) vs. External (between polities) (see Figure 5.1). The first cell houses internal conflict theories. I believe an internal conflict theory explains how the pristine state arose. The other three theories may explain how some secondary states arose. External conflict theories are better known as conquest theories of the origin of the state. There are two versions. In one version, villages are believed to have conquered other villages, thereby creating a two-tier settlement hierarchy. More conquests led to three- and four-tier settlement hierarchies. Some scholars believe three tiers are sufficient for a state; others believe four tiers are necessary. In the other version it is the attacks of nomads—either on foot or on horseback—that led agricultural villagers to wall their settlements. The organizing of residents for defensive purposes led to political centralization and eventually the state. The third cell is home to consensual or integrative theories—the notion that people choose leaders because they perform important societal tasks. Lastly, cooperating polities can become a confederation. This higher order political organization may be a state. And then again it may not. The Huron and Iroquois confederacies did not reach statehood. Fred Gearing studied the rise of the Cherokee of the southeastern United States; he describes how when faced with an external threat—namely the colonists of South Carolina —the Cherokee villages formed a confederacy. Gearing draws parallels between what the Cherokee did and what the early settlers of southern Iraq were once thought to have accomplished, and he calls the process the "Mesopotamian Career to Statehood." [32]

To explain the development of the pristine state I utilize an internal conflict theory. The historic roots of internal conflict theory lie in the writings of Friedrich Engels. Engels argued that with increased agricultural efficiency, people were able to produce a surplus, which gave rise to the cleavage of society into social classes. Government emerged to suppress open conflict between the classes, but government sided with the rich at the expense of the poor. Government or the state thus arose as an institution to maintain wealth-based social classes.[33] Engels grounded his research on the work of Lewis Henry Morgan, the great New York State anthropologist who studied the Iroquois and wrote one of the great classics on evolutionary theory, *Ancient Society*. A follower of Engels, archaeologist V. Gordon Childe, applied the theory to the ancient Near East. In Childe's formulation an agricultural surplus and control of irrigation played major roles. Cultural anthropologist Leslie White, a scholar of Lewis Henry Morgan, set forth a theory of the origin of the state that stressed the role that government played in maintaining social classes.[34]

A "modern" version of the internal conflict theory comes from Morton Fried's *The Evolution of Political Society* (1967). Although clearly following in the tradition of Engels, Fried does not cite or discuss Engels's writings, nor does he discuss Childe or White.[35] Fried set forth a theory of the emergence of ranking, social stratification, and the state by constructing an evolutionary sequence: egalitarian society, rank society, stratified society, and the state. Stratification arises when access to basic resources is restricted.[36] However, stratified society is inherently unstable; governmental institutions of the state rectify the situation. Stratified society is a conjectural stage for which Fried had no examples, either archaeological or ethnographic, yet he stated that "each pristine state certainly had to traverse this stage or level." [37] Fried rejected war as an influence upon the institutionalization of stratification but accepted on the "basis of logic" that "warfare increases in frequency as societies become more complex." Thus, he did not say there was "no war" in those regions where pristine states arose. For Fried the state emerges from stratified society: It is "an organization of the power of society," by which he "means that warfare and killing become monopolies of the state." Once a state exists, "conquest theories of the state fit." [38] A contribution of Fried's 1967 book that did not come into sharp focus until eight years later is Fried's recognition that *tribes* did not precede the emergence of political centralization. Fried, an expert on China, later argued that there were no tribes in China until after the state arose, but he failed to describe pre-state conditions in that region.[39]

In recent years a number of internal conflict theories have been developed that appear, in most cases, not to derive from Fried or from each other. Yet the theories are remarkably similar. Each focuses on an aspect of the process that I believe occurred as agricultural villages (not tribes) evolved into centralized political systems. Fried focused on competition for resources; others focused on status, prestige, power, kinship, elites, factions, intragroup fighting, and coercion. There are probably more that I have missed. I have tried without success to devise diagrams to present the respective theories in a meaningful way. A pie chart would at least prevent me from placing one above the other, but I will discuss my theory first. I have already laid the groundwork for it in chapter 3 in the section titled "The Origin of Fraternal Interest Groups." I have, however, thought of a mechanical way to present the theories. In my office desk is a ten-sided die, numbered 0 to 9, that I use to create sets of random numbers or for making important decisions. It helps in ordering lunch in the cafeteria. If I had a larger ten-sided die, I could describe each theory on one of its faces. Actually, I could number the theories and use the die I have. Then I could roll the die, read about a theory, then roll again. And I could keep doing this. Eventually, all the theories would blur, the so-called Rashomon effect.[40] One or more of the faces of the die would be left blank, leaving room for theories that I failed to find or for theories yet to be devised by scholars unfamiliar with the existing theories. Each scholar (I am no exception) wants his or her own theory, yet the theories seem to be paintings of the same mountain.[41] I suspect that many of us are drawing from a core of knowledge that was constructed by Engels, Childe, and White.

My internal conflict theory of the development of the pristine state derives from fraternal interest group theory. Although the early sedentary hunter-gatherers who domesticated plants and animals probably did not have fraternal interest groups, the likelihood of male children living with or near their father increased as groups became more settled and populations became larger. Differing abilities of individuals and the varying size of kinship groups permitted some groups to accumulate "wealth"—a surplus of food and material objects, such as houses, tools, and domesticated animals. This wealth was a motivation for male children to remain with their family of birth. Competition arose. Rivalry between kinship groups manifested itself materially. Theft, the stealing of a neighbor's property, could have occurred. Indeed, a cross-cultural study of crime by Margaret Bacon, Irving Child, and Herbert Barry found that theft is more likely to occur in communities with a higher level of political integration than in bands.[42] Long-time rivalries could lead to overt conflict between kinship groups within a village. In my recent research on the feuding families of eastern Kentucky, I found examples of such conflict. Competition between "clans" over resources, including the illegal whiskey trade, could turn violent. Often casualties were one-sided, with all or nearly all deaths on one side. Each clan was composed of the descendants of an aggressive male who was willing to kill to further his ends.[43]

While I am not suggesting that homicide necessarily occurred in early agricultural communities, I am suggesting that kinship groups composed of male relatives appeared early in agricultural villages. These are fraternal interest groups. They competed for dominant position within the local group—the village or neighborhood of dispersed homesteads. In the competition for dominance, someone could be killed, which could in turn lead to a revenge killing and another killing—and the development of feuding. As my study of Kentucky feuding shows, deaths occurring in feuding groups are not necessarily symmetrical; they can lead to the demise of one of the rival fraternal interest groups. In early agricultural villages, the dominant fraternal interest group provided the leader of the local group. He and his fraternal interest group became the governing body of the local group. They also became the "upper class."

The government of the local group consisted of the leader, now a village headman, and followers, most likely younger male kinsmen. These "lieutenants," because they had the backing of the headman and their fraternal interest group, were able to coerce other local group members. At a more advanced level of sociopolitical complexity, the leader, now a chief, had followers who might even kill on behalf of their leader. The leader and his followers might live in fortified homesteads. In eastern Kentucky leaders of kinship groups sometimes lived in houses of log construction built in isolated, defensible locations. The leaders might hire assassins, kin or non-kin, to do their killing. A classic ethnographic example is available: In the Trobriand Islands of Melanesia, if a man insults the chief and the chief wishes his disposal, he will instruct "henchmen" to carry out the execution secretly; the killing will be done with spears, from ambush.[44] At the level of sociopolitical complexity that I term the maximal chiefdom/inchoate early state, the chief/king ordered the torture and execution of members of his local group as a means of consolidating political control.[45] Out of this matrix arose the idea of the state. Fortifications were likely to help with control: Captured local group members could be brought to the fortified sites and tortured and executed there. Jails are found almost exclusively in centralized political systems.[46]

In his theory of state formation, archaeologist Malcolm Webb stresses the importance of warfare. The "surplus of defeated groups"— or "loot"—provides the chief with a "source of wealth" that enables him to gather "a group of retainers or a war band large enough to keep in check all other groups in the society." This situation in time generates "a monopoly of coercive force" in the hands of the leader. For Webb, this concentration of power is a radical shift in the "authority of the leadership"—the result is an incipient state system of governance.[47] Thus, the primary element of this theory is coercion. The theory has empirical and logical problems, however. First, warfare is not found prior to the emergence of the pristine state; second, the "loot" or surplus is not specified—if it is food that is carried away, it seems unlikely that warriors would risk suffering casualties to steal food to give to their leader who in turn would give it back to them.

The theory of archaeologist David Webster stresses status rivalry between warring leaders from the same culture. Webster uses my concept of *internal* war—warfare between culturally similar political communities: "Status-rivalry war is war from the top down." It took place between elites and thus "it continually reinforced the gulf between elites and commoners and differentiated among elites themselves."[48] The existing hierarchy itself stimulated intense status rivalry. The goal of war was prestige. Although Webster's discussion of status-rivalry warfare makes it appear similar to ritual warfare, he rejects that formulation: "Warfare may be ritualized internal war between culturally similar factions and still be highly lethal, destructive, and politically significant." In an earlier article, Webster argued that "constant warfare . . . provided an important and highly adaptive managerial function for emergent elite segments of society."[49] Status, as well as elites, are the primary elements of Webster's theory. The lack of evidence for warfare before the pristine state emerged is a weakness of this theory.

Cultural anthropologist Herbert Lewis develops a theory that draws upon his field research with the Galla states in southwestern Ethiopia and upon the theories of Webb and Webster. In his view leaders and followers are "political actors" who make decisions that they believe will further their self-interests. New political patterns are the result of human competition. Lewis further argues that there are "parallel and repeated processes in political evolution." Like Webb and Webster, Lewis views warfare as significant in the foundation of states. In his research on the Galla, a cluster of secondary states, Lewis describes how one local Galla group conquered an important market center on a trade route and then forced neighboring groups to submit to its control. The monarch maintained his position through "eternal vigilance, which is the price of despotism."[50] We will shortly examine the role of despotism in the development of the pristine state.

Archaeologist Jonathan Haas, in a comprehensive review titled *The Evolution of the Prehistoric State,* concludes that "the initial centralization of a social system involves a process of integration through trade, warfare, irrigation, or some other means. The integrative process itself, in turn, results in stratification of the system, with a leadership group gaining increased access to basic resources by controlling either their production or procurement. This control then provides that leadership group with an economic base for exerting coercive power over the rest of the population." He further says, "I have come to the conclusion that while integration played a major role in the original coalescence of governmental institutions, maintenance of a system of stratification and coercion lies at the heart of the first true governments."[51] Haas was highly influenced by Fried. Two features of Haas's analysis are important: First, warfare does not exist or is relatively insignificant before the emergence of the pristine state. It is part of the thesis of *How War Began* that warfare did not emerge until stage III, the maximal chiefdom or inchoate early state. Second, internal conflict manifesting itself in intragroup fighting occurs before the emergence of the state. The winners are able to exercise "coercive power." In my view, the primary element in Haas's theory is intragroup fighting.

For archaeologists John Clark and Michael Blake, political entrepreneurs or aggrandizers are responsible for the emergence of rank societies: "The development of social inequality was . . . a long-term unexpected consequence of many individuals promoting their own aggrandizement." Ambitious males compete for prestige. Clark and Blake "assume patrilocality, with patrilineal descent favored but not strictly necessary." They further assume a numerous population, interest groups of kin and clients, that more wives and children mean more deployable resources, that multiple external ties give the central authority figure an advantage, that raiding (if it occurs) enhances the leader's reputation, that followers receive rewards and become linked in a reciprocal relationship, and that special privileges are passed on to heirs.[52] Prestige, thus, is a primary element of this theory. One strength of this theory is that it does not assume that warfare is necessary for the political process to work.

Archaeologist Richard Blanton develops "a behavioral theory of archaic state politics."[53] He focuses upon the political process—"the competition among various individuals and groups attempting to exert power in such a way as to shape or control the state." Types and sources of power occupy most of his discussion. Blanton is interested in "any behavior that aims to establish and uphold restrictions on the exercise of exclusionary power"; he calls this egalitarian behavior.[54] Although his statements do not directly constitute a theory of the origin of the state, Blanton uses a set of variables similar to those used by other theorists. The primary element of his theory is power.

The internal conflict theories, which have been produced over a span of thirty-five years, deal to some extent with different stages of the road to statehood. My fraternal interest group theory pertains to an early stage, as do Clarke and Blake's prestige-seeking factions and Webb's coercing warrior bands. Webster's leaders engaged in status rivalry, Fried's resource competitors, and Haas's combatants are theoretical formulations that seem to focus upon a middle stage. Blanton's power seekers operate in a newly formed state. What impresses me, however, is that if I throw the metaphorical die and let the theories blend, I see *groups,* whether kinship, non-kinship factions, or elites, engaged in *activities,* including fighting and coercion, the *goals* of which range from resource acquisition to status, power, and prestige. The theories are similar, but different—together they throw light upon the political process that leads to statehood. They take us from the domestication of plants and animals, through early village life, to the threshold of emerging political centralization.

Chiefdoms and States

The terms "chiefdom" and "state" are used to describe categories of political systems. The terms have separate origins, the concept of the state having been developed much earlier than that of the chiefdom. The concept of the state and its origin is generally attributed to late-nineteenth-century German sociologists, although it can be traced to Aristotle and the ancient Greeks.[55] Other European scholars have elaborated upon the concept of the state up to the present. The concept of the chiefdom and its origin is much more recent, appearing in the last half of the twentieth century. In the 1940s, Julian Steward created a category to describe tribal societies in the ancient Caribbean and the land surrounding that body of water. These societies had temples, special residences for chiefs, and storehouses; villages were stratified into three or four classes, with the chief at the top, and wealth was a major factor in their differentiation; in some areas the chief ruled over federations of villages. But it was Kalervo Oberg who in 1955 gave this type of society the name "chiefdom." Steward, who used the term in later writings, saw the chiefdom as an evolutionary stage between tribes and states.[56]

By the late 1960s, Elman Service's evolutionary sequence—bands, tribes, chiefdoms, and states—had become gospel. And it has remained gospel. A recent example is Jared Diamond's treatment of the evolution of the state in *Guns, Germs, and Steel.* In cross-cultural research, I grouped bands and tribes together and called them uncentralized political systems; the chiefdoms and states became centralized political systems.[57] Prior to the 1940s the distinction was between state and stateless societies; states were contrasted with all other societies.[58] An ambiguity developed: Is a centralized political system necessarily a state or could it be a chiefdom? This legacy of research and interpretation has thus left anthropology and the other social sciences with two traditions. Is the state a distinct political entity that we should attempt to identify in the archaeological record, or do we have a continuum from chiefdom to state, with no precise point at which chiefdoms can be differentiated from states?

I opt for the latter approach for two reasons. First, since the late 1960s, in my research and publications I have lumped chiefdoms and states together—not that this practice is a good reason per se, but by continuing to do so I remain consistent. Second, and more importantly, I believe that since the two concepts are the constructions of separate groups of scholars, there is no reason to expect to find a point at which the sociopolitical systems to which the concepts can be applied can be differentiated from each other either archaeologically or ethnographically. Being a state or not is not the same thing as, for example, being alive rather than dead. I believe that, at best, we can only more or less distinguish stages along a continuum. I will identify five stages of the chiefdom-state continuum. I do not find it necessary to distinguish chiefdoms from states.

I constructed the five-stage chiefdom-state continuum by linking two separate typologies—one for chiefdoms, one for states. Each typology has three types, which are arranged in an evolutionary sequence. The typologies overlap, creating a single sequence of five types. Coming out of the Americanist tradition is Robert Carneiro's typology of chiefdoms, while coming out of the Europeanist tradition is Henri Claessen and Peter Skalnik's typology of early states. Carneiro defines a chiefdom as "an autonomous political unit comprising a number of villages or communities under the permanent control of a paramount chief. This is a minimal definition. It focuses on what I consider essential to the concept of chiefdom." Claessen and Skalnik define the early state as "a centralized socio-political organization for the regulation of social relations in a complex, stratified society divided into at least two basic strata, or emergent social classes—viz. the rulers and the ruled—whose relations are characterized by political dominance of the former and tributary obligations of the latter, legitimized by a common ideology of which reciprocity is the basic principle." [59]

The combined typology has the following appearance:

Stage	V	Transitional Early State		
Stage	IV	Typical Early State		
Stage	III	Maximal Chiefdom	=	Inchoate Early State
Stage	II	Typical Chiefdom		
Stage	I	Minimal Chiefdom		

Each of the two typologies was empirically derived; that is, the descriptions of each type were derived by grouping similar chiefdoms and similar states and noting their characteristics. The descriptions of the maximal chiefdom and the inchoate early state are essentially the same. Carneiro and Claessen and Skalnik further listed the societies that conformed to each type. Carneiro lists two maximal chiefdoms—Hawaii and Tahiti—both of which are on Claessen and Skalnik's list of six inchoate early states. Thus, the descriptions and the examples make it readily apparent that the two typologies can be linked.

What goes above and what goes below the typology? The mature state rests on top. Indeed, the transitional early state is seen by Claessen and Skalnik as transitional to the mature state. Although their study of the early state is a lengthy volume, it provides only a brief look at the type of state that developmentally follows the early state.[60] The mature state has an administrative apparatus that is dominated by appointed officials; kinship influences are only marginal aspects of government, and private property prevails in the means of production (as a market economy and overtly antagonistic classes develop).[61] Below the minimal chiefdom is the agricultural village discussed in this and preceding chapters. If these two stages—the mature state and the agricultural village—are added to the ends of the continuum, a seven-stage continuum is the result.

Missing from the typology is a theory of why any society would proceed along the continuum. The internal conflict theory, with its emphases on leaders and followers and competing kinship groups, gets us to the end of the typical chiefdom stage. But something further has to happen. It has been pointed out that the groups that win in the internal conflict may use violence and coercion to achieve control. A second theory takes us further. It is called "political legitimacy theory" by sociologist Steven Spitzer. The theory argues that emerging or recently formed states use a wide range of cruel and repressive sanctions, including torture and capital punishment, to subjugate and control the population. After control is obtained, repressive sanctions are no longer needed; the governing body can rely upon consensus for social regulation. Spitzer suggests that "once states begin to form and arrogate power for their own purposes, they must establish repressive controls to achieve their ends. . . . As soon as the state has achieved a more stable basis for its power and established mechanisms to penetrate the masses and inculcated the 'proper' beliefs, repressive measures can be dropped in favor of more sophisticated incentives and disincentives." A three-stage model is developed: "Stateless societies are regulated through a complex of emergent and consensus-based restitutive controls; pristine states, precisely because they lack legitimacy, must develop and impose harsh, cruel, and highly visible forms of repressive sanctions; developed states, having successfully 're-invented' consensus, can achieve social regulation through a combination of civil law and relatively mild forms of 'calculated' repression."[62] This theory is used by neither Carneiro nor Claessen and Skalnik to explain political evolution, yet it can be fitted to the five-stage continuum: Stages I and II go with the first part of the curvilinear model, stages III and IV with the "pristine state" section of the model, and stage V and the mature state with the "developed state" end of the model.

Ibn Khaldun, a fourteenth-century Arab historian (1332–1406), explained the emergence of statehood with a fully developed theory of political legitimacy. He delineated three stages in the evolution of a state, which correspond approximately to three forty-year generations. The first stage, when rulers are consolidating power, is characterized by despotism—the use of torture and cruel forms of capital punishment by the political leader to intimidate the controlled population. At this stage, the rulers rely on a strong military to secure the obedience of their subjects. During the second stage, despotism is no longer needed to control the subject people; the ruler is less dependent on the military. This stage, in contrast to the first, is marked by the development of a civilian bureaucracy devoted to collecting taxes and administering justice. In the third stage, power becomes concentrated, luxury expands, and docility develops. The state is no longer able to defend itself from attack or prevent internal uprisings. Despotism is no longer available as a means for controlling the population.[63] Ibn Khaldun's three stages in the evolution of the state can also be fitted to the five-stage continuum. However, for the pristine states described in this volume the time period for each stage is much longer than forty years.

Three studies, all cross-cultural, support political legitimacy theory. Anthropologist Yehudi Cohen tested political legitimacy theory by relating newly formed states to the use of capital punishment for sexual crimes. Three stages in the development of statehood were delineated: First, "an inchoate incorporative state is one that has not yet completely subverted local sources of solidarity, allegiance, and authority." Second, "a successful incorporative state is one that has secured the transfer of loyalty and the exercise of authority from local nexuses to the state." Third, "an expropriated nation is a formerly stateless or state society governed by a state organization imposed by force by another state at a much more advanced level of cultural development." Using this developmental sequence, Cohen hypothesizes that "nations characterized by inchoate incorporative states exhibit a unique profile in the regulation of sexual relationships. They adopt laws imposing capital punishment for adultery, incest, and the violation of celibacy." His data show that incorporative states differ from both expropriated states and stateless societies in that they almost exclusively prescribe capital punishment for the three sex crimes listed.[64] An excellent case study utilizing Cohen's theory is Donald Kurtz's "The Legitimation of the Aztec State." He describes the use of terror and capital punishment by Aztec rulers when the state was at the inchoate incorporative stage of development.[65]

A second cross-cultural study that supports political legitimacy the-

ory is by Steven Spitzer. He found that "the relationship between punitive intensity and social development is actually curvilinear—in the
sense that sanctions are lenient in simple egalitarian (reciprocal) societies, severe in non-market (redistributive) complex societies, and lenient in established market societies."[66] The explanation for this relationship is to be found in political legitimacy theory: "If punishment
is instrumental in consolidating a particular system of domination,
then we can explain why greater concentration and complexity lead to
harsher and more extensive punitive controls. This would seem to be
particularly true in societies where the development of political integration has just begun."[67]

In a third cross-cultural study, I tested political legitimacy theory. Of
the twelve states in my sample, seven were despotic and five mature.
Despotic states were distinguished from mature states in this study
largely by using the criterion of torture. If the ethnographic data made
it clear that torture was used to obtain confessions and/or to make death
more painful, the culture was classified as a despotic state. On the other
hand, if few crimes (four or fewer) led to execution, if there were few
(two or fewer) means of executing, and if there were no data describing
torture, the culture was classified as a mature state. I tested the following hypothesis: The newer a state is, the more likely it is to be a despotic
state; and, conversely, the older a state is, the more likely it is to be a mature state. This hypothesis was tested by measuring the chronological
age of each state at the time of the ethnographic description. Support
was found for the hypothesis.[68] All the mature states were more than
two hundred years old, and five of the seven despotic states were less
than two hundred years old. Not only did the test of the hypothesis give
credence to political legitimacy theory but it also provided validation
for distinguishing between despotic and mature states.[69]

I found that the early state was a despotic state. Claessen and Skalnik
do not discuss this feature of the inchoate early state. However, I think
it is extremely important. Despotism explains why chiefdoms that become states are likely not to be waging war—the emerging rulers are far
too busy consolidating their control over both rivals and the lower class
within the chiefdom. Once internal consolidation has been achieved,
the rulers can direct attacks upon neighboring states. The lower class,
now under control, can be conscripted for military service. The conscripts become massed infantry under the direction of elite officers, or
the lower class may be used by the ruler to raise crops, construct fortifications, and become a local defense force.

Internal conflict theory and political legitimacy theory fit well together, just as do the two typologies. Internal conflict and political legitimacy theories can be fitted to the chiefdom-state continuum. The
former covers villages and the first two types of chiefdoms, and the latter covers the three types of early states and the mature state. Indeed,

they can be thought of as one theory. I cannot, however, think of a good term for the combined or composite theory, and I do not believe it is useful to select one label over the other. Perhaps it is best to use them in combination: internal conflict/political legitimacy theory. While the terms "structural" or "political ecology" could be used, I do not believe they convey the precise meaning that the expression "internal conflict/political legitimacy theory" conveys.[70] The evolution of each pristine state described in the next chapter provides support for the combined theory.

Through the village stage and the first two stages of chiefdoms, the minimal and typical, political leaders compete for position within the local group. They do not engage in external conflict or war. At the village stage, one leader and his kinship group or faction may achieve dominance. The larger kinship group may end up on top. At the minimal chiefdom stage the leader and his followers dominate with coercion; they take control of the local group. The leader becomes a chief. By the typical chiefdom stage the chief and his close followers become the government. I believe political evolution can stop here. Chiefdoms in a region could begin to attack each other, but the governments of these polities have not developed to the point where the victors could conquer and incorporate the defeated, and thereby create larger and fewer chiefdoms in the region. Leaders in those chiefdoms that become maximal chiefdoms or inchoate early states (stage III) refrain from warfare while they bring the population under greater control through despotism. They use executions not only to eliminate potential rivals but also to punish prohibited sexual behavior as a means of terrifying and controlling the population. This rapid move toward despotism occurs just as the typical chiefdom is becoming a maximal chiefdom or inchoate early state. Increasing centralization takes place throughout this stage, and with the increase arises the *idea* of the state. I believe that political legitimacy theory as formulated here explains both the origin of the state and the idea of the state that emerged with it.

Once the lower class has been subjugated—and perhaps even become laborers for the upper class—the chief can look outward. At this point one polity is likely to attack another. Conquest and incorporation can occur for two reasons: First, the victors have the political institutions, born of despotism, for subjugating the defeated. A study of state formation in southern Korea (200 B.C.E. to A.D. 300) argues that warfare occurred for the purpose of obtaining slaves. Underpopulation, rather than overpopulation, predicted warfare.[71] Second, the military organizations, unlike in earlier times, are not based on fraternal interest groups but are composed of the chief's followers and members of the upper class. This military organization eventually gives way to a professional army led by aristocratic officers directing massed infantry under coercive leadership. The soldiers may come directly from communal work projects. They are conscripts and are under a coercive command structure. Internal war characterizes this stage; inchoate early states attempt to conquer nearby culturally similar inchoate early states. The conquest theory of the state now can be applied. Once conquests begin, a typical early state (stage IV) emerges.

Many researchers and scholars today are concerned that theories of yesteryear leave out the individual and, in so doing, dehumanize the actors who are so important in social and culture change. Among archaeologists, Joyce Marcus, Kent Flannery, and Elizabeth Brumfiel explicitly feature this aspect of their work.[72] Internal conflict/political legitimacy theory focuses on the individual—a political leader—but it does not exactly humanize him. In the early stages of political evolution, the leader and his followers are likely to use coercion on other villagers; at a later stage the followers may kill rivals of the chief. At the maximal chiefdom/inchoate early state stage they may capture, torture, and execute rivals or anyone else as a means of demonstrating that they have political control of the polity. I would like to leave out the individual, but my theory will not let me.

My theory of how war began in early states differs from a major theory of state formation. I have described above three phases: no war, despotism, and war. During the middle phase subordination develops in civil society. British sociologist Herbert Spencer, considered by many to be one of the great founding figures of that field, argued the reverse: that war occurred first, then subordination developed in the military, and lastly, subordination developed in civil society.[73] In my cross-cultural study *The Evolution of War,* I tested and found support for Spencer's theory.[74] This apparent contradiction—two rival theories appearing to be correct—can be resolved. The theory developed in this section pertains to pristine states, and the theory developed by Spencer pertains to secondary states—states that arose from tribes under the influence of pristine states. The states included in the sample used in my cross-cultural study were secondary states; the sample did not include pristine states.

Pristine States

Four pristine states were chosen. I constructed a matrix describing in general terms the evolution of the pristine state from analyses of the development of each of the four chosen states. This matrix (Figure 5.2) and the description that accompanies it support the internal conflict/political legitimacy theory.

How Many?

How many pristine states were there—six, five, four, three, two, one? An argument can be made for any of these numbers, including a number higher than six. I have selected four, a number that I believe at pres-

Stages	Social and Political Organization	Internal Conflict	War	Military Organization
Mature State	Empire composed of culturally different conquered peoples	Bureaucracy replaces despotism Judicial system with laws	Alliance wars	Light infantry provided by different peoples
V. Transitional Early State	Monarchy with royalty, upper class, commoners, and slaves Four levels to polity: capital, cities, towns, and villages	Consolidation of same-language polities	External war	Distinct military units: massed infantry, troops with projectile weapons, siege train; in Old World, chariot corps
IV. Typical Early State	King heads military aristocracy Four levels to polity: capital, large towns, small towns, and villages Slavery	Lower class taxed Agricultural surplus and labor Men conscripted War captives enslaved Human sacrifice	Internal war	Professional army: officers are aristocrats; conscripted commoners form massed infantry with shields; fortified cities and siege operations
III. Inchoate Early State = Maximal Chiefdom	Chief is despot Chief's village becomes "capital" Three levels to polity: capital, towns, and villages Upper class dominates lower class	Execution of rivals, members of lower class Human sacrifice	Wars of consolidation with close neighbors	"Army" composed of chief, followers, and upper class males; shields and helmets; village fortifications
II. Typical Chiefdom	Chief from upper class, supported by kin Two levels to polity Social classes	Violent conflict between leaders Assassinations	No war	Fraternal interest groups; spears, clubs, and knives; fortified residences
I. Minimal Chiefdom	Chief Large villages Wealth differences	Conflict between leaders begins	No war	None
Villages	Headman Kinship groups with leaders No wealth differences	Minimal conflict	No war	None

Figure 5.2. Stages in the Chiefdom-State Continuum

ent has some degree of consensus. However, the arguments and analysis presented below do not depend upon a precise number. The major effect of having a higher number would be to make this book longer, and a lower number, to make the book shorter.

A pristine state is the first state in a region; there are no prior states in that region or surrounding regions. Indeed, no influences from states elsewhere in the world have had any impact on the region. As Fried has put it, "A pristine situation is one in which development occurs exclusively on the basis of indigenous factors." He further states that "when a pristine state emerges it does so in a political vacuum. That is, there is no other more highly developed state present that might help it toward stateship," or, I might add, prevent it from becoming a state.[75] The above discussion raises two questions. First, which regions of the world were independent of other regions? Second, within a particular region, which was the pristine state? After one state has emerged in a region no other state that arises can be *the* pristine state.

To the first question. There appear to be four independent regions, two in the New World and two in the Old World: Mesoamerica, Peru, Mesopotamia, and northern China. An argument can be made that Mesoamerica influenced Peru since corn, a Mesoamerican crop, is the staple crop of coastal Peru. Corn somehow spread—from group to group or by coastal trade. Did the idea of statehood spread with the corn? I do not believe so, and I have found no one who argues that it did. A factor to consider in researching this conclusion is that the first state in Peru may be earlier than the first state in Mesoamerica, or they may have developed around the same time.[76] The other possibility, that Peru influenced state origins in Mesoamerica, has some plausibility. Temples on platforms, monuments depicting executions, and metallurgy are all earlier in Peru. In the Old World the state developed in Mesopotamia about fifteen hundred years earlier than in northern China. The diffusion of ideas could have taken place for well over a millennium. Numerous features of Chinese society have their Mesopotamian counterparts, such as bronze metallurgy and chariots drawn by equids—two elements important in Old World state-level warfare. Yet many of the shared features, such as writing, are so different that they appear unrelated to each other. Thus, most scholars continue to accept the independence of Mesopotamia and northern China. In spite of present-day consensus, there may be only two pristine states: Peru and Mesopotamia. However, the four pristine states selected appear very different from each other. I am siding with the consensus.

There is also the possibility that China influenced Mesoamerica. Archaeologist Kwang-chih Chang has pointed out the similarities of art styles between the two regions, and from time to time a claim is made that Chinese junks blown off course reached the west coast of Mesoamerica.[77] Nevertheless, the prevailing view among archaeologists is that the evolution of New World states was independent of China, or for that matter any place in the Old World. Early in the twentieth century one scholar argued that all civilization came from ancient Egypt, and at the end of the twentieth century pseudoscholars argued that Mesoamerican civilization derived from western Africa, a claim that has been soundly rejected by reputable scholars.[78]

Two other regions, both in the Old World, could be independent: Egypt along the Nile River and the civilizations along the Indus River. If they were, we would have a total of six independent regions.[79] The Indus River civilizations are probably not independent since the region is close to Mesopotamia and chronologically later.[80] Coast trade almost undoubtedly occurred; furthermore, many features of Indus civilization are strikingly similar to those of the civilization along the Tigris and Euphrates Rivers. Egypt's status as being independent has long been in doubt.[81] Recent research by archaeologist Alexander Joffe has noted the presence of early Mesopotamian styles from Uruk in Egyptian sites and the absence of Egyptian styles in Mesopotamian sites.[82] Nevertheless, Egypt is a good candidate for inclusion on the list of pristine states, maybe as good as northern China. If I felt I needed a fifth case for comparative purposes, I would not hesitate to add Egypt to the list. I have examined the data from ancient Egypt, and it appears to support the generalizations I have derived. The Indus River civilizations also appear to support the generalizations.

To the second question. Which was *the* pristine state within a region? Within a region there were multiple centers where sociopolitical evolution had begun. These centers were in contact, perhaps before, certainly after, the first state emerged. I have selected what appears to be the earliest center to have passed through stage III in each region and then to have gone on to stages IV and V; there is no chiefdom-state demarcation line on my continuum. Rather there is a stage (III) that may span several hundred years. At a future time archaeologists may find sites that indicate that stage III occurred first at another center. At the present time, the most controversial region seems to be Mesoamerica. The Olmec, the Maya, Teotihuacan, and the Zapotec have all been candidates. Dates are approximate, and the dates for the early stages of these cultures are close.[83] Personal rivalries between archaeologists also play a role—and most archaeologists want to find the earliest fossil, artifact, or site. It is possible for Mesoamerica that in the period just before stage III these cultures—explorers, traders, visitors—were in contact and that the contact stimulated development. Recall that pre-state agriculturalists do not engage in war, and Mesoamericans did not war until the Zapotec achieved statehood. Thus, war would not have prevented the movement of small groups of people between regions. I have selected the Zapotec as the first culture to achieve statehood, but it could be one of the others. The establishment of the city of Monte Albán on a hilltop in about 400 B.C.E. is the result of this achievement.[84] If the Zapotec had never existed, one of the other cultures would have become *the* pristine Mesoamerican state.

Peru also presents a problem. Although archaeologists appear to be in agreement that the Moche had the first state in this region, there are a number of North Coast river valleys that vied with each other for the "honor" of being first. The presumed center of the region is the Moche River Valley, but in the early Moche period there were five more river valleys to the north. One of these valleys, Lambayeque, with the site of Pampa Grande, will receive focal attention since Jonathan Haas has applied the internal conflict theory to data from this site.[85] But Haas himself has argued that Chavín de Huántar was a state, as were other sites, beginning about 800 B.C.E., and archaeologist Richard Burger, another Peruvian specialist, concurs.[86] Chavín de Huántar is a highland site with a large ceremonial center. I will describe the evolution of the first Peruvian state as Chavín/Moche. For Mesopotamia consensus holds that Uruk peoples residing in a number of cities, such as Ur, Warka, and Lagash, produced the first pristine states in the world.[87] In northern China the Shang culture has long been considered China's first state, but the state arose earlier, probably during the Erlitou period, or even earlier during the Langshan period.[88] The state preceding the Shang is the Xia or Hsia.

Evolution of the Pristine State

The theory of the origin of the state that I use in *How War Began* has been presented. It is a combination of internal conflict theory and political legitimacy theory. The four regions in which pristine states arose have been selected, and the most likely pristine state in each region has been chosen. Using the five-stage chiefdom-state continuum, I will present in the next chapter the evolution of the state for each of these regions. The evolution of each state fits the continuum, which permits the establishment of a matrix describing in general terms the evolution of the pristine state as it progresses from one stage to the next; each stage is a row of the matrix. Thus, the matrix is a description of how the first state arose in each region. The description itself, derived from the four case studies, shows that the internal conflict/political legitimacy theory accurately predicts the evolution of the pristine state.

In addition to the chiefdom-state continuum, the matrix has four categories, which form four columns. The first category, social and political organization, contains three dimensions or variables: type of political leader, number of hierarchical levels in the political system, and type of social stratification. Political leaders can be classified as either headman, chief, dictator, or king; hierarchical levels can range from one to four or higher; and, social stratification can include the number of social classes, castes (which are endogamous groups, such as military aristocracies), and slaves.[89] These three dimensions taken together describe the social and political organization of any society. The second category, internal conflict, is taken from the internal conflict/political legitimacy theory. Data collected permit direct testing of that theory. War, the third category, and military organization, the fourth category, are, of course, the major topics of this book. Among the types of war are internal war (between culturally similar political communities), external war (between culturally different political communities), and alliance war (separate political communities join to fight one or more other political communities). Feuding, which is not war, takes place within a political community. Military organizations can be classified as being composed of nonprofessional warriors, both nonprofessional and professional warriors, and professional warriors (soldiers).[90]

I have used stages of a developmental sequence not to pigeonhole data but to facilitate the organization of information. If I were focusing on a single case study, it would not be necessary to use these stages of development. Marcus and Flannery set forth the approach that I employ. They argue that "it is the periods of stability, or slow evolution, that look similar. That is where concepts like band, autonomous village, rank society, and archaic state become useful. These abstractions from societies of the recent past allow us to compare the stable periods in different evolutionary sequences. There are stages in the rise of all archaic states that look provocatively similar. One of our goals should be to find out why this is so."[91] *How War Began* attempts to answer this question.

A matrix that has both a time dimension and a series of categories can be read in four ways; each column can be read down, as well as up, while each row can be read across, starting at the top or at the bottom of the matrix. I have chosen to read the chart across, starting at the bottom. This method will show what is happening across the society as each stage develops and evolves into the next, from the village through the stages of the chiefdom-state continuum, to the mature state. For the general matrix, as well as for each of the case studies, seven stages are distinguished (see Figure 5.2).

A summary of what was learned about the evolution of the pristine state follows. At the village level there are kinship groups with leaders, one of whom is the village headman. There may even be a co-headman. Conflict between the leaders of kinship groups is minimal. There is no war. There are no military organizations, although male kinsmen could form fraternal interest groups. Weapons for hunting small game are present, but no weapons are made for military purposes. Villages are not located in defensive locations, no fortifications are present, and residences do not serve for defense.

At the minimal chiefdom level, stage I, the village headman becomes a chief. Wealth differences arise from industry and good fortune, such as many surviving offspring in a family. Wealth and family size become bases for leadership, with some leaders being more important than others. Conflict is still minimal, but conflict between leaders, who may be vying for the chieftaincy, is on the increase. Fraternal interest groups are developing. There is still no war—no military organizations, no military weapons, and no fortifications surrounding villages and residences.

At the typical chiefdom level, stage II, major changes occur. The position of chief is formal and well defined. Stratification based on wealth has occurred: Two social classes, an upper and a lower class, are present. The chief is from the upper class; he is supported by his kin. The chiefdom is likely to consist of multiple villages, with the chief's village being the administrative center of a two-level polity. Rivals of the chief may head other villages within the polity. Conflicts between the chief and these leaders may turn violent. Assassinations and raids upon domiciles take place. Being the chief has privileges, such as multiple mates and freedom from subsistence pursuits, but it also has its risks. To avoid being killed, one must have followers kill potential challengers. War between chiefdoms, however, does not occur. If war—that is, raids, ambushes, and line battles—occurred between chiefdoms, the development path toward statehood would be blocked; no chiefdom would become large enough or strong enough to evolve into the next stage, the maximal chiefdom. At stage II there are fraternal interest group members who form a coersive organization consisting of the leader and his followers, but the administrative organization is so undeveloped that the conquest and incorporation of other chiefdoms cannot take place. Although atlatls, slings, and hunting bows and arrows may still be available, the weapons of choice for assassinations by ambush or raid are thrusting spears and clubs. Knives, often of obsidian, are used to cut off heads and to remove other body parts, such as genitals. The residences of chiefs and village leaders are fortified, and armed followers may provide twenty-four-hour protection.

At the maximal chiefdom or inchoate early state level, stage III, the chief becomes a despot. He, or the leader who has replaced him, has killed through assassination many rivals in the previous stage. Now rivals or potential rivals are openly seized and taken to the chief's "capital," where they are tortured and executed, often publicly. The most serious crime is treason—offenses against the chief.[92] Human sacrifice of rivals, lower class members, and, later, war captives is likely to occur in a public setting as a way to emphasize the power of the emergent state and its ruler. The polity now has three hierarchical levels, consisting of the capital, towns, and villages.

Armies led by the chief and composed of his followers and other members of the upper class constitute a formidable fighting force. Wars against neighboring maximal chiefdoms take place. This situation is the second origin of war. Military equipment abounds. Warriors, in addition to carrying spears, clubs, and knives, are protected by helmets and shields. Projectile weapons are developed for war—the atlatl, the bow and arrow, and the sling. These become weapons of defense. Villages, particularly the "capital," are fortified. Defenders, which may include persons not in the army (lower class males, women, children, and old men), use projectile weapons to drive off or at least attempt to drive off attackers. Attackers, on the other hand, may use the same projectile weapons to drive defenders back from the fortifications. If the fortifications are overrun, defenders—combatants and noncombatants alike —will be slaughtered, enslaved, or taken back to the victor's capital to be publicly executed. At this stage of sociopolitical evolution, the war leader–chief has no greater pleasure than executing the leaders of rival chiefdoms.[93] Survivors of the attack, as well as their territory, are incorporated into the victor's polity. Indeed, a reason for going to war may be to obtain slaves. The coercive political measures that were developed to control the lower class of the winners can be used to control the newly defeated peoples. Once conquests begin, a typical early state arises.

An important point can now be made. A period without war must precede a period of political consolidation within a polity. Only when a chief has firm control over political rivals, as well as the lower class, can he engage in war against neighboring chiefdoms. In other words, not until a chiefdom is a state (stage III) can it successfully wage war. By successfully, I mean that it has the administrative ability to first conquer and then incorporate enemy villages into the state. As stated earlier, states make war, wars do not make states. The above argument derived from the internal conflict/political legitimacy theory has been confirmed by empirical data—that is, the four case studies and the summary of that data.

At the typical early state level, stage IV, the chief becomes a king. The king heads a military aristocracy. This leader came to power by eliminating rivals, subordinating the lower class, and by destroying or incorporating settlements in nearby polities. As king, he has consolidated his position within his polity. However, other polities in the culture may have evolved to the state stage. The king's major fear now comes from the kings and armies of other typical early states that have arisen within the culture. Massive fortifications consisting of moats, walls, and towers are erected around his capital city. His residence, now a palace, remains fortified and serves as a citadel, a place of refuge in case enemy armies surmount the city's defenses. With conquests of rival states the kingdom develops four levels: the capital city, large towns, small towns, and villages. The lower class continues to be oppressed; it is heavily taxed for agricultural surplus—commoners are forced to grow much more than they need. Labor is also required for communal projects, such as erection of the fortifications and the king's palace. Human sacrifice may occur in conjunction with these projects. On the death of the king, his wives and retainers may be buried with him. Irrigation works may also be constructed.

Lower class males are conscripted into the military organization, unless they would be more useful in the agricultural sector or constructing fortifications. They are equipped with shields and spears, formed into massed infantry regiments, and placed under the direction of officers drawn from the military aristocracy. The king is the commander-in-chief. These large armies engage in battles with opposing sides facing each other. The defeated army takes refuge behind the walls of its capital city. To achieve conquest of another typical early state, siege operations need to be brought to bear upon the fortifications of that capital city. A new basic pattern of warfare develops that is based upon line battles and siege operations. Cities are destroyed and war captives are enslaved. Slaves perform construction tasks and toil in the fields for aristocratic owners. Slavery may free lower class males for military duty. Captured enemy may also be sacrificed, as may commoners. These internal wars, wars between culturally similar peoples, may continue for years before one kingdom is able to crush the other. The final outcome is likely to be an even larger kingdom. The typical early state grows in terms of both territorial size and population.

At the transitional early state level, stage V, a monarchy develops around the king. Royalty top a stratified system that has an upper class, commoners, and slaves. Because of the consolidation of same-language polities into the kingdom, there is a growth of bureaucracy. There are four and perhaps even five hierarchical levels to the polity: the capital city, smaller cities (including those conquered), towns, and villages. If there are five levels, larger cities may be positioned between the capital city and the smaller cities. There are distinct units to the military organization: heavy infantry with shock weapons; light infantry with projectile weapons; and siege trains that transport ladders, digging implements, and battering rams. Carts pulled by horses or other animals carry officers and supplies in the Old World. The absence of horses and wheeled vehicles in the New World precluded this development. Eventually the horse-drawn carts become war chariots, the first "high-tech" weapons of war. Cavalry units come centuries later. The distinct military units, working together, form what is known as an "integrated tactical force." In its classic formulation the force consists of infantry, cavalry, and artillery.[94] In my view, two types of infantry working together can also constitute an integrated tactical force. The transitional early state engages in external war—it attacks culturally different peoples. The king now embarks on campaigns to conquer non-state peoples of other cultures. Eventually some of these peoples may imitate the first pristine state in the region and themselves become inchoate early states, then typical early states. The lands and peoples of other cultures, whether or not at the state level of sociopolitical complexity, may be incorporated into the kingdom.

At the mature state level, the monarchy continues, but despotism no longer characterizes internal relationships. A well-developed bureaucracy controls the affairs of the kingdom. A judicial system with laws develops, although different laws may apply to different social classes and the slaves. Conquered peoples, as well as culturally different people choosing to live under the state's protection, transform the polity into an empire. The culturally homogeneous early state becomes a culturally heterogeneous mature state.[95] The warriors from these different cultures may provide light infantry, particularly if they come from hunter-gatherer societies that still possess the skills used in hunting. The state itself is likely to develop foreign relations with other states and empires. Alliances for trade and alliances for war may be formed. Wars between combined armies characterize the mature state level in sociopolitical evolution.

6

Four Pristine States and Their Warfare

Our case studies of pristine states begin with the New World because the Zapotec and the Chavín/Moche, particularly the Zapotec, depict the process of sociopolitical evolution from hunting-gathering bands to mature state in a straightforward fashion.[1] The New World societies have been intensively studied in the past two decades using modern archaeological techniques, and the sites are more recent than the Old World sites; hence, they have been less ravaged by environmental conditions. Furthermore, exogenous factors have not complicated the analyses; the development took place in one area uncomplicated by such issues as absence of plant domestication by the people, the migrations of people into the region, and the availability of the horse for domestication. These issues complicate the discussion of the development of the state in the Old World, where states had evolved in Mesopotamia and in China before village life was beginning in the New World. There is a purity to the New World examples; data from them illustrate feature after feature of the internal conflict/political legitimacy theory. All four of the case studies support the theory—each contributed to the general chart—but it is the New World examples that are the clincher.

Zapotec

The Zapotec were the original settlers of the Valley of Oaxaca, which is composed of three subvalleys producing a Y, or a three-pointed star, and they were the descendants of the hunter-gatherers who first inhabited North America (see Map 2). Archaeologists Joyce Marcus and Kent Flannery have synthesized twenty-five years of research; they describe the Zapotec from the first settlers more than ten thousand years ago through the development of the Zapotec state.[2]

Since Oaxaca is near the west coast of Mexico, it is likely that the pre-Zapotec peoples were in the migration that took a coastal route to the New World. They subsisted on small game, gathering, and river foraging (see chapter 3). Big game hunters, however, did get as far south as the Basin of Mexico, to the north of Oaxaca. In that area there is evidence of two imperial mammoths killed and butchered by hunters using throwing spears or atlatl darts. Ten tools were found with the remains of the

Map 2. Mesoamerica

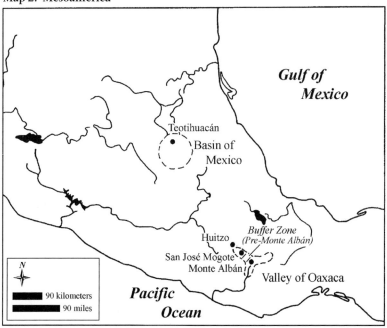

mammoths; three were spear points made farther to the north. Marcus and Flannery believe that the widespread distribution of points indicates that there was exchange with friends—evidence for the existence of an egalitarian society.[3] In addition to friendly exchange, I can think of other explanations for the distribution of points. The points could have been lost, either accidentally dropped or left with an unrecovered spear, and were found by another hunter or warrior years later. Caches of points left in caves might have been discovered. Points may have been in dead animal carcasses or skeletons (these are the ways archaeologists obtain their stone tools, a fact acknowledged by Marcus and Flannery).[4] The original owner could have been killed and his weapons taken (recall the fate of Kennewick Man), or perhaps a camp was attacked and the people fled, leaving their points to be recovered later by others.[5]

The first people to occupy the Valley of Oaxaca were hunter-gatherers who probably lived in bands of about twenty-five people. They ranged over a wide area, hunting the white-tailed deer, pronghorn antelope, Pleistocene horse, jackrabbits, cottontail rabbits, ground squirrel, wood rat, and quail. When the glaciers melted at the end of the last ice age, the climate of the Valley of Oaxaca changed; there were summer rains and dry winters. The antelope and jackrabbits withdrew north; left were the deer, cottontails, collared peccaries, and mud turtles. Hunting parties became smaller, and people relied more upon foraging. Microbands of 4 to 6 persons made up macrobands of 15 to 25 persons. About 75 to 150 people lived in the Valley of Oaxaca, in caves and under rock shelters, during this Early Archaic period from about 8000 B.C.E. to about 3000 B.C.E. In the Late Archaic period, from about 3000 B.C.E. to about 2000 B.C.E., a shift in subsistence took place, from foraging to collecting. Small groups still hunted deer and rabbits, but in place of foraging —the entire band traveling to where the plants were growing—small task groups of collectors were sent out. Wild seeds were collected and planted—bottle gourds, squash, beans, chile peppers, cherry tomatoes, grain amaranths, cotton, and, most importantly, maize or Indian corn. The domestication of corn was under way by 3500 B.C.E.; the cobs were short, with only several rows of small kernels.[6] And with domestication of plants, people spent more time on the fertile valley floor. Grinding stones and storage pits were extensively used. Corncobs grew longer— to a length of about three inches. Together, the corn, beans, and squash made an excellent diet; the latter two domesticates are high in protein, squash seeds in particular. Village life flourished. The earliest settlements date from about 1700 B.C.E.

Settlements of fifty to one hundred persons are found along strips of humid bottom land during an archaeological period known as Tierras Largas (see Figure 6.1). Nineteen permanent hamlets have been located in the Valley of Oaxaca, with nine settlements concentrated in the northwest valley of the Y, where the land was most fertile. One of these settlements, San José Mogote, was much larger, perhaps two hundred persons. There were nine distinct residential areas. Settlements and districts probably had nonhereditary leaders. Total population for the entire valley is estimated at under one thousand. Wattle-and-daub houses were constructed and pottery was made. Domesticated dogs were eaten. There is no evidence of internal conflict, military organizations, or war. The villages are not in defensive locations, and the houses provide no protection from attack. Stone points are absent, but obsidian was obtained and used to make blades for butchering.

Flannery and Marcus, in 2003, reported that on the western periphery of San José Mogote there is evidence of a palisade formed by a double line of posts, spaced in such a way that posts of the second line faced the gaps between posts in the first line. Several posts had been burned.[7] Although the palisade is described as a defense, it is unclear how it could have been used in military activity since evidence of weapons and projectile points is absent at this stage.[8] Furthermore, the other eight settlements in the northwest valley were much smaller than San José Mogote and at this period could hardly have been rivals. Possibly the palisade (or is it better to call it a fence?) was intended to keep out wild animals such as deer and peccaries? Flannery and Marcus also reported a burned house and suggest its destruction could have been the result of

Stages	Social and Political Organization	Internal Conflict	War	Military Organization
Mature State: Monte Albán III, A.D. 200–700	King had royal wife, tombs; Two new cities on hills in Valley of Oaxaca	Kingdom remains intact, although after A.D. 700 Monte Albán declines	Diplomatic negotiations with other states; no alliance war	Military aristocracy
V. Transitional Early State: Monte Albán II, 100 B.C.E.–A.D. 200	King, palaces; Empire; Monte Albán supreme city; Consolidation of valley; Elaborate buildings	Conquest of neighboring peoples; terror used to control; Forced relocation of commoners	External war: outside valley against non-state peoples	Warriors with helmets, round shields, clubs, and thrusting spears form military elites; Commoners defend walls
IV. Typical Early State: Monte Albán I, 500–100 B.C.E.	Chief becomes despot; City-state on hill; Three levels to polity, then four levels	Lower class forced to relocate and produce food for upper class; Canal systems	Internal war: enemy leaders captured and tortured; Valley conquered	Chiefs' relatives lead military aristocracy on raids, battles with spears, and storming of defensive walls
III. Inchoate Early State: Rosario, 700–500 B.C.E.	Chiefs; Four rival centers, three levels to one center; elaborate platforms	Forced labor from lower class	War: centers burned; Buffer zone; Captives executed	Chief or chief's relative leads upper class warriors on raids; Clubs, atlatls
II. Typical Chiefdom: Guadalupe, 850–700 B.C.E.	Chief at each center; Two rival centers, two levels to one center; Two social classes	Minimal conflict; Local leaders co-opted through marriage to upper class women	No war; Rivalry between chiefs of different polities	None
I. Minimal Chiefdom: San José, 1150–850 B.C.E.	Chief; One village much larger; Platforms in villages; Wealth differences in burials	Minimal conflict	No war	None; No weapons in burials
Villages: Tierras Largas, 1400–1150 B.C.E.	Nonhereditary leaders; Villages of 50–100 persons along rivers; one village larger	Minimal conflict	No war	None; Projectile points no longer made

Figure 6.1. Zapotec Matrix: Stages of the Chiefdom-State Continuum

a raid.[9] I think it could have been an accident or the act of a local rival. In the major synthesis of their research on Zapotec civilization, the archaeologists describe a burned house, apparently from a different village, that belonged to a "senior household head, after whose death the house was deliberately burned and its remains buried with him. Alternatively, he and his house might have been the victims of a raid."[10] My skepticism that there was raiding and warfare at this early period, the village stage, is further enhanced by the absence, according to Flannery and Marcus, of any evidence of raiding in the next period.[11]

A minimal chiefdom appeared in the next archaeological period, the San José phase (1150–850 B.C.E.). Rank or hereditary inequality emerged in the Valley of Oaxaca; the primary evidence for this inequality is found in burials. Grave goods, including jade beads, shell pendants, and figurines, were buried with some individuals. No weapons are found in burials. In one burial at San José Mogote, one individual was buried seated above three individuals who are extended; perhaps this individual was a chief. But the burial is in a lean-to attached to a house. No palace yet, but archaeologists consider it to be a "relatively high-status residence."[12] Some infant burials have grave goods, which is evidence for hereditary wealth differences. During this period the number of settlements doubled, to about forty, and the population tripled to more than two thousand. San José Mogote, ten times the size of the next largest settlement, had a population of one thousand; twelve to fourteen villages surrounded the town. Late in the phase pyramidal platforms for public buildings were erected in the town center, evidence that the chief could organize labor.

The typical chiefdom stage arose with the Guadalupe phase (850–700 B.C.E.). The population of the Valley of Oaxaca grew to twenty-five hundred, and the number of settlements increased to forty-five. A rival center, Huitzo, developed about ten miles to the northwest of San José Mogote. Huitzo had its own platform with public buildings as impressive as those of the larger town, but it lacked satellite villages. In contrast, there were sixteen hamlets within five miles of San José Mogote. There was little interaction between the people of Huitzo and of San José Mogote. On the other hand, archaeologists believe that the hamlets surrounding San José Mogote were linked to that center by the strategy of sending a high-status woman to marry the leader of a subordinate community; their children became members of the upper class.[13] Fraternal interest groups appear not to have developed. Although there must have been rivalry between chiefs at the two major centers, there is still no evidence of violence within or between the centers. A possible exception is the finding of three burned houses at a satellite village to the east of San José Mogote.[14] This situation was soon to change.

The maximal chiefdom stage was reached by the Rosario phase (700–500 B.C.E.). For San José Mogote, in the northwest valley of the Y, a three-level settlement hierarchy emerged. The population of the Valley of Oaxaca increased to four thousand and the number of settlements to eighty-five. A chiefly center appeared in the northeast valley of the Y; this center may have held five hundred people out of a valley total of one thousand. Another chiefly center occupied the southern valley of the Y. Similarly, that valley population may have been one thousand. A buffer zone, a strip several miles wide without settlements, separated San José Mogote from the other two valleys. This buffer zone may indicate that raids between chiefly centers were taking place. Competition to build the largest platforms and public buildings appears to have forced male residents to devote considerable effort to their construction. At San José Mogote limestone blocks weighing half a ton were hauled by either volunteers or impressed laborers—without benefit of horse or wheel—from a quarry on the opposite side of the river. I suspect that coercion of lower class males took place.

Warfare erupted. Raids led to the burning of the wattle-and-daub buildings on top of platforms. The Zapotec wanted future generations of archaeologists as well as their contemporaries to know they were a violent people and had warfare. They left a carved horizontal stone slab that archaeologists call Monument 3. The slab depicts a dead and mutilated "naked man sprawled awkwardly on his back, mouth open and eyes closed. . . . [H]is chest had been opened to remove his heart during sacrifice. A ribbon-like stream of blood extends . . . to the border of the monument . . . [and] wrap[s] around the edge of the slab," Marcus and Flannery write. The victim is even named—"1 Earthquake"—by a glyph carved on the stone. We do not know from which settlement he came. The archaeologists state that "this carving of a prisoner, combined with the burning of the temple, . . . suggests that by 600 B.C.E. the well-known Zapotec pattern of raiding, temple burning, and capture of enemies for sacrifice had begun." [15]

Weapons also made their appearance. Obsidian projectile points, probably once hafted on atlatl darts, were found in a tomb. Although direct evidence is lacking, chiefs or high-ranking members of a chief's family probably led raiding parties of upper class warriors, armed with atlatls and perhaps clubs, across no-man's-lands into the land of another chief to burn the important buildings erected on top of platforms and to seize upper class individuals, perhaps members of the chief's family or the chief himself. To return home with the war captive was the major object of the raid. The execution and sacrifice of the captive would have crowned the victory. Every resident of the Valley of Oaxaca would thus learn who was the greater chief. This form of warfare arose so quickly that residences and villages were not fortified and the settlements themselves were not in defensive locations. This situation too was soon to change.

In the buffer zone that screened San José Mogote from the other two arms of the Valley of Oaxaca was, according to Marcus and Flannery, a six-square-kilometer uninhabited mountain, Monte Albán. Sometime around 500 B.C.E. nearly the entire population of San José Mogote moved to that mountain. To move people from their excellent agricultural lands in the valley to inferior lands must have required coercion by the chief, his family — now a military aristocracy — and the upper class. Marcus and Flannery state that a chiefdom seized a hilltop — Monte Albán.[16] I contend that only a state could do this, for relocating two thousand people required a central administration. The move to Monte Albán occurred at the end of the Rosario phase, the maximal chiefdom/inchoate early state stage. This move thus ushered in Monte Albán I (500–100 B.C.E.), the typical early state stage. I suggest two reasons, both military, why the move occurred. First, the rulers at San José Mogote were aware of their vulnerability to raids; they had experienced one burning of their public buildings. Rather than erect fortifications around San José Mogote, they chose to select an easily defensible location and fortify it. Second, the mountain provided a central location in the valley, close to the center point of the three-pointed star. This location would make it easier for the rulers to raid the other Zapotec chiefly centers.

For the next four hundred years both the population and political complexity of Monte Albán rapidly increased. By 400 B.C.E. Monte Albán had more than five thousand inhabitants and by 100 B.C.E., more than seventeen thousand. The entire population of the valley also grew rapidly, to about ten thousand at 400 B.C.E. and by 100 B.C.E., to about fifty thousand. Towns and villages, eventually numbering more than seven hundred, surrounded Monte Albán out to a distance of twenty kilometers from the city, at first producing a three-tier system but soon developing into a four-tier system. The residents of these towns and villages grew much of the corn eaten in the city. Many of the settlements were in defensible localities. Defensive walls were built to protect three kilometers of the more easily climbed north and west slopes of Monte Albán; walls were built at other settlements. Canal systems for irrigating crops were constructed by damming streams that flowed to the river. Raiding intensified and captives were taken. Like Monument 3 at San José Mogote, more than three hundred of the earliest monuments at Monte Albán depict slain or sacrificed enemies. The victims are naked males sprawling in undignified positions with their genitals mutilated.[17] A glyph resembling part of an atlatl on some stones may indicate that the man was taken in battle. Rival centers in the southern and eastern valleys grew larger during 300–100 B.C.E. and in some cases moved to higher and more defensible locations.[18] By 100 B.C.E., the end of the typical early state stage, the entire Valley of Oaxaca was unified under the control of Monte Albán. Although public buildings increased in size and number, no palace has been found. There are, however, elite residences at Monte Albán and in some towns.

A transitional early state appears in the next archaeological period, the Monte Albán II phase (200 B.C.E.–A.D. 100). The Zapotec at this stage became a conquest state. Marcus and Flannery believe that perhaps as many as ten thousand people left the Valley of Oaxaca to colonize other regions; the population declined to about forty thousand. Perhaps these people came from the settlements near Monte Albán—155 settlements that had formed a ring around the mountain were gone. The consolidation of the entire valley meant that food from all parts of the valley could now flow to Monte Albán. Earlier, during the period of warfare between the valleys, food had to come from no farther away than twenty kilometers. The four-tier settlement system continued. At Monte Albán the types and number of public structures increased: palaces, tombs, temples with inner rooms, and ball courts. Among the structures is a building with more than forty carved stone slabs showing regions claimed, either by colonization or conquest. One such region was a long river canyon to the north of the Valley of Oaxaca. Marcus and Flannery believe that one of the slabs depicting conquest (an upside-down head) pertains to this canyon. At the north end of the canyon is a fortress built by the Zapotec. In one of the captured towns there was a rack with sixty-one human skulls arranged in rows; presumably the town's inhabitants had been executed and their heads severed and placed on a rack to discourage uprisings or refusals to pay tribute.

While evidence for warfare and conquest is plentiful, evidence for military organizations is scant. Archaeologist Ross Hassig, the leading expert on Mesoamerican warfare, provides the following interpretation: The Zapotec had an aristocratic military system based upon elite warriors.[19] Ceramic pieces show warriors with their heads inside the open jaws of coyote and puma and in the beaks of raptorial bird helmets. Although these elaborate military outfits indicate elite military orders, the absence of battle standards suggests a lack of formal combat units. Elite warriors used shock weapons—thrusting spears and clubs with stone heads—for which specialized training was required, rather than projectiles. Noble warriors are shown on monuments (steles) with heavy lances in their hands. Carved stones from a later period depict "a well-dressed lord with an atlatl in one hand and a shield and atlatl darts in the other."[20] One noble warrior from San José Mogote was buried with a large spear point broken off in his chest. Warriors wore small, circular shields on the forearm, leaving both hands free and giving spearmen great combat mobility.[21]

Commoners, who were not conscripted because there were sufficient soldiers from the nobility, met their military obligation by constructing fortifications. In case of attack, commoners also would have defended the fortifications with projectile weapons, atlatls, slings, and stones. According to Kent Flannery, "In Oaxaca, our best evidence [for warfare] comes from fortification walls at numerous sites [and] from piles of cobblestones stored as weapons." An integrated tactical force, which Hassig calls "complementary arms groups," was not created. As Hassig puts it, "Monte Albán's army was not large enough to make use of complementary atlatl and spear units without drawing on commoners."[22] Other Mesoamerican armies, such as those from Teotihuacán, did have atlatl units.[23] But for the Zapotec, massed infantry never developed. Indeed, there were few places for massed infantry to engage in battle on the terrain of the Valley of Oaxaca. A typical battle probably took place near or at the walls of a fortified town. The attackers were elite warriors armed with shock weapons, while the defenders had a smaller number of elite warriors supported by commoners with projectile weapons. Attackers often won because they had surprise and number on their side.

Soon after their conquests ceased, the Zapotec passed from the early state stages to become a mature state. Some conquered areas were lost. The Monte Albán III phase (A.D. 200–700) is known as the golden age of Zapotec civilization. The king was a hereditary lord with a royal wife. Tombs were built beneath palaces. Ambassadors were received from Teotihuacán. The population of the valley expanded to 115,000 persons, and Monte Albán's own population grew to more than 16,000. Most significant, however, was the development of two other population centers, one in each of the other two valley arms. The number of fortified sites increased, and two-thirds of the population lived in them. But Monte Albán continued to grow to a population of 24,000, and then its glory faded. Its temples ceased to be maintained, and its population drifted away. It did not fall to military conquest. The one rival state that could possibly have destroyed Monte Albán was Teotihuacán, but diplomatic relations probably kept Teotihuacán at bay. Ross Hassig describes the military supremacy of Teotihuacán but also notes that the fortifications throughout the Valley of Oaxaca would have made a Teotihuacán invasion extremely difficult. However, the threat of a Teotihuacán invasion may explain the large number of fortifications. Studies of Zapotec battles, diplomacy, and fortifications from after the period surveyed here support this interpretation. The wars were with the Aztecs and the Mixtecs.[24] The fortifications appear unrelated to internal conflict.[25]

The rise of the Zapotec from a hunting and gathering society to a mature state supports the basic argument developed in this book to explain the second origin of war. A brief summary makes the case. First, a long period of no warfare prevailed from about 3500 B.C.E. to about 700 B.C.E. (which includes the first three stages on the matrix [Figure 6.1]), during which gatherers domesticated corn and other crops. There were

130 *How War Began*

no military organizations and no weapons. Neo-Rousseauists might call this, rather than the mature state stage, the golden age of the Zapotec. If there had been war, the domestication process would have been disrupted. Second, agriculture led to small settlements, one of which became a focal community, San José Mogote. Later other focal communities arose. Wealth differences led to social classes. Violent conflicts did not develop between leaders in the focal community and its satellite hamlets; rather, upper class males in the focal community gave their sisters in marriage to hamlet leaders, thereby co-opting them. There is no evidence that competing fraternal interest groups struggled for power in early Oaxaca. Third, rivalry between focal communities, now chiefly centers, gave rise to raiding between centers. Captives were taken to the centers and executed in humiliating fashion. The raiding resembles the warfare of many tribal societies, but the degree of political centralization of the chiefly centers is far greater than that of tribes. The chiefly centers are inchoate early states. Although the population expanded, usable land remained available; thus, rivalry between chiefs, not land shortage, gave rise to war. In other words, competition for scarce resources does not explain Zapotec warfare. If raids and war had begun earlier in the developmental process toward statehood, there would have been insufficient political complexity for what happened next to have happened. Fourth, the largest center moved to a central, defensible location—Monte Albán—and constructed walls. The other centers may have done the same, but it did not save their leaders. They were captured and executed and their centers incorporated into the expanding typical early state centered at Monte Albán. Going to the mountaintop was a great strategy for the chief and leaders who left San José Mogote. Because of the unique environmental circumstances of the Valley of Oaxaca, we should not expect to see this happening in our other pristine states, but we should expect to see a highly developed polity that has grown large in size defeat and incorporate culturally similar polities.

Chavín/Moche

Peru, our second region in which pristine states arose, presents complexities that make analysis difficult. It is necessary to simultaneously examine cultural sequences in both the highlands of Peru and in the valleys along the coast of the country. To establish what happened in prehistoric Peru I have had to draw upon the works of archaeologists who have specialized in the different regions (see Map 3). The matrix describing the development of the state in Peru thus shows two columns for each category (see Figure 6.2). First, an overview.

The Moche of the North Coast are considered by many to be the first true state in the region.[26] On this coast thousands of years earlier foragers of marine life erected platform mound structures. Archaeologists and other scholars have attempted to link these early peoples with the later Moche by constructing a sequence of stages. Perhaps the best known of these sequences is found in Julian Steward's study of "irrigation civilization." Since irrigation developed early in the river valleys along the coast, the early agriculturalists were viewed by Steward as the link between the early foragers and the later Moche. In the 1950s, when Steward was writing, anthropologists considered irrigation to be the prime mover toward statehood: Control of irrigation canals led to political centralization.[27] Warfare was considered to be absent, based on archaeological research in one of many valleys—the Viru Valley.[28] However, later research in other valleys found evidence of warfare.[29] Since the Moche were a conquest state, these findings fit into Steward's sequence, and warfare replaced irrigation as the prime mover toward political centralization.

Less well known is what was happening in the highlands at the same

Map 3. North Coast Peru

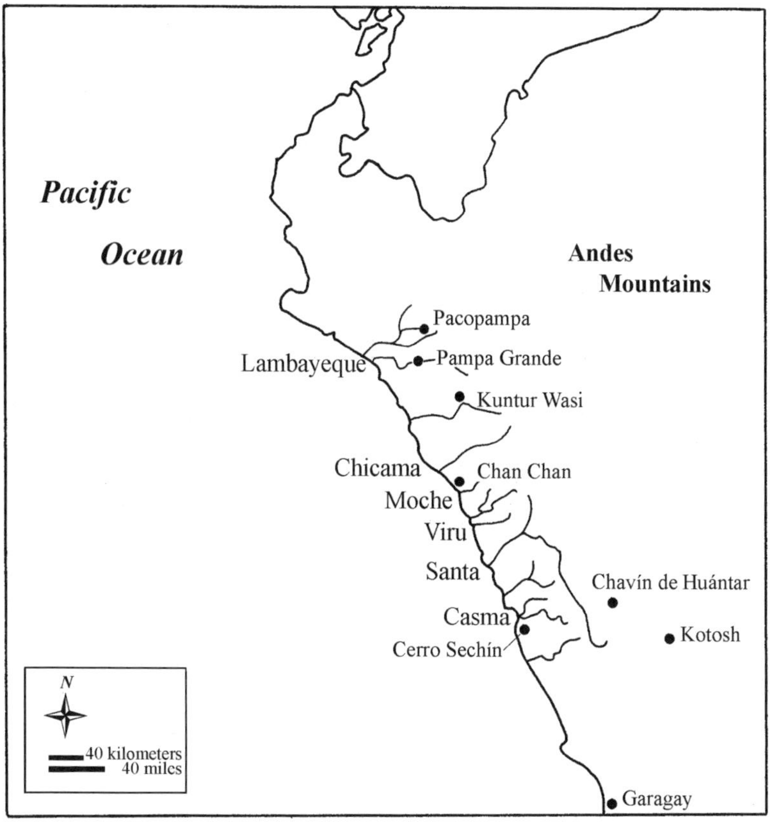

	Social and Political Organization		Internal Conflict		War		Military Organization	
	North Coast	Highlands	North Coast	Highlands	North Coast	Highlands	North Coast	Highlands
Mature State: Late Intermediate Period, A.D. 1000–1470	Chimú Chan Chan is capital city King Palaces Empire		Sacrifice of harem		Inca conquer Chimú		King heads army of elite warriors	
V. Middle Horizon, A.D. 600–1000	Two large polities arise Wari influence the Moche area		Internal tensions lead to abandonment of cities		External war		Elite warriors from upper classes	
IV. Early Intermediate Period 200 B.C.E.–A.D. 600 V IV III II I	Moche declines Four-level polity Four social classes Monumental architecture Centralized irrigation canals Three-level polity	Chavín disintegrates 200 B.C.E.	Residential separation with walls Locals tortured Human sacrifice		V. Loss of valleys to south IV. Conquest of valleys to north III. Conquest of valleys to south I. & II. Six valleys Consolidated		Warriors equipped with spears, clubs, shields, darts, and knives for removing heads	

Figure 6.2. Chavín/Moche Matrix: Stages of the Chiefdom-State Continuum

Period								
III. Early Horizon, 800–200 B.C.E.II.	Small two-level polities that are not at Stage III Corn	Chavín ideology spreads Hereditary social classes Three-level polity	Minimal conflict	Cannibalism?	Intra- and Inter-valley warfare	No war	Fortresses	None
II. Initial Period, 1800–800 B.C.E.	Temple complexes Irrigation canals: beans, squash, potatoes No classes Pottery	Kotosh Religious Tradition continues Wealth differences Pottery	Minimal conflict	Cannibalism?	Internal war Raids, heads taken Captives executed	No war	No fortifications Warriors dressed alike, pillbox helmets, circular shields, darts Weapons: club, spear, slings	None
I. Late Pre-ceramic Period, 3000–1800 B.C.E.	Pyramids Irrigation canals No classes	Kotosh Religious Tradition Domestication of potato	Minimal conflict	Minimal conflict	Internal war uncommon	No war		None
Villages: Early Pre-ceramic Period, 4500–3000 B.C.E.	Platform mound structures Foragers	Hunter-gatherers Domestication of llama and guinea pig	Minimal conflict	Minimal conflict	No war	No war	None	None

time. There the llama and the guinea pig were domesticated by hunters centuries before the potato was domesticated. There also, before plant domestication, large ceremonial centers with numerous public buildings were erected. After plant domestication, irrigation did not become important and warfare did not arise; the two alleged prime movers of coastal society were not present. Yet the communities in the highlands continued to develop through the maximal chiefdom/inchoate early state stage. Chavín de Huántar is the best known of these sites in the highlands.

On the coast at this same time warring polities were failing to conquer each other; sociopolitical evolution came to an end. Some archaeologists have suggested that climatic conditions might in part be responsible. El Niños may have caused shifts in wind that changed water temperatures and killed plants and animal life.[30] My analogy in chapter 5—that warfare is like an El Niño wind blowing west to east and ripping off the top of a developing hurricane—came to my mind as I read the Peruvian materials. However, I do not believe it was El Niño winds that prevented the state from developing on the North Coast. It was warfare. Contrary to conquest theories of the origin of the state, I believe that for typical chiefdoms to evolve into states warfare must be absent. On the North Coast warfare drove the two-level polities to defensive locations where the people built elaborate fortifications consisting of walls and citadels.

In the highlands, peaceful Chavín culture spread for five hundred years, then for reasons unclear to archaeologists the various centers of the culture declined. Warfare, as well as internal political weakness, have been suggested as reasons. In their decline, the Chavín people transmitted to the coast ideas of statehood as well as other aspects of their culture, such as gold metallurgy. One recipient was the Moche people of several North Coast valleys. The Moche developed into first an inchoate early state, then a typical early state. Eventually the Moche were able to conquer people residing in hilltop fortifications. Now, to return to the beginning.

The peoples of Peru were probably in the migration to the New World that took a coastal route. On the west coast of South America they found abundant marine life—anchovies, sardines, larger fish, mussels, clams, sea snails, crabs, sea lions, and ocean birds. Those that ventured into the highlands encountered an abundant animal life. They hunted a giant ground sloth that became extinct about ten thousand years ago, as well as deer, guanaco, and a rodent that was to be domesticated later (about 4000 B.C.E.)—the guinea pig. Permanent residence at high elevation was achieved by 7000 B.C.E.[31] Both the peoples on the coast and the peoples in the highlands had atlatls as their main hunting device; they also used stone-tipped and fire-hardened wooden spears.[32] The guanaco was domesticated (about 3500 B.C.E.) and became the llama. By

2500 B.C.E. the llama and its close relative, the alpaca, were fully domesticated, the llama for its cargo-carrying capacity, the alpaca for its wool-like hair.[33] These animals were also eaten. The llama, while not strong enough to carry a person (no chance for cavalry here), could carry loads over rough, high-altitude terrain. The llama facilitated the transportation of goods from the tropical forests of eastern Peru to the coast and shells from the coast to the highlands. Settlements in the highlands became trading centers, a possible indirect reason why states first arose there. Trade led to wealth differences, which led to distinct social classes.

The foragers of marine life and the hunters and herders of the highlands were able to establish villages before they domesticated plants (in the highlands only) and invented pottery. In the highlands the potato, quinoa, lima bean, peanut, and squashes were domesticated by 3500 B.C.E.[34] On the coast platform mound structures dating to 3000 B.C.E. were erected. At this village stage of sociopolitical complexity, there is no evidence of internal conflict or warfare either on the coast or in the highlands. And, of course, there were no military organizations. Nevertheless, hunting weapons were available but probably seldom used by the coastal foragers. In the highlands hunters became herders.[35]

Minimal chiefdoms emerged in the Late Pre-Ceramic period. Pyramids were erected on the coast, and temple complexes were constructed in the highlands. At Kotosh and other highland centers ceremonial practices appear to have arisen; archaeologist Richard Burger refers to them as the Kotosh Religious Tradition.[36] These centers date to as early as 2800 B.C.E. Burger states, "It would appear, therefore, that small, mostly unstratified theocratic polities appeared in the highlands at almost the same time as on the coast. The two developments must be considered as two interrelated elements within a single developmental process." By the Late Pre-Ceramic period deer and other wild game animals were no longer a major source of meat.[37] Domestic animals had taken their place. Domesticated food crops and other plants of economic importance were introduced, including corn from Mesoamerica, but on the coast the marine component remained more important.[38] Irrigation was practiced on a small scale. There is no evidence for social classes. Although the highlands are free of military organizations and warfare, on the coast warfare may have made an appearance, as can be inferred from the presence of weapons: "a wooden club embedded with sharks' teeth, plus pointed spears and woven slings." Burger continues, "These finds do not imply that warfare was an important force at the time, only that it exists. Most major sites flourished for centuries in locations that would have made them vulnerable to attack, and fortifications were completely unknown during the Late Preceramic."[39] At a small village in the Santa Valley dating to about 3000 B.C.E., according to John Topic and Theresa Topic, "discrete piles of slingstones bound the village on two sides. These piles are arranged in two rows, one on each side of the site. . . . The average spacing of the piles is consistent with the spacing required between individual slingers." There are no major walls at the village.[40] Were animals or birds being repelled?

The typical chiefdom arose during the Initial period, starting about 1800 B.C.E. Agriculture became more important. Beans, squash, and potatoes were watered by irrigation canals in the valleys along the coast. In the highlands the potato dominated. In both areas pottery finally made its appearance. On the coast social classes were still absent, but in the highlands wealth differences were present. The Kotosh Religious Tradition continued to flourish. The significant difference, in this Initial period, between the highlands and the coast is that warfare occurs on the coast but not in the highlands. I cannot explain this occurrence. There was no large game hunting tradition, the resources of the region seem plentiful, and nothing in the ceremonial centers of the Late Pre-Ceramic period seems to demand war and war captives. The only suggestion I can make for the presence of warfare on the coast in the Initial period is that it was always there at a low level of intensity. With increasing population, warfare increased. Yet there were no fortifications.

The military organization consisted of similarly dressed warriors who wore "spotted pillbox helmets" and flowing loincloths. "Pillbox" is the term Richard Burger used to describe trapezoidal-shaped headgear. The warriors presumably carried clubs, spears, and slings—weapons of the previous period. Now they were protected by circular shields and they carried darts. The evidence comes from stone carvings on large granite blocks, dated to 1500 B.C.E., at Cerro Sechín in the Casma Valley and at Garagay farther to the south.[41] The warriors are shown in military procession in two columns amidst the carnage of their adversaries. At the head of each column is a banner, probably emblematic of the victorious group. Tactics consisted of raids in which both heads and captives were taken. A slain enemy would be decapitated; a captured enemy warrior was taken to a ceremonial center and executed there. Victorious warriors constitute about 7 percent of the approximately four hundred stone sculptures at Cerro Sechín. One is shown with decapitated heads hanging as trophies from his waist. Trophy heads in net bags are depicted farther north. Sometimes the heads are shown stacked in columns; other times single heads appear to have blood flowing from the top and the base. Richard Burger's description of the scene emphasizes the mutilation of the enemy. The nude bodies are portrayed in agonizing positions, with bulging eyes, hands flailing, sliced torsos, and with entrails and blood gushing forth. The decapitated heads comprise about 70 percent of the stone carvings. The head is usually shown lifeless with its eyes closed; on some pieces blood flows from the eyes, mouth, scalp, or neck. Other severed body parts, such as arms, legs, rows of eyes, and stacks of vertebrae, complete the gruesome scene. On one sculpture a victim, with eyes open, is "writhing in agony while his intestines spill from his body."[42] There are striking similarities between this sculpture and Monument 3 at San José Mogote (Zapotec, Valley of Oaxaca). While archaeologist friends tell me the sculptures are unrelated, both pieces appear to be from the same "school" of art. Since Monument 3 is much later, could it be possible that the idea for such sculpture diffused north into Mesoamerica, or even that an itinerant artist traveled to the Valley of Oaxaca?[43]

In the highlands during the Initial period, wealth differences became pronounced, suggesting the presence of social classes. Pacopampa is the northernmost Initial period center in the Peruvian highlands known to have public architecture. Pottery from distant lands suggests that it was a trading center and that social classes were present. Meat consumed came primarily from deer. Richard Burger writes that "an unexpected discovery in the . . . refuse was that human remains were second in frequency only to deer. These bones are frequently cut, calcined, and gnawed, and the existence at Pacopampa of some sort of ritual cannibalism must be considered a serious possibility." Richard Burger does not suggest who the victims were. I suspect that internal conflict may have arisen and that it manifested itself in cannibalism. Since there is no evidence for military organizations or warfare, those consumed probably were not war captives; the likelihood is that they were the losers in an internal power struggle. Several hundred years later, in the next period, in a temple gallery at Chavín de Huántar, evidence for cannibalism again appears. Mixed with the abundant food waste were the bones of at least twenty-one children, juveniles, and adults. The full spectrum of body parts appears to be represented. "The calcination, fragmentation, and context of these bones raises the possibility of ritual cannibalism," Burger states.[44] And there is still no evidence of military organizations and warfare: "The centers of Chavin civilization were not fortified, nor were they located in defensible locations." In the conclusion of his study of Chavin culture, Burger sets forth an interpretation consistent with internal conflict theory: "Warfare is not the only form of coercion. If a subgroup . . . claimed economic and social prerogatives previously absent, and could implement these privileges through their association with supernatural forces . . . , the other households might have found themselves in a [difficult] situation . . . [They could] either accept the new asymmetric socioeconomic arrangement or risk perishing in unsettled areas where no infrastructure exists."[45]

In the Early Horizon period, beginning about 800 B.C.E., Chavín de Huántar reached the maximal chiefdom/inchoate early state stage. Hereditary social classes formed, and Chavín ideology spread northward.[46] A major site, Kuntur Wasi, appeared at that time. Since there was no military organization to spread the religious traditions of Chavín, it has been assumed by archaeologists that it was the great prestige of Chavín de Huántar that led other peoples to adopt their beliefs. According to Burger, "Some [coastal] groups also appear to have sought from the highlands a religious ideology better equipped for dealing with social and economic upheaval, thereby facilitating the spread of the Chavín cult."[47] On the coast the small two-level Moche polities that developed in the Initial period increased in size and number, in part aided by the addition of corn from Mesoamerica to the local diet of beans, squash, and potatoes. The polities did not increase in sociopolitical complexity, however. Warfare, both within and between valleys, became serious. Elaborate fortresses were constructed on hilltops, presumably in response to increasing head-hunting raids.[48] Polities were not large enough to field a sufficient number of warriors to overrun fortifications, nor were they politically complex enough to conquer their neighbors. Warfare, as I said in chapter 5, does not lead to the state if it occurs early in the evolutionary sequence.

The Early Intermediate period saw the decline of Chavín, the gradual rise of Moche to first the inchoate early state stage at the beginning of the period, and then the typical early state stage throughout the period, before the Moche state declined. Since our focus now shifts from the highlands to the North Coast, the matrix columns for the highlands will be left blank (see Figure 6.2). Chavín, figuratively speaking, hands the baton to Moche. Although the manner in which this transfer actually happened is hard to visualize, archaeologists are of the belief that it occurred. (I cannot imagine a Chavín ruler telling a Moche chief that it is now his turn. The Chavín ruler is a priest, while the Moche chief a warrior.) Richard Burger informs us that Chavín endured as an ancient center of sacred power and that the Moche began to revive the style and motifs of Chavín for decorating their ceramics.[49] Archaeologist Garth Bawden believes that Chavín influenced the Moche because broader concepts of sociopolitical integration replaced local communal forces: "This was achieved in the ideological domain with the widespread adoption of a formal religious cult to enhance and justify political authority. . . . North Coast elites were able to distance themselves socially from their subjects to an unprecedented degree, an hierarchical trend that is reflected in the increasing richness of elite burials of the period."[50]

The valleys along the North Coast were the home of numerous culturally similar peoples at the beginning of the Early Intermediate period. The evidence provided by fortifications indicates that warfare was widespread. Yet in some areas villages were not fortified. These unfortified villages grew in size; perhaps size was their defense. Agriculture flourished and canals were extended to areas previously not watered. Towns of several thousand inhabitants developed near the coast in both the Moche and Viru Valleys. Great adobe platforms were erected, indicating the growth of central political authority.[51] By A.D. 100, Moche culture emerged on the North Coast. The apparent absence of warfare in these areas permitted the development of three-level polities, an indication that the maximal chiefdom/inchoate early state stage had been reached. Social classes formed, and eventually there were four hereditary classes.[52]

Internal conflict probably accompanied the development of social classes. The upper classes had residences that were spacious and spatially separate from the residences of the lower classes and had walls to prevent unwelcome visitors. For one late Moche residence at Pampa Grande Jonathan Haas concludes, "This high-status residence is . . . a highly defensible stronghold against any possible internal acts of aggression or hostility." Since Pampa Grande is neither in a defensive location nor fortified, it is clear "that the elaborate defensive measures surrounding the single high status residence are addressed to internally rather than externally originating aggression."[53] Coercive sanctions were used to punish individuals, presumably from the lower classes, who trespassed and stole or perhaps refused to participate in the construction of platforms or residences for the upper classes. Artwork on some Moche pottery depicts disfigurement, mutilation, and torture. Noses and lips have been cut off, individuals are shown bound to a stake or in stockades, and bound individuals are shown attacked by carnivorous birds. Others have been flayed or had their limbs or genitals amputated, and scantily clad individuals are herded in a line by others brandishing whips.[54]

Scholars have divided the period of Moche ascendancy into five stages indicated by Roman numerals. During Moche I and II (Early period) the semi-independent Moche polities consolidated their hold in six valleys. In the Moche III phase the two southern polities in the Moche and Chicama Valleys consolidated and expanded southward, consolidating six more valleys into a single polity. During Moche IV, the northern four polities expanded, with two becoming consolidated. In the Moche V phase the polity that had resulted from amalgamation expanded further. Its capital was at Pampa Grande in the Lambayeque Valley. Also in the Moche V phase the Moche Valley polity lost control over the valleys to the south.[55]

Moche armies were composed of elite warriors from the upper classes and were led by royal officers. They were well equipped for hand-to-hand combat. They wore conical helmets with decorative projections on top and skirted tunic-like garments that differed for each warrior, and they carried rectangular or circular shields. The mace was the principal weapon. Two types were used; one had a conical end, the other was star-shaped. Warriors depicted on Moche III pottery are shown holding the mace in both hands, with the shield not being used. Other weapons included spears, atlatls, and perhaps slings. Battles took place away from habitations. Sometimes cacti are shown in drawings, suggesting that the battles took place in desert locations. In a battle scene, repeatedly reproduced, Moche warriors engage a culturally different people, perhaps from another valley or perhaps from the highlands. The enemy are less well attired, sometimes not even wearing helmets. They carry small circular shields and maces. One warrior appears to be hurling a stone at his Moche opponent. Heads were taken; warriors carried *tumi*—or ax-shaped bronze weapons—for severing heads. A dead warrior was stripped of his clothing and his weapons taken. When possible, enemy warriors were captured. Drawings depict enemies being pulled to the ground by their hair and ropes placed around their necks; they are disrobed. Naked and bleeding prisoners were transported, sometimes by seagoing craft, to the captors' capital. Archaeologist David J. Wilson concludes that drawings "lend support to the assertion of interregional rivalries of some time depth, fierce battles in defense of regional autonomy, and the apparent defiance of prisoners even in defeat" (one prisoner is turning his head back and giving his captor "the finger" as blood drips from his nose).[56] Murals at temple complexes show the victims being marched in procession to their deaths. At grand public occasions they were executed with the *tumi*.[57]

Since individual combat between uniquely dressed warriors is depicted, it is tempting to describe Moche armed combat as ritual warfare. What is depicted looks like a duel between champions from each side. Drawings of combat between a warrior and a dangerous supernatural being contribute to this interpretation.[58] The "sacrifice ceremony" or "Presentation Theme" involving the drawing of blood from the neck of a bound prisoner, its placement in a goblet, and its presentation to an official further contributes to the idea that Moche combat is ritual warfare.[59] The depiction of the ceremony is replete with supernatural beings portrayed by Moche participants. The recent discovery of the burials of rulers with goblets confirms that the sacrifice ceremony actually occurred. Nevertheless, Moche warfare is much more than ceremony. Combat may have ritual aspects, but it is not ritual warfare in the sense of low casualties. The depictions of combat, on pottery and in murals, make it clear that warriors were killed and beheaded on the battlefield and that captives were later killed. Excavations confirm that towns and cities in other valleys were conquered. For example, a Moche ceremonial center with a throne was discovered in the Viru Valley, one of the valleys conquered during the Moche III phase.[60] The overall effect of the sacrifice ceremony must have been to cow the conquered peoples into submission.

During the Moche V phase, the typical early states that had been formed by the Moche peoples went into decline. An important external factor was a thirty-year drought (A.D. 562–94) resulting from El Niños.[61] Archaeologist Brian Fagan has argued that the environmental destruction caused by El Niños forced the Moche capitals in the Moche and Lambayeque Valleys to move inland and upstream, twenty kilometers and sixty-five kilometers, respectively. The two polities became more centralized, thus gaining greater control over precious irrigation water. It was, according to Fagan, an inflexible system, whereas the highland state of Wari to the south, with a flexible, decentralized administration, was able to expand into the weakened Moche domains.[62]

I believe an important internal factor in Moche decline was the failure of the Moche to develop a method of record keeping or a rudimentary written language. For large armies to be barracked and maintained in the field, there must be ways to determine the size of forces, what the supply needs are, and where both are located. There is no evidence on ceramics, metalwork, or walls that soldiers were counted or that the number of containers with grain at a storehouse was recorded. Likewise, there is no evidence of records of conquest. Recall that the Zapotec drew glyphs that named individuals and recorded the towns and cities they had conquered. The later Inca of Peru tied knots in strings for record keeping. Without the ability to keep records, Moche rulers must have been severely handicapped in conducting wars and in controlling conquered territories. It is not surprising to me that they lost territories—they had no way of keeping track of armies, supplies, or conquered lands.

The Middle Horizon on the North Coast, which witnessed the decline but not the disappearance of the Moche, is the transitional early state stage. In the highlands to the south two large states arose: the Wari and the Tiwanaku. The former influenced the valleys on the coast. Politically, its influence resulted in a reduction in the size of the Moche state's territory and, subsequently, a transfer of the seat of power from the Moche Valley to the Lambayeque Valley.[63] Moche V cities were eventually abandoned and the population dispersed throughout the coastal valleys. Garth Bawden believes that since "internal tension was an integral part of urban formation," cities like Pampa Grande could no longer hold their populations. Izumi Shimada uses an internal revolt theory to explain the selective burning of buildings that forced abandonment of Pampa Grande around A.D. 700.[64] In the aftermath of the abandonment, Moche traditions and Wari ideology merged to form a new order known as the Lambayeque or Sican culture.

Out of the new order arose the Chimú kingdom, a mature state. Its capital city of Chan Chan stood on a low rise northwest of the floodplain of the Moche Valley. Upon the death of a Chimú king, his successor received the reins of state but did not inherit his predecessor's estates. These estates passed to junior heirs, who were charged with venerating the dead king. Their duties to the deceased king included managing his property and holding his conquered lands. In death a king was also served by two hundred to three hundred young women, probably members of his harem, who were sacrificed at, or soon after, the time of his death. Each new king had to build his own palace compound and conquer his own lands, which were then taxed, organized, and administered for his benefit while he lived and for his veneration after his death.

Each new king had to have his own army to conquer and hold territory; his posthumous administration needed to hold that territory. The army on campaign was probably headed by the king; elite warriors were drawn from the upper classes and royalty. With each new king the number of compounds increased, and each living king shared Chan Chan with the remains and bureaucracy of his predecessors. Without the benefit of record keeping, this system must have been confusing. Somehow the system did work. The Chimú kingdom expanded both north and south of the Moche Valley and lasted nearly five hundred years, until it was conquered by the Inca in A.D. 1470. The Inca had a more efficient military organization based on massed infantry.[65]

The rise of the Chavín from a hunting and gathering society in the highlands and the Moche from a foraging society along the coast supports the thesis of this book. The first Peruvian state arose in the highlands. The hunting of game declined, animals were domesticated (one of which—the llama—became a herd animal), and the potato was domesticated. No warfare was present. Chavín ceremonial centers arose out of the lives of these peaceful mountain peoples. On the coast warfare practices that reached back to the time of the earliest settlers persisted. Warfare was infrequent, but as sociopolitical complexity increased, so did warfare. Eventually the warfare drove people to mountains where they built fortifications, and the typical chiefdoms that had developed ceased to evolve further. Only when the influence of states in the highlands spread to the coast were the chiefdoms able to continue their development. It also appears that this development was preceded by a short period of peace in some valleys. The Moche then became a typical early state and embarked on conquests. Their military organization had its roots in the basic pattern of warfare established centuries before. With the emergence of hereditary social classes, combat personnel came exclusively from the upper classes. This form of military organization persisted through Chimú times.

Uruk/Sumer

The first states arose more than five thousand years ago on the alluvial plains of Mesopotamia between the Tigris and Euphrates Rivers and in the piedmont zone between these Mesopotamian lowlands and the Zagros Mountains to the east (see Map 4). The latter region had sufficient rainfall in winter for dry farming and large rivers for irrigation in dry seasons. Irrigation farming probably arose here. The alluvial plain to

Map 4. Mesopotamia

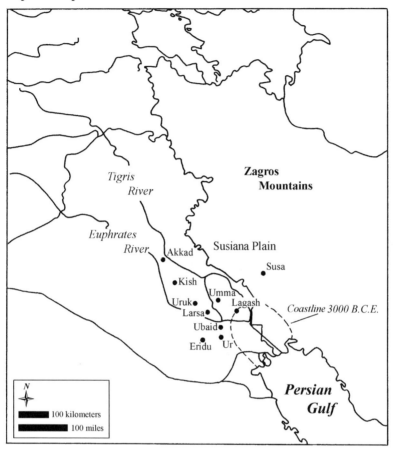

the west required irrigation if agriculture was to flourish there. Domestication of plants and animals did not occur in either region but instead happened farther north along the Fertile Crescent. The first settlers brought with them domesticated plants and animals (wheat, barley, and lentils, and sheep, goats, and cattle, respectively). The migration took place, probably in stages, nearly twenty-five hundred years before the rise of the first states, in 3500 B.C.E. Most significantly, settlers did not bring warfare into the region with them. Although warfare had arisen along the Fertile Crescent by perhaps 7000 B.C.E., it is likely that these early settlers were already farmers and that they had not experienced warfare and did not have military weapons. These Ubaid peoples lived in numerous small villages.

The physical environment of Mesopotamia is critical to the development of the first state. The land was flat, unwooded except along

Stages	Social and Political Organization	Internal Conflict	War	Military Organization
Mature State: Akkadian 2350–2150 B.C.E.	Empire Sargon is King Conquest of city-states	Codified law	Internal and external war	Infantry and archers Composite bow, 2250 B.C.E.
V. Transitional Early State: Early Dynastic III 2600–2350 B.C.E.	Monarch Ur emerges as major state	Human sacrifice at 2600 B.C.E.	Stele of Vultures War between city-states, 2600 B.C.E.	Ruler, officers ride in "chariots" Massed infantry in phalanx; copper helmets, shields, pikes, socket axes
IV. Typical Early State: Early Dynastic I & II 3000–2600 B.C.E.	Sumerians: Lagash & Ur—about 13 city-states; kings Uruk declines, 2700 B.C.E. Writing develops, beginning 3100 B.C.E.	Slaves	Standard of Ur Buffer zones gone Internal war	Infantry support chariot corps; copper helmets, capes, and spears Fortifications, bronze weapons
III. Inchoate Early State: Uruk 3700–3000 B.C.E.	Warka population 50,000 at 3000 B.C.E. Colonies and outposts King (*Lugal*) Temple complexes, four levels Chief-priests (*En*), three levels Social classes	Coercion based on priestly authority Mace heads used by assistants of officials?	Susiana state splits War at 3200 B.C.E. No-man's-land Widespread trade	Warka walled Elite warriors with maces, bows and arrows, and spears
II. Typical Chiefdom: Late Ubaid 4350–3700 B.C.E.	Warka population 10,000 at 3800 B.C.E. Potters wheel Number of villages declines Several large centers, two levels Temples, chief-priests	Burning of storage building (uprising?)	Peaceful contacts and trade	No fortifications
I. Minimal Chiefdom: Early Ubaid 4750–4350 B.C.E.	Villages of a few hundred people Temple platforms, priest-farmer Minimal wealth differences	Minimal conflict	No war	No military organization
Villages: Eridu 5700–4750 B.C.E.	Small villages, irrigation Temple at 4750 B.C.E. Priest-farmers No wealth differences	Minimal conflict	No war	No military organization

Figure 6.3. Uruk/Sumer Matrix: Stages of the Chiefdom-State Continuum

rivers, and fertile. It was also hot and had little rainfall, but the rivers and their tributaries provided abundant water. The fertility was renewed annually by a flood caused by melting snow from the rivers' mountain sources. The floodwaters formed marshes and often caused the rivers to change course.[66] During this period sea levels rose and the Persian Gulf extended northwestward nearly as far as the ancient cities of Ubaid and Eridu, the two principal cities of the Ubaid peoples. Sea levels stabilized in about 3000 B.C.E.[67] A major change occurred in approximately 3500 B.C.E. or earlier, when the Euphrates River separated from the Tigris River and formed a channel to the west. Population size and the number of settlements expanded greatly after this separation occurred.[68] Settlements were sometimes forced to move. Buildings were of reed-and-clay construction and, later, mud brick. To bring water from the marshes to dry land, the villagers dug canals; each year the canals had to be cleared of silt. Irrigation thus came early to Mesopotamia, and irrigation required cooperative labor with others. Sociologist Michael Mann describes the social consequences of irrigation: "As soon as improvements began, the inhabitants were territorially caged. . . . Territory also caged people because it coincided with substantial labor investment to secure a surplus—a *social cage.*"[69] The significance of this environment is that it was conducive to agricultural intensification and, as a result, a surplus was produced. Because of the surplus, the population increased, newcomers could be accommodated, and wealth differences between individuals and families arose.

By the end of the village stage, Eridu had the earliest known structure assumed to be a temple: a single long room with smaller rooms flanking it on the long sides and, at the end of the central hall, an altar.[70] The position of priest had emerged by this time. Prayers and magic may have, in the minds of the priests and in the minds of the farmers, ensured that the floods would come each year. These priest-farmers may have supervised canal construction and cleaning. A minimal chiefdom formed.

During the Early Ubaid phase (see Figure 6.3) villages grew larger, temple platforms were erected, and wealth differences arose. The minimal chiefdom stage became fully developed. The number of small settlements increased dramatically in many areas. At older towns, such as Eridu, the temple became taller as structures were built one upon the other. The manufacture and use of ceramics proliferated. Stamp seals made of stone and carved with distinctive designs on one surface made their appearance. Some seals depict elite figures, nonhuman in appearance.[71] Others have a "master of animals" motif consisting of a human figure holding fish or snakes.[72] I suggest that these human figures represent the priest-farmers who conducted ceremonies at the temples. There is no evidence of internal conflict, military organizations, or war.

Brian Fagan describes what might have been the process that started the Ubaid peoples on the road to political complexity. As the oceans rose, the Persian Gulf rapidly spread inland, and "communities near the water's edge had to move several times within a generation. In a tightly packed farming landscape, even a minor move altered jealously guarded territorial boundaries and sent political and social ripples through a wide area." The movement of villages led to serious disputes that could be resolved only by "village kin leaders." "Centuries later," Fagan writes, "their powerful descendants became the spiritual and political leaders of communities of much greater complexity."[73]

By Late Ubaid times several large centers had emerged and a two-tier hierarchical settlement pattern developed in some areas. Typical chiefdoms made their appearance. Temples grew larger, sometimes two stories high. Large storage buildings were constructed, the rooms of which held sealed storage jars. A stamp seal, pressed into the clay sealings, may have been used to identify contents or owner. Seals with elaborate designs were used more frequently than seals with simple designs. This organized system of storage of produce suggests that the priest, turned chief, was controlling some of the surplus for his own use and that of his kin.[74] In a community in the region between the Tigris River and the Zagros Mountains known as the Susiana Plain, a storage building was destroyed by fire and the community was abandoned. Internal conflict was probably the cause; the occurrence of deliberate burning may be evidence of a peasant uprising.[75] Another possibility is that the fire was set by a rival and his followers within the settlement. Since there are no fortifications around settlements, it seems likely that the chiefs of settlements did not fear attack from other chiefs and their followers, nor did they fear attack from nomads. Herders in southern Mesopotamia were probably village residents who spent part of the year with their animals—cattle, sheep, and goats—away from their settlements. There is no evidence for conflict and warfare between villagers and nomads, probably because the herders were not separate populations pursuing their own interests.[76]

Peaceful contacts and trade with distant peoples seem to have occurred. Among the inventions of this period was the potter's wheel, a mechanical device that would have greatly facilitated the production of high-quality ceramics. Indeed, Ubaid-style ceramics are widespread, having been found in central Turkey, in the Arabian plateau, and in highland Iran. Thus, there is evidence of villages having full-time craft specialists producing pottery and full-time traders distributing the ceramic wares. These specialists were provided sustenance from the stored produce. The potter's wheel is also important because it links two wheels on an axle. When two such axles connecting pairs of wheels are placed under a box, a cart is created. Once an animal is harnessed to a cart, the first "chariot" is created. But this comes later.[77]

The trend toward urbanization continued. By 3800 B.C.E. Uruk or

Warka had reached a population size of about ten thousand. (Usually scholars refer to the city as Warka and to the people and their culture as Uruk.) A three-tier settlement pattern developed. A maximal chiefdom or inchoate early state was in place. By early Uruk times cylinder seals were developed; when rolled across damp clay they repeat the pattern on the seal. The figures on seals indicate a change in relationships and the emergence of social classes. On some seals, several figures are shown in reciprocal relations; on some, one figure is dominant over the others. The figures represented on these seals indicate that social classes were present. Seals depicting reciprocal relations show upper class individuals, while the other seals show an upper class individual dominating lower class members. Only members of the upper class would have seals made for themselves. Another indicator of social class differences in late Uruk times is a larger-than-life figure (ruler?) on a stele, shown drawing back an arrow in a simple, single-arc bow.[78] This figure was clearly an important person. Stamp seals continued to be used, along with cylinder seals, to seal containers as well as storage room door locks. Archaeological evidence indicates that during lean years the doors and containers were opened by officials, and presumably during good years produce was put into storage as well as used to "pay" full-time craft specialists, such as potters.[79] And produce must also have been collected to support the officials and the rulers residing in urban centers.

Both along the Tigris and Euphrates Rivers and on the Susiana Plain, chiefdoms evolved into states. The people on the alluvial plains, known as the Sumerians, are said to have invented the first of nearly everything; archaeologist Samuel Noah Kramer lists twenty-seven "firsts."[80] A four-tier settlement pattern emerged, with large centers, small centers, large villages, and small villages. The famous city of Ur started, while Eridu, just to the southwest of Ur, was abandoned. The large centers had numerous temples, residences for chief-priests, and storehouses. The first palace has not been identified.[81] The archaeological data leave the impression that these inchoate early states were smoothly running entities. The sociopolitical order was flexible enough to adjust to environmental changes. In lean years, all members of society were supported and sustained. When rivers shifted course, new villages were started and old ones abandoned. New canals were constructed. Although officials must have had assistants to guard storehouses, there is no evidence of military organizations. These assistants, however, must have been able to force recalcitrant farmers to contribute what the officials thought was their share of produce and to contribute their time to canal construction and maintenance. It appears that the sociopolitical order was able to develop and mature because the polities did not go to war with each other. Resources, including personnel, did not need to be diverted to supporting military organizations. All that was required was a minimum of internal coercion. While not a conquest state, apparently, Warka had influence and perhaps control extending from the Persian Gulf in a northwesterly direction for six hundred miles.[82]

The paucity of natural resources, such as stones and metals, on the alluvial plains was rectified, in part, by trade. Uruk "colonies" or "outposts" existed, and some archaeologists contend that they were established to ensure a supply of stone, obsidian, metals, and luxuries such as semiprecious stones. Other archaeologists suggest that at least some Uruk colonies or outposts may have been founded by the refugee elites of losing factions in Uruk power struggles, accompanied by their political followers.[83] The colonies do not appear to be military outposts, although some of the raw materials obtained by trade or from colonies were essential for making weapons. During later Uruk times at Susa on the Susiana Plain mace heads were manufactured. Archaeologist Henry Wright describes the workshop: "There also are four alabaster and calcite maceheads of a type fixed onto a handle with straps, some finished and some unfinished, perhaps for social coercion or display."[84] I doubt they were for display. They were more likely for the assistants of officials who, as argued above, exercised "social coercion" over recalcitrant farmers. I also think it is possible that they were made not just for a "police force" but also to equip a military organization. There are scenes on cylinder seals of kneeling captives with their arms bound behind them being presented to a standing ruler wearing a garment and holding an inverted spear. Guards (soldiers?) stand behind the bound figures, and they are holding what may be clubs (which do not appear to have separate mace heads). Rather than clubs they may be open devices—like tennis racquets without strings—that can be placed over the heads of captives for leading them. Both prisoners and guards appear naked.[85] It is unclear what is to become of the captives.

In late Uruk times war made its appearance. By 3200 B.C.E. conflict broke out between the elites of Susa and a city to the east, whose elites archaeologist Gregory Johnson believes were attempting to establish independence. Scenes of violence appear on cylinder seals. Many villages and small centers were abandoned, and a no-man's-land developed between the two cities. Settled population declined rapidly, a process that would continue into the third millennium B.C.E.[86] Along the Euphrates River similar events occurred. The warfare that arose seems to have been generated from within Mesopotamia rather than introduced by nomadic raiders from other areas. The simultaneous abandonment of small settlements in the countryside and construction of city walls—probably by workers from the smaller settlements—supports the interpretation that war arose from within. If raiders had begun to enter Mesopotamia, the response would have been to attempt to prevent invasion by establishing military outposts on the fringes. This attempt does not seem to have occurred. There was widespread abandonment of almost all the rural settlements surrounding Warka; the city of Warka grew rapidly to fifty thousand people, who now lived behind substantial defensive walls. This change must have been the result of refugees fleeing or of forcible transference of the population from the distant outskirts into the city.[87] Warka also lost its influence over the other cities of Mesopotamia.

Although data on military organizations seem not to be available, except for scenes on cylinder seals, I conjecture that the first "armies" of Mesopotamia consisted of the upper class followers of chief-priests.[88] It is likely that the soldiers of these armies were the same men who directed canal construction and enforced the collection of produce. These elite warriors were equipped with maces, bows and arrows, and spears. The iconography depicts a ruler with an arrow drawn back.[89] Perhaps soldiers wore body armor consisting of capes and copper helmets. These last two items of military equipment are prominent in the next period, the Early Dynastic. Besides armor for individuals, the sheer size of cities must also have provided great protection; the addition of walls must have made it nearly impossible for small, elite military organizations to penetrate the fortifications. The limited information available suggests that wars were fought for political independence, over boundary disputes, and to obtain captives. Whether the captives were made slaves or sacrificed is unclear. Centuries later both fates awaited them.

The remarkable recording system developed for keeping inventories slowly evolved into a written language. The first pictographs appear about 3100 B.C.E. From this beginning came a written script that utilized phonetic units. These records still survive, housed at many of the great museums and libraries of the modern world. They exist because the scribes wrote on clay tablets. Cuneiform writing, as it is called, was a great stimulus to the economy; inventory accounts and contracts abound.[90] It also helped in the procurement of military supplies and the management of the military organization that was soon to become a standing army.

By 3000 B.C.E., the start of the Early Dynastic period, a typical early state had developed. Mesopotamian warfare had become modern in the sense that wars of conquest occurred; soon battles would be fought with massed infantry under the command of a ruler who would ride in an "armored car," and siege operations would be used to surmount and penetrate the fortifications surrounding cities. Sumerian warfare is dear to the hearts of those who love to read military history. All the ingredients of classic warfare are in place: specialized weapons, integrated tactical forces, set-piece battles, and protracted sieges. It is not an exaggeration to say that true warfare was invented five thousand years ago by the Sumerians. The term "true warfare" is used by many military historians to describe what they believe is rational, efficient warfare. In spite of the many fine accounts of Sumerian warfare, I will offer an interpretation that differs from those available. Most accounts collapse the evidence and present a composite picture that purports to be accurate for the period from 3000 to 2000 B.C.E. I look for changes in weapons and tactics over time, and the reasons why the changes occurred and what the consequences of the changes were. I used this method in the 1960s in my analyses of Iroquois and Zulu warfare.[91] Military historians had been using the method.

The sociopolitical system, which was finely adjusted to the physical environment, took more than two thousand years to develop. It was possible for this system to develop only in the absence of war. Indeed, if war had been present in lowland Mesopotamia, irrigation agriculture could never have developed and flourished. The people would have remained hunter-gatherers or at most simple farmers and herders living around the marshes. When warfare arose it totally disrupted the sociopolitical system and a completely new adaptation arose, one that incorporated warfare. There were no hills to which the people could flee, no hills on which easily defended new settlements could be erected. The only thing they could do was to fortify their largest centers and to move from the small centers and towns into the largest centers. Thus, walled cities surrounded by uninhabited farmlands sprang up all over the alluvial plain. At Warka the walls are more than seven meters tall and equally thick, with gates and towers distributed along the walls. The walls are often bigger and better built than military requirements would demand, presumably to impress both the inhabitants and visitors to the city. The earlier walls were carefully constructed using regular bricklaying patterns, as at Warka; later walls had a mud-brick façade with rubble fill.[92]

Warring cities, each a city-state, dotted the landscape. They were often only about ten miles apart. There were probably ten thousand to twenty thousand people on average in each of about thirteen city-states, Warka perhaps being the largest.[93] The closeness of cities to each other suggests there was no prior period of warfare; if warfare had been present early, I would expect the cities to be much farther apart. Michael Mann describes the scene: "In the Early Dynastic I period a town would exercise . . . political control over perhaps 20,000 persons. The radius of such a zone would vary from about five to fifteen kilometers. . . . In Mesopotamia it is especially striking that the most important cities, Eridu and Ur, and Uruk and Larsa, were within sight of one another!" Eridu was abandoned when Ur started, but palaces were later erected at Eridu.[94] Cities were within sight of each other because the temples, what we term ziggurats, reached hundreds of feet into the sky. From the ground their tops could be seen from a long distance.[95] From their upper levels approaching enemy forces could be observed. With the element of surprise gone, raids by elite warriors would have been ineffective against cities, but men who had to work fields some distance from the cities were subject to attack and capture by elite warriors. Sometimes word of an impending attack would reach those working in the fields, other times not. Even if the farmers made good their escape from the raiders, crops could be plundered and irrigation canals destroyed.

A new type of military organization was devised to fight new kinds of war. The farmers, long accustomed to being under the control of officials, were conscripted into the military and uniformly equipped by the state. A city could now put a larger force into the field, one that could attempt to protect the irrigation system and defend those tending the crops. The enemy responded similarly. Thus, each side had an army that could march forth and do battle somewhere on level ground between the rival city-states. Set-piece battles developed, and particular locations may have been chosen for battlefields. "Diplomats" may have arranged for battles to take place on a particular day on a particular battlefield. Was this sort of conflict ritual warfare? Of course not. These armies did not cease combat when the first casualty occurred; they fought until one side fled. Then the victors pursued the defeated, killing and capturing as many of the enemy as they could. The defeated would attempt to take refuge behind the walls of their city, but real security did not come to the winners because the enemy city was still there. To destroy the enemy city, the winners had to undermine, penetrate, or surmount the protective walls. To do this, siege operations were developed using the two basic devices for overcoming walls: scaling ladders and battering rams.

A new basic pattern of warfare arose: line battles with massed infantry and siege operations. In Mesopotamia line battles went through two stages. The evidence for the stages comes from two famous pieces of "art": the Standard of Ur and the Stele of Vultures, both dated to about 2500 B.C.E., although the former is, I will argue, earlier. C. Leonard Wooley, the excavator of Ur, dated the Standard of Ur to 3500 B.C.E. and the Stele of Vultures to 2800 B.C.E.; when he described each he presented different pictures of warfare.[96] Although Wooley's dates are no longer accepted, he recognized that the two pictures of warfare were fundamentally different. The Standard of Ur depicts a style of warfare that is developmentally less complex than the style depicted on the Stele of Vultures. Scholars do not know the function of the Standard of Ur, which is from the royal tomb at Ur. It is a panel of mosaic in shell and lapis lazuli. One side is referred to as the "peace side" because it shows provisions being brought to a banquet. The other side is the "military side" because it shows combat and the presentation of captives to the ruler.[97] There are three registers or rows of illustrations, which clearly are to be read from the bottom up. The first register shows four "chariots" (carts) or four views of the same; if the latter, they can be read as one reads a comic strip. In the first view a driver and warrior with javelins are being transported in a four-wheel cart drawn by four animals that resemble horses or donkeys (i.e., equids).[98] In the second view a spear is raised and a slain enemy lies under the animals pulling the cart; in the third scene a socket ax is raised, and two slain enemy lie by the animals. In the fourth view the spear is raised and a slain enemy lies under the animals.[99] The second register shows eight similarly dressed soldiers with spears, helmets, and studded capes; they are not carrying shields.[100] The eight soldiers are in a row or column, and there are four more soldiers in combat, preceding the column, who appear to be equipped the same as the warrior in the chariot; two enemy are slain and seven are retreating. The enemy appear to be equipped with spears and helmets but not capes. Damage to the mosaic makes interpretation difficult, however. In the third and top register, the standing king, with a chariot and three guards behind him, receives a procession of captives. The standard is damaged in this area, but there may be seven captives and four guards. The king's vehicle is not used as a war chariot; it does not have a quiver holding javelins at the front of the cab. The guards are armed with socket axes and spears and the driver, with a socket ax.

The usual interpretation of the lower two registers is that one depicts the charge of a phalanx and the other, the charge of a chariot.[101] Military historian Arther Ferrill takes the interpretation a step further: "Sumerians are depicted in close order advancing with chariot support. . . . The advantages of combining mobility (chariots) and security (pikemen) with short-, intermediate- and long-range firepower (spears, javelins, and bows) were recognized early in the ancient Near East."[102] My interpretation is different; I "read" the Standard of Ur from the bottom up. Bottom register: A chariot commanded by an elite warrior (there are presumably other chariots on the battlefield) is used as a shock weapon against an enemy infantry who is not equipped with chariots. The elite warrior and his driver are highly skilled. Some enemy soldiers are killed. Middle register: The infantry, equipped only with thrusting spears, advances slowly. They are commoners who, although unskilled with weapons, are equipped by the state with mass-produced weapons. They are preceded by elite warriors, perhaps from the chariots, who engage the enemy in combat, killing some while others flee. Top register: The soldiers also capture and bind some enemies. Later the captives are presented to the king, who apparently played no role in the battle. The same elite warriors, armed with socket axes, javelins, and spears, appear in all three registers. The guards are probably also elite warriors. The battle is a frontal attack of chariots against infantry. The victor's heavy infantry, presumably the soldiers of Ur, kill the wounded and collect prisoners and weapons.

The other "document," the Stele of Vultures, unlike the Standard of Ur, is a fragment with two registers. The fragment came from a carved stone monument that commemorated the victory of the city of Lagash over Umma. The cuneiform writing on the stele details the claims of Lagash to a piece of land along the border with Umma. The ruler of Lagash is Eannatum. The upper register or panel depicts a victorious phalanx walking on the bodies of fallen enemies. The soldiers are in a column organized six files deep, with a nine-man front. Each soldier carries a rectangular shield and a long spear or pike and wears a helmet. The pikes are leveled, their points thus extending beyond the front of the phalanx. The spears are held by both hands; shields must be suspended from the shoulder. The column is led by the ruler on foot. In the lower panel the ruler rides alone in a two-wheeled chariot with javelins in a quiver at the front of the cab, his spear is raised, and he carries a sickle-sword, cast in the curved shape of a sickle, made of bronze. Behind the ruler march soldiers with their pikes over their shoulders. They carry socketed penetrating axes but no shields. Richard Gabriel and Karen Metz conclude that "the stele provides the first evidence of a standing professional army." [103]

The great expert on ancient warfare, Yigail Yadin, interprets the upper panel as a "charge over bodies" (but the battle is over) and the lower panel as the ruler as he "leads charging troops" (but spear points are high in the sky). I believe that the ruler would not lead a charge into an enemy phalanx, assuming that the enemy had phalanxes—which I think was the case. Military historian Robert O'Connell interprets the upper panel as a "full-fledged phalanx" (I agree) with willing troops (I believe they were coerced). The lower panel, he claims, shows the ruler seeking "individualized combat" (I see no evidence for this; the other ruler is not shown). [104]

My interpretation, starting with the upper panel, is that a phalanx is used as a shock force; the ruler directs from behind the lines on foot, or possibly from his cart. The enemy is crushed—the battle is won and the ruler moves to the front of his victorious phalanx. In the lower panel, the ruler rides in triumph in his chariot (which sounds better than "cart") or "parade vehicle" at the head of his marching troops. Ruler and soldiers both display their weapons. It looks like a Memorial Day parade. [105] If the stele is "read" from the bottom up, as one reads the Standard of Ur, the lower register shows the army on the march. (The shields are presumably carried in carts.) The upper register depicts the defeat of the enemy. I wish there had been a middle register. If reading down, it should show bound captives being presented to the ruler; if reading up, it should show phalanxes from each side in combat. A middle register, thus, might tell us which direction to read the stele. Another fragment of the Stele of Vultures shows a burial mound of enemy corpses after the battle. [106] They appear to be naked but not bound, mutilated, or beheaded. The victors are clothed and appear to be carrying baskets of dirt on their heads, presumably to be dumped on the mound of corpses.

The battles on the Standard of Ur and the Stele of Vultures differ from each other. In the Ur battle the forces employed four-wheel carts as shock weapons; infantry played a supporting role. Two kinds of soldiers were present: elite warriors, who fought from battle platforms on the carts, and common soldiers, who used thrusting spears. The Lagash army employed phalanxes. The two-wheel chariots were for transporting the ruler, perhaps officers, and supplies. The phalanx appears similar—perhaps nearly identical—to the phalanx developed by Philip of Macedonia and his son Alexander the Great. The Lagash-Umma battle must have been a set-piece battle on a chosen battlefield between two city-states. The resemblance to Macedonian warfare two thousand years later is remarkable, leading me to wonder how much of the Greek experience I and others have read into ancient Mesopotamian warfare. Could the Sumerians really have invented phalanx warfare two thousand years before the Greeks?

At least one historian, Doyne Dawson, thinks not. He argues that Early Dynastic warfare was siege warfare and that field armies resembled the fighting forces of earlier times. He emphatically states that Sumerian armies did not have war chariots and phalanxes of heavy infantry. He also suggests that the warfare between the city-states was "less serious and destructive than the typical warfare of advanced chiefdoms." I agree that the equid-drawn carts were not chariots, but the infantry with large rectangular shields and long pikes could not have fought except in dense formation. Dawson, I believe, undermines his argument by recognizing that Sumerian armies were large "conscript armies." Earlier combatants were not conscripts. I have argued that there are two fundamentally different types of military organizations, the professional and the nonprofessional, the former being full-time and the latter being part-time. Conscript armies are full-time and professional. In addition, Dawson emphasizes the importance of siege warfare in early Mesopotamia.[107] The shields and pikes would have been nearly useless in a siege, however. Soldiers had such weapons because they engaged in combat organized as phalanxes.

The Ur battle appears to be a stage between the combat of elite warriors of the Uruk period, who were equipped with maces and probably bows and arrows and spears, and the massed infantry battle between Lagash and Umma (see Figure 6.3). The copper helmets of the Early Dynastic period provided excellent protection against blows from maces and probably led to the discarding of the mace as a battle weapon. Richard Gabriel and Karen Metz provide experimental evidence that a copper helmet with a leather cap underneath disperses the crushing power of a mace. Such helmets have been found by archaeologists. The soldiers at the Ur battle wore helmets and studded capes, which would probably also have blunted the blows of maces. Presumably their opponents were protected in the same way, although they may not have worn capes. The soldiers of Ur carried spears, which probably could pierce felted wool cloth or perhaps leather body armor; they did not carry maces. The soldiers at the Lagash-Umma battle carried socketed penetrating axes, the narrow blade of which was designed to pierce metal helmets. The bronze socket and blade were cast in one piece. Again, experiments by Gabriel and Metz show that such axes will pierce armor—the metal helmets and, I presume, also the body armor.[108] Thus, a technological analysis of weapons supports the argument that there were three stages in Mesopotamian warfare, and it also establishes the Ur battle as having been earlier than the Lagash-Umma battle.

Not only weapons but also military organizations underwent change. In the first stage, elite warriors from the upper class attacked similar forces on a battlefield or farmers working in fields. In the next stage, the army was composed of elite troops, who fought from carts drawn by equids, as well as soldiers conscripted from the lower class. There was, thus, an integrated tactical force of a mobile command and an infantry. In the third stage professional soldiers under the command of the ruler, and presumably other officers as well, constituted the army. The mobile force seems to be absent.

Tactics also underwent great changes. Late in the Uruk period, surprise and the skill of elite forces drove farmers to take refuge behind city walls. The landscape of Mesopotamia changed as farmers abandoned towns and villages and moved into the cities. Cities grew larger. Farmers had to walk several miles to their fields and were vulnerable to attack while working there. In order to gain military superiority over the other cities on the alluvial plain, Ur conscripted commoners and outfitted them with helmets and body armor so that they could stand up to attack from elite warriors. Other cities may also have followed this practice. To defeat such infantries, the elite troops were placed aboard carts drawn by four equids. In addition to the driver, the carts may have held up to three warriors. These "armored vehicles" lacked mobility but could be used in a frontal attack. Elite troops hurled javelins down upon infantry and hoped to hit unprotected areas of soldiers' bodies. There is no evidence that "chariot battles" took place. In the third stage, to prevent infantry from being overrun by elite troops fighting on mobile battle platforms, Lagash and perhaps other city-states reequipped their infantry with shields and pikes. If a cart drove into a wall of spear points, the equids would be killed and infantry with socketed penetrating axes could engage the elite troops in hand-to-hand combat. They would outnumber and defeat the elite troops, who could not flee in vehicles since the equids had been killed. This argument is similar to the one offered by historian Robert Drews to explain why the Bronze Age came to an end about 1200 B.C.E. Drews argues that light infantry, with javelins and long swords, could overwhelm the chariots of elite forces that were restricted to level fields. Years earlier, another scholar of ancient military, F. E. Adcock, similarly argued that Alexander the Great used light infantry to defeat the chariots deployed by Darius at the Battle of

Gaugamela (331 B.C.E.).[109] In Mesopotamia the four-wheeled vehicles, having lost their effectiveness on the battlefield, became relegated to transporting supplies, perhaps carrying officers, and to chauffeuring the king in victory parades. Drews contends "that in Mesopotamia, at least, kings had all along ridden to the battlefield—on stately, heavy wagons in the third millennium and in chariots after the development of the spoke wheel."[110]

Warfare did not hurt the growing prosperity of the city-states. Because of high agricultural yields and the development of numerous craft specialties, which stimulated trade, the affluence of Mesopotamian cities increased throughout the third millennium B.C.E. Kings and other members of the upper class lived in splendor. Merchants and traders formed a prosperous middle class. Slaves furnished field and other labor following the urban population explosions that resulted from massive migration to the cities. Warfare even helped the growth of the economy by stimulating invention and trade. The population of southern Mesopotamia probably reached 200,000.

In the middle to late part of the third millennium B.C.E. the typical early state became a transitional early state. During the Early Dynasty III period, Ur grew, many large buildings were constructed, and the royal cemetery was expanded. Cuneiform documents attest to the accomplishments of Ur's dynasty.[111] Underground masonry tomb chambers, approached by descending ramps, led to the bodies of the kings and queens. Gold and silver jewelry, as well as luxury items such as harps and gaming boards, accompanied the deceased. The Standard of Ur was among the items.[112] So was a gold helmet and dagger. Human sacrifice was probably practiced; groups of retainers were put to death at the time of burial—soldiers, charioteers, and ladies-in-waiting. The numbers approach one hundred for several tombs. The ladies-in-waiting wore golden headdresses. There is no evidence that the victims resisted.[113]

The mature state stage came about under Sargon of Akkad (2371[?]–2315[?] B.C.E.), the first great conqueror of history. Sargon, an outsider to Mesopotamia, probably came from a land to the north where there was both irrigation agriculture and upland pasture lands. Through his victories Sargon was able to unite all of Sumer under a hegemonic empire. Some city-states were apparently conquered, including Lagash, Umma, and Ur; their walls were razed and Akkadian governors installed.[114] Akkad, his capital, has not been located, but scholars believe it lay in the vicinity of Kish.[115]

Sargon began his career as a professional soldier in the service of the king of Kish, a northern Sumerian city-state. How he became the head of an army is unknown. What is known is that he became famous for his speed of attack, despite his use of heavy infantry. To this military force he added archers who used the composite double-convex bow, a weapon developed by hunting peoples to the north. With an effective range of two hundred meters, this bow could propel arrows into an advancing phalanx before the two battle lines met. Any disruption to the enemy's infantry before contact would have increased the likelihood of victory for Sargon's army. However, the first visual evidence for the composite bow in Mesopotamian warfare comes later, during the reign of Sargon's grandson, from a victory stele dated to about 2340 B.C.E.[116]

During Sargon's reign the chariot, drawn by equids, did not play a role in combat. The chariot, however, was to make a comeback in the centuries to come. By approximately 2000 B.C.E. the peoples of Mesopotamia were obtaining domesticated horses from pastoral peoples to the north. They attached the horse to their two-wheeled chariot.[117] The vehicle, however, underwent major changes. It became lighter, stronger, and had spoked wheels. Probably the first peoples to create what archaeologist Stuart Piggott calls the "chariot package-deal" were the Babylonians.[118] After the fall of the Akkadian dynasty founded by Sargon (2350–2150 B.C.E.), only 350 years elapsed until the first dynasty of Babylon (1800–1600 B.C.E.). The Babylonians created a vehicle with great military potential. One reason I believe that the chariot is an indigenous development in Mesopotamia is that there is an evolution of the vehicle itself within the region. The lightweight spoked wheels of these later chariots are construction marvels that could be created only by teams of full-time artisans working in urban centers. How the chariot's military potential was realized in the Near East and elsewhere is another story.

The rise of Warka and the other Mesopotamian city-states provides evidence that the basic evolutionary sequence I have identified for the emergence of the pristine state is correct. A period of nearly two thousand years without warfare and with minimal internal conflict, during which irrigation canals and large villages with temple complexes were constructed, was followed by a period of internal conflict. Lower class members were coerced into providing produce for common storage facilities, and rival members of the upper class struggled to gain control over the administrative apparatus of the growing urban centers. The result was increasing political complexity, and yet there was no warfare. Not until late in the Uruk period does evidence of warfare appear—weapons, fortifications, fissioning polities, and no-man's-land. The rapid rise of warfare occurred from about 3200 to 3000 B.C.E. The countryside was abandoned and the size of cities rapidly increased. The vulnerability of small settlements to the attacks of elite warriors from the upper class who sought captives for slaves led to a rapid change in the built landscape. The large populations of the cities made possible a military organization composed of both elite warriors and commoners, many of whom had fled from the countryside or been brought into the cities by the rulers. The craft specialists resident in the cities were able to mass produce weapons and protective armaments for the lower class males conscripted into the military organization. From this basis three types of armies evolved: an attack force of elite warriors riding in carts, followed by lower class infantry; a standing army composed of massed infantry organized into phalanxes led by the king; and a professional army composed of phalanxes and archers equipped with the composite double-convex bow.

Hsia/Shang

More than four thousand years ago states arose in northern China. They were the culmination of a long evolutionary process that began more than six thousand years earlier. Hunter-gatherers were widely distributed over much of China, along rivers and near the coasts and large lakes. A layer of loess, extremely rich soil, covered northern China. The Yellow River cut through the loess plateau, frequently changing course (see Map 5). People living along the river specialized in fishing. This warm, moderately rainy area had great agricultural potential. About 7500 B.C.E. the more sedentary peoples—those who depended on gathering and fishing—domesticated two forms of millet, a cereal grass that produces a nutritious grain. Three kinds of beans, including the soybean, as well as the pig and silkworm were also eventually domesticated. (Rice was domesticated in southern China.) At the village stage these farming communities clustered into three regional cultures; the culture in the region where the Hsia and Shang states arose is known as the Peiligang (see Figure 6.4). The early farmers lived in subterranean circular pit houses.[119]

The Yangshao culture grew directly out of the earlier Peiligang culture. Individual self-sufficient villages were the primary social unit. The minimal chiefdom stage had been reached. One of the largest villages was arranged into five complexes, each with a large house surrounded by ten to twenty smaller ones. Perhaps five clans, each with a head, resided within the village. The clans were patrilineal and probably acted as fraternal interest groups. The only evidence of possible warfare is a "defensive moat" that surrounded the village, an indication that attacks may have been feared.[120] Archaeologist Kwang-chih Chang describes the culture: "Yang-shao is the culture of millet farmers and pig breeders. . . . Farming villages, inhabited by members of clans or lineages, were evidently the basic social unit; there is no evidence for political groups larger than the village, nor evidence of war or social stratification." A large building at one site could have been a chief's house or meeting hall.[121] Periodically villages were abandoned and reoccupied, perhaps because the people practiced slash-and-burn agriculture. Or perhaps changes in the course of rivers forced the abandonment.

A transitional phase, known as Miao-ti-Kou, links Yangshao culture with the next major culture, the Longshan. Miao-ti-Kou can be thought

Map 5. North China

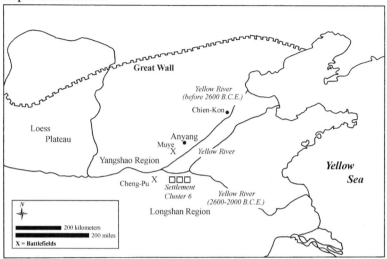

of as a Late Yangshao or an Early Longshan culture. The villages were typical chiefdoms. Silk weaving was developed during this phase. There is evidence of a possible execution that occurred at this time; at a burial site one person had "both hands bound at the time of burial." [122] This burial is the first indication of internal conflict in the first three stages of our sequence, and it occurs during what is apparently a period of peaceful relations between villages. There is as yet no evidence for military organizations or war.

Village life began to change and to change rapidly after people began to cultivate the same fields each year. Annual floods renewed soil fertility. Domestic animals—pigs, poultry, sheep, and cattle—became more important. Villages were occupied for longer periods of time; they grew larger, but the same settlement pattern of pit houses arranged around a central large building continued. In some villages rectangular houses on low platforms were constructed. The platforms may have been built to keep the houses above the annual floodwaters. Some of the villages were surrounded by walls of "stamped earth"—loess and clay were pounded by workers into compact walls about six meters high and nine meters wide. Burials interpreted as human sacrifice have been found under walls at one site.[123] The culture of these people, which stretched across northern China, is known as the Longshan; with it, the maximal chiefdom stage had been reached. Three-tier settlement hierarchies came into being. Burials show great wealth differences. Full-time craft specialists may have made the excellent jade ornaments and well-turned pottery found in graves. The practice of marking the pottery with emblems of lineages and clans may be the origin of Chinese

Stages	Social and Political Organization	Internal Conflict	War	Military Organization
Mature State: Chou 1045–221 B.C.E.	Extensive kingdom; Great Wall—300 B.C.E.; Irrigation works; Iron—500 B.C.E.	Decline of sacrifice	External and internal war; Cities besieged—400 B.C.E.; Battle of Cheng-Pu—632 B.C.E.	Massed infantry armies, cavalry—300 B.C.E.; Swords, crossbow—400 B.C.E.; Conscription—600 B.C.E.
V. Transitional Early State: Shang 1750–1045 B.C.E.	King, nobility; Royal capital, Anyang—1400 B.C.E.; royal tombs; Domain of many city-states; Written inscriptions on oracle bones; writing—1200 B.C.E.	War captives worked fields and were sacrificed	Battle of Muye—1045 B.C.E.; External and internal war	Chariots—1200 B.C.E.; Chariots and infantry, composite bows, knives, halberds; Hundreds of walled towns, some may have moats
IV. Typical Early State: Hsia 2200–1750 B.C.E.	Warrior nobility; Palaces; Ruling clans and lineages; Bronze Age begins, 2200 B.C.E.	Human sacrifice—war captives	Internal war; Towns captured	Walled towns, citadels; Elite warriors; bows and arrows, halberds, knife
III. Inchoate Early State: Longshan 2500–2200 B.C.E.	Two- and three-level polities; Intervillage leagues with rulers; Wealth differences; Copper-bronze metallurgy	Human sacrifice; Decapitation, scalping, burial alive of war captives or feud victims	Intervillage warfare?	Spears, bows and arrows; Walled villages—for defense or flood control
II. Typical Chiefdom: Miao-ti-Kou II (Early Longshan) 3200–2500 B.C.E.	Two-level polity; Potter's wheel; Silk weaving—2700 B.C.E.	Burial with hands bound (execution?)	No war?	No military organization
I. Minimal Chiefdom: Yangshao 5000–3200 B.C.E.	Individual villages composed of complexes; Chief's house or meeting hall	Minimal conflict	No war? Moat around village	No military organization
Villages: Peiligang 6500–5000 B.C.E.	Farming communities; Millet, soybeans	Minimal conflict	No war	No military organization

Figure 6.4. Hsia/Shang Matrix: Stages of the Chiefdom-State Continuum

writing.[124] Foretelling the future through scapulimancy, a practice that extended back to hunter-gatherer times, was fully developed. The religious specialist, perhaps working for a chief, would draw symbols on bone (often a scapula), heat the bone until it cracked, then interpret the pattern of cracking. Copper metallurgy also had its beginning in Longshan culture.

Leagues of villages were formed under a full-time ruler. Evidence for warfare or internal conflict has been found. Chang states, "At Chienkon, there is the earliest [c. 2200 B.C.E.] direct evidence of violence against people in Chinese prehistory."[125] Abandoned water wells within a house foundation yielded five layers of human skeletons, both males and females, young and old. Some had been decapitated and some showed postures of struggling. Six skulls showed signs of blows and scalpings, apparently indicating that the victims were scalped after having been killed. Stone arrowheads and spear points were recovered at the site.[126] If the victims were the residents of the house, this violence might indicate warfare; perhaps village fortifications, if any, were overrun. On the other hand, the skulls could have been the severed heads of enemy chiefs or warriors—again, evidence for warfare. If the victims were killed by fellow villagers, the burials indicate serious internal conflict—perhaps fighting between clans arising out of feuds. Since children are among the deceased, these killings are unlikely to be executions for crimes; since there is decapitation and scalping, these killings are unlikely to be human sacrifice.

Across northern China chiefdoms with both two-tier and three-tier settlement hierarchies have been identified by archaeologist Li Liu. The number of villages composing the settlement hierarchies increased through the Longshan period; villages differed greatly in size. Liu classifies them as either major center, minor center, or village. Several of the larger centers in the east were walled, and a few of the villages were as well. The walled sites were on or near rivers, which occasionally flooded and changed course. The course of the Yellow River made a major change from north to south around 2600 B.C.E. and then again from south to north around 2000 B.C.E. The latter change may have been facilitated by the deepening and widening of channels, an activity undertaken by the first ruler of the Hsia dynasty, Yu (see below). Liu has analyzed the distribution of the settlement hierarchies and the villages that composed them and concluded that shifts in the course of rivers as well as "intense intergroup conflict" resulted in frequent movement of villages.[127]

The stamped-earth walls have been universally interpreted by scholars as evidence for warfare, either raids between villages or raids by nomads.[128] I suggest another interpretation. I believe that the walls may have served to protect the villages not only from raids (if there were raids in the region) but also from floods. If walls could prevent floodwaters from destroying homes, villagers might reason that the expenditure of a huge amount of labor in wall construction was worth the time spent (see the section "Walls and Fortifications" in chapter 7). When rivers changed course, however, even if houses and possessions were saved, moving the villages might have become necessary. In one cluster of settlement hierarchies three walled towns are shown on maps by Liu. Liu reports that at two of these walled towns floods destroyed the enclosures.[129] Were the walls erected in the first place to control flooding? If so, maybe they did their job for many years before they failed. I believe that Longshan stamped-earth walls are for flood control, not for defense from attacks by neighbors or nomads.

At another site within the cluster, walls fell into disuse, as indicated by "cultural remains" covering the walls, even though the town continued to be occupied. The presence of cultural artifacts on the walls suggests that there never was a threat of attack and that the walls were built for flood protection. If raids were a threat, keeping the top of the wall clean would have facilitated the movement of defending combatants. If floods were a threat, keeping the top of the wall clean would not have been necessary. Liu, however, offers another interpretation: "The town wall probably ceased to function not long after the initial construction. [Why?] Evidence of violence indicated by dismembered and incomplete human skeletons in burials has been found . . . at the site, dated to the late Longshan period, suggesting that intergroup conflict may have continued after the town wall ceased to function." Dismemberment is not necessarily evidence for "intergroup conflict"—it may just as well indicate *intragroup* conflict. I lean toward the latter interpretation. If there was *intergroup* conflict—I presume Liu means raids and war—why would the residents not continue to maintain their walls? Liu does, however, provide an answer to my "why?" question: The town "may have been one political center that emerged in the beginning of the late Longshan period, but which then weakened or was replaced because of other polities in the region."[130] This idea still does not explain the neglect of the walls. If raids were a threat, then the wall should have been maintained.

Support for my explanation comes from traditional Chinese history. The mythical ruler-sage Yu, who is said to have founded the Hsia dynasty in 2205 B.C.E., is referred to as conqueror of floods.[131] Today Yu is accepted as a historic figure and the Hsia dynasty as being archaeologically represented at the type site of Erlitou. Yu succeeded in resolving the flooding problems that China had faced for a long time. His father, Gun, whom the Chinese credit with the invention of the town wall, had tried to solve the problem by building dikes to hold back the floodwaters. The dikes failed, though, because they were not high enough. Gun's failed attempt to solve the problem was followed by Yu's success. Yu's innovation was to open and then widen and deepen channels that controlled the path of the water as it flowed to the sea. He also cleared hills and mountains of superfluous timber and used the wood to build places of refuge for the people. Many towns, including the seat of government, were moved. This history, often treated as legend, is presented in detail by Kuo-Cheng Wu, and it supports my argument that town walls were for flood control, not military defense.[132]

It has been argued for decades that attacks by nomads, perhaps mounted on horses, caused the early Chinese to construct village fortifications. Villagers built walls out of fear. Organizing to build walls and then organizing for defense led to the formation of the state. This theory has been favored by historians from Owen Lattimore to William McNeill to Robert O'Connell.[133] The theories of all three historians have in common that pastoral peoples practiced war and carried it to peaceful agriculturalists. The often cited phrase "wars make states, and states make war" fits well with their version of the external conflict theory of the origin of the state. In the nineteenth century it was the conquering pastoralists who supposedly created the state; in the twentieth century it was the innocent villagers who, in defending themselves, created the state. Evidence advanced by historians to support the theory comes from later historical records dating from about 600 B.C.E., which describe barbarian invasions (the Great Wall was erected three hundred years later), the presence of walls surrounding villages, and the observation that walls and war seemingly came abruptly to China in about 2500 B.C.E. Robert O'Connell argues that building walls was a response to steppe nomads riding horses. Later these pastoral peoples brought the horse-drawn chariot to the Shang in about 1200 B.C.E.[134]

The theory that attacks by nomads led to state formation in China stumbles on several grounds. First, there is no archaeological evidence of nomads being present during the Longshan period; no material remains have been found. Second, anthropologists and archaeologists who specialize on ancient China—Kwang-chih Chang, Morton Fried, and Li Liu—describe a smooth transition through a series of stages from the early Neolithic to the first Chinese states. Their evidence for war consists of walls and the burials of dismembered bodies.[135] These casualties are attributed to internal war—war between the villages and towns of the same region. Never do they suggest that the victims might have met their deaths at the hands of outsiders. Third, the walls may be—as I argued—for flood control, in which case they do not provide evidence of either internal or external war. Furthermore, the location of the walled settlements is not where one would predict them to be if steppe nomads attacked from the west or northwest. Liu argues that the three-tier settlement hierarchies lay to the west and "defensive facilities such as town walls . . . were absent."[136] This region experienced a rapid expansion in population due to natural increase and immigration. To the east, north, and south of the major bend of the Yellow River lay the two-tier systems.[137] Here were found walled settlements along rivers. Other walled sites are even farther to the east, along the northern course of the Yellow River, which formed after 2000 B.C.E. Thus, raids of nomads from the west and northwest cannot explain this distribution of Longshan walled settlements.

The maximal chiefdom/inchoate early state in ancient China emerged after four thousand years of gradual development, from small farming communities to three-tier settlement hierarchies. This transition occurred in the absence of warfare. When walls were erected, they were intended to prevent the encroachment of floodwaters, not rival villages or nomads. The violence that is represented in the archaeological record I attribute to rivalry between clans within a settlement. The village headman became a chief early. Struggles between clans to choose the chief turned violent at times. The winners of the struggle chose the chief; he and his followers became the "government" of the settlement. Villages fissioned and fissioned again due to population increase, producing two- and three-tier settlement hierarchies. Since this multiplication of settlements occurred in the absence of warfare, I suggest that close relatives of the chief founded the satellite villages. The leaders of these villages became heads of lineages, lineages that were linked to each other, the whole group of settlements with their lineages being a single clan.

Agricultural intensification occurred after 2000 B.C.E. in the region where the Yellow River flowed south and then turned eastward. More land was brought under cultivation, and the population increased.[138] The Longshan culture gave way to the Erlitou culture, which was characterized by cities, state hierarchies, palaces, temples, monumental art, social stratification, elaborate burials, writing, and a state-controlled bronze industry. Bronze was used for weapons: arrow points, spearheads, and a distinctive blade (*ko*) attached to a shaft, thereby creating a dagger-ax or halberd. However, horse-drawn chariots were not present.[139] The sociopolitical system maintained a strong continuity with the Longshan period and persisted through the Shang and Chou periods.

China's first three dynasties, which span two thousand years, have roots in Erlitou culture. As Kwang-chih Chang has stated, "The Hsia, Shang, and Chou shared the same culture and only differed from one another in matters of detail. . . . In social organization and level of societal development, the Hsia, Shang, and Chou shared a very important feature, namely lineages in walled towns serving as the ruling instrument."[140] To live in the luxury that is shown by the archaeological record, rulers must have physically coerced the lower classes to extract ever greater productivity from the soil. The nobility, freed from toil themselves, were able to engage in warfare and hunting, their two favorite pursuits.[141] When horse-drawn chariots first made their appearance in China in about 1200 B.C.E. they were probably used by the nobility in both hunting and warfare. I have suggested that hunting and warfare were linked in the Upper Paleolithic; I believe that in ancient China the chariot was a "weapon" highly useful in both hunting and warfare. Hunting honed archery skills, while warfare provided captives for sacrifice. For defensive reasons, walls were erected around towns and cities after 2000 B.C.E. Within cities, walls and even moats were constructed around the palaces. These fortifications amounted to citadels where the nobility could defend itself if the main walls were overrun. These interior walls also provided defense from attack by the lower classes, who may well have desired the destruction of their oppressive rulers. Archaeologist Jonathan Haas, who has championed the internal conflict theory, points out that these interior fortifications isolate and separate higher status residences from lower status residences. Of the four pristine states, he regards the Shang dynasty of northern China as offering the "best archaeological evidence" of a "conflict-based state." In other words, Shang civilization supports the internal conflict theory.[142]

With firm control over their polities Hsia kings were able to focus upon rivals. Members of the ruler's lineage formed a warrior nobility. Honor became a key element in the rivalry, rivalry that led to war.[143] Early Chinese warfare dating from the typical early state stage was facilitated by the availability of bronze for making weapons and by the presence of walled cities. The warfare engaged in by the Hsia kings probably consisted of arranged set-piece battles that took place on level ground somewhere between the walled capitals of the rivals. The combatants were members of the warrior nobility. Non-nobility—the artisans, the lower classes, and the peasantry—did not participate in battle. Because of the great wealth of the kings and the nobility, warriors were probably dressed in the finest of silk clothing; body armor may have been worn. Combat opened from a distance with bows and arrows. As the battle intensified, the warriors would draw closer and engage in hand-to-hand combat with the halberds. Held in two hands, halberds were probably swung like a mace or slashing sword. If needed, a bronze knife could be drawn from its sheath. Individual combat brought honor to the victorious noble warrior. Capturing an enemy might have brought more honor than killing him, since captives were often the subjects of human sacrifice, a practice that had occurred for hundreds of years.[144] I believe that in earlier times sacrificial victims were rivals of a chief within a polity. Hundreds of years later it was rivals from another kingdom who were executed, thus satisfying the need to offer human sacrifice. If one "army" thoroughly defeated the other, the victorious king and his warrior nobility would seize the villages, towns, and capital of the other kingdom. These battles were "dynastic wars" in the same sense that European wars were dynastic wars until the time of the American and

French Revolutions. Although Hsia battles would have superficially appeared to be ritual combat, they were no more ritual wars than was the Battle of Hastings (A.D. 1066), after which William the Conqueror seized England.

Battles between elite warriors who were members of the nobility, including the king and chiefs from towns and villages, constitute the first stage in early Chinese warfare. Near the end of the Shang period, about 1200 B.C.E., horse-drawn chariots made their first appearance in China and thus began the second stage in early Chinese warfare. The horses that pulled chariots must have come from the west, brought by pastoral peoples who had been living on the steppe. Two theories have been offered. The first is that the Shang themselves were a steppe people who invaded China and replaced the Hsia. Historians John Keegan and William McNeill appear to still adhere to this "barbarian invasion" theory.[145] However, the cultural continuity that has been demonstrated through the archaeological record rules out this possibility. The second theory, which has been offered by historian Robert O'Connell, is that neighbors of the Chinese adopted the chariot, which had been used as "prestige transport in the deep steppe." The neighbors had not learned to ride horseback. O'Connell believes the horse-drawn chariot was introduced when some of the populations that gathered along the outskirts of China found the chariot offered military advantages.[146] Archaeological research supports O'Connell's conclusion.

The horse was domesticated in the steppe in Ukraine and southern Russia, north and east of the Black Sea. In this region, by 1500 B.C.E., there are chariot burials. The chariots are structurally similar to the chariots found three hundred years later in China, which strongly suggests that either the chariots themselves or the knowledge of the techniques for their construction spread across the steppe of Asia to the Shang Chinese.[147] Archaeologist Robert Bagley concludes, "Anyang chariot burials thus seem to indicate a substantial interaction with northern neighbors beginning about 1200 B.C.E.: not an invasion, but not a border incident either. The mere capture of enemy chariots and horses would not have brought the skills required to use, maintain, and reproduce them." Chinese material culture was so advanced by this time that the rulers could adopt the "chariot package-deal," the phrase used by archaeologist Stuart Piggott.[148] The Chinese apparently even had a symbol for "chariot-maker"; they may also have had "horse-fitting-manufacturers." As a domesticated animal the horse was bred by the Chinese; however, I suspect horses had to be continually imported.[149]

Military historians speak of the "Chariot Revolution."[150] Chariots dominated the battlefields of the Old World until about 1200 B.C.E. in the eastern Mediterranean, until about 600 B.C.E. in northern Mesopotamia, and until about 400 B.C.E. in China. Drews attributes their demise in the eastern Mediterranean to light infantry tactics, McNeill in Mesopotamia to the Assyrian development of cavalry, and Mark Edward Lewis in China to "mass infantry armies composed of peasant levies, complemented by the mounted cavalry that appeared in the fourth century."[151]

Chariot battles in China, which occurred from about 1200 B.C.E. to about 400 B.C.E., constitute the second stage in early Chinese warfare. Since the period spans nearly a thousand years of Chinese history, it encompasses both the Shang and Chou dynasties, the transitional early state and mature state stages. The development of the chariot was eagerly supported by Chinese rulers for a very simple reason: It allowed them to ride in style to the battlefield, rather than to walk or be carried by retainers. Another probable reason for the eager adoption of the chariot, as I noted earlier, was its usefulness in hunting. Even the closest battlefields might lie ten to twenty miles from the king's capital. An army on foot can march at a rate of two to three miles an hour. Battlefields could be a day's march away. Armies can move much faster in chariots, perhaps as much as five miles an hour, thirty miles a day. "Combat speed," however, according to Richard Gabriel and Karen Metz, "was between 8 and 12 miles per hour, the speed of a cantering horse." The maximum speed of a chariot was approximately twenty-five miles per hour, the speed of a galloping horse.[152] A warrior or a commanding officer could not handle his weapons at this speed, but he surely could make a quick getaway if his forces lost the battle. If his army had won, he could attempt to cut off the retreat of the enemy ruler who would be fleeing toward his own capital city. Numerous battlefields could now be reached in one day, many more in several days. Certainly for this reason alone the frequency of warfare increased during the Shang dynasty. The intensity of this warfare seemingly explains why the Shang capital was moved several times before it ended up at Anyang.[153]

More than twenty Shang chariots have been recovered from tombs; they are described by Chang: "The basic structures of all of them are similar: the chariot consisted of five major parts: wheels, axle, body mounted on the axle, pole, and yoke, and it was pulled by two horses."[154] Skeletons of horses were found lying on either side of the pole in one tomb. Chang describes the ornamentation: "Both chariot and horses were richly decorated with bronze and turquoise ornaments, and the chariot body was perhaps painted with animal designs."[155] Sacrificial burials suggest that Shang charioteers were organized as follows: Five chariots formed a squadron, and five squadrons formed a company. Each chariot had three charioteers. The middle one was driver, carrying a whip; the one on the left was striker, carrying a *ko*-halberd; and the one on the right was archer, carrying bow and arrows.[156] Large shields (thirty-two by twenty-six inches) were carried in the chariots.

They consisted of a wooden frame with a leather or basket surface, with tiger patterns painted on the outside. The archer's double-convex bow —a composite bow made of cattle sinew and horn—when strung was equal to a man's height (five feet, four inches); arrows half the length of the bow were feathered and tipped with stone, bone, antler, shell, or bronze. The Shang bow was unusually long, probably giving it great range, perhaps as far as two hundred meters (see Figure 4.1).[157] The *ko*-halberd consisted of a bronze blade hafted onto a wooden shaft about forty-four inches long. It was probably wielded with two hands.[158]

In addition to the chariot companies (twenty-five chariots and seventy-five warriors per company), foot soldiers and archers were organized into companies of one hundred soldiers each. Three companies formed a regiment. Soldiers and archers carried the same weapons as were carried in the chariots, except their shields were smaller. All soldiers carried a bronze knife about eight inches long, in a sheath, and a sharpening stone. The knife was not dagger-shaped but had a wide drop-point blade. In other words, the Shang knife was for cutting, not stabbing. It may have been used for cutting off ears to get a body count.[159] The nobility wore helmets and body armor; the ordinary soldiers apparently did not. Richard Gabriel and Donald Boose inform us that "officers and aristocratic warriors wore silk gowns, helmets, heavy circular bronze neck protectors (rather like loose, high collars), and armored breastplates made of bronze or leather." On the other hand, "Common soldiers wore knee-length hemp gowns, gathered at the waist with a belt or length of rope." Some aristocratic warriors wore two-piece armor that protected their chests and backs; their bronze helmets had a rounded crown, and the sides and back came down low over the ears and the nape of the neck.[160] Bronze helmets were found in the tomb of a king at the Shang capital of Anyang.[161] Officers and the archers who fought from chariots were probably members of the ruling lineage; the other soldiers were specialists who worked for the ruling lineage when not at war. Soldiers of the Shang army would have resided at the various towns within the kingdom. When a decision was made to go to war, each town's leaders, who were also military commanders, brought their companies and regiments to the battlefield.

The earliest battles in which chariots were used probably resembled the battles that took place during the Hsia period, except that the king and other important members of the nobility rode to the battlefield in chariots. Many of the chariots found in burials support this interpretation. The chariots were used for prestige transport, not combat, since weapons have not been found in conjunction with the chariots in half of the burials. Compared with Near Eastern chariots they have a larger floor area and the sides of the box are lower. As Bagley notes, these chariots are suited more for transport than for combat: "The use of such chariots in battle is uncertain. They could have served as showy vehicles for commanders or as transport for shifting special troops rapidly from one part of the field to another; kneeling archers could perhaps have fought from them." [162] Retainers walked.

Combat continued to occur on foot, but eventually the military potential of the chariot was realized. Well after the introduction of the chariot, I believe that combat could, and probably did, take place from chariots. Stuart Piggott notes, "Within China warfare at the aristocratic level was conducted as between chivalrous gentlemen, with an agreed battlefield prepared by leveling up irregularities of the ground to avoid accidents on either side." The king and other members of the nobility were the archers. Archery was an aristocratic pursuit in ancient China; the nobility held archery contests. [163] In the chariot with the archer, besides the driver, was a shield bearer whose job was to protect his king or master. He carried a *ko*-halberd.

Sinologist Edward L. Shaughnessy suggests that the Shang army made limited use of the chariot in combat. On the other hand, the western Chou employed chariots more extensively in combat. At the Battle of Muye or Shepherd's Wild in 1045 B.C.E. the Chou decisively defeated a larger Shang force. Shaughnessy states that "the Zhou had already moved beyond the stage of using the chariot as a mobile command platform and had begun to employ it in large numbers as a tactical weapon." He further states that "the Zhou conquest of Shang was achieved in part through their superior use of chariotry." Shaughnessy also credits "King Wu and Shangfu, . . . the commander of the Zhou army, for their strategy of risking a Yellow River crossing to attack the Shang capital from the south, thus bypassing the hitherto impenetrable Shang western defenses." The Chou enjoyed advantages in weaponry, from an improved design of the *ko*-halberd to a reliable stabbing sword and perhaps even to a composite bow. "Yet . . . it may well have been the chariot," Shaughnessy concludes, "that gave the Zhou the decisive military advantage that day on the field of Muye." [164] Shaughnessy believes that at the battle the Chou and their allies may have employed as many as forty-five thousand troops and three hundred war chariots. [165] The legendary history told by Kuo-Cheng Wu supports these figures and adds that the king of the Chou and his commander "had especially mustered three hundred war chariots and, also, three thousand elite troops selected for outstanding bravery, speed, and prowess, called 'bolting tigers.' All in all, he had a force of 45,000 men bearing arms." [166] The elite troops might have been organized into ten regiments with one war chariot company assigned to each. [167] The Shang army, with probably fewer war chariot companies, was apparently quickly overpowered. The Shang king fled to Anyang, where he committed suicide by setting fire to his palace. Shaughnessy writes that "the Zhou celebrated their victory by executing 100 of the Shang officials." [168]

The golden age of chariot warfare now developed, with the chariot becoming the dominant battlefield weapon by 800 B.C.E. According to Shaughnessy, "Battles in this region had already developed into contests pitting chariotry against chariotry. This style of combat gradually spread throughout the rest of China proper during the first half of the Spring and Autumn period [770–484 B.C.E.], when even minor states became capable of fielding armies of several hundred chariots."[169] Armies, however, rarely exceeded ten thousand troops. A high frequency of wars characterized this period, due in part to the large number of states—172, of which 13 were major powers. States gobbled up states. By the end of the period only 22 states survived, the largest possessing four thousand chariots and the smallest, only six hundred chariots.[170]

Combat between chariot crews, much like aerial duels between twentieth-century fighter pilots, was probably one-on-one, with the potential of "interference" from another chariot. If commanding officers, kin of the ruler, saw the king being endangered or defeated, they might drive their chariots into the flank of the ruler's opponent. Thus, I visualize an early chariot battle as a melee, with chariots dashing back and forth across the battlefield. Foot soldiers were bystanders until horses were wounded, chariots broke down, and warriors fell from chariots. They then rushed in to either defend their masters or to dispatch wounded enemy. The battle was over when one side, probably with the greater casualties, fled. Surviving charioteers of the victorious army pursued the defeated. I am doubtful that these were massive charges by hundreds of chariots, as suggested by later Chinese texts.

The first adequate description of a "chariot battle" comes from the Eastern Chou period (770–256 B.C.E.). It is the Battle of Cheng-Pu (632 B.C.E.), between the Ch'in and Ch'u dynasties. The account left by Chinese chroniclers is complete enough to permit sinologist Frank Kierman to draw three charts showing troop movements on the battlefield.[171] Each side had three "armies" or divisions facing each other: a center and two wings. Duke Wen of Ch'in joined combat with an advance of both wings. The left wing of Ch'in defeated the right wing of Ch'u; the right wing of Ch'in faked a retreat. The chariots of Ch'in, which had been deployed between the center and the now retreating right wing, swept across the front of the retreating right wing dragging tree branches, creating clouds of dust that obscured the view. The right wing of Ch'in re-formed and counterattacked the advancing enemy left wing. That advancing left wing of Ch'u was attacked on its left flank by the chariots, presumably no longer pulling trees, and on its right flank by a section of the Ch'in center. A pincer attack, or double envelopment, crushed the Ch'u left wing. The chariots of Ch'u seem to have played no role in the battle, but the claim is made that one hundred chariots were captured by Ch'in. There is no battle of chariot squadrons, no one-on-one, no frontal charge of chariots against infantry;

archers with their firepower and foot soldiers with their defensive weapons (shields and halberds) could inflict serious damage on horses and charioteers.

Gabriel and Metz describe the vulnerability of horses and chariot crews to archery fire: "Once a chariot or cavalry charge began, if the infantry stood its ground and gave the archers time enough to fire, a hail of arrows into the charge would cause havoc as wounded horses fell to the ground, spilled their riders, and caused one machine to crash into another. The bow, therefore, was a weapon to be feared among charioteers and cavalry and encouraged the charioteer and the cavalryman to become bowmen themselves."[172] The chariots were therefore kept out of harm's way. This situation is analogous to a modern one, in which U.S. commanders keep expensive bombers out of range of ground fire; they rarely are shot down and they inflict little damage upon enemy ground forces.[173] In Gulf War II helicopters were used against enemy ground forces; they inflicted heavy damage, were often shot up, and sometimes were brought down by ground fire. The best use of chariots was transportation of officers, reconnaissance, special maneuvers, and pursuit of defeated enemy. Nevertheless, the Battle of Cheng-Pu shows a well-organized, highly professional military organization in operation. The army had come a long way from the individual combat of the first stage of early Chinese warfare and the first uses of chariots.

A major transformation in Chinese warfare took place about 600 B.C.E., shortly after the battle just described. Armies grew immensely larger, due to conscription. Massed infantry armies dominated the final centuries of the Chou dynasty, which was in the mature state stage. Sinologist Mark Edward Lewis describes the change: "In 530 B.C.E., the king of Chu boasted that his four greatest cities could each provide a thousand chariots, and in the following year [the state of] Jin carried out a general mobilization for a hunt that put an army of 4,000 chariots into the field. [At the Battle of Cheng-Pu each army had only eight hundred chariots.] This means that in half a century the military levies of the larger states had increased by a factor of five, a result that was particularly impressive because the king of Chu's remark suggests that much of the levy still came from the vicinity of major cities."[174] The larger states grew huge. By the end of the Chou period one state has been estimated to have had a population of five million.[175]

New weapons were developed: laminar armor (made of overlapping rows of hard, lacquered leather plates), swords, and crossbows. Iron replaced bronze in weapons. Both massed infantry and their cavalry made appearances. Lewis informs us that "it was in the middle of the sixth century B.C.E. that the Zhou states first introduced armies composed entirely of infantry. . . . Over the next two centuries mass infantry armies composed of peasant levies, complemented by the mounted cavalry that appeared in the fourth century, completely supplanted

the chariot armies of the aristocracy." Shaughnessy describes the introduction of cavalry: "By the end of the Spring and Autumn period in
484 B.C.E., horse-mounted warriors had already made their first appearance along China's northwestern borders. . . . In the course of the next
two or three centuries, chariotry gradually reverted to its original function as a mobile command platform and a vehicle of prestige."[176] During this time books that discussed military strategy were written. The
most famous of these was *The Art of War,* attributed to legendary strate-
gist Sun Tzu, the chief of staff for the ruler of Ch'i, a major state in the
fourth century.[177]

Sinologist Cho-yun Hsu suggests two reasons why chariots were replaced by infantry: First, chariots were expensive in comparison with
infantry and cavalry; second, chariots were vulnerable or unusable in
swampy and mountainous terrain. Infantry and cavalry were infinitely
more suited to fighting non-Chinese tribes of the mountainous regions
in the north.[178]

The threat of invasion by pastoral peoples to the north arose, and
walls were constructed to prevent their advance. Later these walls were
connected to form what is known as the Great Wall of China. Substantial irrigation works were constructed; irrigation was not important
in the earlier stages of the development of the Chinese state. Human
sacrifice declined. War and battles with huge armies took place between rival states; having 100,000 soldiers on a battlefield, with approximately 50,000 soldiers in each army, was probably not unusual.[179]
The massed infantry of the last century of the Chou dynasty have been
dramatically presented to the modern world in the form of more than
7,000 life-size terra-cotta soldiers unearthed within the burial complex
of the last Chou emperor, who died in 210 B.C.E. after creating the empire known as China in 221 B.C.E. The main body of the actual army
may have totaled 600,000 men.[180] Wars often lasted longer than a year.
Walled cities were sometimes besieged. Lewis notes that "armies dug
tunnels under the walls of besieged towns in order to enter the city or
bring the walls down." Scaling ladders were also used. Hsu writes that
"hundreds of thousands of men were required to seize large cities, and
wars often dragged on for several years."[181]

I have shown how the state in China evolved—in the absence of warfare—from small farming settlements to three-tier settlement hierarchies, a sequence that again supports my thesis. By the inchoate early
state stage, violent power struggles between rival clans within the larger
towns resulted in many deaths. The winners formed ruling lineages that
controlled a growing peasantry who grew millet, domesticated there
four thousand years earlier, and crops obtained from elsewhere. Warfare
between ruling elites of different polities developed. Bronze weapons
were cast. Three major stages of early Chinese warfare can be identi-

fied: (1) a pre-chariot stage in which elite warriors from ruling lineages fought their counterparts from other polities with both projectile and shock weapons; (2) a chariot stage that has three phases—a phase in which elite warriors were transported to battlefields but continued to fight on foot, which eventually gave way to combat between chariot crews drawn from the nobility and finally chariot squadrons performing specialized military tasks on the battlefield; and (3) a post-chariot stage in which massed infantry and cavalry formed an integrated tactical force.

Reflections

In order to construct the descriptions of the four pristine states, it was necessary for me to draw upon archaeological materials as well as descriptions and interpretations by archaeologists. The majority of these archaeologists used interpretations that can be classified as internal conflict theories; for the early stages of the societies they studied, they describe conflict within the polities and not warfare between them. This reliance upon internal conflict theory does not prove the thesis of this book, but it helped me describe the evolution of each pristine state. Together, these descriptions detail an evolutionary track that supports my thesis. While perhaps the majority of archaeologists and military historians subscribe to external conflict theories or conquest theories of the origin of the state, those archaeologists who have directly studied one of the pristine states have a different view.

I have described four pristine states. The striking similarities between them made it possible for me to construct a matrix that outlined the evolution of the pristine state in general terms. It is a description, thus, of how the first state in each region arose, as well as a general statement that supports the internal conflict/political legitimacy theory of the development of the state. I will not repeat that description here.

I will, however, point out the salient features of the evolutionary progression of the pristine state. Through the village, minimal chiefdom, and typical chiefdom stages military organizations and warfare are absent. At the typical chiefdom stage intense rivalry develops among the leaders of kinship groups. At the critical maximal chiefdom/inchoate early state stage factions within polities begin to sort themselves into winners and losers. The winners become the ruling class and select the chief, who becomes a despot. The losers become a victimized lower class. They are forced to contribute to the support of the ruling class, they may be forced to relocate, and they may be subject to human sacrifice—possibly even to cannibalism. I strongly suspect that the human sacrifice that is found in all four of the pristine states in this study originated in the violence that took place just prior to centralization. First it was the killing of rivals and their families; once in a position of dominance, the ruling class killed members of the lower class whenever they chose. A belief system that demanded human sacrifice developed.

Once the ruling class has consolidated its position it engages in combat with the ruling class of another polity. Elite warriors carry out attacks against the settlements of other typical early states. Warfare is a prerogative of the ruling class; the lower class is needed for subsistence activities. Furthermore, the rulers do not want the lower class armed and skilled in weapons use. Rulers fear the prospect of peasant uprisings, so they deliberately leave the lower class unarmed and continued to fortify their own residences. In the New World, elite warfare continued through the next two stages. In the Old World, conscription, producing massed infantry, arose early in Mesopotamia and later in China. This phase of massed infantry was preceded in the Old World by a phase in which rulers attempted to achieve military supremacy by creating mobile, animal-drawn firing platforms, better known as chariots. Massed infantry later appeared in the New World. The progression of warfare shown in Figure 5.2 applies to the Old World states. When the military needed a larger number of soldiers, conscription, massed infantry, and an integrated tactical force were developed. In an evolutionary sense this need developed later in the New World than in the Old World.

I identified an evolutionary sequence that goes from no war, to internal conflict, to combat between elite warriors, to battles between massed infantry. In the Old World, battles in which chariots were used preceded the battles between massed infantry. This evolutionary sequence is not a general one that pertains to all polities—it pertains only to the development of pristine states. In different terms, at the village level we find cooperation within and between villages; at the chiefdom level we find feuding within polities; at the state level, internal war waged by elite warriors; at the empire level, external war waged with massed infantry. For the pristine state, political development means the expansion of coercion from within groups to between groups—from internal coercion to external coercion.

I argued in the last chapter that plant gathering and cultivation in the absence of war led to state formation, that is, *plants* plus *no war* led to *the state*. Our four case studies permit elaboration of that statement. The physical environments in which each of the pristine states arose were different, yet they had in common two ingredients that must be present if agriculture is to flourish: fertile soil and water. The plants were greatly different, but that did not matter: corn in Mesoamerica; the potato and, later, corn from Mesoamerica in Peru; emmer wheat from the Fertile Crescent in Mesopotamia; two species of millet in northern China and, later, rice from southern China. Thus, *plants* plus *soil and water* plus *no war* led to *the state*.

Populations appear to have increased very slowly until the maximal chiefdom stage was reached. Once coercion backed by despotism arose, agricultural intensification occurred. Populations increased. It is the increasing centralization of the polity that is responsible for the increasing productivity— rulers force peasants to grow more produce so they can supply the elites. In this sense, it can be argued that the state produced agricultural intensification rather than that agricultural intensification produced the state. It is during the early state stages that irrigation works were constructed, dams erected, and canals dug. These were "public works" projects undertaken by the state using forced labor. Again, the state produced irrigation, rather than irrigation producing the state.

In the wake of agricultural intensification is to be found the origin of written language in three of the four pristine states. In Mesopotamia the connection is direct. Agricultural produce, which the rulers probably obtained through coercion, was stored in locked rooms in central locations. The content of storerooms was enumerated on clay seals and tablets. Scholars seem to be in unanimous agreement that the cuneiform language arose from this source.[182] Not only can jars of grain be counted, but so can soldiers. Writing must have facilitated the development of a professional military organization in the Early Dynastic period. Commanding officers could receive lists of the number of soldiers available to them and their locations.

In northern China the origin of written language reaches back to the Neolithic. Pottery inscriptions, according to Kwang-chih Chang, "were markers and emblems of families, lineages, clans, or some division of one of these." He further notes, "Membership in one's kin group was the first thing that the first writing recorded, because it was the key to ancient Chinese social order." [183] By the Shang dynasty writing appears on pottery, oracle bones, bronze vessels, wooden bamboo strips that were rolled up, and probably silk. The system of characters that came to form the Chinese written language also had military applications. These uses included the enumeration of captives, the writing of treaties, and the sending of messages. As sinologist Herrlee Creel stated many years ago, "Even in Shang times the sending of letters from one place to another seems not to have been uncommon. In the conduct of war, for instance, reliance was not placed in verbal commands. Written orders were sent, to assure that there would be no mistake in carrying out the projected campaign." [184] When conscription occurred in about 600 B.C.E., it was facilitated by a well-developed written language.

In Mesoamerica, probably starting with the Zapotec in about 600 B.C.E., glyphs were used to list who was killed and later to record events, including cities captured.[185] Written language thus served military affairs, although it did not seem to play a role in organizational matters. In Peru written language did not develop. I believe the lack of a written language greatly hampered the development of the administration of both the state and the army. In Chimú times an unusual and awkward system of separate, overlapping administrations developed. I argued that the failure of Peruvians to devise a writing system was responsible for this unusual sociopolitical system. Or perhaps it was the unusual political system that made it unnecessary to develop a written language.

Written language appears not to be an inevitable consequence of chiefdoms becoming states. On the other hand, the existence of a written language influences matters of statehood and military activities. The uniqueness of each of the three languages, however, caused them to have different impacts upon their respective polities and their military organizations. Languages do not make states, states may or may not make languages.

7
Early States

The description and comparison of the four pristine states raises a number of issues that pertain to not only these states but also early states in general. An extremely important issue is how warfare spreads, first within a region, then beyond, making secondary states out of agricultural villages and herding peoples and also transforming hunter-gatherers and agricultural villagers into tribes. (The development of tribes will be covered in the next chapter.) A second issue is the military organization itself—its structure, how and why it came into being, and the activities it performs. Specifically, two types of professional military organizations are identified: the first, which draws its personnel only from the upper class, and the second, which includes not only the upper class but also lower class personnel conscripted to serve in the military organization. Professional military organizations engage in a pattern of warfare based on battles and sieges. Moreover, the placement of shock weapons in the hands of professional soldiers produces highly lethal warfare. Casualties run high for both sides. A third issue that loomed large in the discussion of each pristine state was the presence of walls and fortifications and their functions. Were walls built to keep out neighbors, raiding parties from other polities, or floodwaters? The topic deserves much more attention. The famous walls of Jericho were largely ignored, and deliberately so, in the chapter on early agriculturalists because I do not believe that they were fortifications. More discussion of Jericho's walls is necessary. A fourth issue concerns the killing of captured enemies—whether warriors or women and children. Captives were subject to human sacrifice in all four pristine states. Through cross-cultural studies it will be shown that the practices of killing captured enemies and human sacrifice are found in early states.

How Secondary States Arose

Warfare spread within a region by attacks and conquests by pristine states. The conquests might have been of other pristine states, or they might have been of chiefdoms or villages within the region. Our four case studies of pristine states amply illustrate these scenarios. After Monte Albán consolidated its position in the Valley of Oaxaca during the typical early state stage, the Zapotec expanded northward out of the valley, conquering less politically developed peoples during the transitional early state stage. An empire was established. Peru presented a more complex situation. Chavín, in the highlands, developed into an inchoate early state but did not develop a substantial military organization. On the North Coast, however, typical chiefdoms of the Moche developed warfare and failed to evolve further until the idea of statehood diffused to them from the Chavín. This pattern is typical of the basic way that new states arose. Leaders of a complex non-state polity learned of the institutions and practices of a state, whether it was a pristine or secondary state, and instituted these practices in their polities. During the typical early state stage the Moche conquered similar peoples to the south and north along the Peruvian coast. During the transitional early state stage they engaged in warfare with culturally different peoples. In Mesopotamia during the Uruk period pristine states developed across the alluvial and Susiana plains. During the typical early state stage city-states waged intense internal wars. Conquests occurred during the transitional early state stage. Eventually Sargon of Akkadia was able to conquer most of the city-states in the region and embark upon campaigns against culturally different peoples. The idea of statehood spread widely. In northern China internal war enabled leaders of towns of the Hsia culture to conquer one another during the typical early state stage. In the Shang period, the transitional early state stage, wars were waged against not only other Chinese peoples but also non-Chinese to the west and northwest. Thus, the four case studies illustrate how the first state-level warfare began within each region between culturally similar peoples and then, as these early states grew larger through conquests, expanded into regions occupied by culturally different peoples. Thus, over time the nature of warfare shifted, from internal to external conflicts.

The idea of statehood, as we have seen, slowly evolved in the four regions where pristine states developed. Henri Claessen and Peter Skalnik, in their comparative study of the early state, found that only two factors were common to all early states: the ideology of statehood and a surplus.[1] Although Claessen and Skalnik viewed these two factors as necessary conditions for the emergence of the state, the four pristine states offer evidence that a substantial degree of centralization preceded the production of a surplus. Wealth differences between individuals or kinship groups in the early stages of sociopolitical development do not constitute a surplus. It was the coercive power of the inchoate early state that forced lower class members to work to produce more than they needed for their own subsistence, thus producing a surplus for the use of the upper class. Susan Pollock refers to this as a tributary economy.[2] A surplus did not create the state, but it was necessary for the continued growth of the state. This statement still leaves the question of how the

idea of statehood arose. Both the internal conflict theory and the supporting archaeological data from the four regions of pristine states suggest that it arose out of factionalism. Once one group was able to dominate another group, the realization that this domination could occur
—and could be advantageous to the dominating group—established
the idea of the state.

A third factor is also present in all early states, whether they be pristine or secondary states: an efficient military organization. Initially the
military organization consisted of supporters of the chief who were able
to hone their martial skills because lower class members were coerced to
produce more and to contribute to the support of the upper class. When
conflict between leaders of rival polities arose, these supporters became
elite warriors who constituted the military organization of the recently
formed state. The major finding of my book *The Evolution of War,* first
published in 1970, made it absolutely clear that a centralized political
system cannot retain its statehood unless it has a military organization
that is militarily sophisticated—a military organization that is as strong
as or stronger than its neighbors'. Moreover, political communities
with high military sophistication scale scores are likely to have expanding territorial boundaries. These efficient military organizations usually
have professional military personnel.[3] This finding is corroborated by
Claessen and Skalnik's comparative study of early states: Most early
states had standing armies, the sovereign was the supreme commander,
and there were military specialists.[4] Thus, the presence of an efficient
military organization appears to be a third necessary condition for state
formation. Indeed, the other two necessary conditions for the formation of a typical early state can be viewed as contributing to the development of a large, efficient, military organization: The idea of statehood
carries with it the notion of sovereignty (a situation that can be maintained only if an efficient military organization is present), and a surplus permits a concentration of people and a channeling of resources
into weapons and subsistence for full-time military personnel.[5]

Once the idea of statehood developed, the idea could diffuse within
the region to agricultural villagers and herding peoples. If those villagers and herders had the potential to produce a surplus, they would
likely become states—secondary states. If not, they would become
tribes. Village leaders, although not able to increase production, would
be able to adopt the weapons and martial values of the elite warriors of
the encroaching state. As it was well argued by Morton Fried, states
make tribes, but tribes do not become states.[6] The idea of statehood
could diffuse further, beyond the region to lands occupied by herding or
hunting and gathering societies. In these new regions there was little
possibility of a surplus being produced unless the size of large animal
herds could be increased. As I argued in the last chapter, plants and fertile, well-cultivated soil, as well as the absence of war, led to the forma-

tion of states. Hunters and gatherers without plants and fertile land could not become states even if their leaders had learned what a state is and how it operates. On the other hand, herding peoples can possibly become states if the circumstances are favorable: if the idea of statehood becomes known to their leaders; if a surplus in, say, cattle can be amassed; and if an efficient military organization can be developed. In chapter 8 I discuss how the Zulu, a cattle-raising Nguni tribe, became a chiefdom and then a state that conquered other Nguni tribes.

Secondary states could arise not only because of the stimulus to development that occurred when the idea of the state became known to non-state agricultural or herding peoples but also when a pristine state or a secondary state fissioned. The breakup of a state, perhaps because rival population centers were able to establish their political independence, resulted in new states. In other words, subordinate leaders developed military organizations loyal to them and thus were able to break away from the capital city. Thus, stimulus diffusion and rebellion are two major ways that new states were created. As new states arose through rebellion or fissioning, more of the earth was ruled by states. This process of state formation continues today (see chapter 9).

Early State Warfare

The cardinal characteristic of the early state is coercion, which lies at the base of early state warfare. It manifests itself in four areas. The first is taxation, or the extraction of a surplus from the lower classes. All four of our pristine states appear to have had tributary economies. This surplus made possible a professional army—a full-time military supported by the lower class. The second area of coercion is conscription, that is, the requirement of military service. By definition, conscription is involuntary service. If elite warriors from the upper class are insufficient in number to produce an efficient military organization, conscription will be instituted. (More details are provided below.) Third, in the military itself, a coercive command structure requires soldiers to follow orders. Military leaders, including the sovereign, can force soldiers to fight even when outnumbered; corporal and capital punishment can be used to enforce compliance. Desertion is usually a capital offense. Fourth, in diplomatic relations, coercive diplomacy dominates. Negotiators from a city-state or multi-tiered polity with a large army threaten attack if a city-state with a small army does not pay tribute or subordinate itself to the larger polity.

Military Organization

The military organizations of early states share many characteristics other than coercion, although coercion is the underpinning of these military organizations. Our four pristine states give us our first look at a type of military organization that nearly all states, including both early states and mature states, have had for the past five thousand years. What is remarkable about this type of military organization is that once developed, it has persisted as an institution virtually unchanged over the millennia. Its chief characteristic is the professionalism of the personnel: They are full-time soldiers, men usually, who train with weapons and also practice in maneuvers.[7]

The pristine states revealed two types of professional military organizations. In the first type, military organizations consisted of elite upper class combatants, soldiers, or warriors. Their leaders were likely to be close kin of the monarch. The military organizations controlled internal security matters and also engaged in armed combat with similar military organizations from rival states. Because of their dual role—keeping the lower class subordinate and battling external enemies—membership in the military was restricted to the upper class. The Zapotec, Moche, Uruk, and Hsia had military organizations with this structure. These military organizations were small in size, and the warriors were well equipped with both offensive and defensive weapons. The primary weapon, however, was a shock weapon that required that the soldiers develop skill in its use. These elite warriors, although organized into units under a royal officer, fought as individuals. Combat was hand-to-hand. Strength, agility, and bravery—particularly bravery—were essential to success. Death or injury and capture befell the soldier who faced a more skilled adversary. The weapon in all four regions was a sophisticated descendant of the club. The Zapotec warrior carried a club with a stone head; the Moche soldier, a mace with a conical or star-shaped head; the Uruk combatant, a stone-headed mace and later a socket ax; and the Hsia warrior, a halberd.

The second type of professional military organization drew members from both the upper and lower classes. Typically the upper class provided the officers and elite forces and the lower class furnished conscripts. The conscripts formed a massed infantry organized into identical units under upper class officers. They were equipped with identical weapons manufactured by full-time craft specialists under governmental supervision. The primary weapon of such a force was either a shock weapon, such as a spear, lance, or pike, or a projectile weapon, such as a bow and arrow, sling, or atlatl. Indeed, it is possible to have both shock weapon units and projectile weapon units in the same army. When an army has two or more kinds of units operating in conjunction, an integrated tactical force has been created. This second type of professional military organization generally arises when there is need—for either defense or attack—for a large army, an army much larger than can be derived from only the upper class. The New World did not produce such military organizations until polities larger than the Zapotec or Moche made their appearance. In the Old World, in Mesopotamia, a massed in-

fantry organized into phalanxes emerged by 2500 B.C.E., and in northern China conscription in about 600 B.C.E. led to the formation of huge
massed infantry formations. Specialized units consisted of first chariots
and then cavalry, in both regions. These elite forces were drawn from
the upper class.

Was this second type of military organization entirely professional or
composed of both professionals and nonprofessionals? I believe these
ancient armies were entirely professional. The conscripts were full-time
military personnel who were equipped by the government and trained
for combat as a unit. A military organization, however, can be composed of both professionals and nonprofessionals if lower class males
join the army for a battle or campaign and bring their own weapons.
In the English-speaking world until the twentieth century, nonprofessional soldiers were formed into militias. Among nonliterate peoples,
armies composed of both professional and nonprofessional soldiers
frequently are found. In my cross-cultural study of war, I found such
armies occurring in nearly 25 percent of the societies in the sample;
armies composed only of professional soldiers were found in approximately 20 percent.[8]

Weapons Control and Conscription

It was suggested above that a military organization that draws from
both the upper and lower classes is present when there is a need for a
large army. Several years ago I developed a theory to predict the conditions under which weapons control and conscription would occur.[9] The
paucity of data in the ethnographic record has prevented me from conducting a cross-cultural study. I present the theory below, illustrating it
with three historical examples and two ethnographic examples. Although I have not been able to prove the theory, I believe the theory and
examples help us to understand the formation of military organizations
in the pristine and early states.

It is a truism that warfare profoundly affects those polities that engage in armed combat—fighting with weapons. One possible result is
the militarization of the political communities, forcing a soldier's life
upon the male population of the polities. One requirement of being a
soldier is ability in the use of weapons. But which males will be allowed
or required to become soldiers is a key issue for a political community.
Thus, those men destined to be soldiers will be required to learn to use
weapons, while men excluded from the military may be prohibited
from owning weapons.[10]

In bands and tribes (uncentralized political systems) every able-
bodied man learns to use weapons from an early age. There is no weapons control imposed by political leaders because leaders do not have the
power to prevent men from having weapons: Men own and keep their
weapons. The training of youth is informal. Youth often make the

weapons for themselves as they reach adulthood. The weapons are likely to be general-purpose projectile weapons used primarily in hunting. What boys learn about using these weapons for the hunt is directly transferred to using them in war. Empirical results from a cross-cultural study of hunting and gathering bands showed that societies dependent upon hunting have a high frequency of warfare. (This study is discussed in the section "Hunting and Gathering Bands" in chapter 4.)

In chiefdoms and states (centralized political systems), both the size of the military aristocracy and the occurrence of warfare influence weapons control and conscription. The size of the ruling/warrior class, in terms of its percentage of the total population of a political community, influences who has weapons in the ways described below.

If the ruling warrior class is large, commoners will not be permitted to have weapons. Commoners are not needed as military, and an armed populace poses an ever-present threat of overthrowing the ruling class. There is also no military conscription of commoners. This situation prevailed at the maximal chiefdom/inchoate early state stage in the development of the pristine state.

If the warrior class is small, commoners must be proficient in the use of weapons if the political community is frequently engaged in warfare. They are needed as military manpower; hence, conscription occurs. This situation prevailed in the later stages of the development of the pristine state, later in the New World, earlier in the Old. Although there is the danger that armed commoners will overthrow the ruling class, the need for help from commoners in waging war is so great that the political leaders must chance it. Furthermore, the wars make the militarized conscripted commoners concentrate on defeating the enemy, diverting them from considering the possibility of overthrowing the ruling class.[11] However, when the political community is not engaged in war, commoners will be prohibited from owning weapons. For a generation, of course, they will retain the knowledge of how to use weapons.

If there is no ruling/warrior class in a political community that frequently engages in warfare, most or all able-bodied men must be able to use weapons. In times of war there is military conscription. In times of peace there is of course no conscription, and although there is no ruling class that could be overthrown, the political leaders may attempt to prohibit weapons ownership. The reasons for this prohibition seem to be diverse; they include crime control and suppression of ethnic conflict. This situation exists in many modern nations, such as the United States.

In centralized political systems, that is, in all three of the situations described above, the training with weapons is likely to be formal as well as informal. Formal training may begin at an early age. Weapons will be specialized, that is, intended for war. They probably are made by full-time craft specialists. The weapons may be issued to rather than owned by the warriors.[12] The theory is summarized in Figure 7.1.

Figure 7.1. The Relationship between Size of Warrior Aristocracy and
Warfare Frequency, and Weapons Control and Conscription.

Type of Situation	Size of Warrior Aristocracy	Frequency of Warfare	Resulting Weapons Control for Commoners	Conscription
I	Large	(Irrelevant)	Prohibited weapons	Absent
II A	Small	Frequent	Weapons encouraged or required	Present
II B	Small	Infrequent	Prohibited weapons	Absent
III A	None	Frequent	Weapons encouraged or required	Present
III B	None	Infrequent	Prohibited weapons	Absent

Examples illustrate and support the theory. The Japanese provide a fine illustration of the first portion (I) of the theory. Historian Noel Perrin, in *Giving Up the Gun,* describes the successful efforts of shoguns and the ruling samurai nobility to outlaw firearms beginning in the early 1600s.[13] Samurai warriors did not want to be killed with guns by non-samurai, or, for that matter, by samurai. The prohibition thus covered samurai as well. Although the Japanese were at war with neighboring countries, such as Korea, the size of and percentage of men in the ruling/warrior class—7 to 10 percent of the population—meant that non-samurai were not needed on the battlefield.[14] Thus, commoners were prohibited weapons, particularly guns, and they were not conscripted into the military.

The second portion of the theory (IIA and IIB) is well supported by English history. The English ruling class has always been small; Perrin pegs it at six-tenths of a percent for the sixteenth century.[15] When military requirements were such that non-nobility needed to be armed, all men were required to possess arms and become proficient in their use. This situation prevailed for seven hundred years. Sen. Orrin Hatch has described the historical situation: "Under the laws of Alfred the Great, whose reign began in 872 A.D., all English citizens from the nobility to the peasants were obliged to privately purchase weapons and be available for military duty."[16] After 1066 archery was encouraged as the national sport. Under the Assize of Arms of 1181, freemen were required to possess certain arms. Then in 1252, during the reign of Henry III, another Assize of Arms required all forty-shilling freeholders to possess a bow and arrow.[17] Senator Hatch writes that in 1511 Henry VIII not only required men to own and practice with the bow and arrow but also required fathers "to purchase bows and arrows for their sons between the age of 7 and 14 and to train them in longbow use."[18] However, in 1514 a ban was placed on firearms. A series of ordinances in 1523, 1528, and 1533 limited possession to those whose incomes were at least one hundred pounds a year. War with France in 1543 led Henry to revoke the controls. "By proclamation," Perrin notes, "he authorized any male from the age of sixteen up to own and use a gun. When peace came again, Henry revoked the revocation. . . . In 1557 there was another war, again with France. Again the gun laws were repealed."[19] Thus, as war waxed and waned for the English, so did weapons control. When there was war, weapons were required; when there was peace, weapons were banned among the lower classes.

A similar situation developed in colonial New England. Authorities in Massachusetts and Connecticut in the 1600s, because of fear of Indian attacks, tried, although not very successfully, to curb Indian ownership and use of firearms. According to historian Patrick Malone, however, "in 1652, the general court of Massachusetts Bay Colony ordered certain Indians to train with muskets in the militia. . . . The threat of war with the Dutch and their Indian allies undoubtedly stimulated the action of the Bay Colony. From 1652 to 1656 all male Indians from sixteen to sixty living with or working as servants of Massachusetts colonists had to attend training days."[20]

The third portion (IIIA and IIIB) of the theory is supported by recent U.S. history. The absence of a military aristocracy and the high frequency of wars, many of a major magnitude, for more than two centuries meant that American males had to be proficient in the use of firearms and had to serve in the military. As the cold war mentality of the post–World War II period subsides, more and more calls are being made for gun control.[21] The theory predicts that calls for gun control will continue, in part driven by the desire to reduce firearms use in crimes. Legislation may follow. However, if the United States becomes involved in major wars again, the theory predicts that such calls will decline and proposed gun control legislation will be set aside. In 2002 and 2003 the United States entered into major combat in Afghanistan and Iraq. It appears that calls for more gun control legislation have declined.

Two excellent examples from the ethnographic literature—the Zulu and the Tonga—also support the third portion of the theory. Under King Shaka (1787–1828) the Zulu evolved from a tribe to a state. How and why this transformation occurred will be described in detail in the next chapter. The increasing frequency and intensity of warfare during the period of Shaka's reign forced military participation upon all adult males. A military aristocracy never had a chance to develop. By the time young Zulu males reported to military kraals in their late teens, they had undergone intensive informal training with weapons. Initiation into age-grade regiments was a mandatory form of conscription.[22] The pattern persisted through the nineteenth century, as the Zulu engaged first one, then another European army in battle.

The Pacific islands of Tonga at this same time period had no warrior aristocracy, although they did have chiefs. As one chief attempted to conquer another chief, the frequency and intensity of internal war increased. That all young men were encouraged to become proficient in weapons use can be inferred from descriptions of both hunting and military bows, as well as the manner in which some men became "professed" warriors. By 1800 conscription was in place.[23]

This brief analysis of weapons control and conscription suggests that warfare per se is a powerful stimulus for weapons use: When war is present, a substantial proportion of the adult male population must become proficient in the use of weapons; when war is absent, at least in centralized political systems, it is likely that a substantial proportion of the adult male population will be prohibited from owning and using military weapons—there will be weapons control and no conscription.

The analysis further shows that within a political unit, warfare, weapons control, and conscription are related. The relationship depends upon the structure of the sociopolitical system—the level of political complexity and the nature of the social stratification system. In uncentralized political systems, which do not have powerful leaders, the ownership of weapons cannot be controlled. In centralized political systems, the presence and size of the military aristocracy—the ruling/warrior class—affects the control of weapons: If the aristocracy is large, it forms the military organization, and it is in the aristocracy's interest to restrict commoners' access to weapons. If there is no warrior/ruling class, or if it is small, commoners must be armed and skilled in the use of arms so that they can participate in the military organization led by military specialists or by the military aristocracy.

When this theory is applied to pristine states, it helps us to understand how military organizations evolved in each region. Both in Mesoamerica and in Peru the aristocracy that emerged in the inchoate early state stage was large in comparison with the lower class, a pattern that continued during the typical early state stage. Zapotec and Moche military organizations were thus composed entirely of warriors drawn from the upper class. Lower class members, however, used simple projectile weapons, such as stones and slings, to defend walled settlements. They did not own or train with maces.

Both in Mesopotamia and in northern China, the first military organizations that we encounter were drawn from the aristocracy. In both regions, in the typical early state stage, the kings developed specialized weapons—cart or chariot squadrons—to give them a military advantage. This stage is one that I identified in both regions as lying between the elite warrior stage and the massed infantry stage. During this second stage some commoners, perhaps retainers, entered the military. During this stretch of time agricultural intensification increased, and so did the population. With an increase in warfare and the emergence of walled city-states, some of the laborers who had produced the surplus that supported warrior aristocracies needed to be enlisted in the military. The newly enlisted persons were probably conscripts, perhaps volunteers. I am only guessing, but I suspect that the size of the lower class grew at a faster rate than the size of the upper class. To increase military efficiency, the rulers of early states in both regions conscripted large numbers of commoners, perhaps reluctantly, because they probably would have preferred that commoners remain in subsistence pursuits or in the manufacture of elite weapons and luxury goods. These armies based on massed infantry are huge, even by modern standards. An army that did not adopt conscription would probably not have been able to achieve victory. There is no evidence that commoners possessed their own weapons, although in Mesopotamia during the Akkadian period weapons have been found in households of the well-to-do.[24] All evidence suggests that in both the second and third stages that I delineated, soldiers were supplied with weapons, generally a spear—a weapon that required little training. Weapons that required skill, such as driving a war chariot or shooting a bow and arrow, remained exclusively in aristocratic hands.

The manner in which military organizations evolved in the four pristine state regions suggests that the theory of weapons control and conscription outlined above is valid. Where data can be found, the theory appears to be supported.

In addition to coercion and professionalism, the military organizations of early states have a number of other characteristics in common. Claessen and Skalnik found that most early states had standing armies, that the sovereign was the supreme commander, and that there were military specialists.[25] It is unfortunate that the data on our four pristine states are scant for these three attributes. Nonetheless, by the time conscription was in place, standing armies were central to the political organization of these societies. There is every indication that the monarch was the supreme commander whether or not he accompanied his army into the field. If he did, the type of leadership he displayed was probably command style—he directed from behind the lines. But the monarch may have exercised heroic style by leading his troops into battle and fighting with the front lines.[26] The Stele of Vultures, from Mesopotamia, shows the king in front of a phalanx that is walking over the defeated enemy. While this sort of leadership might have taken place, I suspect that the portrayal of heroic style is more propaganda than reality.[27] In the Old World there certainly were military specialists; charioteers, the men who drove the chariots, were definitely specialists, and the soldiers—spearmen or archers—who fought from the chariots were specialists also.

Weapons and Tactics

The warfare of early states is based upon battles and sieges. This pattern of war is basic for professional standing armies with a coercive command structure. Deceit in diplomatic negotiations probably played a large role in political relations of early states. Overtures of cooperation and trade may have masked expansion intentions. If a city-state could be assured that it had nothing to fear, it could be vulnerable to a surprise attack. If a surprise attack on a city did not succeed, the attackers and defenders might mass troops and engage in frontal assaults on a battlefield near the defenders' city. Although both ambushes and lines were used, maneuver and flank attacks of the sort later developed by great commanders such as Rameses II, Hannibal, and Alexander did not occur. The larger army was more likely to win; since the largest city-states would have the largest armies, the largest cities would survive. Armies of similarly equipped soldiers that engaged in frontal attacks were found in all four pristine state regions. They are also found among secondary states throughout the world. Coercive diplomacy would have developed. Complex fortifications developed to prevent surprise attack and to make it possible for a city-state with a small army to resist coercive diplomacy and avoid battle with a superior force. Siege operations developed.

Battles and siege warfare thus became the two major tactics of warfare employed by early states. The line was used in battles, but the soldiers in a line were organized into units with their own officers. The only tactic employed was the frontal assault. Battles with such tactics are depicted on buildings and monuments and are recounted in writing. Casualties for this type of battle were high for both sides, with the loser often having extremely high casualties.[28] These high casualties contrast sharply with the line battles that occur in hunting and gathering societies, where either side may withdraw after one or a few casualties, having tested the strength of a rival political community. State-level battles are intended to destroy the adversary, not to test its strength. Classicist Victor Hanson argues that the quest for victory in a *decisive* battle of this sort originated in Greek hoplite warfare (650–338 B.C.E.), but it appears that Thutmose at Megiddo (1458 B.C.E.) and Rameses II at Kadesh (1285 B.C.E.) were seeking decisive victory in battle.[29] I also believe that Sargon of Akkadia, a thousand years earlier, sought victory in decisive battles. Susan Pollock argues as much, noting that "the imagery on the Sargon Stele depicts a military victory complete with the killing and taking of captives."[30]

Siege warfare developed in response to fortifications surrounding towns, cities, or military fortresses. Depending upon whether the polity was a pristine or a secondary state, fortifications had different origins. Regardless of the origin of the walls surrounding settlements, once they are used as fortifications they are maintained, rebuilt, or expanded when there is frequent warfare (see "Walls and Fortifications," below). Sieges consist of encircling a fortified settlement with military forces. The intent is to prevent breakout or escape and to starve the inhabitants into submission. Thus, the encircling army must be prepared at all times to engage in battle an army that comes out from behind its walls. The attacking force might erect walls to provide protection from sudden attack by the defenders. Sieges also consist of attacks upon the settlement's fortifications. For such attacks armies developed techniques for destroying, penetrating, or surmounting the ditches and walls surrounding settlements. Undermining walls by tunneling so that the walls collapse was one means of destruction. Battering rams were used to penetrate gates and walls. Placing scaling ladders against walls permitted soldiers to climb to their top. The walls without defenders would not be fortifications. If there were no defenders, breaking through gates or going over the walls would be easy. What makes walls true defenses is the presence of soldiers with projectile weapons who can shoot the men trying to penetrate the walls or surmount them—an active defense. To prevent these countermeasures, the attackers might house the battering ram in a movable covered structure and place the soldiers in enclosed towers that could be positioned against the walls. These elaborate devices made their appearance well after the emergence of the first states. Siege machines, along with chariots, were the "superweapons" of the Bronze Age. Other elaborate devices, designed to throw rocks or boulders, were developed by the time of Alexander. Usually termed catapults, they were the artillery of the ancient world.[31] By the fourth century B.C.E. catapults were used, first to provide cover for storming parties and later by defenders to keep at bay attackers who were armed with catapults, battering rams, and siege towers.[32]

Fortifications are nearly universally found among centralized political states. My cross-cultural study of war further showed that siege operations were associated with centralized political systems (six out of seven cases—only societies with fortified villages were included in the analysis). Specifically, it showed that if a polity is centralized and if villages in other cultures are fortified, siege operations will be used (seven out or nine cases conformed to the hypothesis).[33]

Walls and Fortifications

Hunters and gatherers did not build walls around their camps; early agriculturalists did not build walls around their settlements. Walls were built only by groups of people who had achieved a level of sociopolitical complexity termed either maximal chiefdom or inchoate early state. Most scholars interpret walls around settlements to be fortifications, and because they are considered fortifications their presence leads to an inference of warfare. However, walls can serve functions other than defense against enemy attack. My assessment of the data in the four case studies, particularly the information about the walls of northern China, has led me to be cautious about assuming that the presence of walls indicates the existence of warfare.

Walls may be constructed for several reasons, and it takes an organized group to erect them. First, walls physically secure a site. A wall can divert floodwaters away from the houses, as I believe was the case in northern China; a wall can block winds that produce dust storms, as might have occurred in the alluvial plains of Mesopotamia, an area also prone to flooding; and, they can block the force of the winds of tropical storms, which occurred along the coast of Peru. Second, walls keep animals and children in, whether the walls are around the settlement or around the houses. This "imprisonment" is for their protection—the walls prevent animals and children from walking or running away.[34] Walls may also keep adults in. When despotism arises, as in the inchoate early state stage and the typical early state stage, the monarch may use walls to prevent the subjects from leaving. Third, walls keep out enemies from other settlements as well as neighbors from within one's settlement. The walls around settlements may be fortifications that block the progress of attackers and provide an elevated platform from which missiles can be launched. The walls around houses may keep out covetous neighbors.[35] In Peru and northern China walls appear to have served the last function. In both locations, for the walls to "work" there must have been residents inside who possessed weapons that could be used against those seeking to enter (an "active defense"). Walls not only provide protection to the inhabitants but also prevent thieves from stealing animals and portable objects. Although harvested produce is usually stored in buildings, walls may protect gardens—the yet-to-be harvested produce—from being damaged or consumed by animals and children who have wandered from their owners or caretakers. Fourth, walls that are wide and flat on the top may be roads or beltways. This situation was probably not a frequent occurrence, but the Great Wall of China had a road on top, and I suspect that the walls of some cities could serve as beltways.[36]

Walls, like all structures built by humans, do not last forever. First, walls can be destroyed by natural disasters—floods, hurricanes, and earthquakes. Destruction by fires is unlikely since most walls, particularly those intended for flood protection or defense, are built of nonflammable materials, such as earth or stone.[37] Second, an uprising of the oppressed lower class can lead to the destruction of walls, as seems to have occurred in North Coast Peru and on the Susiana Plain of Mesopotamia. Third, an attack by raiders or an enemy army can destroy walls, either through siege operations that successfully undermine and breach walls or by deliberate destruction after the settlement or city has been seized. In such attacks, many residents are usually killed—combatants and noncombatants alike. Since walls symbolize the prosperity and permanence of a city, their destruction by attackers has symbolic meaning. Conquerors in Mesopotamia frequently made claims in cuneiform writing that they had destroyed the walls of cities they had conquered.[38] Fourth, a settlement may move to a different location and thus abandon its walls, or the population of a settlement can grow and spread into the area beyond the walls. There would, of course, be no up-keep of such walls; indeed, material from the walls might be used to build new structures.

In the areas where our four pristine states arose, it appears that walls were constructed in the following sequence. Since states arose in these areas before warfare arose, the first walls were built to physically secure sites. However, the walls around residential compounds within larger settlements were fortifications since they separated the upper class from less affluent neighbors. The lower class may have resented their ex-ploitation. Uprisings in Peru and Mesopotamia seem to confirm this theory. Later, forts were constructed at the borders of regions, as in the Valley of Oaxaca and coastal Peru, suggesting that these structures were defenses against attacks by nomads and/or by enemies at a similar level of sociopolitical complexity, most likely an inchoate early state or a typ-ical early state. These forts may also have been staging areas for attacks against other early states. Finally, cities themselves were walled after statehood was firmly established and internal war between city-states became frequent. The sequence for wall construction for pristine states can be diagrammed as follows:

State → Fortifications → War

The diagram, which exaggerates, emphasizes that fortifications and warfare follow—not precede—the development of the pristine state.

The development of fortifications in areas where secondary states arose follows a different sequence; warfare preceded the construction of fortifications and the emergence of the early state. The diagram for the secondary state sequence is the above diagram reversed:

War → Fortifications → State

Although our case studies thus far have been of pristine states, we find evidence to support this sequence in several cross-cultural studies uti-lizing samples that include secondary states.

Perhaps the first cross-cultural study to examine the relationship be-tween the level of political complexity and the presence of fortifications is my study, *The Evolution of War.* That study demonstrated that fortified villages were found in nearly all centralized political systems (that is, chiefdoms and states—thirteen out of fifteen societies) but that only two-fifths of uncentralized political systems (bands and tribes) had fortified villages (ten out of twenty-five societies). There is thus a rela-tionship between political centralization and the erection of fortifica-tions; centralized political systems are more likely than uncentralized political systems to have fortifications.[39] I offered the following expla-nation for the relationship: There must be a sufficient degree of political centralization in the society for fortifications to be constructed. Only leaders in centralized political systems—chiefs and kings—have the authority to organize the villagers for the purpose of building fortifications. Political authority goes hand-in-hand with the construction of fortified villages, a relationship that supports the second half of the paradigm. Are fortifications the result of warfare? The relationship between the frequency of internal war—war with other polities within the culture—and the presence of fortifications, the first half of the paradigm, can be examined with data from my study.[40] Nearly every society that had fortified villages engaged in continual or frequent internal war (fifteen out of eighteen societies), and just over half of the societies without fortified villages had continual or frequent internal war (ten out of nineteen societies). There is thus a relationship or correlation between the frequency of internal war and village fortifications.[41] It should be noted that village fortifications predict continual or frequent warfare (fifteen out of eighteen societies), while war does not predict village fortifications (fifteen out of twenty-five societies).[42] The three societies with fortifications that did not have frequent internal war engaged in continual or frequent external war—war with polities of different cultures. Thus, all societies with village fortifications do have warfare with either culturally similar or culturally different polities.

Two other cross-cultural studies have examined fortifications and warfare frequency. Anthropologist Donald Griffiths explicitly designed a cross-cultural study to provide archaeologists with an ethnographic analogy that would allow them to infer warfare from the presence of village fortifications. Nearly every society that had village fortifications had a high frequency of war (twelve out of fifteen societies), and less than one-quarter of the societies without village fortifications had a high frequency of war (ten out of forty-four). Moreover, the presence of village fortifications predicted war (twelve of fifteen societies), but war did not predict village fortifications (twelve out of twenty-two societies.)[43] Griffiths furthermore conducted a multivariate analysis, including as a variable mid-range sociopolitical level (that is, societies that fall between bands and states in their social and political complexity); he derived the following causal model:

Warfare → Village Fortifications → Mid-Range Sociopolitical Level

This model matches the diagram that I posited for the secondary state sequence.[44]

Another cross-cultural study, by archaeologist Peter Peregrine, developed a permeability scale. Various architectural features of a settlement were evaluated as to the degree to which they would impede the advance of attackers; the scale ranged from 0 to 4, with 4 representing the most elaborate and effective set of fortifications. Peregrine found that the permeability scale was related to the frequency of warfare. A high permeability scale score (3 or 4) was associated with a high frequency of war (3, 4, or 5 on a 5-point scale) (seven out of seven societies), while a low permeability scale score (1 or 2) was associated with a low frequency of war (1 or 2) (ten out of fifteen societies). Specifically, a high permeability scale score predicted a high frequency of warfare (all seven out of seven societies), but war did not predict a high permeability scale score (only seven out of twelve).[45]

Thus, three cross-cultural studies have demonstrated a relationship between the frequency of warfare and village fortifications. Furthermore, they show that village fortifications predict a high frequency of war, while war does not predict fortifications.[46]

Several interpretations can be drawn from these cross-cultural studies. First, a low frequency of warfare went hand-in-hand with the absence of village fortifications. Second, warfare was likely to precede village fortifications in an area. The distribution of the data suggests the following: Cases of warfare and no fortifications outnumber cases of no warfare and fortifications (that is, if there is no war, why have fortifications?). Third, once warfare was established in an area, large settlements became fortified. Fourth, as warfare spread, villages became fortified. These interpretations support the secondary state sequence, diagrammed above.

No discussion of walls and fortifications would be complete without an examination of the walls of Jericho. Most scholars uncritically view them as evidence of early warfare. Given the correlations between warfare and fortifications found in the ethnographic record, as discussed above, this view seems reasonable. Jericho, the first town, dated to about 8300 B.C.E., was surrounded by a moat and wall; inside the wall was a tower. Moats, walls, and towers are considered the three basic elements of military architecture until the gunpowder age.[47] Scholars who interpret the walls as evidence for warfare include Claudio Cioffi-Revilla, Barbara Ehrenreich, Arther Ferrill, John Keegan, Robert O'Connell, and Richard Wrangham and Dale Peterson.[48]

Some voices, including my own, question whether the walls were fortifications and hence evidence for early warfare. Archaeologist Marilyn Roper contends that "aside from the defensive structures . . . there are no further signs of warfare." Richard A. Gabriel suggests that the walls were "to protect the fields against animals. . . . Later, and somewhat incidentally, the walls would have served as protection against scavenging by semi-nomadic bands."[49] The most serious doubts come from archaeologist Ofer Bar-Yosef, who, after a detailed investigation of the site, concludes "that a plausible alternative interpretation for the Neolithic walls of Jericho is that they were built in stages as a defense system against floods and mud flows."[50] It was Bar-Yosef's conclusion that the walls of Jericho were for flood control that led me to interpret the walls around early settlements in northern China as flood protection. At Jericho the moat could have been produced as a by-product of wall construction; it also would serve to divert water from the walls and town. A tower inside a wall, such as Jericho's, has limited military usefulness. In later times towers were erected against the outer walls of fortifications. Positioned there, sentries, archers, and slingers could easily see and take aim at any attackers attempting to breach or climb the walls. Jericho's tower inside the wall is an enigma. It was constructed of solid stone with a staircase in the center.[51] Bar-Yosef suggests "ritual significance," but this explanation does not indicate how the tower was used for any ritual. The only suggestion I can offer is that it was a means for climbing to the top of the wall, where villagers could look out to see approaching visitors and wild animals.

I believe there are three good reasons for doubting that the walls of Jericho were fortifications. First, there is no evidence for warfare at or near the walls, such as embedded arrow points or piles of sling stones, nor are such artifacts found in the region. This lack of evidence for war has been noted by both Roper and Bar-Yosef. The masterful summary of the Neolithic of the Near East by James Mellaart provides no evidence for warfare, although he accepts the walls as fortifications.[52] Second, Jericho was a settlement of perhaps two thousand people occupying about ten acres with their round houses and fields. The wall probably had a circumference of at least seven hundred meters. The inhabitants of Jericho cultivated wheat and barley apparently brought from the uplands to the east. They had no domesticated animals. Although they were hunters of gazelles—a factor that might lead us to predict warfare—hunting was on the decline because the population of migrating gazelles was declining. The walls would have prevented migrating gazelles from entering the village in the spring and foraging on the villagers' crops. Possibly the walls were, in part, erected for that purpose, and the tower could have served as a lookout station. The people of Jericho thus were early agriculturalists who had recently been settled hunter-gatherers. According to the theory I set forth in chapter 4, the people of Jericho had put warfare behind them. Third, Jericho was at the village stage of sociopolitical organization, or possibly the minimal chiefdom stage. The people of Jericho erected their walls more than five thousand years before the first states arose in Mesopotamia; 8300 B.C.E. is not a period of complex sociopolitical organization. It is doubtful that there could have been sufficient political leadership, in what must have been a kinship-based society, to require adults to serve as sentries. Furthermore, if Jericho was attacked, leaders would have needed to mount an active defense: They would have needed to send parties of soldiers to stations on the walls to prevent the enemy from scaling them. Walls are not fortifications unless there is a military organization that utilizes them in warfare. Even if the walls and moat were built as fortifications, they probably never saw a battle. Without other evidence of warfare in the area, they remain an anomaly of no significance to the study of the origins of war.

Killing of Captured Enemies

Battles between early states resulted in high casualties for both the losers and the winners. For military analysts the term "casualties" includes both dead and wounded. In battles between massed infantry, casualties may have been nearly equal until one side—the losers—fled or retreated. Fleeing soldiers, wounded and captured or captured uninjured, were likely to be killed immediately, killed at the end of the day, or taken to the victors' capital and there publicly executed. These latter killings may be human sacrifice. This type of human sacrifice occurs in all four pristine state regions and in many other early states.

In my cross-cultural study of warfare I examined casualty rates, which I defined as deaths upon the battlefield. If more than one-third of the combatants were usually killed while the military organization was employing its most efficient type of military formation, the society was classified as having high casualty rates; if less than one-third were usually killed, the society was classified as having low casualty rates.[53] I argued that military organizations with a high degree of sophistication are able to sustain direct and prolonged contact with the enemy. This tactic is efficient because the military organization can inflict heavy casualties upon the enemy at close quarters and for an extended period of time. But the enemy in turn has the same opportunity to inflict heavy casualty rates. I found that the higher the degree of military sophistication, the higher the casualty rate.[54]

Recently I conducted a cross-cultural study to establish the extent to which victorious warriors kill captured enemy warriors as well as women, children, and other noncombatants, and to examine the conditions under which such postcombat killing occurs. I sought and found those conditions in the type of political system of the victor.[55] Of the forty-two societies for which the relevant data were available, thirty-nine killed captured enemy warriors. Captured warriors were never spared in twenty-eight of these societies; thus, only in fourteen societies—one-third—were captured enemy soldiers spared or sometimes spared. The political systems most likely to kill captured soldiers were despotic states (early states), chiefdoms, and dependent native people (nonliterate peoples incorporated into a state). These political systems are also the most likely to kill all enemies, combatants and noncombatants alike. It is the societies that nearly always kill captured enemy warriors that kill women and children; half of the despotic states, chiefdoms, and dependent native peoples do not spare women and children. I concluded, "Presumably the killing of women and children is part of the pattern of terror that these societies pursue."[56] The findings of this study are consistent with the finding that the four pristine states definitely killed captured enemy warriors and probably their wives and children.

In the study I also focused upon four types of uncentralized political systems: first, tribe with a council of elders and no feuding; second, tribe with a council of elders and feuding; third, tribe with no council and feuding; and, fourth, band.[57] The vast majority of these societies spare women and children (twenty-two out of twenty-six). When the centralized political systems were contrasted with the uncentralized political systems, I found that the former were three times more likely to kill women and children. Additional data collected, but not included in the study, showed that women are often taken as mates and their children adopted, whether the victors are from centralized or uncentralized political communities. Women and children might also be made slaves or sold into slavery. More than half of the centralized political systems took captives as slaves (nine out of seventeen societies). Surprisingly, more than one-fourth of the uncentralized political systems took captives as slaves (seven out of twenty-six societies); the captives were sometimes sold to members of centralized political systems. I concluded that "it appears that the vast majority of societies want women and children—indeed, the acquisition of women and children may be a goal or reason for going to war."[58] I went on to note that even societies with feuding seldom kill noncombatants (one out of five). A possible reason is that feuding societies are often polygynous and can easily incorporate captive women as wives.[59]

The killing of captured enemy warriors may, in some societies, become an institutionalized religious practice. The sacrifice of war captives may have arisen in the following fashion: The faction that came to power in the inchoate early state stage achieved its dominant position through killing rivals and members of their families. Once the upper class was established, it could select lower class members from time to time to be executed. The executed might be criminals (a likely crime would be a property crime against an upper class person), or they might be innocents selected for human sacrifice. The next stage was to execute prisoners of war. Captives might be killed at the battlefield site or taken to the victors' capital, where they were executed in public, with the entire populace able to attend—if they wished—as spectators. In pristine states the practice is expanded and connected to beliefs in the supernatural. In his cross-cultural study, sociologist Dean Shiels describes human sacrifice as a way to "approach the spirit world" and as an "institutionalized religious practice."[60] Just as mutilation of victims within the polity occurred during the inchoate early state stage, mutilation of war captives occurred during the typical early state stage. Degrading the enemy thus was a feature of the killings. The four pristine states in this study differ in their practices. The Zapotec removed hearts and genitals, the Peruvians cut off heads, the Chinese bound and buried, and the Mesopotamians may have followed the last practice, but the record is unclear. Executions were ceremonially elaborate and connected to beliefs in the supernatural; in pictorial representations from ancient Peru the execution ritual looks like a masquerade party with extravagant costumes for the participants. Often the intent was to appease or please a deity. I believe that in many situations there is a fine line between the execution of war captives and human sacrifice. In the first case, the captive may be hated or deemed a criminal; in the second, the motive may be to please ancestors or supernatural beings.[61]

Various functions are served by human sacrifice. Help from deities is obtained; an enemy is disposed of; public entertainment is provided; in the New World, where the sacrificed were eaten, protein was added to the diet; and the power of the monarchy is shown. One feature of human sacrifice, and indeed executions in general, is often the degradation and humiliation of the victims. They may be naked, they may be tortured, and body parts—genitals, intestines, and hearts—may be removed. Death, certainly in the New World, was made as painful as possible for the victims.

Allowing condemned persons to commit suicide, as in Japan, is a way of allowing victims to retain their high status. It also prevents someone of lower status from executing the condemned.[62] Indeed, Japanese general Hideki Tojo attempted suicide prior to the Tokyo war crime trials after World War II. He survived and was tried, convicted, and hanged.[63]

Dean Shiels showed human sacrifice to be common in 18 out of 106 societies in the Human Relations Area Files. He further showed a relationship between human sacrifice and the presence of slavery and full-time craft specialists.[64] Thus, human sacrifice appears to arise in societies with a surplus, which is generated by slaves and full-time craft specialists, and a surplus, as we saw earlier, arises after centralization has emerged. My cross-cultural study of the killing of captured enemies suggests that human sacrifice may be restricted to those centralized political systems that are chiefdoms and despotic states; they are also the societies most likely to kill captured enemy warriors. Twenty-one societies in Shiels's study are in the Human Relations Area Files 60-society sample that I used in both my cross-cultural study of capital punishment and my study of the killing of captured enemies. Nine are centralized political systems; thus, it is possible with these societies to test the hypothesis that despotic states and chiefdoms are more likely to have human sacrifice than are mature states and dependent native peoples (see Figure 7.2). Although the numbers are small, there is a relationship. The 1 chiefdom and 4 despotic states had human sacrifice; it was "common" in 4 societies and occurred "sometimes" in 1 society. On the other hand, of the 3 mature states and 1 dependent native people, only 1 case had human sacrifice; there were 3 societies in which human sacrifice was "absent."

The remaining twelve societies from the overlapping samples provide another interesting result. If tribes with councils of elders are con-

Figure 7.2. Relationship between Type of Political System and the
Occurrence of Human Sacrifice

Type of Political System	Occurrence of Human Sacrifice		
	Absent	Sometimes	Common
Chiefdom and Despotic State	0	1	4
Mature State and Dependent Native People	3	0	1
Tribe with Council of Elders	1	4	2
Tribe with No Council and Band	5	0	0

trasted with tribes without councils and bands, another strong relationship is found. Of the seven societies with councils only one does
not have human sacrifice, while four sometimes have human sacrifice
and two commonly do. Of the five societies without councils (tribes and
bands), none had human sacrifice. This relationship clearly shows that
to have any human sacrifice, councils must be present.[65] Although not
predicted in advance, as was the relationship of despotic states and
chiefdoms to human sacrifice, this relationship makes sense. Human
sacrifice is an act of a community as a whole. While kinship groups or
sections of a community could sacrifice one of their own, as in the biblical story of Abraham and his son Isaac in Genesis, chapter 22, the data
suggest that it does not occur. The communal nature of human sacrifice
suggests a sixth function, namely, that the social solidarity of the
community, whether it be a tribal society with a council, a chiefdom, or
a despotic state, is enhanced. Many social scientists have argued during the past hundred years that ceremonies performed publicly bring
people together so that they can reaffirm their beliefs in front of fellow
villagers.[66]

8
Tribes

A tribe is not an evolutionary stage between a hunting and gathering band and a chiefdom. Tribes derive from bands, hence the warfare patterns of bands and tribes are similar. Tribes do not conquer each other and become chiefdoms, nor do tribes become states. Three examples of warring nonliterate peoples serve to illustrate why this transformation does not occur.

Tribal Warfare

Tribal warfare, like the warfare of hunting and gathering bands, follows a basic pattern consisting of ambushes and lines. Bands became tribes after they adopted agriculture and/or animal husbandry and became less dependent on their hunting and gathering way of life. Even with the change in sociopolitical structure that followed the adoption of new subsistence technologies, they did not develop a new pattern of warfare—they continued to use ambushes and lines. However, the warfare of tribes differs in scope from that of bands of hunter-gatherers. It also, of course, differs greatly from the warfare of early states, which as we have seen is based upon a pattern of battles and sieges. Bands became agricultural villages when seeds and the knowledge of how to grow plants and how to harvest crops spread or diffused to the hunter-gatherers who occupied lands where agriculture could flourish. Bands adopted animal husbandry when domesticated animals and the knowledge of how to breed them and utilize them for food and for work diffused to the hunter-gatherers whose lands were suitable for raising livestock. Diffusion occurs in culture contact situations, whether the contact between the peoples is friendly, such as trading, or hostile, such as war. Trade may arise between hunter-gatherers and agricultural villagers; war may arise from the spread of villages into the hunting and gathering territories of bands, or from the attacks of hunter-gatherers upon villages. Indeed, war may arise simultaneously in both ways.[1]

Since military organizations and the way they wage war emerge from the sociopolitical organization of a society, it is necessary to first focus briefly on that organization before describing tribal warfare in detail. The hallmark of most tribes is a system built from kinship groups.

Hunter-gatherers have nuclear families consisting of mother, father, and children; extended families spanning three generations; and, sometimes, fraternal interest groups. All are kinship groups. The classic interpretation of how tribes emerged from bands of hunter-gatherers is that through fissioning of a group, two or more groups of related people come to occupy adjacent territories. The kinship groups now cut across local groups (local groups that are now sedentary) and form pan-tribal sodalities or lineages. Lineages are descent groups, either patrilineal or matrilineal, and it is possible to find kin groups based upon both patrilineal and matrilineal descent. If the core membership of a sodality is male, the kin groups are known as patrilineages; if the core membership is female, matrilineages. Patrilineages are far more common than matrilineages; probably three times as many cultures in the ethnographic record have patrilineages as have matrilineages. This fact is related to the great likelihood that male kin reside together: Males live with or near their fathers and bring their wives to live with them — the custom of patrilocal residence, which creates fraternal interest groups. In the classic interpretation, patrilocal residence also leads to patrilineal descent. On the other hand, if females live with or near their parents and bring their husbands to live with them, a custom known as matrilocal residence arises. Matrilocal residence leads to matrilineal descent.[2]

Related males living together are able to cooperate in activities such as hunting and defense. If animals have declined in number in a region and people have become sedentary — and agriculture promotes that transition — hunting and defense are likely to be of less importance. Matrilocal residence can arise in such an environment. Such villages preceded the emergence of chiefdoms. Tribes, on the other hand, emerged from bands through the expansion of chiefdoms and states, and tribes engaged in warfare. While the classic interpretation is that matrilocal residence arose in peaceful agricultural villages, one anthropologist, William Divale, has a different explanation. Divale argued that matrilocal residence was a response to the extreme warfare that occurred when a tribal society — which was probably patrilocal and patrilineal — migrated into a region occupied by other peoples. Intense warfare led to high male casualties. Under such circumstances fathers, who may have lost sons, insisted that their daughters remain at home and that men who wished to marry the daughters must agree to reside with their fathers-in-law. In two separate studies, Divale found that recent migration was associated with war between culturally different societies and with matrilocality.[3]

A tribal-level political unit with patrilineages probably has a military organization drawn from these lineages. Unlike fraternal interest groups that, by definition, are localized groups, lineages have members in multiple adjacent villages. The major implication of this is that there may be dozens of military organizations within a tribe. If the region where the villages are located is densely populated, hundreds of warriors may be able to converge on a battlefield in several hours. Yet the basic military units—the components of the larger lineage-based military organization—may be fraternal interest groups, one or more drawn from each village. The potential for conflict between fraternal interest groups, even from the same lineage, is an ever-present possibility, but being in a state of war with neighbors often results in greater cohesiveness of the lineage. On the other hand, the military organization of a political unit with matrilineages is likely to be drawn from the male population of a large number of villages that have peaceful relationships with each other. The basic military units, composed probably of unrelated males, come from each village. Although the military organization of the entire network of villages will have members related to each other, kin will be in different basic units. These military organizations also may be able to put hundreds of warriors into the field.

In the military organizations of patrilineal political units, the military leaders are the leaders of their kinship groups, with the head of the lineage in command; in those of matrilineal polities, the military leaders are village leaders, with the headman of the most important or largest village in command. In both types of military organizations men who are highly skilled in combat may become both military and political leaders; indeed, in some societies military ability is an attribute of political leadership. A skilled warrior may become the head of a fraternal interest group in his village. Or, as occurs in some societies, those men who are skilled enough to lead successful raids or to kill adversaries on the battlefield may be honored with a special designation. The Higi of northeastern Nigeria had, in addition to a war leader, *katsala*.[4] These men can be viewed as the equivalent of American fighter pilots who become aces after shooting down five enemy planes.

Except for isolated peoples such as the Toda and Tikopia, discussed earlier, tribes almost invariably have warfare. There is, however, great variation in the types and frequency of warfare. I have distinguished between internal and external warfare. Internal war takes place between polities within the same culture, and external war takes place between polities in different cultures. The rationale for the distinction is simple—waging war is a part of a culture. Peoples within the same culture probably wage war in the same way, using, for example, the same types of military organization and weaponry, while peoples from two different cultures probably wage war differently. In a cross-cultural study I have shown that societies with fraternal interest groups are likely to engage in internal war.[5] Using the same sample, I later demonstrated that societies with a high degree of military sophistication, whether they were uncentralized or centralized political systems, were likely to attack culturally different neighbors, that is, to engage in offensive external war, and to expand territorially.[6] Divale later found a relationship between migration and external war. A high degree of military sophistication seems to both create the offensive external war and lead to migration-expansion. A culture that expands territorially I deem to be militarily successful. Thus, the two types of warfare are caused—perhaps too strong a term, but I believe an accurate one—by different features of the sociopolitical system: Fraternal interest groups lead to internal war, while a high degree of military sophistication leads to external war.

The basic pattern of ambushes and lines has a logic that has not been recognized by most scholars who have studied the warfare of nonliterate peoples. Historians in particular have focused on line battles, noted the low casualty rates, and concluded that primitive warfare is ritual. They have overlooked the importance of ambushes; in many tribal societies, and band societies as well, heavy casualties occur in ambushes.[7] One frequently finds uncentralized political systems with the basic pattern of warfare: ambushes, often in conjunction with raids, yielding high casualties, and line battles, yielding low casualties. Line battles appear to be a testing of strength, whereas the ambush is the tactic chosen to inflict great casualties or to destroy an enemy village. It was suggested in chapter 4 that Tiwi arranged battles may have been a testing of strength and the sneak attacks a means to kill adversaries.[8]

The testing of strength in a line battle is also well illustrated by the Dani, a tribal group in Highland New Guinea. The Dani arranged line battles that produced few casualties, staged ambushes that produced a few more, and launched massive dawn raids that killed hundreds. Battles were a means of testing the strength of an adversary. Over a several-month period punctuated by the occasional battle or ambush, one side would slowly succumb to more casualties than the other side. If this polity appeared weak in the eyes of its adversary, the adversary and a neighboring polity might join forces and annihilate the weaker one in a dawn raid.[9]

The use of an ambush or a dawn raid breaks a stalemate. Parity in group size and weaponry can make tribal warfare indecisive. To break a stalemate political leaders devise strategies for overcoming the indecisiveness of battle. The Dani dawn raid is such a strategy. In South America, the Yanomami of the Amazon raided each other, but their fortified villages defended by fierce warriors generally kept attackers at bay. To break the stalemate one village would secretly ally itself with an ally of its enemy. The betraying friend would invite its erstwhile ally to a feast. Then the hosts and their new allies, who had secretly surrounded the village, would attack. As the guests fled the village, many males would be killed. The women, who remained within the village, would be seized and divided between the two new allies.[10]

Tribes Do Not Become States

Although peaceful agricultural villages once became states, tribes—whether their subsistence is based upon agriculture, herding, or hunting—rarely become states. Since nearly all tribes have warfare, and tribes are politically less complex than chiefdoms and states, many social scientists have been "tricked" into believing that centralized political systems arise when the villages of tribal peoples conquer each other—the conquest theory of the origin of the state. It is a conjectural theory; there is no empirical basis for it. Neither archaeological nor ethnographic data support the theory; the data from the four pristine states do not support the theory, nor do data from a huge number of ethnographies of tribal societies.

I have chosen three societies to illustrate what happens when warring tribes engage in intense, frequent, offensive external war—two patrilocal-patrilineal, the other matrilocal-matrilineal. The societies are among anthropology's best described cultures, and their members have played significant roles for centuries in the countries where they reside—Sudan, the United States, and South Africa. They are the Nuer, the Iroquois, and the Zulu. The Nuer and Zulu are pastoral peoples at the northern and southern ends of the East African Cattle Area. The Iroquois are a horticultural and hunting people. The Nuer and Iroquois cases clearly show that "conquest" does not lead to the state. The Zulu are the only example I have found that appears to support the conquest theory of the state. I have included the Zulu because they appear to be the exception that proves the rule—tribes do not become states.[11]

Nuer versus Dinka

The first case study examines the conflict between the Nuer and the Dinka. Both the Nuer and the Dinka were polygynous patrilineal cattle herders. Cattle were valuable not only for sustenance, but for bride price—payment for wives.[12] The rapid expansion of the Nuer at the expense of the Dinka in the nineteenth century has been called a "conquest."[13] Use of the term "conquest" implies political incorporation, which could be the initial stage in the development of a state. But political incorporation did not occur. The Nuer conquest was a territorial expansion that drove the Dinka from their lands. The classic explanation for Nuer territorial expansion is that they had a segmentary lineage system based upon patrilineal descent. With population growth a lineage fissioned and the new lineages would feud, thus forcing these new segments apart and onto new lands. If the lands were occupied by other peoples, usually Dinka, war resulted. Former feuding Nuer lineages would unite—at least temporarily—to battle the Dinka. In order for the lineages to unite, their feuds needed to be resolved, mediated by "leopard skin chiefs," who were religious leaders, not war leaders. In warfare,

Nuer killed Dinka males and seized cattle and women. Nowhere in the literature on this conflict is there a suggestion that the Nuer increased in political complexity as a result of their territorial expansion. There is also not the slightest hint that the line battles that occasionally occurred were ritual warfare. What happens when warring tribes engage in intense and frequent external war is that one tribe is the winner and the other the loser. The tribe that is the winner may expand territorially, but it does not become a state. The case study that follows attempts to answer the question: Why did the Nuer expand?

I suggest that when one group expands at the expanse of another it is because of superior military efficiency. In reviewing theories of war in 1973, I asked if it were the military abilities of the Nuer that were responsible for their geographical expansion.[14] My question was not answered, so in the 1990s I attempted to answer it myself. E. E. Evans-Pritchard, Raymond Kelly, and Douglas Johnson provide information indicating that the Nuer were superior in military efficiency to their Dinka neighbors. Evans-Pritchard was an ethnographer who studied the Nuer in the field, Kelly is an anthropologist who based his research on published and primary sources, and Johnson is a historian who did the same.[15] Primary information comes from nineteenth-century English explorer John Petherick.[16]

The major period of Nuer expansion was about 1820 to 1860.[17] I suggest that it developed in the following manner. I use the term "expansion"; the term "conquest," used by Evans-Pritchard, I think is too strong. It is states that conquer each other; tribes such as the Nuer and Dinka typically defeat each other, with the defeated withdrawing and the winner expanding. Evans-Pritchard states that "absorption and miscegenation" were the result of the "conquest" (expansion). Indeed, Johnson speaks of "extensive intermarriage and mixed settlements." Since the Nuer and the Dinka are closely related peoples who speak similar languages, absorption and intermarriage easily occurred.[18]

Three sets of material causes displaced some settlements of Nuer, as well as Dinka. Johnson describes how both environmental and social factors led to conflict in the early nineteenth century. First, floods forced Nuer across major rivers. When waters rose, one group would drive another off high ground. Second, internal political disputes split both Nuer and Dinka groups. Further disruption of peoples in the area was caused by displaced groups of Nuer attacking Shilluk, who in turn attacked Nuer. According to Johnson, Nuer raids did not cause the migrations—they "were incidental to the original reasons for migration."[19] Third, first Egyptian, then Arab military expeditions for slaves took hundreds of Dinka captive from 1821 onward, weakening those people and putting them on the defensive. The Nuer were relatively unaffected by the slave trade, at least directly.[20]

When displaced settlements came in contact, fighting was often the result. The initial cause could have been either the desire or need for sustenance (in this case cattle and grain), habitation sites, or women. (I believe these are the three basic or primary reasons for going to war.) Habitation sites may have been the most likely cause. Once fighting led to displacement, the domino effect would have spread warfare across the region. Thus, defense/revenge, a universal reason for going to war, would have drawn all the Nuer and Dinka groups into a "war system."[21]

Those groups with superior military efficiency would win and displace the less efficient groups. The Nuer needed a lot of cattle to pay bride prices, which Kelly indicated were much higher than Dinka bride prices, but that economic necessity does not explain Nuer military efficiency.[22] It may have made Nuer warriors eager to go on cattle raids, just as Plains Indians such as the Sioux and Cheyenne readily raided their neighbors for horses, but going on a raid to fill an economic need is no guarantee of military success.[23] If the stolen cattle are for bride prices and Dinka women are also captured in raids, it can be argued that women, not cattle, are the major reason the Nuer went to war. No bride price is paid for a captured bride. A brief analysis of Nuer military weapons and tactics makes clear why the Nuer won.

John Petherick and his wife obtained limited information on Nuer combat from a chief, Shotbyl, on April 22, 1863, on the White Nile near the mouth of the Bahr el Ghazal. Their published diary contains this description:

> The Nouaer tribes are greatly divided, each community having an independent chief. They frequently war on each other for the sake of cattle; no prisoners are made, but men's lives were taken without scruple, whilst the women and children are ever respected. If threatened by enemies not of their tribes, feuds between themselves are suspended temporarily, and they fight in common against the invaders. Shotbyl can raise nine hundred fighting men. They carry a bow turned like a shepherd's crook at both ends, a club, and a large lance; the club is thrown at an enemy, but the lance is never parted with. . . . Men killed in battle are left on the field, but the wounded are carried off.[24]

The use of weapons is described at other points in the diary. Each warrior, including chiefs, carried a wooden club and a lance.[25] The club can be "dexterously thrown" and, in the case reported, it killed a man.[26] In an attack upon missionaries the Nuer warriors "suddenly dashed at them, and, hurling their clubs with vexatious precision, followed up their villainous attack with lances." The Dinka, who "reside in far-distant, isolated stockaded enclosures," would have been vulnerable to surprise attack and outnumbered by the attacking Nuer if the chief's figure of nine hundred fighting men is correct.[27] The stockaded enclosures were probably, according to anthropologists Charles G. Seligman and

Brenda Seligman, "cattle kraals, sometimes but not always surrounded by a thorn fence."[28]

For the major period of expansion, Nuer/Dinka military history is described in some detail by Douglas Johnson. Floods, as noted above, set populations in motion. At the beginning of the nineteenth century one Nuer group, the Jikany, "was virtually annihilated in war with the Western Dinka; this was one reason the Jikany looked for safer lands to the east," Johnson wrote. The eastward-moving Jikany attacked Nyiel Dinka settlements: "Their tactic of infiltrating Nyiel camps at night and then attacking at dawn simultaneously from within and without was designed to scatter the Nyiel warriors, leaving cattle, women, and children behind undefended." As Nuer entered the region north of the Sobat River, they established settlements. Tensions developed between old and new settlers, with the newcomers "initiating raids against Dinka to the east and north." Another group of Nuer, the Gaawar, moved eastward in the 1830s when their land was flooded, and at Pakuem they attacked the Lauc Dinka, who had an abundance of cattle and grain. They were apparently successful, Johnson writes, because "the two halves of Gaawar, Radh and Bar, combined to fight the Dinka."[29]

Nuer military organization was village based—men fought by villages—and each military unit was based on a local group. Unlike cattle-herding people to the south, such as the Zulu, the Nuer did not employ age-grade regiments cutting across local groups.[30] Nuer warriors could travel rapidly on foot for two days, carrying nothing but spears, not even food. The shield, says Evans-Pritchard, was not carried because the Nuer regarded fighting the Dinka "so trifling a test of valour." From Petherick we know that clubs and lances were carried, not shields. The shield, if they even had shields, would have been an unnecessary encumbrance. Spears or lances, as described above, were used as shock rather than projectile weapons. Dinka villages or camps were attacked at dawn. Surprised and probably outnumbered, the Dinka "seldom put up any resistance, but loosened their cattle and tried to drive them away." Women of marriage age, boys, and girls were taken captive. Old men and women and babies were clubbed to death.[31] Wounded Dinka warriors were probably killed ("men's lives were taken without scruple," states Petherick); Dinka are reported as killing fallen warriors.[32] Nuer, rather than Dinka, were usually the attackers since it was they who were more frequently displaced from their villages by floods. The Dinka were already "softened up" by Egyptian and Arab slave raids. The weapons and tactics used gave a definite advantage to the attacker.

Twentieth-century accounts of Nuer tactics describe a more complex tactical situation than the dawn raid. Evans-Pritchard states that "Nuer fight in three divisions [presumably the village-based units that are referred to as "war companies"] with two or three hundred yards between each, and if one division is engaged the others advance or retreat parallel to it. . . . A party of scouts are in advance of the central division and they charge up to the enemy, hurl their spears at them, and fall back on the main body."[33] I wonder if the three divisions are an inference from the chief's assertion to Petherick that he could "raise nine hundred fighting men." I also question Evans-Pritchard's statement that the Nuer "hurl their spears"; a Nuer warrior would not throw away his spear—his only weapon. Raymond Kelly, drawing on early twentieth-century sources, states that a Nuer "army" might be organized into five columns, apparently Evans-Pritchard's companies or divisions, that would simultaneously attack as many Dinka communities and later re-group at a captured village to await any counterattack.[34] Such complex tactics would ensure success. The Dinka appear to have fought in lines when able and to have used slim, medium-length spears (as projectile weapons), forked clubs, and shields.[35] But even if these more complex Nuer tactics had not been developed in the early nineteenth century (I doubt they were), the surprise attack by a single company or column on a sleeping Dinka village would have meant success. Both the use of am-bushes and lines and the use of shock weapons are efficient military practices that contribute to a high level of military sophistication.[36]

The data suggest that over a period of a hundred years Nuer/Dinka warfare changed from surprise raids upon villages to battles in which the warriors faced each other in lines. The type of weapons used shifted from shock to projectile weapons. I suspect that attempts by the En-glish to control the region may have produced the shift. Recall the in-fluence the English had upon Tiwi warfare (see the section "Warfare" in chapter 4). Battles are better than raids for demonstrating the valor of warriors, and they cause fewer deaths than raids on villages. A dawn raid may wipe out a village—a military action that colonial authorities would try to prevent. But since Nuer expansion occurred prior to 1860, it is the earlier practice of dawn raids in which shock weapons were used that is relevant to any discussion of the so-called Nuer conquest.

Many of those scholars who have studied the Nuer see their rapid ex-pansion at the expense of the Dinka as unusual and therefore seem to believe that a complex explanation is required.[37] I do not. Rapid expan-sion is not unusual in the ethnographic record, and when it does occur it can almost always be attributed to the military superiority of one group over the other. The Iroquois and Zulu, to be described below, are examples.[38] Kelly's complex explanation, which has been ques-tioned in both reviews and article-length critiques, is not needed.[39] To explain Nuer expansion it is necessary only to show how the initial contact came about, what competing interests led to conflict, and the relative military strength of the cultures in confrontation. For the Nuer and the Dinka it was segmentation of communities and floods that resulted in migration, competition for women and cattle, and Nuer mil-itary superiority.

Iroquois versus Huron

The second case study examines the seventeenth-century conflict between the Iroquois and the Huron.[40] Like the Nuer, who expanded at the expense of the Dinka, the Iroquois expanded at the expense of their northern neighbors, the Huron. Although from time to time I have heard a reference to an Iroquois "empire," the Iroquois defeat of the Huron was no more a conquest than was the Nuer defeat of the Dinka. No political incorporation occurred; the Huron were annihilated. Huron were killed and some were taken captive, their villages were burned, and the small number of survivors fled the lands of the Huron, known as Huronia. Huronia became an Iroquois hunting territory.

Iroquoian-speaking peoples have for centuries occupied the region south of Lake Ontario and the Saint Lawrence River, present-day New York State; the Huron occupied the region north of Lake Ontario and the Saint Lawrence River, the present-day Canadian province of Ontario. The Iroquois and Huron spoke closely related languages belonging to the Iroquoian language family. The standard interpretation of Iroquoian history is that both groups consisted of hunters and gatherers who received crops—corn, beans, and squash—by diffusion from Mesoamerica. A recent alternative interpretation of Northern Iroquoian history is that the peoples migrated from what is today central Pennsylvania in about A.D. 900 and the years following, bringing with them their matrilineal and matrilocal social organization, as well as horticulture based upon the classic three crops grown in North America.[41] By 1500 Iroquoian subsistence was firmly based upon a form of horticulture known as shifting cultivation, hunting, and fishing. Their hunting provided not only food but also furs—a product desired by the French, Dutch, and English, who arrived in the area by the 1600s. In spite of the excellent diet, the population did not increase rapidly. The total population of the Iroquois and the Huron probably never exceeded twenty-five thousand for either culture. Furthermore, the subsistence economy was not conducive to producing wealth differences.

The Iroquois and Huron people lived in palisaded villages of longhouses, with several longhouses to a village. These longhouses, shaped like a loaf of bread, were home to matrilineages and matriclans; they were occupied by several families, all of them related through the maternal line. A monogamous family consisting of a woman, her husband, and their children occupied one side of a segment of a longhouse. The woman's sister's family might occupy the other side of that segment, with the sisters sharing a centrally placed hearth. Because residence was usually matrilocal and marriage was monogamous, the Iroquoian peoples did not have fraternal interest groups. The husbands, members of clans different from that of their wives, usually came from nearby villages. Since males were often living in villages in which they had not been born, cross-cutting kinship ties linked the villages, and conflict within and between villages was probably minimal. Indeed, the sources for most types of conflict were absent, since wealth differences had not arisen, a rule of monogamy reduced competition for multiple spouses, and there were no fraternal interest groups.

In the 1500s Iroquois villages were grouped into five separate polities scattered across what is today New York State; the Huron villages were likewise grouped into either four or five separate polities, near Lake Ontario early in the sixteenth century and, later, near Georgian Bay on Lake Huron, where the growing season was longer and they were out of reach, they hoped, from Iroquois raids. The Iroquois and the Huron polities, or nations as they are called, formed separate confederacies late in the 1500s. Iroquois mythology says they took this action to stop feuding (I would call it internal war) between the nations. Since the Iroquois and the Huron were matrilocal-matrilineal and did not have fraternal interest groups, I doubt if feuding or internal war was a frequent occurrence. Rather, I suspect that it was war between the Iroquois and Huron polities—external war—that prompted political leaders, called chiefs, to form confederacies. Following William Divale's argument, the intense external warfare that developed would have maintained the practice of matrilocal residence and earlier might have been conducive to its development. I believe the process of confederacy formation consisted of first two nations uniting, then the others joining one by one. In any case by the early 1600s two confederacies faced each other across Lake Ontario.

The confederacies were not alliances but political communities with a governmental organization that met in a centrally located "capital" city. Female members of matriclans, composed of matrilineages, selected male representatives to attend council meetings. The creation of a new governmental structure represented an increase in political complexity. Both the Iroquois and the Huron are considered to be chiefdoms. This transition from tribe to chiefdom appears to have occurred because of external warfare. However, political development soon ceased. The increasing warfare of the early 1600s did not lead to conquest, incorporation, and the state. The Iroquoian peoples can probably be classified as minimal, possibly typical, chiefdoms; they had two-tiered polities. But the Iroquois and Huron do not resemble many chiefdoms. Their governments consisted of councils of chiefs, chiefs who were equal and subject to recall by the matriclans. Council chiefs did not go to war. Younger men were selected by the matriclans to be war chiefs. Government operated by consensus. Although a leading chief was selected, he lacked executive powers.[42] In spite of their chiefdom status, the Iroquois and the Huron retained many features that make them resemble tribes.[43]

After 1600 warfare between the confederacies intensified. Weapons and tactics changed. I have identified three periods in time when the discrepancy between weapons and tactics gave an advantage to the Iroquois over the Huron and other Indian nations. Prior to the changes in weapons and tactics the Indians of the Northeast wore body armor, carried shields, and fought with bows and arrows. The opposing sides formed two lines in the open and discharged arrows at each other. The Indians also erected field fortifications—log forts in which they could spend the night before battle. Each "army" might number as many as two hundred warriors. War chiefs led the military organizations and, I believe, opened combat by advancing in front of their "troops." Individual combat between champions probably preceded a general battle. The defeated could flee to their fort. Evidence for this description of Iroquois warfare comes from Samuel de Champlain, the French explorer. Champlain was with Algonquins who were warring with the easternmost nation of the Iroquois, the Mohawk. Champlain, who became the Algonquin champion, left an account of a battle in which he took part in 1609:

> I saw the enemy come out of their barricade to the number of two hundred, in appearance strong, robust men. They came slowly to meet us with a gravity and calm which I admired; and at their head were three chiefs. Our Indians likewise advanced in similar order. . . . Our Indians put me ahead some twenty yards, and I marched on until I was within thirty yards of the enemy, who as soon as they caught sight of me halted and gazed at me and I at them. When I saw them make a move to draw their bows upon us, I took aim with my arquebus and shot straight at one of the three chiefs, and with this shot two fell to the ground and one of their companions was wounded who died thereof a little later. I had put four bullets into my arquebus. . . . The Iroquois were much astonished that two men should have been killed so quickly, although they were provided with shields made of cotton thread woven together and wood, which was proof against arrows.[44]

The panic-stricken Iroquois fled to their fort, where they were attacked and severely defeated.

The Iroquois changed tactics, ushering in the first period of Iroquois superiority. In order to cope with the enemy, small war parties of Mohawks would pretend to retreat and thus draw the advancing Algonquins into ambushes.[45] The dissected Allegheny Plateau and the Adirondack Mountains of present-day upper New York State are ideally suited for hiding war parties and staging ambushes. Tactics consisted of rushing upon the enemy and engaging in hand-to-hand combat before the Algonquins could do much damage with their matchlocks and bows and arrows.[46] In these attacks the Mohawks discarded their shields but not their body armor; thrusting spears and war clubs replaced their bows and arrows. Shields and bows were still carried on the march, but they were not used in a charge. The enemy were probably still wearing body armor and would perhaps have chosen to fight in a battle line if possible. Although the Iroquois were on the defensive during this period, they were able to maintain control of their hunting area through what is today known as guerrilla warfare. Wiping out enemy raiding parties was undoubtedly a means of obtaining needed weapons.

In the second period, beginning in the 1640s, firearms, obtained from Europeans by trading furs, began to play a key role. These arquebuses, flint guns with better firing mechanisms than the earlier matchlocks, were adapted to the existing tactics. In 1642 the Iroquois attacked a French fort at Quebec; their tactics consisted of charging up to the walls of the fort and firing through the loopholes. In the open field the arquebuses were likewise used as assault or shock weapons. The Iroquois would charge the enemy battle line, fire their muskets at close range, and fall upon the fleeing enemy who had been dislodged from their position by the onslaught. By 1647 the Huron had developed tactics for coping with such an attack. The Huron warriors would form a crescent; just as the Iroquois were ready to fire their guns, the Hurons would drop to the ground. After the Iroquois had discharged their weapons, the Hurons would rise, fire their own guns, and countercharge the enemy. The Iroquois made more effective use of the arquebus, however, by positioning themselves along river banks and ambushing canoe convoys laden with furs.[47] Guns loaded with chain-shot could sink canoes whose crews consequently had little chance for defense and none for counterattack. The captured furs were used to purchase more arquebuses from the English. By 1649 the Iroquois were better armed than the Huron, who were allies of the French.[48]

These small battles, raids, and ambushes led up to the major war and battles that took place in March, 1649. Evidence for what happened in that month comes from reports by French Jesuit priests residing in Huronia. The Iroquois had refused to accept missionaries; indeed, when they captured French priests they burned them at the stake.[49] Military organizations in the field grew larger in the forty years between Champlain's defeat of the Iroquois and what I have called the Iroquois Campaign of 1649. Huronia was invaded by an Iroquois force of about one thousand, many of them equipped with firearms, the others with bows and arrows. All carried steel tomahawks or war clubs. The Huron lived in large palisaded villages of longhouses. The walls surrounding villages consisted of upright poles anchored in the earth. Tomahawks and fire could destroy palisade walls. On March 16, the superior Iroquois army overwhelmed first one, then a second Huron village. Complete surprise was achieved in the first attack. In the second village eighty warriors and two priests remained to fight the Iroquois. Women and children had time to flee to the safety of the French missionary fort before battle commenced.

The next day, the Iroquois advanced upon the French fort where the priests and many Hurons resided. In a morning battle about 300 Hurons routed the advance column of about 200 Iroquois, who retreated to the second village captured by the Iroquois the day before. The Hurons pursued the Iroquois and defeated them, taking possession of the village. There, perhaps 150 Hurons awaited the attack of the main body of the Iroquois army, perhaps 500 strong. An intense battle raged throughout the afternoon and into the night. Reinforcements from other Huron villages never arrived, largely, I believe, because they did not know the battle was taking place. Having already been battered by two previous battles, the palisaded walls did not hold. The Hurons who had been victorious in the morning were annihilated. The casualties for both sides were enormous. For the Huron probably 500 warriors lost their lives, as did a noncombatant population of perhaps 300 in the first village attacked. For the Iroquois perhaps nearly 350 warriors were killed out of an attacking force of about 1,000. In terms of percentages, the casualties were enormous—this was no ritual war.

The next day, March 18, passed without combat, both sides being in terror. On March 19 the Iroquois retreated in disorder from Huronia; some captives were used to carry captured supplies, the others were tied to stakes in various longhouses, which were then set on fire. The retreating Iroquois were pursued by a large Huron force, perhaps seven hundred warriors, from a large village on the southern periphery of Huronia. But no battle took place. The remaining Huron nations and villages, once they learned of the destruction of two villages, viewed themselves as a defeated people. In fear of future Iroquois attacks, both the Huron and the priests abandoned their villages and mission station. Some Hurons fled westward, and the priests and some other Hurons fled to an island in Georgian Bay, where the following winter many of them starved.[50]

While in a sense there was a conquest of the Huron by the Iroquois, there was no incorporation of Huron villages into an Iroquois empire. There was no increase in political complexity, and an Iroquois state did not develop. Huronia became a region available to the Iroquois for long-distance hunting expeditions. Even if Huronia had been more circumscribed, with physical barriers to prevent escape, the result would not have been the incorporation of villages into an emerging Iroquois state but more attacks upon Huron villages, which would have resulted in the killing of both combatants and noncombatants. The Iroquois confederacy simply was not structured to incorporate the Huron villages or nations into its political system. Even if the confederacy had been able to incorporate the remaining Huron, no increase in political complexity would have occurred. In the next century a sixth nation, the Tuscarora, moved into present-day western New York and became part of the Iroquois confederacy (ca. 1722). No state resulted.

Following the defeat of the Huron, the tactics of the Iroquois changed, and a third period can be identified in which the Iroquois had an advantage over their enemies. In the 1660s the English began to supply the Iroquois with more firearms. Iroquois warriors no longer wore body armor; they went into action wearing only a loincloth and moccasins, thus achieving greater mobility. Before the end of the seventeenth century Iroquois fighting tactics had changed so much that the warriors were no longer proficient in the use of tomahawks and clubs. The Iroquois now relied heavily upon snipers, who fired from the cover of any available object. Their enemies, who were not as well armed, had to continue relying upon war clubs and in-fighting, which gave them some advantage in meadows and open fields but left them greatly outclassed in the forests. The Iroquois battle line was extended as much as possible. When the battle line advanced, each wing tried to envelop the enemy forces.

In my studies of Iroquoian warfare, I have addressed the question of why the Iroquois won. Of the several explanations that have been offered, I find the most convincing to be that the Iroquois had a strategic position between the western fur supply and the eastern market, that they had access to guns and ammunition, and that they used superior tactics at critical times during the seventeenth century.[51] The 1649 victory is an example of the use of superior tactics. In these battles, as well as earlier in the seventeenth century, the Iroquois showed a military ability greater than that possessed by their enemies. It appears that, in the case of the Huron and Iroquois, a military analysis of the wars they fought provides evidence that superior military ability—weapons and tactics—was a major factor in why the Iroquois won.

Zulu versus Nguni

The third case study, Zulu versus Nguni, derives from a study of the evolution of Zulu warfare.[52] Probably the best, and possibly only, example of a tribe becoming a chiefdom and then a state comes from the cattle-herding peoples who speak Nguni languages. For approximately three hundred years prior to 1800, Nguni tribes had been migrating into southeast Africa, now Zululand and Natal, from the northwest. Rivalry between the sons of the tribal leader frequently led to fissioning of the royal patrilineage. Such splitting kept the tribes small and scattered. The economy, based on shifting cultivation and cattle raising, also contributed to this dispersion by requiring tribes to constantly seek better land.[53] By 1800 the increase in population and the dwindling availability of unoccupied land created a situation in which fissioning could no longer solve the problem of dynastic disputes. The amount of available land declined because the Dutch occupied the lands to the south, mountains ran north-south to the west, and the Indian Ocean lay to the east. In addition to warfare and circumscription, three other factors essential for the transformation to statehood appear to have been present.

First, this area to the west of the Indian Ocean was within the shadow of several states that had arisen thousands of years earlier, in Egypt, in Mesopotamia, and along the Indus River. Trade had occurred back and forth across the Indian Ocean for centuries. Also in the region was the ancient state or kingdom of Zimbabwe. Later, Portuguese explorers and slave traders ventured up and down the coast of eastern Africa for four hundred years before the Zulu state developed.[54] The possibility that the idea of statehood could have diffused to Nguni leaders is great.

Second, a particular type of sociopolitical institution, probably unique to eastern Africa, was already well developed and greatly facilitated the uniting of villages: age grades. This institution had as its foundation a group ceremony that initiated young males from neighboring villages, probably from the same patriclan, into manhood. Initiation ceremonies occurred every five years or so. After initiation the group of men belonged to an organization distinct from the age grades of their elders and distinct from the classes of initiates who followed. Thus, neighboring villages were united by a series of age grades; a man's classmates lived in different villages.

Third, not one, but two men of great ambition—who may have learned how states are organized from European explorers and Portuguese slave traders—through their innovations seem to have "lifted" the Nguni from one level of sociopolitical complexity to the next. The first "lift" came from Dingiswayo, a leader of the Mtetwa tribe, who organized the age grades of young warriors into regiments of soldiers.[55] This move transformed fraternal interest group–based military organizations into professional military organizations. The age grades later came to be housed in their own barracks. The three youngest age grades generated three regiments that could be placed side by side in battle line, creating a center and two wings. The second "lift" came from Shaka, a Zulu warrior who was a protégé of Dingiswayo. Shaka's innovations included changes in weapons and further changes in tactics.[56]

A summary of the evolution of Zulu warfare reveals how new ideas in social organization combined with military innovations led to the formation of the Zulu kingdom. Prior to 1805, when conflict arose between tribes, a day and a place were designated for settling the dispute by combat. On that day the rival tribes marched to battle, the warriors drawing up in lines at a distance of about one hundred yards apart. Behind the lines stood the remaining members of each tribe, who during the battle cheered their kinsmen on to greater efforts. The warriors carried two or three light javelins and oval shields five feet tall. These rawhide shields,

Figure 8.1. Types of Zulu Warfare

Categories of Comparison	Dueling Battles	Battles of Subjugation	Battles of Conquest	Campaigns
Sociopolitical System	Tribe	Chiefdom	State	Empire
Goals of War	Settling disputes	Subjugation	Conquest	Plunder
Type of Military Organization	Patrilineage	Age-grade regiment	Age-grade regiment	Age-grade regiment
Type of Formation	Lines	Lines	Envelopment	Envelopment
Type of Weapon	Projectile	Projectile	Shock	Shock
Casualty Rate	Very low	Low	High	Low

when hardened by being dipped in water, could not be penetrated by the missiles. Chosen warriors, who would advance to within fifty yards of each other and shout insults, opened the combat by hurling their spears. According to *Shaka Zulu* author E. A. Ritter, eventually more and more warriors would be drawn into the battle until one side ceased fighting and fled, "whereupon a rush would follow for male and female prisoners and enemy cattle, the former to be subsequently ransomed [for cattle], the latter to be permanently retained."[57] If the pursued dropped their spears, it was a sign of surrender and no more blood would be shed. Since wounds were seldom fatal, the number of casualties was low. Dingiswayo changed the nature of Nguni warfare by introducing a new goal of war and a new military organization. With his age-grade regiments he was able to achieve military success. Without altering weapons or tactics but simply by increasing organizational efficiency and hence the discipline and size of his forces, he was able from 1806 to 1809 to defeat more than thirty tribes and establish for himself a chiefdom. "After subduing a tribe with as little slaughter as possible," anthropologist Max Gluckman writes, "he left it under its own chiefly family, perhaps choosing from it a favorite of his own to rule, though the young men of the tribe had to serve in his army."[58] These military innovations are summarized in Figure 8.1.[59]

Around 1810 Shaka, the illegitimate son of a Zulu chief, invented a new technique of fighting while he was an officer in Dingiswayo's army. He replaced his javelins with a short, broad-bladed stabbing spear; he retained his shield but discarded his sandals in order to gain greater mobility. By rushing upon his opponent he was able to use his shield to hook away his enemy's shield, thus exposing the warrior's left side to a spear thrust. Gluckman writes that Shaka also changed military tactics by arranging the soldiers in his command—a company of about one hundred men—into "a close-order, shield-to-shield formation with two 'horns' designed to encircle the enemy or to feint at his flanks, the main body of troops at the center and the reserves in the rear ready to

exploit the opportunities of battle."[60] Dingiswayo, however, always refused to use the formation and to adopt the short spear because it meant
high casualties for both sides.

In 1816, when Shaka's father died, Dingiswayo helped him to become chief of the Zulu. Shaka immediately outfitted his army of five
hundred soldiers with the short spear and taught them the new tactics.
Although he remained within Dingiswayo's chiefdom, he began to
conquer tribes on his own. Early in 1818 Shaka prepared to join with
Dingiswayo in a campaign against the Ndwandwe tribe ruled by Zwide.
Dingiswayo foolishly left the army without an escort and was captured
and killed by Zwide before the regiments of Shaka and Dingiswayo
could join forces. Shaka was forced to retreat and establish a defensive
position on Qokli Hill, from which he defeated Zwide. After the battle
the Mtetwa and several small tribes joined Shaka. The following year,
1819, the Ndwandwe again invaded Shaka's domain and were defeated
at the Battle of Umhlatuze.

Following the consolidation of his kingdom, Shaka launched a series
of wars for the next three years that expanded the kingdom into an empire of eighty thousand square miles. However, once the empire was secure the army—which by then totaled thirty thousand men—had few
military duties. What does a nation do with a large army that is necessary only for defensive purposes? Shaka's answer to the question (although the soldiers herded Shaka's cattle and worked his fields) was to
send it on long-range campaigns; usually the army returned with plunder consisting primarily of cattle. These campaigns occurred during the
last four years of Shaka's reign, until he was assassinated by his brothers
in 1828.

The evolution of Zulu warfare can be analyzed in terms of a progression of types of wars, the types named for the goals of war. The first type
can be characterized as "dueling battles" between small tribes whose
warriors agreed upon the time and place of the battle and who fought
for cattle. Since spears were used only as projectile weapons, casualties
were slight. The nature of war changed when Dingiswayo—for the purpose of conquering other tribes—created a more efficient military force
by organizing his warriors into age-grade regiments. Thus, he created a
new concept of war by using the newly formed army as an instrument
of political expansion. These "battles of subjugation," in which there
were still few casualties, constitute the second type of war. Shortly after
the establishment of Dingiswayo's chiefdom, Shaka invented a short
stabbing spear and enveloping tactics, which he had no opportunity to
use until he became leader of the Zulu. Upon the death of Dingiswayo
and the breakup of his domain, Shaka was forced to defend Zululand
from invasion. The use of these new weapons and tactics and new motives for fighting resulted in a third type of war in which casualties were
very high. The defense of Zululand was followed by a series of success-

ful offensive battles in which casualty rates remained high; these "battles of conquest" resulted in the creation of an empire. The fourth type of war was the series of long-range "campaigns" into enemy territory, the aim of which was to keep the army busy rather than to conquer new peoples. Casualty rates became low again, as they had been prior to 1816. It should be noted that each of these four types of war corresponds to a different level of sociopolitical development. In terms of Elman Service's taxonomy, "dueling battles" occurred on the tribal level, "battles of subjugation" led to the development of chiefdoms, "battles of conquest" brought about the emergence of the state, and with the eventual development of empires long-range "campaigns" became the dominant form of war.[61]

This review of the evolution of Zulu warfare and sociopolitical organization shows the importance of five factors: first, intense warfare; second, circumscription, which produced an increase in population density that in turn led to population pressure; third, the idea of statehood, perhaps introduced early by traders, almost undoubtedly by the eighteenth century by Europeans, which influenced Nguni leaders; fourth, an indigenous institution—the age grade—which provided ties across villages as well as groupings of young males who could be utilized as professional military organizations; and, fifth, two intelligent leaders, who were able to accept new ideas and transform local institutions into tools for their own political advancement. The Zulu are our best—and perhaps only—example of a tribe becoming a state via the chiefdom route. It is also the best example of the circumscription version of the conquest theory of the state. But—and this must be emphasized strongly—the Zulu are *not* a primary or pristine state. They are a secondary state. They were, of course, a newly formed state, hence an early state, and they were a despotic state (although the despotism has not been described in the above summary). The Zulu are an excellent example of secondary state formation: the idea of statehood diffused to a people whose subsistence base permitted the development of a centralized political system.

9
Conclusion

The two types of military organizations—the nonprofessional and the professional—engaged in serious warfare.

From my childhood reading I had learned about kinship-based military organizations of American Indians—these were nonprofessional military organizations—and about armies of the ancient world—these were professional military organizations. In 1960, I became acquainted with the concept of the fraternal interest group. After that time, my thinking came to equate the nonprofessional, kinship-based military organization with the fraternal interest group.

I believe that the concept of the fraternal interest group is one of anthropology's seminal ideas. The term was coined by Dutch anthropologists H. U. E. Thoden van Velzen and W. van Wetering; they used fraternal interest group theory to explain why some local groups were peaceful internally and others were not.[1] Included among their several measures of nonpeacefulness was feuding; kinship groups that seek revenge are usually fraternal interest groups. In carrying out vengeance, such groups form raiding parties, thus creating kinship-based military organizations.

In 1964, my wife-to-be and I conducted a cross-cultural study of feuding, and we found that fraternal interest groups and feuding were related.[2] It was only a short step for me to generalize the finding: If the vengeance group is a military organization, that same military organization can conduct raids upon neighboring polities within the same culture. I created the concept of internal war (contrasting it with external war), conducted another cross-cultural study, and found that fraternal interest groups and internal war were related. Fraternal interest groups, I concluded, were responsible for both feuding and internal war.[3]

In conducting these two studies I also demonstrated that nonliterate societies were characterized by great variation in these two types of violence. Since the late 1960s I have viewed any statement that asserts that such societies are either peaceful *or* warlike as simplistic to the point of being incorrect. Many nonliterate societies are violent and many are not. Fraternal interest group theory provides an explanation for the variation.

The equating of the second type of military organization, the professional armies of the ancient world, with the armies of some state-level nonliterate peoples has taken place for years. For example, the Zulu army has been compared to hoplite soldiers from Sparta and the Inca army to the Roman legions.[4] Nothing in this study suggests that this equating should not be done. The armies of the four pristine states that we have examined in detail are similar not only to each other but also to the armies of other early states, as well as to the armies of the ancient world. I recognized these similarities in the 1960s. Shortly after compiling of my collected papers on feuding and warfare for publication in 1994, I intensified my reading of military history.

Each type of military organization has had a separate career. The first, the fraternal interest group–based nonprofessional military, arose early —how early is a subject of debate. Although I trace it from *Homo habilis,* I do not believe that early warfare was frequent. It was a rare occurrence, probably, until the emergence of modern *Homo sapiens.* I also believe, and have for more than ten years, that as hunting weapons improved, big game hunting increased in importance. Concomitant with this change was an increase in the frequency of warfare. Although this view, known as the hunting hypothesis, has been under attack since the 1960s, I believe the attack is largely ideologically driven. The horrors of war—and the fighting in Vietnam was a horrible war—have led numerous social scientists and others to seek peoples in prehistory and in history that had little or no war. They found what they were looking for—prehistoric peoples and hunter-gatherers who did not have war. To find what they were looking for required that they deny the evidence or define warfare in such a fashion that the armed combat of nonliterate peoples was not considered warfare. This view has been called the Myth of the Peaceful Savage.[5]

I found, as noted above, that numerous small-scale societies had kinship-based military organizations and that these societies were likely to have feuding and internal war. More recently I found that hunter-gatherers whose subsistence relied heavily upon hunting, particularly large game hunting, were likely to engage in frequent warfare.[6] Only recently was this understanding applied to the Upper Paleolithic. Doing so created a serious intellectual problem. I had long been aware that primary states did not have warfare in their early stages. Julian Steward in the 1950s had noted the absence of war in five regions where he found that early states arose.[7] I learned this in graduate school, and, as a professor, I covered it later in lectures on evolutionary theory. Then in the 1960s Elman Service argued that the leaders of chiefdoms, which he positioned between tribes and states, were consensual leaders, not war leaders. Thus, he argued that warfare arose after the state formed.[8] In my 1997 article on the origins of war I noted what Steward and Service had found and concluded, "Primary states arose in regions where warfare was not prevalent. Only after the state developed did warfare become a central concern to these polities."[9] The intellectual problem confronting me was how to get from warring peoples in the Upper Paleolithic to peaceful agriculturalists in the regions where the first states arose. A major part of *How War Began* explains how I crossed that chasm. I noted a decline in the hunting of large game and, accompanying this decline, a decline in warfare. Peaceful peoples settled river valleys, where they either domesticated crops or received crops through diffusion. In the absence of warfare, political complexity arose. Only after statehood was reached did the second type of military organization, based first on elites, later on massed infantry, arise. I traced in detail, in chapter 6, the career of the military organizations in the regions where the four pristine states arose.

The joining of the two perspectives, that early hunters engaged in warfare, while early agriculturalists did not, is, I believe, a synthesis worthy of serious consideration. It resolves the dispute between the hawks and doves by bringing the two perspectives together. In the section "Hawks and Doves" in chapter 2, I describe the two warring camps. I am in both camps. Recently doves have attacked me for distinguishing the two camps, denying that there are two such entities.[10] It is ironic that scholars who believe in "the natural history of peace" are so ready to mount attacks upon fellow scholars who do not share completely their views. Their attacks prove the existence of two camps: The enunciation of their position defines the doves' camp, and it also defines the hawks' camp by stating what they disagree with. Attacks by hawks upon the doves' position likewise define the hawks' position while establishing the existence of the dove position.[11] Each group views the other as wrong. I see them both as right. *How War Began* is a synthesis of the two positions.

How War Began challenges several established notions, first, the notion that there was no warfare before the Neolithic period. I have argued that *Homo* species earlier than *Homo sapiens* occasionally engaged in armed combat and that *Homo sapiens* in their migration out of Africa swept the other *Homo* species aside. Efficient hunting weapons, in particular the atlatl, made possible this advance at the expense of other *Homo* species. And *Homo sapiens* fought other *Homo sapiens*. Direct evidence for *Homo sapiens* killing other *Homo sapiens* consists of rock art and projectile points in bone. Warfare also appears to be linked to an increasing reliance upon hunting. Second, I challenge the notion that early agriculturalists, including the first residents of Jericho, engaged in warfare. I have argued that the first farmers did not go to war. Walls, as at Jericho and along the Yellow River, are not necessarily evidence of war or deterrence; there may be other reasons for walls, such as protection from rampaging rivers. Third, I dispute the notion that military conquests led to the first states. I have argued that there were no conquests until there were states. States led to war; war did not lead to states.

Although I have challenged several established notions, I recognize that there are diverse opinions on some issues and that I could be wrong. In the years to come new evidence could change the interpretations I have made and reestablish the notions that I have challenged: that there was no warfare before the Neolithic; that early agriculturists engaged in warfare; and that conquest led to the state. I believe I have refuted these notions.

However, particular types of evidence could conceivably support these three disputed notions. First, new evidence may already have been found that there was no warfare before the Neolithic. Although the current view is that *Homo neanderthalensis* was a separate species driven to extinction, a view I accept, this was not the concensus for thirty years. From the 1960s to the 1990s modern humans and the Neanderthals were considered subspecies: *Homo sapiens sapiens* and *Homo sapiens neanderthalensis*. Interbreeding was considered a distinct possibility. Once again some experts on fossil humans question the independence of the two species. Recently physical anthropologist Alan Mann has examined the dentition of the two populations and noticed striking similarities in the patterns of tooth enamel, which suggest a single species.[12] Archaeologist G. A. Clark sees a lack of evidence to support the replacement theory. Rather, he sees continuity in changes in tool technology over a long period of time within the Mousterian culture itself.[13] If the single species view is once again established, it suggests that interbreeding, not genocide, occurred between the Neanderthals and the modern *Homo sapiens* who settled in the Near East. (Of course, genocide and interbreeding can occur simultaneously.) This view would be a blow to the Out of Africa hypothesis, which posits a rapid, nonpeaceful expansion of *Homo sapiens* into Europe.

Second, if settled gatherers, those who were the precursors of early agriculturalists, are found in some instances to engage in warfare, it would suggest that warfare did not decline after the extinction of large animals. It also suggests that war increased gradually over time, accompanying a gradual increase in political complexity. Raymond Kelly refers to this gradual change as "the early coevolution of war and society."[14]

Third, if warfare is found in minimal and typical chiefdom stages in those regions where pristine states arose (meaning that perhaps the first states arose from warring chiefdoms), this suggests that warfare and conquest could be the cause of state formation. Coastal Peru is instructive in this matter. When I first examined the literature on Peru, Jonathan Haas's *The Evolution of the Prehistoric State* persuaded me that the Moche were an example of a pristine state that developed without warfare.[15] Since Haas is an archaeologist who had carried out excavations in Peru, I had confidence in his conclusions. Indeed, I thought that the Moche would be the best example of how a pristine state arises. It was not to be. An examination of more recent sources revealed that warfare was present on the coast from hunting-gathering times. This finding gave me great concern for the validity of the internal conflict/political legitimacy theory of the origin of the state. Only the discoveries that Chavín in the highlands reached statehood earlier than did the Moche and that Chavín had no history of warfare saved the theory. The next research task was to find out how the Moche actually did become a state, since they had a prior "history" of warfare, which defies the rule that states make wars but wars do not make states. It appears that the idea of statehood, as well as crops, diffused to the coastal peoples that became the Moche. Without Chavín my theory would be in trouble. Accordingly the second example of a pristine state is labeled "Chavín/Moche," rather than simply "Moche."

Lessons for Tomorrow

Any discussion of lessons to be learned from scholarly research is plagued by the possibility that the investigator has viewed the data through the lens of his or her personal belief system. Depending on the political stance of the reader, various conclusions may be drawn from *How War Began.*

A scholar who believes that gun ownership is a major cause of homicide may find in the discussion of weapons development (the spear, the atlatl, and the bow and arrow) an important truth: With each new technological advance the ease of killing someone without fear of injury to oneself increased. The observation can be expanded to include specialized weapons for war such as the chariot and battering ram. Increases in the range and efficiency of military weapons lead to higher battlefield casualties and facilitate the killing of noncombatants. A scholar who believes that military preparation is responsible for war can find in the discussions of the warfare of early states the truth he or she seeks. The lessons drawn from both discussions lead to the conclusion that gun control is desirable, as is military disarmament.

A scholar who believes that the natural propensity of humankind is to live in peace and harmony can find in the discussion of the early agriculturalists support for his or her position. It should be welcome news to such a scholar that communities can survive for thousands of years without warfare. Such a scholar has often sought warless societies among hunter-gatherers; the best place to look, however, appears to be the settled gatherers who first domesticated plants and animals. In the Near East, the settlement of Abu Hureyra, occupied from 9500 to 5000 B.C.E., is a wonderful example—nearly five thousand years of continuous occupation and no warfare. This scholar's position is further strengthened by the finding that hunter-gatherers who hunted large game and engaged in warfare ceased hostilities when the supply of wild game dwindled to very low levels. This finding provides evidence that even a society that has become warlike can, nevertheless, reverse direction and become peaceable again.

The data and interpretations in *How War Began* do not seem to support the conclusions of two comprehensive studies of warfare by noted military historians. John Keegan believes that modern society should follow the lead of warriors in nonliterate societies who limited their combat.[16] I do not see limitations, however. My study of the killing of captured enemies shows, as do other data, that there are no limitations. Robert O'Connell believes that war has become so horrible that polities in the future will turn to peace.[17] The horrors of war in the past—the destruction of cities and the killing of noncombatants—never led to the end of war. It is hard to find in the despotism, warfare, and human sacrifice of the four pristine states any clues to suggest that there would be a unanimous cry of "Enough!"

The lesson I draw is taken from the discussion of the inchoate early state stage in the evolution of the pristine state. The emergence of factions that became social classes in the typical chiefdom stage laid the groundwork for what was to come. In the struggle for political leadership, the leaders of the losing faction were killed. The leaders of these early states became despots. They took from the losers. The "haves" soon wanted more. A police-like organization ensured that the "haves" got more. Indeed, they probably were able to force farmers and craft specialists to produce a surplus, a surplus that could make the leaders' lives comfortable and that could be used to support an army. Once despotism was firmly established, the leaders could use their army—now a full-time professional force supported by the surplus—to attack other polities, first culturally similar, then culturally different ones.

Thus, the lesson I find in *How War Began* is that early states both brutally suppress their own populations and attack their neighbors. Pristine states lie thousands of years in the past, but inchoate early states are constantly being produced. With the continuing breakup of polities, a steady supply of inchoate early states or despotic states is being created. Their existence guarantees that there will be numerous places throughout the world where civilians are terrorized as despots attempt to consolidate their political control. Once consolidation occurs, peaceful neighbors may be attacked.

This is the bad news. But there is good news. Although the number of polities steadily increased throughout the twentieth century, the number of polities whose citizens enjoy a high degree of political and civil freedom increased even faster. In 1900 there were 55 sovereign polities, in 1950 there were 80 sovereign polities, and in 2000 there were 192 sovereign polities. The decline in colonies and protectorates since 1950 accounts for some of the increase (about 75 polities), and some resulted from the breakup of sovereign polities. In 1900 about 12 percent of humankind lived under a democratic form of government; in 1950 there were 22 democratic states, which accounted for 31 percent of the world's population; and in 2000 there were 120 electoral democracies, which accounted for 58 percent of the world's population. A recent survey "finds that 85 of the world's 192 countries (44 per cent) are free, meaning that these countries maintain a high degree of political and economic freedom and respect basic civil liberties." This number represents an increase in a ten-year period from 61 to 85; the number of "not free" states declined from 62 to 48 (59 polities were classified as "partly free").[18]

Conflict, both within and between nations, has accompanied this steady increase in the number of polities. Following World War II the number of conflicts seemed to be on the increase, and this pattern continued in the aftermath of the cold war.[19] I suggest that this increase resulted from the formation of new states, whether they had been colonies or protectorates or segments of larger states that had fractured. Since 1992, however, the trend appears to be downward. According to Adrian Karatnycky, "Conflicts reached a peak in 1992, but have since gradually decreased across all regions; while an annual average of 48.3 interstate and intrastate conflicts took place in the period 1989–1994, this annual average fell to 35 in the period 1995–1998."[20]

Two factors may account for this seeming decline. First, over time despotic states become mature states. The survey cited above provides strong evidence that polities in the modern world are moving in that direction. Second, as more and more polities enter the free and partly free ranks there will be fewer and fewer polities racked by internal conflict that could lead to fissioning and the formation of new states. By definition a free society is a polity in which internal conflicts are peacefully resolved. While a polity that is free and has an electoral democracy may have a strong military organization that could attack other polities, many scholars believe that democracies do not fight each other, although they do war with nondemocratic nations.[21] If this view is correct, then it is logical to expect that as the percentage of democratic polities increases, the frequency of interstate warfare will decline since there are fewer nondemocratic polities to engage in warfare with each other and with democracies.[22] Political scientist Bruce Russett has stated, "The more democracies there are in the world, the fewer potential adversaries we and other democracies will have and the wider the zone of peace."[23]

Why do democracies not war with each other? Since *How War Began* does not focus upon democracies or mature states, it does not provide a direct answer. The only society studied that resembles an electoral democracy was the Iroquois. These native New Yorkers were internally peaceful, but they warred with their equally democratic Huron neighbors. Thus, no answer to the question can be found here. The answer I now provide is drawn from two sources: studies of the "democratic peace" and of "freedom and development."[24] Democracy is good for peace and good for development. The humanistic values that accompany democracy are counter to militaristic values. Democracies, while they may build military organizations that are capable of successfully engaging in offensive warfare, do not build military organizations with the intent to conquer neighbors. Furthermore, while some democracies may have the resources—the surplus—that can be used to build an efficient military organization, strong demands may be made by the electorate to channel resources into domestic needs rather than into the military. Only a perceived threat to national security will persuade citizens and their leaders to provide a strong military. This scenario seems to be happening in the wake of the terrorist attacks upon the World Trade Center and the Pentagon on September 11, 2001. As democracies increase in number and despotic states decrease in number, the nations of the world, I predict, will build smaller and smaller military organizations. Fighting terrorism will require special kinds of military organizations—it is too early to predict what an effective counterterrorism strike force will be like. The frequency of war between nations should decline. The fight against terrorism will continue. Hopefully a new eternal triangle will emerge, with democracy, development, and peace at the points of the equilateral triangle.

> "The farther backward you can look,
> the farther forward you are likely to see."
> —Winston Churchill

Notes

Preface

1. Holling, *The Book of Indians*, pp. 43–44, 86–88.

2. The current location of that war bonnet is unknown. My classmate, Chase Putnam, has a degree in anthropology and for years was the director of the Warren County Historical Society, located in our hometown of Warren, Pennsylvania. Each summer when we get together, I press him to look for the war bonnet. He has been unable to find it. To stop my nagging Chase and his wife Mary, during the summer of 2003, presented me with a headdress made from wild turkey feathers they had collected.

3. The term "primitive war" would fit better here, but in anthropological circles it has become politically incorrect in the last twenty-five years. Even the terms "native peoples" or "nonliterate peoples" may be politically incorrect by the time you read this book. Historians continue to use the term "primitive warfare."

4. Classicist Victor Davis Hanson, who is also a military historian, takes his colleagues to task for writing histories that leave out killing: "There is an inherent truth in battle. It is hard to disguise the verdict of the battlefield, and nearly impossible to explain away the dead, or to suggest that abject defeat is somehow victory. Wars are the sum of battles, battles the tally of individual human beings killing and dying. . . . Euphemism in battle narrative or the omission of graphic killing altogether is a near criminal offense of the military historian. . . . War is ultimately killing. Its story becomes absurd when the wages of death are ignored by the historian" (Hanson, *Carnage and Culture*, pp. 7–8).

5. Carneiro, *Evolutionism in Cultural Anthropology*, p. 288 (italics in the original).

6. At Pennsylvania State University my advisor was archaeologist Fred Matson. I attended archaeological field school at the University of Arizona's field station at Point of Pines.

7. See Otterbein, "Warfare: A Hitherto Unrecognized Critical Variable," p. 706; and Otterbein, ed., *Feuding and Warfare*, p. xvii.

8. At the University of Pittsburgh my doctoral dissertation on family organization in the Bahamas was directed by George P. Murdock. The dissertation was published in 1966 as *The Andros Islanders: A Study of Family Organization in the Bahamas* (University of Kansas Press).

9. Upon my return I married Charlotte Swanson, a psychologist. As I tell my students, my interest in marriage and the family shifted at that time to feuding and warfare.

Chapter 1

1. See Edgerton, *Warrior Women*.

2. A political community is a group of people whose membership is defined in terms of occupancy of a common territory and who have an official with the special function of announcing group decisions—a function exercised at least once a year. The term "political community" is synonymous with the term "polity." The official is a political leader. There is usually more than one political community in a cultural unit, which is an ethnic unit composed of contiguous political communities that are culturally similar. In most instances the cultural unit is the same as a society or culture (Otterbein, "Clan and Tribal Conflict," p. 289).

3. In my comparative study of the warfare of fifty nonliterate societies, I found

that the patterns described above did occur. Of the forty-six societies with military organizations, more than two-thirds of the centralized political systems (chiefdoms and states) had professional military organizations, and nearly two-thirds of the uncentralized political systems (bands and tribes) had nonprofessional military organizations (Otterbein, *The Evolution of War,* p. 8).

4. Otterbein, "The Origins of War," p. 265.

5. McRandle, *The Antique Drums of War;* Jones, *Women Warriors;* Wrangham and Peterson, *Demonic Males;* Ehrenreich, *Blood Rites;* Keegan, *A History of Warfare.*

6. Sanders, "Warriors, Anthropology of," 3:773.

7. See Otterbein, "Dueling."

8. Keegan, *A History of Warfare,* p. xvi.

9. Ibid., p. 387.

10. Otterbein, "The Origins of War"; and "A History of Research on Warfare in Anthropology."

11. Keegan, *A History of Warfare,* pp. 387–89.

12. O'Connell, *Ride of the Second Horseman,* pp. 69–83.

13. Keegan, *A History of Warfare,* pp. 389–91.

14. See Hanson, *The Western Way of War;* and *Carnage and Culture.*

15. Keegan, *A History of Warfare,* p. 392.

16. Peters, *Fighting for the Future,* pp. 32, 34–47, 188.

17. Otterbein, "Five Feuds," 240. "Feudists as Soldiers" is the title of the relevant section in my study of Kentucky feuding.

18. I do not suggest that the warriors of the world should be conscripted into standing armies as a way of controlling them. As Peters points out, when armies demilitarize they release into civilian populations unemployed males who are trained in arms (Peters, *Fighting for the Future,* pp. 36–37).

19. Millett and Maslowski, *For the Common Defense,* p. xiii.

20. Otterbein, *The Ultimate Coercive Sanction,* pp. 9–13.

21. See Otterbein, "The Anthropology of War," p. 923; "Clan and Tribal Conflict," p. 290; *Comparative Cultural Analysis,*

p. 146; *The Evolution of War,* p. 3; and "Internal War," p. 277.

22. In a cross-cultural study of nonliterate people, I found that one-third of the attacking war parties kill women and children (see the section "Killing of Captured Enemies" in chapter 7).

23. Julian Steward describes the period between the small local community and the multicommunity state as being characterized by "comparative peace" (Steward, *Theory of Culture Change,* p. 192). Elman Service argues that warfare arose after the state formed (Service, *Origins of the State and Civilization,* pp. 270–73, 297–99).

24. Marcus and Flannery, *Zapotec Civilization,* p. 32.

25. Ibid.; Peregrine, "Ethnology versus Ethnographic Analogy," pp. 316–18.

26. Peregrine, "Ethnology versus Ethnographic Analogy," pp. 319–21; and "Cross-Cultural Comparative Approaches in Archaeology," 2–6.

27. I have set forth the basic methodology of the cross-cultural study (Otterbein, "Basic Steps in Conducting a Cross-Cultural Study"), as well as several methodological aspects of its use (Otterbein, "Sampling and Samples in Cross-Cultural Studies"; "Samples and Samples—An Update"; "Two Styles in Cross-Cultural Research"; and M. Ember and Otterbein, "Sampling in Cross-Cultural Research").

28. For example, Raoul Naroll, another pioneer in the cross-cultural method, conducted a cross-cultural study for the purpose of determining the amount of floor area one person occupies. The figure of ten square meters per person has come to be known as "Naroll's constant" (Naroll, "Floor Area and Settlement Population"). Barton Brown's restudy argues that six square meters per person is the appropriate figure. With this constant an archaeologist can derive population size. The starting point is the number of people who share the dwelling floor area of a culture's typical dwelling, that is, the household (B. Brown, "Population Estimation from Floor Area"). If the number of dwellings in a settlement can be ascertained or estimated, then the population of the settlement can be estimated. I was a doctoral student of George Peter Murdock, and, later, a colleague of Raoul

Naroll. And Barton Brown was my student.

29. See McGrew, *Chimpanzee Material Culture.*

30. For the recent comparative study of six chimpanzee populations, see Boesch and Tomasello, "Chimpanzee and Human Cultures."

31. R. Brown, *Explanation in Social Science,* pp. 113–93; Diesing, *How Does Social Science Work?* pp. 303–306.

32. Aristotle, *The Politics,* trans. Carnes Lord (Chicago: University of Chicago Press, 1984), pp. 149–55; Bunge, *Causality,* pp. 31–33; Dray, *Perspectives on History,* pp. 71–92; Millett, "American Military History," p. 15.

33. Gould, "Introduction: The Scales of Contingency and Punctuation in History," p. xi.

34. Vayda's pioneering theories were published in 1961 in his article, "Expansion and Warfare among Swidden Agriculturalists." For his recantation and new focus on "context-relatedness of purposeful human behavior," see Vayda, "Explaining Why Marings Fought," p. 173.

35. Vayda, "Phases of the Process of War and Peace among the Marings of New Guinea," 4–6.

36. Marcus and Flannery, *Zapotec Civilization,* pp. 244–45. (see also the section "Chiefdoms and States" in chapter 5.)

37. Brumfiel, "Factional Competition and Political Development in the New World: An Introduction," p. 3.

38. Gearing, *Priests and Warriors,* p. vi.

39. I have engaged in this pastime. In the conclusion to my study of Huron versus Iroquois warfare I speculate as to what might have happened if the Hurons, not the Iroquois, had won (see Otterbein, "Huron vs. Iroquois"; and *Feuding and Warfare*). Recently two volumes of articles explicitly focusing on answering the "what if" question for a number of historical events have been compiled by military historian Robert Cowley (*What If?* and *What If?™2*). The answer to a "what if" question is referred to as counterfactual history. If something does not occur, the situation is referred to as reverse counterfactual. For examples of the war gamers' work, see Wells, *Little Wars,* and Morschauser, *How to Play War Games in Miniature.*

Chapter 2

1. Cartmill, *A View to a Death in the Morning.*

2. Wrangham and Peterson, *Demonic Males;* Stanford, *The Hunting Apes.*

3. Cartmill, *A View to a Death in the Morning,* pp. 191–96.

4. Ibid., pp. 196–99.

5. Malinowski, "An Anthropological Analysis of War"; "War—Past, Present, and Future." (The former is an expanded version of the latter.)

6. Q. Wright, *A Study of War,* pp. 546, 560–61.

7. White, *The Science of Culture,* p. 131.

8. Newcomb, "Toward an Understanding of War," pp. 328–29.

9. Beals and Hoijer, *An Introduction to Anthropology,* pp. 502–503, 524.

10. Service, *Primitive Social Organization.*

11. Fried, *The Evolution of Political Society.*

12. Carneiro, *Evolutionism in Cultural Anthropology,* pp. 138–39.

13. Otterbein, *The Evolution of War,* p. xxix.

14. Otterbein, *The Evolution of War,* 2nd ed., p. xxi.

15. Cioffi-Revilla, "Ancient Warfare," pp. 86–88.

16. Kelly, *Peaceful Societies and the Origin of War,* p. 136.

17. Ibid., pp. 6, 140.

18. Dart, "*Australopithecus Africanus.*"

19. Cartmill, *A View to a Death in the Morning,* p. 9.

20. See Ardrey, *The Hunting Hypothesis.*

21. Lorenz, *On Aggression;* Ardrey, *The Hunting Hypothesis.*

22. Otterbein, "The Anthropology of War," p. 928.

23. Tiger, *Men in Groups,* pp. 165–93.

24. Cartmill, *A View to a Death in the Morning,* pp. 15–20.

25. Ibid., p. 18.

26. Wrangham and Peterson, *Demonic Males,* pp. 46–47, 198.

27. Sussman, "The Myth of Man the Hunter/Man the Killer and the Evolution of Human Morality," p. 128.

28. See Stanford, *The Hunting Apes.*

29. Stanford, *Significant Others*, pp. 11, 54–55.

30. For examples see Otterbein, "A History of Research on Warfare in Anthropology," p. 797.

31. Otterbein, "A History of Research on Warfare in Anthropology," p. 801.

32. R. B. Ferguson and Whitehead, eds., *War in the Tribal Zone*, pp. 3, 8–12. A second edition of the book was published in 1999.

33. R. B. Ferguson and Whitehead, eds., *War in the Tribal Zone*, pp. 17–18.

34. Ibid., pp. 19–25.

35. Ibid., pp. 26–27.

36. Otterbein, *The Evolution of War*, pp. xxiii–xxiv.

37. Claessen and Skalnik, eds., *The Early State*, pp. 562–63, 587, 629; see also Fried, *The Evolution of Political Society*, pp. 231–42.

38. Otterbein, "The Origins of War," pp. 266–70. This section on hawks and doves is adapted from that article.

39. Howard, *The Causes of Wars and Other Essays*, p. 5; see also pp. 2–5.

40. Ibid., p. 242. My stance embraces elements from both positions. I like guns and believe children should be taught firearms safety in schools (perhaps in the same class where they are taught safe sex). I also believe that the sale of handguns and semi-automatic weapons should be restricted and that such weapons should be regulated. I also believe that the United States should have a strong military for national defense, while at the same time I advocate reductions in military forces. These are not contradictory positions. My views on this subject have been set forth in my essay "The Dilemma of Disarming."

41. See Sponsel and Gregor, eds., *The Anthropology of Peace and Nonviolence*; Sponsel, "The Natural History of Peace"; and "Response to Otterbein."

42. Malinowski, "An Anthropological Analysis of War," pp. 521, 531.

43. Goldschmidt, "A Perspective on Anthropology," p. 800 (italics added for emphasis).

44. Carneiro, "The Chiefdom," pp. 63–68.

45. Ferrill, *The Origins of War from the Stone Age to Alexander the Great*, p. 13.

46. See Keegan, *A History of Warfare*, pp. 124–25, 139–42.

47. Cioffi-Revilla, "Origins and Evolution of War and Politics," pp. 1, 12; and "Origins and Age of Deterrence," p. 249. "Conquest" is his term.

48. McRandle, *The Antique Drums of War*, pp. viii, 164.

49. O'Connell, *Of Arms and Men*, p. 30 ("The Origins of War," p. 15, restates the same position in different words); and *Ride of the Second Horseman*, p. 29.

50. Wrangham and Peterson, *Demonic Males*, pp. 26, 47, 171–72.

51. Ehrenreich, *Blood Rites*, pp. 22, 118.

52. Kroeber and Fontana, *Massacre on the Gila*, pp. 165–74.

53. Keeley, "Giving War a Chance," p. 332.

54. P. Walker, "A Bioarchaeological Perspective on the History of Violence," pp. 584–87.

55. LeBlanc, *Constant Battles*, p. 9.

56. E.g., O'Connell, *Ride of the Second Horseman*, p. 58–61; Ehrenreich, *Blood Rites*, p. 121.

57. Bar-Yosef, "The Walls of Jericho"; Keeley, *War before Civilization*.

58. Service, *Primitive Social Organization*, pp. 143–77; see also Service, *Origins of the State and Civilization*.

59. Hallpike, *The Principles of Social Evolution*, p. 116; the chapter covers pp. 81–145.

60. Gabriel, *The Culture of War*, pp. 20–30.

61. Sponsel and Gregor, *The Anthropology of Peace and Nonviolence*.

62. Sponsel, "The Natural History of Peace," pp. 103, 105, 107; emphasis has been removed from the first quotation.

63. Gregor, ed., *A Natural History of Peace*, p. xvi.

64. Haas, "War," p. 1360.

65. Haas, "The Archaeology of War," p. 7.

66. Cioffi-Revilla, "Origins and Evolution of War and Politics," p. 12.

67. Keeley, "Giving War a Chance," p. 332. In this review chapter in a book on prehistoric Southwestern warfare, Keeley states, "I regard the contributions to this volume as signaling a healthy return to our scientific senses about prehistoric and

'primitive' warfare after four decades of increasing irrational meandering in a neo-Rousseauian, postmodernist 'woo-woo land'" (p. 342).

68. Chapple and Coon, *Principles of Anthropology*, pp. 616, 628–35.

69. Otterbein, *The Evolution of War*, p. 33.

70. Otterbein, *The Evolution of War*, pp. 63–70.

71. Naroll, "Does Military Deterrence Deter?" p. 17. Naroll served in the U.S. Army in World War II. He was stationed at Pearl Harbor on December 7, 1941, and later in Germany. He earned his Ph.D. in history. For more on the life of Raoul Naroll see "Obituary: Raoul Naroll (1920–1985)," *American Anthropologist* 89 (1987).

72. For Divale's passage, see Divale, *Warfare in Primitive Societies*, pp. xxi–xxii.

73. Keegan, *A History of Warfare*, pp. 98–99. As indicated by the ellipses, Divale's description is longer than this. Keegan shortened the original statement. The quotation here is taken from Keegan and shortened a bit further.

74. Divale, *Warfare in Primitive Societies*, p. xxii.

75. Sociobiology Study Group of Science for the People, "Sociobiology—Another Biological Determinism," p. 184.

76. The members of the Sociobiology Study Group of Science for the People listed are: L. Allen, B. Beckwith, J. Beckwith, S Chorover. D. Culver, N. Daniels, E. Dorfman, M. Duncan, E. Engelman, R. Fitten, K. Fuda, S. Gould, C. Gross, R. Hubbard, J. Hunt, H. Inouye, M. Kotelchuck, B. Lange, A. Leeds, R. Levins, R. Lewontin, E. Loescher, B. Ludwig, C. Madansky, L. Miller, R. Morales, S. Motheral, K. Muzal, N. Ostrom, R. Pyeritz, A. Reingold, M. Rosenthal, M. Mersky, M. Wilson, and H. Schreier.

77. Livingstone, "The Effects of Warfare on the Biology of the Human Species." pp. 8–11.

78. Gabriel, *The Culture of War*, p. 25.

79. For the New Guinea expert's statement on Highland arrows, see Heider, *Grand Valley Dani*, p. 104.

80. Gabriel and Metz, *From Sumer to Rome*, p. 3.

81. Chaliand, "Warfare and Strategic Cultures in History," p. 7.

82. Dawson, *The Origins of Western Warfare*, pp. 13–14. See also Dawson, *The First Armies*, p. 57. In this second source Dawson recognizes that "these ritual battles ... can easily escalate to much bloodier combats with hand-to-hand weapons."

83. Perlmutter, *Visions of War*, pp. 46, 48.

Chapter 3

1. Ehrenreich, *Blood Rites*, p. 22.

2. I believe the idea is original with me. If I am wrong, readers can correct me. For a discussion of defensible space and fortress architecture, see Otterbein, *Feuding and Warfare*, pp. 185, 190.

3. Kortlandt, "Wild Chimpanzees Using Clubs in Fighting an Animated Stuffed Leopard."

4. Gowlett, *Ascent to Civilization*, pp. 72–73.

5. Thieme, "Lower Paleolithic Hunting Spears from Germany."

6. See Bigelow, "The Role of Competition and Cooperation in Human Evolution"; Knauft, "Culture and Cooperation in Human Evolution"; and "The Human Evolution of Cooperative Interest."

7. Otterbein, *The Evolution of War*, pp. 5, 108.

8. Carneiro, foreword to *The Evolution of War*, by Otterbein, p. xii.

9. See Bower, "Ultrasocial Darwinism."

10. Otterbein, *The Ultimate Coercive Sanction*, pp. 49–60.

11. Behavior in accordance with norms may be the result not only of positive societal sanctions but also of genes that permit the individual to be readily socialized. Those rare individuals who cannot become socialized may have genes that prevent the normal functioning of the autonomic nervous system. In a sense they may have "genes for asocial behavior," that is, they may be genetically unsocializable. Studies by psychologists on the heritability of criminal behavior strongly suggest that some types of criminal behavior are genetically determined (Eysenck, *Crime and Personality*). The autonomic nervous system of asocial individuals appears to differ from that of individuals in the noncriminal population. The heritability of asocial behavior may be attributed to the heritability of autonomic nervous system mechanisms;

genes for asocial behavior appear to relate to emotional reactions determined by the functioning of the autonomic nervous system, specifically, slow electrodermal recovery and hyporeactiveness. Both of these have been found to predict delinquent behavior and to be highly associated with prison populations (see, e.g., Siddle, "Electrodermal Activity and Psychopathy"). See Otterbein, "Capital Punishment: A Selection Mechanism," p. 634.

12. Bingham, "Human Evolution and Human History," pp. 248, 251.

13. Palmer and Wright, "On Cultural-Selection Mechanics."

14. For a lengthy treatise on the relationship between cooperation and war, one should consult Peter A. Corning's "Synergy Goes to War: An Evolutionary Theory of Collective Violence."

15. Otterbein, *The Evolution of War,* p. xxii.

16. de Waal and Lanting, *Bonobo,* pp. 1–4.

17. Ibid., p. 63.

18. Ibid., pp. 2, 108–13.

19. Otterbein, "Feuding," p. 79; and "Clan and Tribal Conflict," p. 290.

20. The differences between the two chimpanzee species have been described in Itani, "Inequality versus Equality for Coexistence in Primate Socieites"; Kano, "Commentary: Social Regulation for Individual Coexistence in Pygmy Chimpanzees (*Pan paniscus*)"; and de Waal and Lanting, *Bonobo,* pp. 22–47, 72–85.

21. de Waal, "The Social Behavior of Chimpanzees and Bonobos," p. 407.

22. For the specialized anomaly, see Wrangham and Peterson, *Demonic Males;* on minimizing the differences, see Stanford, "The Social Behavior of Chimpanzees and Bonobos"; "The Hunting Apes"; and "Significant Others." Craig Stanford has pointed out that wild bonobos are more similar to wild chimpanzees than are the zoo-raised bonobos; they engage in sexual intercourse with the same frequency as do wild chimpanzees; their estrus cycle is shorter than that of zoo bonobos; and bonobos in the wild eat meat and engage in meat sharing, as do wild chimpanzees (Stanford, "Significant Others," pp. 28–29).

23. Boesch and Tomasello, "Chimpanzee and Human Cultures"; McGrew, *Chim-*

panzee Material Culture; de Waal and Lanting, *Bonobo,* p. 42.

24. For Wamba, see Kano, "Commentary: Social Regulation for Individual Coexistence in Pygmy Chimpanzees (*Pan paniscus*)"; and *The Last Ape.* For Lomako, see Fruth and Hohmann, "How Bonobos Handle Hunts and Harvests."

25. Blanchard, "Applicability of Animal Models to Human Aggression," p. 59; Blanchard, Hebert, and Blanchard, "Continuity vs. Political Correctness," p. 7. The male who responds aggressively to challenges is a common feature of modern American life. More than twenty-five years ago, two physicians described such individuals as having a Type A behavior pattern. They state that for such a behavior pattern "to explode into being, the *environmental challenge must always serve as the fuse for this explosion* (Friedman and Rosenman, *Type A Behavior and Your Heart,* p. 84 [italics in original]). I suspect that there were Type A males in prehistory, the equivalent of the alpha male chimpanzee of the primatologists. Furthermore, I suspect that such males, with the backing of their fraternal interest groups, were likely to issue challenges and to respond aggressively to challenges.

26. Dollard et. al., *Frustration and Aggression,* p. 1 (italics in original).

27. Stanford has asserted that "there are three sorts of benefits to group living: group defense of food, protection against predators, and a steady supply of mates" (Stanford, "Significant Others," p. 38). These three benefits parallel my three basic reasons for war.

28. Blanchard, Hebert, and Blanchard, "Continuity vs. Political Correctness," p. 9.

29. Blanchard, "Applicability of Animal Models to Human Aggression," pp. 57–60.

30. Ross, "Social Structure, Psychocultural Dispositions, and Violent Conflict," pp. 281–82.

31. Thoden van Velzen and van Wetering, "Residence, Power Groups and Intrasocietal Aggression," pp. 179–80.

32. See Coser, *The Functions of Social Conflict.*

33. E. Wilson, *On Human Nature,* p. 13.

34. van der Dennen, *The Origin of War.*

35. Charles Darwin, *The Descent of Man and Selection in Relation to Sex*, p. 116.

36. The terms "power grip" and "precision grip" were coined by John Napier in the 1960s (see A. Walker and Shipman, *The Wisdom of Bones*, p. 107). John Gowlett depicts the differences between ape and human extremities (*Ascent to Civilization*, p. 15).

37. Experiments in stone throwing and club wielding undertaken by physical anthropologists Mary Marzke and William Kimbel at Arizona State University seem to confirm that early hominids had these abilities. These statements were suggested in an episode of the PBS television series *Scientific American Frontiers*, "Life's Really Big Questions," broadcast on December 19, 2000, and hosted by Alan Alda. Experiments at Arizona State by Marzke and Kimbel showed chimpanzees throwing and striking, and they said that the Australopithecines had these capabilities. Some years ago Marzke suggested that the hands and anatomy of *Australopithecus afarensis* (Lucy belonged to this subspecies of Australopithicine) permitted the forceful overhand throwing of small round objects (Marzke, "Joint Functions and Grips of the *Australopithecus afarensis* Hand").

38. Oman, *The Art of War in the Middle Ages*, pp. 73–74.

39. Goodall, *The Chimpanzees of Gombe*, p. 533 (emphasis in original); see also pp. 488–534.

40. Some of the earliest weapons manufactured by humans were formed from stones by flaking—striking one stone against another to produce sharp edges on flakes. A bonobo or pygmy chimpanzee, Kanzi, has been taught to do stone flaking, but the flakes he made were crude. The technique that worked better for him was to throw a rock onto a hard surface so that it shattered, producing flakes (de Waal and Lanting, *Bonobo*, pp. 37, 44; Kline, *The Human Career*, pp. 232–33, 236; Tattersall and Schwartz, *Extinct Humans*, p. 120). Kanzi has been called an "anthropoid genius" (de Waal and Lanting, *Bonobo*, p. 44). Bonobos in the wild do not make or use tools (de Waal and Lanting, *Bonobo*, pp. 37, 42). The shaping of stones by flaking, to produce useful flakes and other tools, requires a precision grip. Perhaps Kanzi has shown us a technique used by early humans before the development of the technique of flaking.

41. See Mitani and Watts, "Demographic influences on the Hunting Behavior of Chimpanzees."

42. Mercader, Panger, and Boesch, "Excavation of a Chimpanzee Stone Tool Site in the African Rainforest," p. 1452.

43. See Vogel, "Can Chimps Ape Ancient Hominid Toolmakers?"; de Waal, "The Social Behavior of Chimpanzees and Bonobos," pp. 227–28, 239–46; McGrew, *Chimpanzee Material Culture*, pp. 115–20, 218–22.

44. McGrew, *Chimpanzee Material Culture*, pp. 180–81.

45. Boesch and Tomasello, "Chimpanzee and Human Cultures," p. 593.

46. A comprehensive review of chimpanzee behavior unequivocally concludes that many behaviors are customary or habitual (thirty-nine behaviors were found by comparing seven long-term studies). The nine authors of the study explicitly relate the behaviors to "imitative learning" (Whiten et al., "Cultures in Chimpanzees"). Frans de Waal, a student of both the chimpanzees and of the bonobos, has recently argued forcefully that his favorite animals have culture (de Waal, *The Ape and the Sushi Master*).

47. See Thieme, "Lower Paleolithic Hunting Spears from Germany."

48. See Kelly, *Peaceful Societies and the Origin of War*.

49. *Homo neanderthalensis* is today considered a fourth *Homo* species, but the emergence of the Neanderthals cannot be considered a major event. Some paleontologists recognize more *Homo* species.

50. Experts disagree as to which *Australopithecus* species was the ancestor of *Homo habilis* (see Gibbons, "In Search of the First Hominids"). Indeed, a recent fossil find from the Lake Chad region, dated to 7 million years ago, resembles *Homo habilis* in facial anatomy (Guterl, "All in the Family"). Perhaps this ape-human was the ancestor of both *Australopithecus* and *Homo*. The find, however, has generated controversy. Some scholars have questioned its alleged hominid status ("Celebrity-Skull Toumai Debated," p. 24).

51. See Whittaker and McCall, "Handaxe-Hurling Hominids."

52. See Balter and Gibbons, "A Glimpse of Humans' First Journey Out of Africa"; Gabunia et al., "Earliest Pleistocene Hominid Cranial Remains from Dmanisi, Republic of Georgia."

53. The fossil finds uncovered at Dmanisi show great variability in size. Some finds resemble *Homo habilis* more than they resemble *Homo erectus*. Several African animals, such as the ostrich and the short-necked giraffe, apparently accompanied these first pioneers (Gore, "New Find"). The pairing of early *Homo erectus/Homo habilis* with Oldowan tools is not surprising.

54. A. Walker and Shipman, *The Wisdom of the Bones*, pp. 230–46.

55. Johanson and Edey, *Lucy*, p. 287.

56. Leakey, *The Origin of Humankind*, p. 83. The archaic *sapiens* have been classified as *Homo heidelbergensis*. Both African and European examples are known (Johanson and Edgar, *From Lucy to Language*, pp. 194–210). In Europe these hominids evolved into *Homo neanderthalensis*, in Africa, into *Homo sapiens*. Ian Tattersall and Jeffrey Schwartz state, "Provisionally, the indications are that *H. heidelbergensis*, or the group to which it belongs, arose in Africa and emigrated [*sic*] to Europe. It also made it as far afield as China, if, for example, the Dali cranium . . . actually belongs to this species" (*Extinct Humans*, p. 170).

57. Hublin, "The Quest for Adam," p. 35.

58. See Gore, "New Find."

59. See Thieme, "Lower Paleolithic Hunting Spears from Germany."

60. Vencl, "Stone Age Warfare"; LeBlanc, *Constant Combat*, p. 59.

61. Balter, "In Search of the First Hominids," p. 1221.

62. Shea, "Middle Paleolithic Spear Point Technology," pp. 81–84.

63. Gowlett, *Ascent to Civilization*, p. 115.

64. Farmer, "The Origins of Weapon Systems," p. 681.

65. Johanson and Edgar, *From Lucy to Language*, p. 256.

66. Farmer, "The Origins of Weapons Systems," p. 681.

67. For the displacement of the Neanderthals and Asian *Homo erectus* see Tattersall and Schwartz, *Extinct Humans*, pp. 219–21, 235–36, and pp. 162–164, 224, respectively. See chapter 9 for a discussion of the implications of Neanderthal–*Homo sapiens* interbreeding.

68. There is evidence that Neanderthals and *Homo sapiens* resided in close proximity in the Levant (eastern Mediterranean lands) from about 100,000 to 47,000 years ago; they shared the same Mousterian tool tradition (Tattersall and Schwartz, *Extinct Humans*, p. 234).

69. Shea, "Neanderthals, Competition, and the Origin of Modern Human Behavior in the Levant," p. 184; Farmer, "The Origins of Weapons Systems."

70. Lemonick, "How Man Began."

71. Kline, *The Human Career*, p. 586. My section on the evolution of humankind is derived from the 1999 edition of Kline's encyclopedic, eight-hundred-page text. I have incorporated into this description the new information on early *Homo erectus* in Georgia (Balter and Gibbons, "A Glimpse of Humans' First Journey Out of Africa") and the first spears from Germany (Thieme, "Lower Paleolithic Hunting Spears from Germany"). This information enhances Kline's interpretation.

72. Diamond, *Guns, Germs, and Steel*, pp. 59–69.

73. R. Clark, *The Global Imperative*, p. 31.

74. See MacDonald and Hewlett, "Reproductive Interests and Forager Mobility."

75. Weiss, "In Search of Times Past," p. 137.

76. See Holliday, "Evolution at the Crossroads."

77. Farmer, "The Origins of Weapon Systems," p. 680.

78. Dickson, "The Atlatl Assessed," p. 20; Farmer, "The Origins of Weapon Systems," pp. 680–81.

79. Cattelain, "Hunting During the Upper Paleolithic," p. 214.

80. Corning, "Synergy Goes to War," p. 60.

81. Demographic modeling shows that only a 1 or 2 percent rise in mortality would have extinguished Neanderthal populations within a thousand years (see Zubrow, "The Demographic Modeling of Neanderthal Extinction").

82. Leakey, *The Origin of Humankind*,

pp. 94, 99; Tattersall, *The Last Nean-derthal,* pp. 200–202 (Tattersall's "revised edition" [1999] is identical, except for publisher and dedication, to the first edition [1995]); Tattersall and Schwartz, *Extinct Humans,* p. 221.

83. Tattersall, *The Last Neanderthal,* pp. 199–200.

84. Ibid., pp. 199, 203. This rapid replacement of *Homo neanderthalensis* by *Homo sapiens* appears to be similar to a phenomenon that I have observed at bird feeders in my backyard in western New York. Twenty-five years ago, many purple finches (*Carpodacus purpureus*) were feeding. A similar species, the house finch (*Carpodacus mexicanus*), seems to have replaced the purple finch population almost completely. House finches were introduced into the eastern United States about 1940 and have spread rapidly from their point of release in the New York City area (Roger Tory Peterson, *A Field Guide to the Birds: A Completely New Guide to All the Birds of Eastern and Central North America* [Boston: Houghton Mifflin, 1980], pp. 270–77 and range map no. 356). The house finches have the adaptive trait of being able to tolerate many companions at feeders; purple finches do not. Today I see house finches that look, to me, like purple finches, and I suspect interbreeding. But my serious birdwatcher friends insist that the two are separate species that do not interbreed.

85. Although modern *Homo sapiens* may have reached Australia shortly after forty thousand years ago, some scholars believe that there might have been an early migration of southeastern Asian peoples about sixty thousand years ago. The megafauna survived alongside *Homo sapiens* for a considerable period, with the large marsupial mammals, such as the giant kangaroo, not becoming extinct until perhaps twenty-five thousand years ago (Gowlett, *Ascent to Civilization,* pp. 136–39).

86. See Laughlin and Harper, "Peopling the Continents," pp. 16–17.

87. For a summary of the evidence that indicates an early coastal route to both North and South America, see Begley and Murr, "The First American" (this *Newsweek* article includes a map). Both *National Geographic Magazine* (December, 2000) and *Scientific American* (September, 2000) also summarize new evidence for the early coastal route and present maps (see Parfit, "Dawn of Humans"; and Nemecek, "Who Were the First Americans?").

88. Dillehay, *The Settlement of the Americas,* p. 5. These are radiocarbon dates. Some scholars correct them by adding two thousand years, for radiocarbon dates of around eleven thousand years (T. Flannery, *The Eternal Frontier,* pp. 174–75).

89. Farb, *Man's Rise to Civilization,* p. 198.

90. Dillehay, *The Settlement of the Americas,* p. 287; Kline, *The Human Career,* pp. 559–65.

91. Dillehay, *The Settlement of the Americas,* p. 284.

92. Chatters, "The Recovery and First Analyses of an Early Holocene Human Skeleton from Kennewick, Washington."

93. Crawford, *The Origins of Native Americans,* pp. 21–31.

94. On the bow and arrow, see the section "Weapons Development" in chapter 4; for projectile injuries and warfare patterns in western Canada, see Lambert, "Patterns of Violence in Prehistoric Hunter-Gatherer Societies of Coastal Southern California," and Maschner, "The Evolution of Northwest Coast Warfare," respectively.

95. For Crow Creek massacre see P. Willey, *Prehistoric Warfare on the Great Plains;* for warfare on the Gulf Coastal Plain see Baker, *No Golden Age of Peace;* for chiefdoms and fortifications in the Southeast see Pauketat, *The Ascent of Chiefs;* for warfare in the Southwest see Billman, Lambert, Leonard, "Cannibalism, Warfare, and Drought in the Mesa Verde Region during the Twelfth Century A.D."

96. See Linton, "Nomad Raids and Fortified Pueblos"; Rice and LeBlanc, *Deadly Landscapes;* Wilcox and Haas, "The Scream of the Butterfly: Competition and Conflict in the Prehistoric Southwest."

97. Tattersall, *The Last Neanderthal,* p. 202.

Chapter 4

1. In the Levantine (eastern Mediterranean) Mousterian assemblages, Levallois points were probably hafted to shafts that were thrust or thrown a short distance, but evidence for hafted stone spear

point use in the European Mousterian is inconclusive (Shea, "Middle Paleolithic Spear Point Technology," p. 99). Mousterian tools are from the Middle Paleolithic.

2. Dickson, "The Atlatl Assessed," p. 8.

3. Ibid., pp. 9–14.

4. Cattelain, "Hunting during the Upper Paleolithic," p. 230.

5. Kline, *The Human Career,* pp. 540–42; Cattelain, "Hunting during the Upper Paleolithic," p. 220.

6. Thomas, *Exploring Ancient North America,* p. 58; Blitz, "Adoption of the Bow in Prehistoric North America," provides similar dates.

7. Blitz, "Adoption of the Bow in Prehistoric North America," p. 135.

8. Ibid., p. 136.

9. The composite, double convex bow makes its first appearance on a victory stele in Mesopotamia in about 2250 B.C.E. during the reign of a grandson of Sargon the Great (Gabriel and Metz, *From Sumer to Rome,* p. 167; see Yadin, *The Art of Warfare in Biblical Lands,* pp. 47–48, 150–51). Yigail Yadin believes that the composite bow made it possible for the Akkadians to conquer and gain domination over Mesopotamia and beyond. He describes its "comparatively long range . . . as revolutionary" (p. 48). I believe that the spear thrower with a greater range than a throwing spear was likewise a revolutionary weapon that permitted *Homo sapiens* to enter Europe and displace the Neanderthals.

10. Dickson, "The Atlatl Assessed," pp. 21–24.

11. In 1998, I observed a modern atlatl competition and participated in a practice session. I can personally attest to both the initial difficulty in obtaining accuracy and the skill and effectiveness of serious competitors.

12. Cattelain, "Hunting during the Upper Paleolithic," pp. 221, 230–31.

13. Ellis, "Factors Influencing the Use of Stone Projectile Tips," p. 63.

14. Kline, *The Human Career,* pp. 564–65. Tim Flannery argues that it was Clovis hunters—not climatic change—that wiped out most of the megafauna of North America (*The Eternal Frontier,* pp. 173–205). Flannery states, "The Clovis people made their stone points for an extraordinarily brief period—300 years is what has been determined from uncalibrated radiocarbon dates. These lethal yet elegant sculptures became useless around 12,900 years ago, I believe because . . . the last of the very large creatures they were designed to kill had all fallen victim to their efficiency" (p. 183).

15. Figure 4.2 has been developed from a graph in Scupin and DeCorse, *Anthropology* (p. 172). I have given it greater time depth, distinguished between small and large game, and generalized it so that it pertains to all regions in which pristine states arose.

16. Stiner, Munro, and Surovell, "The Tortoise and the Hare," p. 58.

17. K. Flannery, Comment on "The Tortoise and the Hare" by Stiner, Munro, and Surovell, p. 64. Charles L. Redman has stated that

> archaeologists have identified the cultures of Western Europe at the end of the Pleistocene (terminal Wurm) as *Mesolithic.* The tool inventory and the way of life of the people living then were strikingly different from those of their Upper Paleolithic ancestors. Some scholars have used the term Mesolithic in referring to cultures of the Near East at the end of the last Ice Age. However, these cultures and their tools are not so markedly different from those of their predecessors; hence, most Near Eastern archaeologists refer to this period as *Epipaleolithic.* Important changes nevertheless did take place in the lifestyle of the Epipaleolithic people. Among the changes were a continued increase in the size of communities and more technological specialization, especially with the introduction of such facilities as storage pits and grinding stones. (*The Rise of Civilization,* p. 51)

18. Stiner, Munro, and Surovell, "The Tortoise and the Hare," p. 58.

19. Diamond, *Guns, Germs, and Steel,* pp. 110–11.

20. Numerous technical and popular sources that I perused make no mention of this occurring, e.g., Burenhult, *People of the Stone Age;* Cauvin, *The Birth of the Gods and the Origins of Agriculture;* Diamond, *Guns, Germs, and Steel;* Harris, *The Origins and Spread of Agriculture and Pastoralism in*

Eurasia; Harris and Hillman, *Foraging and Farming;* Henry, *From Foraging to Agriculture;* MacNeish, *The Origins of Agriculture and Settled Life.*

21. Roper, "A Survey of the Evidence for Intrahuman Killing in the Pleistocene," p. 447; the drawings at Peche Merle and Cougnac are shown in Bachechi, Fabbri, and Mallegni, "An Arrow-Caused Lesion in a Late Upper Paleolithic Human Pelvis," p. 136, and in Kelly, *Peaceful Societies and the Origin of War,* pp. 153–54.

22. Kelly, *Peaceful Societies and the Origin of War,* pp. 153–54.

23. Otterbein, "The Origins of War," p. 255.

24. See Lee, *The Dobe !Kung,* pp. 95–96; also in Otterbein, *The Ultimate Coercive Sanction,* pp. 37–39.

25. Ferrill, *The Origins of War from the Stone Age to Alexander the Great,* p. 211; Kelly, *Peaceful Societies and the Origin of War,* pp. 154–55. Kelly, however, views the scene as warfare, rather than capital punishment: "The execution group . . . vividly portrays collective responsibilities for vengeance encoded in the practice of pincushioning" (p. 155).

26. Ferrill, *The Origins of War from the Stone Age to Alexander the Great,* p. 22.

27. O'Connell, "The Origins of War," pp. 10, 13.

28. Tacon and Chippendale, "Australia's Ancient Warriors," pp. 214–24, 226–27. Tacon and Chippendale are explicitly following my evolutionary scheme (Otterbein, *The Evolution of War*) and Bruce Knauft's thoughts on human evolution (Knauft, "Culture and Cooperation in Human Evolution").

29. R. B. Ferguson, "Violence and War in Prehistory," p. 322.

30. See Bachechi, Fabbri, and Mallegni, "An Arrow-Caused Lesion in a Late Upper Paleolithic Human Pelvis"; Wendorf and Schild, "The Wadi Kubbaniya Skeleton."

31. Bachechi, Fabbri, and Mallegni, "An Arrow-Caused Lesion in a Late Upper Paleolithic Human Pelvis," p. 137. These authors present in tabular form the data on the six sites with pierced human bones, as well as from two sites where animal bones are pierced. The artifacts include a fragment of a triangle, an "arrow head," fragments of backed tools, a fragment of backed point, a backed point and fragments of backed tools, microlithic backed tools, and spear points.

32. Wendorf, *The Prehistory of Nubia,* p. 993. The sex of one individual could not be ascertained; hence the number of men, women, and children killed totals twenty-three, not twenty-four.

33. Kelly, *Peaceful Societies and the Origin of War,* p. 151.

34. Wendorf and Schild, "The Wadi Kubbaniya Skeleton," p. 62; Wendorf quoted in Gore, "People Like Us," p. 111.

35. Kelly, *Peaceful Societies and the Origin of War,* p. 174.

36. Wendorf, personal communication, October 26, 2000.

37. Forensic anthropologist Phillip Walker makes the following observation: "According to my calculations, in frontal view a person's skeleton occupies about 60% of the target area a body presents to an assailant. This means that about half of the time a projectile randomly shot at a person would not impact bone. Thus, we can safely assume that the frequency of injuries detected in ancient skeletal remains is just the 'tip of the iceberg' in terms of the actual incidence of injuries" ("A Bioarchaeological Perspective on the History of Violence," p. 584).

38. Brian Ferguson has noted that "the 'classic' combat related injury is a parry fracture—a forearm broken as if warding off a blow—but this could happen in many ways" ("Violence and War in Prehistory," p. 323).

39. Chatters, "The Recovery and First Analysis of an Early Holocene Human Skeleton from Kennewick, Washington," pp. 291, 298.

40. Ibid., pp. 309–10, 312.

41. The controversy has been reviewed by archaeologist David Hurst Thomas in *Archaeology,* pp. xix–xxvi, 231–38, 279.

42. McManamon, "K-Man Undergoes Complete Physical," pp. 21–22; Lathrop, "Policy Monitor," p. 26; Begley and Murr, "The First American."

43. Owsley and Jantz, "Biography in the Bones," p. 58.

44. Smith, "Osteological Indications of Warfare in the Archaic Period of the Western Tennessee Valley," pp. 250–56. The projectile points are not pictured or described.

45. Ibid., p. 259.

46. Defleur et al., "Neanderthal Cannibalism at Moula-Guercy, Ardèche, France"; Culotta, "Neanderthals Were Cannibals, Bones Show," p. 18.

47. Johanson and Edgar, *From Lucy to Language*, pp. 93–96. The evidence for cannibalism has recently been reviewed by Phillip Walker, "A Bioarchaeological Perspective on the History of Violence," pp. 584–86.

48. Malinowski, *A Scientific Theory of Culture and Other Essays*, pp. 95–99.

49. Fried, *The Evolution of Political Society*, pp. 27–49.

50. Ibid., p. 34.

51. Boehm, "Egalitarian Behavior and Reverse Dominance Hierarchy," pp. 232, 240. For a less technical discussion of this research, see Boehm, *Hierarchy in the Forest*, pp. 64–124. In a published comment upon Boehm's 1993 article, I rejected the concept of egalitarian society as utterly meaningless, arguing that it was a monolithic stereotype that masked tremendous variation in behavior. Great variability exists among hunters and gatherers (Otterbein, Comment on "Egalitarian Behavior and Reverse Dominance Hierarchy" by Christopher Boehm, p. 244; see also by Otterbein, Comment on "Reconsidering Violence in Simple Human Societies" by Bruce M. Knauft; Comment on "On Semai Homicide" by Robert K. Dentan; Comment on "The Human Community as a Primate Society" by Lars Rodseth et al.; and Comment on "Violence and Sociality in Human Evolution" by Bruce Knauft). The same variability exists among horticultural and pastoral tribal peoples. Boehm replied to my criticism:

> Otterbein indicates that "egalitarian behavior" is simply too general a concept to be useful in cross-cultural analysis. But decisive control of the abuse of power by leaders (and others) in little-centralized societies that subscribe to *primus inter pares* ethos is empirically distinguishable from the situation of centralized polities that lack an egalitarian ethos, and this is a distinction that can be useful for typological and processual analysis if one is interested in larger questions. (Boehm, "Egalitarian Behavior and Reverse Dominance Hierarchy," p. 246)

I agree with his reply, which contains a point that I will elaborate upon in chapter 5 in the section "How the State Arose." On the other hand, Boehm does not address my charge that the notion of the egalitarian band is a monolithic stereotype. Boehm only contrasts little-centralized societies with centralized societies. Meanwhile, however, what I am disputing is the notion that there are egalitarian societies, not the existence of leveling mechanisms. Whether an egalitarian ethos is universal among both bands and tribes is doubtful, although Boehm asserts that it is so.

52. The only community that I am familiar with that approaches the notion of the egalitarian society is Garrison Keillor's Lake Wobegone, "where the women are strong, all the men are good-looking, and all the children are above average" (Keillor, "In Search of Lake Wobegone," *National Geographic Magazine* 198 [December 2000]: 90). A basic reference on the community of Lake Wobegone can be found in Keillor, *Lake Wobegone Days* (New York: Viking, 1985). In the December, 2000, issue of *National Geographic Magazine* Keillor described how he created Lake Wobegone, conceived when he was residing in Stearns County, Minnesota. He states, "I respect Stearns County for its egalitarianism. It may look down on strangers, but it looks down on all of them equally, and it doesn't look down on people because they have less money or do dirty work" (Keillor, "In Search of Lake Wobegone," p. 108).

53. Otterbein, *The Ultimate Coercive Sanction*, pp. 49–60, 105, 108. On page 108, I stated, "Group survival theory argues that any act that is seen by the members of a band as threatening the survival of their group will subject the perpetrator of that act to capital punishment. Findings that support predictions from the theory include: Those offenses that endanger the welfare of the group—incest, sacrilegious acts (such as sorcery, witchcraft, and violations of taboos), and homicide—are capital offenses. The community decides upon the execution. The execution occurs in secret, with weapons."

54. Salzman includes Elliot Fratkin and Eric Roth in his "revisionist" category (Salzman, "Toward a Balanced Approach to the Study of Equality," p. 282; Fratkin,

Roth, and Nathan, "When Nomads Settle"; Roth, "On Pastoral Egalitarianism").

55. Anthropologist Herbert Lewis has well described the relationship between leaders and followers and how each benefits from the other (H. Lewis, *Leaders and Followers,* pp. 50-5-50-6). For multiple mates as a reward see French anthropologist Claude Lévi-Strauss's "The Social and Psychological Aspects of Chieftainship in a Primitive Tribe," which describes for the Nambikuara of South America the several young females who act as the leader's consorts and aid him in his activities. Sociologist George C. Homans, in *Social Behavior: Its Elementary Forms* (1961), describes the reciprocal relationship between high status and low status individuals—the high status individual receives deference and in turn rewards low status individuals with recognition and goods.

56. Otterbein, *The Evolution of War,* pp. 20-21.

57. Rivers, *The Todas,* p. 586.

58. Firth, *We, the Tikopia,* pp. 312, 374.

59. There are other societies that were not in my sample that have not engaged in warfare in their recent history. They, like my sample societies, are isolated both physically and socially. They are generally refugee groups, meaning defeated peoples who have fled their original homeland, or they are enclaved peoples who totally lack political independence (see Dentan, "The Rise, Maintenance and Destruction of Peaceable Polities"; and "Surrendered Men").

60. Stefánsson, *My Life with the Eskimo,* p. 70.

61. Huntingford, "The Political Organization of the Dorobo," p. 134.

62. Otterbein, *The Evolution of War,* p. 21.

63. Hobhouse, Wheeler, and Ginsberg, *The Material Culture and Social Institutions of the Simpler Peoples,* pp. 228-33; Q. Wright, *A Study of War,* p. 556; Otterbein, *The Evolution of War,* pp. 145-48; C. Ember, "Myths about Hunter-Gatherers," p. 444; Otterbein, "Killing of Captured Enemies"; Kelly, *Peaceful Societies and the Origin of War,* p. 52.

64. On the frequency of war see Otterbein, Comment on "Violence and Sociality in Human Evolution" by Bruce Knauft; on the frequency of homicide

and capital punishment see Otterbein, Comment on "On Semai Homicide" by Robert K. Dentan.

65. Hart and Pilling, *The Tiwi of North Australia,* pp. 79-87; Pilling, "Discussion: Predation and Warfare," p. 158; Pilling, "Sneak Attacks," pp. 93-95.

66. Hart and Pilling, *The Tiwi of North Australia,* p. 99. The section entitled "Warfare" covers pp. 83-88.

67. Hart and Pilling, *The Tiwi of North Australia,* p. 83.

68. Pilling, "Discussion: Predation and Warfare," p. 158.

69. Hart, Pilling, and Goodale, *The Tiwi of North Australia,* 3rd ed., pp. 93-95.

70. Kelly, *Peaceful Societies and the Origin of War,* p. 159 for the quotation; on origination of war, pp. 138-39; for cave painting and burial interpretations, pp. 148-58.

71. See Dickson, *The Dawn of Belief,* pp. 176-89.

72. Otterbein, *The Evolution of War.*

73. Tom Wintringham, *The Story of Weapons and Tactics from Troy to Stalingrad,* p. 22. Wintringham's book is a favorite of mine. I read it while in high school and later, while in graduate school, obtained my own copy, used, but with dust jacket, from a famous bookstore in Philadelphia. Because of my love for this book, I have cited it several times in this section. I learned from this book an important theory of how weapons and tactics evolve, a theory I put to use in my first paper on the Iroquois. I have acknowledged my debt to Wintringham in my collected papers (Otterbein, "Why the Iroquis Won," p. 56; Otterbein, *Feuding and Warfare,* pp. xxiii, 2).

74. Ferrill, *The Origins of War from the Stone Age to Alexander the Great,* pp. 18-19; Ardrey, *The Hunting Hypothesis,* p. 172; Wintringham, *The Story of Weapons and Tactics from Troy to Stalingrad,* pp. 22-23.

75. Otterbein, *The Evolution of War,* p. 44; Otterbein, "The Anthropology of War," p. 928; Woodburn, "Egalitarian Societies," p. 436.

76. Otterbein, *The Evolution of War,* p. 40.

77. Richard Edward Connell's 1924 short story, "The Most Dangerous Game," tells the tale of a shipwrecked sailor who is

hunted by the island's sole resident, a big game hunter who believes that the most challenging quarry is another human being (Connell, "The Most Dangerous Game," in *Great Tales of Terror and the Supernatural,* ed. Herbert A. Wise and Phyllis Fraser [New York: Modern Library, 1944). With this story perhaps in mind, Sherwood L. Washburn and C. S. Lancaster wrote in 1968, "And until recently war was viewed in much the same way as hunting. Other human beings were simply *the most dangerous game"* (Washburn and Lancaster, "The Evolution of Hunting," p. 22; italics added).

78. Wintringham, *The Story of Weapons and Tactics from Troy to Stalingrad,* p. 22; Tiger, *Men in Groups,* p. 95; Morris, *Manwatching,* p. 159; Feest, *The Art of War,* p. 17; Ferrill, *The Origins of War from the Stone Age to Alexander the Great,* p. 20.

79. Biolsi, "Ecological and Cultural Factors in Plains Indian Warfare."

80. This subsistence economy variable, with accompanying codes for societies, is in Murdock's *Atlas of World Cultures,* p. 92. It contains five components: [1] collection of wild plants and small land fauna; [2] hunting, including trapping and fowling; [3] fishing, including shellfishing and the pursuit of large aquatic animals; [4] animal husbandry; [5] agriculture.

For each component Murdock estimated the relative dependency of the coded society on that subsistence activity. The numbers used represent percentages; for each society the five numbers, representing the five components, total 10 (the equivalent of 100 percent). Hunter-gatherers have zero scores for [4] and [5]. Since many of the hunter-gatherers fish, [1] and [2] need not total 10 (or 100 percent) and thus are not the complement of each other. Therefore, in statistical analyses, hunting and plant gathering should be treated as separate variables.

81. Carol R. Ember provides warfare frequency codes for hunter-gatherers. The points on the variable are defined as follows:

a = warfare occurs almost continuously all year round
b = warfare occurs almost continuously within a season of the year
c = warfare occurs at least once every two years

d = warfare occurs occasionally
e = warfare occurs rarely or never

Some societies were coded, however, as "ab," "cd," "de," or ">c." The last of these notations was used when the data were not clear as to whether warfare was "a," "b," or "c" but when it seemed to be at least "c." For the present analyses, the codes are assumed to be at least an ordinal scale (C. Ember, "Residential Variation among Hunter-Gatherers," p. 223).

82. The correlation coefficient for these thirty-one societies is $+.45$; it is significant at the .01 level. The product-moment correlation r is used for analyses, although not all assumptions are met; its robustness has been demonstrated. Furthermore, its use permits the comparison of correlations in analyses and the examination of the combined prediction through multiple correlation.

83. Otterbein, *The Evolution of War,* pp. 20–21.

84. The correlation coefficient is $-.30$; it is significant at the .05 level.

85. If both the positive correlation between hunting and warfare and the negative correlation between gathering and warfare are used in combination, the accuracy of the prediction of warfare increases slightly; the multiple correlation coefficient is $+.48$; it is significant at the .025 level. Statistically, the multiple correlation takes into account any relationship between the two independent variables—hunting and gathering. It is interesting that the use of the two variables in a prediction equation increases the accuracy, although it does not increase the significance of the prediction. The correlation coefficient for the relationship between fishing and the frequency of warfare is $+.18$; it is not significant.

86. Murdock and Morrow, "Subsistence Economy and Supportive Practices," pp. 47–48. The variable was developed and used for the standard cross-cultural sample. The points on the variable are defined as follows:

F = hunting consists predominantly of the snaring, netting, or shooting of waterfowl or other birds
S = hunting consists predominantly of the trapping, netting, or shooting of small animals

L = hunting consists predominantly of the killing of large game, e.g., buffalo, deer, guanaco, or kangaroos

V = hunting assumes two or more of the above forms, no one of which preponderates.

Codes for eighteen societies in Figure 4.4 are available (Murdock and Morrow, "Subsistence Economy and Supportive Practices," pp. 51–55). For hypothesis testing, "L" is contrasted with "F," "S," and "V." Note that the "V" category can include hunters who may occasionally kill large game but for whom this form of hunting does not predominate because they also kill small mammals and/or birds; however, it is not possible, with the codes of Murdock and Morrow, to discriminate these groups from groups who hunt only small game and waterfowl or other birds.

87. The correlation coefficient for Figure 4.6 is +.39; it is significant at the .05 level of probability. Although it would be interesting to include this as a third variable in a prediction equation, the small number of cases makes it unreasonable to do so (eighteen cases, with four variables). The correlation may have been lowered because some societies classified as "V" hunt large animals.

88. Statistically, least-squares regression lines could be fitted to the data to describe the relationship between subsistence and warfare. To do so would suggest more precision of measurement than is justified by the nature of the measures.

Chapter 5

1. The assertion that agriculture and village life are inextricably linked is an overstatement made for the sake of emphasis. In recent centuries some native peoples whose subsistence depends on hunting and gathering have on occasion been able to live in permanent settlements. Examples include Indians of the Northwest Coast of North America and native peoples of Alaska. In the Near East, permanent settlements, as at Jericho, precede the domestication of plants (Cauvin, *The Birth of the Gods and the Origins of Agriculture*, pp. 15–21).

2. Henry, *From Foraging to Agriculture*, p. 232.

3. Fagan, *Floods, Famines, and Emperors*, pp. 71–95; Lewin, *In the Age of Mankind*, pp. 188–204; Wenke, *Patterns in Prehistory*, pp. 268–330.

4. Lewin, *In the Age of Mankind*, pp. 199–200; Moore, Hillman, and Legge, eds., *Village on the Euphrates*, pp. 477–78; Rowley-Conway, "Abu Hureyra," p. 27.

5. Legge and Rowley-Conway, "The Exploitation of Animals," p. 449.

6. Moore, Hellman, and Legge, eds., *Village on the Euphrates*, pp. 494, 507.

7. I have also discussed the site of Abu Hureyra with its chief excavator, Andrew Moore, on January 23, 2003, and he also concludes that the people of Abu Hureyra did not engage in warfare.

8. Moore, Hellman, and Legge, eds., *Village on the Euphrates*, p. 288; see also pp. 266, 450.

9. Thomas, *Archaeology*, pp. 283–87; Diamond, *Guns, Germs, and Steel*, pp. 114–30.

10. Diamond, *Guns, Germs and Steel*, p. 100.

11. Price and Brown, eds., *Prehistoric Hunter-Gatherers;* Henry, "Preagricultural Sedentism"; Lewin, *In the Age of Mankind*, pp. 193–97.

12. For the definition of domesticated animals, see Diamond, *Guns, Germs, and Steel*, p. 159; see also pp. 157–75.

13. Diamond, *Guns, Germs, and Steel*, pp. 141–42; Henry, "Preagricultural Sedentism," p. 376; Legge and Rowley-Conway, "The Exploitation of Animals," p. 439; Rowley-Conway, "Abu Hureyra," p. 27. Legge and Rowley-Conway believe that the primary method of hunting gazelles was pole and pitfall animal traps or "desert kites," rather than stalking and then shooting with arrows ("The Exploitation of Animals," pp. 447–50). This kind of hunting is not conducive to the development of raiding and warfare.

14. Gowlett, *Ascent to Civilization*, p. 161.

15. Bar-Yosef, "The Walls of Jericho"; Cauvin, *The Birth of the Gods and the Origins of Agriculture*, pp. 34–39. The walls of Jericho are discussed further in the section "Walls and Fortifications" in chapter 7.

16. Jared Diamond asserts that plants were domesticated in at least nine regions (*Guns, Germs, and Steel*, p. 100).

17. Cavalli-Sforza and Cavalli-Sforza, *The Great Human Diasporas*, p. 131; Diamond, *Guns, Germs, and Steel*, p. 135; Wenke, *Patterns in Prehistory*, p. 287.

18. Breasted says he "suggested the term" Fertile Crescent in the high-school history text *Ancient Times* (1916): "The term has since become current and is now widely used. . . . Its western end is at the southeastern corner of the Mediterranean, the center lies directly north of Arabia, and the eastern end is at the northern end of the Persian Gulf. It lies like a horseshoe opening southward with one side stretching along the eastern shore of the Mediterranean and the other reaching out to the Persian Gulf, while the center has its back against the northern mountains" (*The Conquest of Civilization*, p. 116). Breasted is very clear that the Fertile Crescent included the first states in southern Mesopotamia.

19. On crop domestication in western Africa, see Diamond, *Guns, Germs, and Steel*, p. 100; on Bantu peoples, see Murdock, *Africa*, pp. 35–39.

20. Claessen and Skalnik, eds., *The Early State*, pp. 9–17; Haas, *The Evolution of the Prehistoric State*, pp. 34–85.

21. The "mantra" has long been accepted by many social scientists. A variant of it was used by Ronald Cohen in a chapter subtitle of *Warfare, Culture, and Environment* (1984): "Warfare and State Formation: Wars Make States and States Make Wars."

22. See Carneiro, "The Chiefdom," pp. 45–46, 70–71; K. Flannery, "The Ground Plans of Archaic States," pp. 15–21, 55–56; G. Johnson, *Local Exchange and Early State Development in Southwestern Iran*, pp. 2–3.

23. See Heider, *Grand Valley Dani*.

24. Otterbein, "Why the Iroquis Won"; and "Huron vs. Iroquois"; Hunt, *The Wars of the Iroquis*; Engelbrecht, *Iroquoia*.

25. Ferrill, *The Origins of War from the Stone Age to Alexander the Great*, pp. 30–31; Roper, "Evidence of Warfare in the Near East from 10,000–4,300 B.C.," pp. 321–23.

26. "Unlike any other community of this period and area, access to the rooms of Catal Huyuk was only by ladder through the roof—there are no front doors—and the close packing of structures is such that much of the movement among the houses must have been on the roofs. The roof access may reflect a need for defense, for once the inhabitants had pulled up the ladders on the outside walls, the settlement would have been difficult to attack" (Wenke, *Patterns in Prehistory*, pp. 392–93). This and other interpretations never mention the possibility that attackers could have carried their own ladders and launched their attack at night.

27. Cauvin, *The Birth of the Gods and the Origins of Agriculture*, pp. 93–95.

28. Gowlett, *Ascent to Civilization*; Wenke, *Patterns in Prehistory*, p. 393.

29. Roper, "Evidence of Warfare in the Near East from 10,000–4,300 B.C.," pp. 327–31.

30. Teggart, *Rome and China*.

31. H. Lewis, "Warfare and the Origin of the State," p. 217.

32. Gearing, *Priests and Warriors*, pp. 106–12.

33. Engels, *The Origin of the Family, Private Property, and the State*.

34. Childe, *Man Makes Himself;* and *What Happened in History;* White, *The Science of Culture*. I was familiar with the writings of Childe and White while I was a student, both undergraduate and graduate, in the 1950s. Paperback copies of their books, read at the time, still stand on my shelves.

35. On April 3, 1980, Henri Claessen, coauthor of *The Early State* (1978), discussed with me Engels's influence on Fried, and I pointed out to him that Fried did not cite Engels.

36. Fried's theory diverges sharply from Elman Service's theory of the origin of centralized political systems. Service views the chief as a redistributor of basic resources (see his book *Primitive Social Organization*). Fried and Service were office mates at Columbia University and remained good friends throughout their lives (Harding, "Obituary: Elman Rogers Service," p. 162).

My wife has pointed out the irony of their names. Fried should have a theory about freedom, and Service should have a theory about servitude. Somehow, names and theories became reversed. Fried's theory involves "Servitude," while Service's theory posits "Freedom."

37. Fried, *The Evolution of Political Society,*

p. 185. When I first read Fried's book in the spring of 1968, while conducting ethnographic fieldwork in the Bahama Islands, I rejected his theory on the basis that he had no supporting examples. Jonathan Haas, his student, had the same concern (Haas, *The Evolution of the Prehistoric State*, p. 55).

38. Fried, *The Evolution of Political Society*, pp. 214, 230, 232.

39. Fried, *The Notion of Tribe*, p. 10; see also Fried, "Tribe to State or State to Tribe in Ancient China?"

40. *Rashomon* is a Japanese movie from 1950. A bandit attacks a couple on a road and kills the man, a samurai. Later each tells the story of what happened, the samurai through a medium. There is also a witness, a woodcutter (Heider, "The Rashomon Effect," p. 74). I believe that by the end of the film viewers are unable to keep the conflicting versions separate. I certainly was unable to do so. The film is based on a short story titled "In a Grove," by Ryunosuke Akutagawa. It was translated into English by Takashi Kojima as the first story in a collection, *Rashomon and Other Stories*. The second story is titled "Rashomon," which is the name of the largest gate in Kyoto, Japan's ancient capital. After reading the story "In a Grove" I was able to keep the four versions separate in my mind. And I believe I know what happened. All three major versions are self-serving and incorrect. The New Testament provides a second example of the Rashomon effect. Each of the four gospels tells the Jesus story, but each gospel differs from the others. Without a chart in front of me, I cannot remember which gospels have the nativity narration and which the resurrection (see Craig L. Blomberg, *Jesus and the Gospels* [Nashville, Tenn.: Broadman & Holman Publishers, 1997], p. 127, for such a chart).

41. I am thinking of Mont Sainte-Victoire, near Aix, France, which Paul Cézanne repeatedly painted (seventy-five times) and which today is painted by artists working at the same location where Cézanne stood (Helen Dundas, "Cezanne's Endless Quest to Parallel Nature's Harmony," *Smithsonian* 27, no. 1 [1996]: 82–90).

42. Bacon, Child, and Barry, "A Cross-Cultural Study of Correlates of Crime"; see also Otterbein, "Crime."

43. Otterbein, "Five Feuds."

44. Malinowski, *Argonauts of the Western Pacific*, pp. 64–65. "Henchman" is Malinowski's term.

45. Otterbein, *The Ultimate Coercive Sanction*, pp. 73–82. See also Y. Cohen, "Ends and Means in Political Control."

46. Otterbein, *The Ultimate Coercive Sanction*, p. 92.

47. Webb, "The Flag Follows Trade," pp. 157, 185; see also Webb, review of *The Early State*, by Henri J. M. Claessen and Peter Skalnik.

48. Webster, "Warfare and Status Rivalry," pp. 314, 340; see also Otterbein, "Internal War."

49. Webster, "Warfare and Status Rivalry," pp. 340–47; Webster, "Warfare and the Evolution of the State," p. 469.

50. H. Lewis, "Warfare and the Origin of the State," pp. 204–205; H. Lewis and Greenfield, "Anthropology and the Formation of the State," pp. 12–13. For a description of the Galla states, see H. Lewis, "The Galla State of Jimma Abba Jifar," pp. 323, 336; for a discussion of leaders and followers, see his 1974 publication, *Leaders and Followers*.

51. Haas, *The Evolution of the Prehistoric State*, pp. 209, 216–17.

52. J. Clark and Blake, "The Power of Prestige," pp. 17, 18, 19–21.

53. Blanton, "Beyond Centralization," pp. 141.

54. Ibid., pp. 140, 151.

55. Otterbein, "The Anthropology of War," pp. 947–48. I singled out Ludwig Gumplowicz (*The Outlines of Sociology*) and Franz Oppenheimer (*The State: Its History and Development Viewed Sociologically*).

56. Steward, *Handbook of South American Tribes*, vol. 4; Oberg, "Types of Social Structure among the Lowland Tribes of South and Central America"; Steward and Faron, *The Native Peoples of South America*. Robert Carneiro ("The Chiefdom") provides a detailed review of the history of the concept of chiefdom, discusses the origin of chiefdoms, and provides a typology of chiefdoms.

57. See Diamond, *Guns, Germs, and Steel*, pp. 267–81; Otterbein, "Internal War"; Otterbein, *The Evolution of War*.

58. Fortes and Evans-Pritchard, introduction to *African Political Systems*.

59. Carneiro, "The Chiefdom," p. 45; Claessen and Skalnik, eds., *The Early State,* p. 640. Malcolm C. Webb, after reviewing *The Early State,* edited by Claessen and Skalnik, argues that the upper end of chiefdoms and the lower (inchoate) end of early states overlap (Webb, review of *The Early State,* by Henri J. M. Claessen and Peter Skalnik, pp. 274–75). Nevertheless, Webb distinguishes chiefdoms from states according to whether or not the government can prevent fissioning (p. 275). But if a "state" fissions, does that mean it was not a state? This often-used criterion is flawed since it defines only chiefdoms, that is, a chiefdom is a centralized political system that can fission. But there is a logical problem here also; if a "chiefdom" never fissions, is it a state?

60. Claessen and Skalnik, eds., *The Early State,* pp. 22, 23, 588, 605.

61. The concept of the mature state is described further in Otterbein, *The Ultimate Coercive Sanction,* pp. 79–82.

62. Spitzer, "Notes toward a Theory of Punishment and Social Change," pp. 209–10.

63. Ibn Khaldun, *An Arab Philosophy of History,* pp. 109–26.

64. Y. Cohen, "Ends and Means in Political Control," pp. 659–61, 662, 663–64.

65. See also Kurtz, "Strategies of Legitimation of the Aztec State." The Aztecs are in Cohen's sample. The coder for Cohen's study was Donald Kurtz, who states that he did an "analysis of the social and political organizations of 28 state formations . . . for Y. A. Cohen in 1966 and 1967" (Kurtz, *Political Anthropology,* p. 187). Kurtz's case study is included in Claessen and Skalnik's edited volume, *The Early State.* The Aztecs, however, are not a pristine state. Recently Kurtz has reformulated Cohen's theory (see Kurtz, *Political Anthropology,* pp. 170–88).

66. Spitzer, "Punishment and Social Organization," p. 633. This 1975 study preceded by four years Spitzer's full formulation of political legitimacy theory.

67. Spitzer, "Punishment and Social Organization," p. 632.

68. The Phi coefficient for this relationship is 0.71; it is significant at the .05 level, using Fisher's Exact Test.

69. Otterbein, *The Ultimate Coercive Sanction,* pp. 78–79.

70. Archaeologist Elizabeth Brumfiel uses an internal conflict theory in her case study of the origin of the Aztec state (a secondary, not a pristine state). She calls it a structural approach—"a theory that explains the state as a consequence of conflicts arising from political, rather than economic structures." She has a "special concern for political ecology: how ecological variables present obstacles and opportunities to individuals pursuing their political goals in various structural contexts" (Brumfiel, "Aztec State Making," pp. 264, 266). Donald Kurtz's study of the legitimation of the Aztec state is highly compatible with Brumfiel's theory (Kurtz, "The Legitimation of the Aztec State"; and "Strategies of Legitimation and the Aztec State").

71. Kang, "A Reconsideration of Population Pressure and Warfare."

72. Marcus and Flannery, *Zapotec Civilization,* pp. 236–45; Brumfiel, "Factional Competition and Political Development in the New World," p. 3. Brumfiel explicitly names cultural ecology and Marxism as two theories that leave out the individual. She wants an agent-centered theory.

73. Spencer, *The Principles of Sociology,* 2:337.

74. Otterbein, *The Evolution of War,* pp. 27–28.

75. Fried, *The Evolution of Political Society,* pp. 111, 231–32.

76. Archaeologist Richard Burger reviews the arguments for and against contact between Peru and other parts of the world and concludes that "there is widespread consensus among archaeologists that Andean civilization developed *in situ* without significant input from other autochthonous civilizations" (Burger, *Chavin and the Origins of Andean Civilization,* p. 222).

77. Chang, *The Archaeology of Ancient China,* pp. 419–22. He attributes the similarities to a common deep cultural heritage based upon a system of shamanistic cosmology and rituals (p. 421). Betty Meggers has presented the evidence for the theory about Chinese junks reaching Mesoamerica (Meggers, "The Transpacific Origin of Meso-American Civilization").

78. Haslip-Viera, Ortiz de Montellano, and Barbour, "Robbing Native American Cultures."

79. This number of regions—six—had been my view for years. Indeed, in my 1997 paper "The Origins of War" I listed six regions, citing Julian Steward's *Theory of Culture Change* (1955) and accepted that number (Otterbein, "The Origins of War," p. 263). I was in error, however; Steward does not list the Indus with his five.

80. See Possehl, "Sociocultural Complexity without the State."

81. Fried, *The Evolution of Political Society*, p. 233.

82. Joffe, "Egypt and Syro-Mesopotamia in the 4th Millennium."

83. Haas, *The Evolution of the Prehistoric State*, pp. 184–92.

84. Marcus and Flannery, *Zapotec Civilization*, pp. 139–54. Zapotec stage III is Rosario (700–500 B.C.E.); Monte Albán I (500–100 B.C.E.) is stage IV.

85. Bawden, *The Moche*, pp. 10, 203; Haas, *The Evolution of the Prehistoric State*, p. 91.

86. Haas, "The Exercise of Power in Early Andean State Development," p. 35; Burger, *Chavin and the Origins of Andean Civilization*, p. 181.

87. H. Wright, "Uruk States in Southwestern Iran."

88. Liu, "Settlement Patterns, Chiefdom Variability, and the Development of Early States in North China," p. 276.

89. I have described these terms in Otterbein, *Comparative Cultural Analysis*, pp. 129–32, 126–27, and 67–69, respectively.

90. Otterbein, *Comparative Cultural Analysis*, pp. 137–48. A glossary with definitions of these terms can be found in Otterbein, "Clan and Tribal Conflict," pp. 289–90. I first distinguished internal war from external war in Otterbein, "Internal War," p. 277.

91. Marcus and Flannery, *Zapotec Civilization*, p. 245.

92. In a previous work I have described treason as follows:

> *Treason* refers either to the betrayal of the political community to enemies in other political communities or to insults directed to the political leader and members of his family. While current, popular use of the term treason refers to betrayal—e.g., the role

that Benedict Arnold played in the American Revolution—the historical meaning pertains to acts directed toward the ruler. Edward III (1327–1377) of England defined treason by statute as "compassing or imagining the king's death, or that of his wife or eldest son, violating the wife of the king or of the heir apparent . . ." (*Oxford English Dictionary*, 1971, p. 2291). The Trobriand example . . . [see the section "How the State Arose" in chapter 5] is one of numerous cases that can be found in the ethnographic literature of capital punishment for insulting the ruler. (Otterbein, *The Ultimate Coercive Sanction*, p. 26)

93. Executing the leaders of defeated polities is a common practice. For example, following World War II the Allied powers, between 1946 and 1949, conducted war crimes trials in Germany and Japan. At the major trial in each country leading political and military figures were sentenced; the Nuremberg trials led to the hanging of ten German leaders and the Tokyo trial, to the hanging of seven Japanese leaders. Hermann Goering committed suicide by poisoning himself just before he was to be executed. For political reasons, the emperor of Japan was not tried. There were numerous minor trials, some conducted in other nations, in which lesser officials were executed. Sources are unclear, but the figure is probably more than eight hundred executions for each theater of war (see Brackman, *The Other Nuremberg;* Ginn, *Sugamo Prison, Tokyo;* Tusa and Tusa, *The Nuremberg Trial*).

94. Ferrill describes the "military revolution" in Greece at about 350 B.C.E. as resulting from the creation, by Philip and Alexander of Macedon, of an integrated tactical force (Ferrill, *The Origins of War from the Stone Age to Alexander the Great*, pp. 149–50).

95. The concepts of culturally homogeneous political community and culturally heterogeneous political community are described in detail in my book *Comparative Cultural Analysis*, pp. 122–26.

Chapter 6

1. The Moche, however, present one complication—the state evolved in the

highlands (Chavín), but further evolution took place on the coast (Moche).

2. Most of my information in this section comes from *Zapotec Civilization* (1996) by archaeologists Joyce Marcus and Kent Flannery. The book is appropriately subtitled *How Urban Society Evolved in Mexico's Oaxaca Valley.*

3. Marcus and Flannery, *Zapotec Civilization,* pp. 44, 47, 62.

4. Ibid., p. 45.

5. To use an ethnographic analogy: American males never throw out knives. They gather them and sometimes even create collections. I only gather. As a youngster I found a hunting knife in the woods, which I still have. I have knives, made by native blacksmiths, that I brought home from northeastern Nigeria in 1965 after my fieldwork stay in that region, and I have a native-made knife from the northern Philippines, given to me by a colleague. I have lost two Swiss Army knives; I am sure the finders have put them to use.

6. Marcus and Flannery, *Zapotec Civilization,* pp. 67–69.

7. K. Flannery and Marcus, "The Origin of War."

8. Marcus and Flannery, *Zapotec Civilization,* p. 83. The palisade or fence is not described in *Zapotec Civilization.*

9. K. Flannery and Marcus, "The Origin of War."

10. Marcus and Flannery, *Zapotec Civilization,* p. 84. For evidence of warfare I like to see more than burned fences and houses. Convincing archaeological evidence of warfare can consist of fortifications, weapons (particularly special purpose weapons designed for combat), body armor and shields, skeletal injuries (such as projectile points in bone and fractures caused by weapons), warrior burials, and pictorial evidence (paintings and sculpture). All of this evidence is found in later stages of Zapotec civilization.

11. K. Flannery and Marcus, "The Origin of War."

12. Marcus and Flannery, *Zapotec Civilization,* p. 103.

13. Steven Spitzer suggests a reason why this political marriage strategy existed:

In contradistinction to the political legitimacy hypothesis, . . . ideological and economic controls become far more important than political controls when certain types of pre-industrial states are first attempting to establish effective rule. In situations where local officials . . . must be counted on to support the interests and objectives of the state, coercion may be tried. But in the absence of fine-grained political control and penetration by the state, it was usually far easier to rely on ideological and economic co-optation of local rulers than to undertake a thoroughgoing "reign of terror." ("Notes toward a Theory of Punishment and Social Change," pp. 220–21)

14. K. Flannery and Marcus, "The Origin of War." The houses are not described by Marcus and Flannery in *Zapotec Civilization.*

15. Marcus and Flannery, *Zapotec Civilization,* pp. 129–30.

16. Ibid., p. 157. They also argue that it was atop Monte Albán that the Zapotec became a state (pp. 160–65). (Note: The use of metric units of measure in this section reflects Marcus and Flannery's usage.)

17. John Scott presents the argument that these are slain corpses (*Danzantes of Monte Alban,* 1:26–30). He provides a catalogue of photographs of all three hundred-plus figures (*Danzantes of Monte Alban,* vol. 2). Unfortunately, weapons and clothing are not shown.

18. Marcus, "The Peaks and Valleys of Ancient States," p. 69.

19. Hassig, *War and Society in Ancient Mesoamerica.*

20. K. Flannery, "Zapotec Warfare," p. 319.

21. Marcus and Flannery, *Zapotec Civilization,* p. 230; Hassig, *War and Society in Ancient Mesoamerica,* pp. 63–65.

22. K. Flannery, "Zapotec Warfare," p. 322; Hassig, *War and Society in Ancient Mesoamerica,* p. 67.

23. See Hassig, *War and Society in Ancient Mesoamerica,* pp. 50–51, 67.

24. Ibid., pp. 66–70; Marcus, "Aztec Military Campaigns against the Zapotecs"; K. Flannery, "Zapotec Warfare."

25. Feinman, "Scale and Social Organization," pp. 129–31.

26. See, for example, Shimada, *Pampa Grande and the Mochica Culture*, p. 6.

27. Steward, *Theory of Culture Change*.

28. G. Willey, *Prehistoric Settlement Patterns in the Viru Valley, Peru*.

29. D. Wilson, "Reconstructing Patterns of Early Warfare in the Lower Santa Valley"; Topic and Topic, "The Archaeological Investigation of Andean Militarism."

30. Bawden, *The Moche*, p. 179; Burger, *Chavin and the Origins of Andean Civilization*, p. 190; Wenke, *Patterns in Prehistory*, pp. 625, 631.

31. Aldenderfer, *Montane Foragers*, p. 174.

32. Burger, *Chavin and the Origins of Andean Civilization*, p. 29.

33. Aldenderfer, *Montane Foragers*, pp. 275, 300.

34. Diamond, *Guns, Germs, and Steel*, pp. 100, 126–27.

35. Aldenderfer, *Montane Foragers*, pp. 301, 307.

36. Burger, *Chavin and the Origins of Andean Civilization*, pp. 45–53.

37. Ibid., pp. 42, 43.

38. Ibid., p. 30.

39. Ibid., p. 37.

40. Topic and Topic, "The Archaeological Investigation of Andean Militarism," p. 50.

41. Burger, *Chavin and the Origins of Andean Civilization*, pp. 65, 78–79.

42. Ibid., p. 78.

43. Gold objects were made earlier in Peru than in Mesoamerica. If the advent of gold metallurgy is viewed as an indicator of which state arose first, then Peru gets the nod. Could it be possible that Peru is the region in which the first pristine state in the New World arose, and that Mesoamerica's states are secondary states in the same sense that Egypt and the Indus are secondary states?

44. Burger, *Chavin and the Origins of Andean Civilization*, pp. 108–109, 138.

45. Both quotations from ibid., p. 225.

46. Ibid., p. 203.

47. Ibid., p. 190.

48. D. Wilson, "Reconstructing Patterns of Early Warfare in the Lower Santa Valley"; Topic and Topic, "The Archaeological Investigation of Andean Militarism."

49. Burger, *Chavin and the Origins of Andean Civilization*, p. 229.

50. Bawden, *The Moche*, p. 183.

51. Ibid., pp. 187–88.

52. Shimada, *Pampa Grande and the Mochica Culture*, p. 178.

53. Both quotations from Haas, *The Evolution of the Prehistoric State*, p. 109.

54. Haas, *The Evolution of the Prehistoric State*, pp. 120–21.

55. Garth Bawden provides three maps showing these expansions and contractions (*The Moche*, p. 203), while Izumi Shimada provides four maps (*Pampa Grande and the Mochica Culture*, pp. 78–79).

56. D. Wilson, "Reconstructing Patterns of Early Warfare in the Lower Santa Valley," pp. 67–68; Bawden, *The Moche*, p. 67.

57. Pictures depicting the behaviors I have described are found in the following sources: Bawden, *The Moche*, pp. 67, 125–26, 130, 238, 278; Donnan, *Moche Art and Iconography*, pp. 27, 29, 38, 39, 56, 57, 111; Shimada, *Pampa Grande and the Mochica Culture*, pp. 19, 108–10, 233; D. Wilson, "Reconstructing Patterns of Early Warfare in the Lower Santa Valley," pp. 66–68.

58. Bawden, *The Moche*, p. 278.

59. Donnan, *Moche Art and Iconography*, pp. 117–29. Michael Moseley refers to "one-on-one armed conflict" as "ritual combat" (Moseley, *The Incas and Their Ancestors*, p. 193).

60. Bawden, *The Moche*, pp. 114, 241–42.

61. Shimada, *Pampa Grande and the Mochica Culture*, pp. 2, 249–50.

62. Fagan, *Floods, Famines, and Emperors*, pp. 133–36.

63. Mackey, "The Middle Horizon as Viewed from the Moche Valley," p. 330; Bawden, *The Moche*, pp. 320–21.

64. Bawden, *The Moche*, p. 329; Shimada, *Pampa Grande and the Mochica Culture*, pp. 247–54.

65. The kingdom of Chan Chan is well described in the 1982 book edited by Michael Moseley and Kent Day, *Chan Chan: Andean Desert City*. For the Inca

military, see Bram, *An Analysis of Inca Militarism, pp.* 45–56.

66. Archaeologist Susan Pollock has well described the early environment (*Ancient Mesopotamia,* pp. 28–44).

67. Fagan, *Floods, Famines, and Emperors,* pp. 94–95. An excellent map showing the shoreline is in Algaze, "Initial Social Complexity in Southwestern Asia," p. 202.

68. Pollock, *Ancient Mesopotamia,* pp. 71–72, 76.

69. M. Mann, *The Sources of Social Power,* 1:80 (italics in original).

70. Floor plan in Pollock, *Ancient Mesopotamia,* p. 51; also K. Flannery, "The Ground Plans of Archaic States," p. 38.

71. H. Wright, "Uruk States in Southwestern Iran," p. 178.

72. Pollock, *Ancient Mesopotamia,* p. 92.

73. Fagan, *Floods, Famines, and Emperors,* pp. 93–94.

74. Pollock, *Ancient Mesopotamia,* p. 92.

75. Wenke, *Patterns in Prehistory,* pp. 402–403.

76. Pollock, *Ancient Mesopotamia,* p. 70.

77. In the New World, there were no wheels used for pottery or for transportation.

78. Algaze, "The Uruk Expansion," pp. 574–75; Pollock, *Ancient Mesopotamia,* pp. 184–85.

79. H. Wright, "Uruk States in Southwestern Iran," pp. 179–82.

80. See Kramer, *History Begins at Sumer.* Kramer's list includes such accomplishments as writing and a murder trial, but it fails to include other "firsts"—such as the first despotic state or the first army (although government and war are included).

81. K. Flannery, "The Ground Plans of Archaic States," p. 37.

82. Algaze, "The Uruk Expansion"; Marcus, "The Peaks and Valleys of Ancient States," p. 80.

83. Marcus, "The Peaks and Valleys of Ancient States," p. 80.

84. H. Wright, "Uruk States in Southwestern Iran," pp. 185–86.

85. Postgate, *Early Mesopotamia,* pp. 24–25; Pollock, *Ancient Mesopotamia,* p. 97.

86. G. Johnson, *Local Exchange and Early State Development in Southwestern Iran,* pp. 141–55; and "The Changing Organization of Uruk Administration on the Susiana Plain."

87. Wenke, *Patterns in Prehistory,* p. 404. Annual rates of settlement abandonment and founding are presented in Pollock, *Ancient Mesopotamia,* pp. 72–75.

88. For cylinder seal data, see Postgate, *Early Mesopotamia,* pp. 241–42.

89. See Algaze, "The Uruk Expansion," pp. 574–75; Pollock, *Ancient Mesopotamia,* p. 185.

90. Pollock, *Ancient Mesopotamia,* pp. 149–72.

91. Otterbein, "The Evolution of Zulu Warfare"; and "Why the Iroquois Won." Paul Bohannan selected both of my articles, which had been recently published, for his edited book *Law and Warfare* (1967). This widely read compendium brought the method I used to the attention of anthropologists, and both articles have been widely cited. I included them in my volume of collected papers, *Feuding and Warfare* (1994). In discussing my research in the preface to that volume, I noted, "My research is placed in a developmental (in the sense of change) or evolutionary framework. The case studies of the Iroquois and Zulu explicitly take into account changes over time, changes that in part came about due to the diffusion of military technology. . . . I see changes in sociopolitical organization as occurring because of new military practices, and in turn I see the emergence of more complex sociopolitical organization as a stimulus for the acquiring of military technology" (*Feuding and Warfare,* p. xxii).

92. Pollock, *Ancient Mesopotamia,* pp. 47, 178, 181.

93. Ibid., pp. 63–64.

94. M. Mann, *The Sources of Social Power,* 1:97; H. Wright, "The Southern Margins of Sumer," pp. 325, 327.

95. My wife and I have twice experienced travel in flat countryside where one can indeed see a tall structure ten miles away in spite of the earth's curvature. While driving across Kansas in the 1960s, my wife and I would play a game—how far away is that grain elevator? At first we would see only its top; as we got closer it became taller. The typical grain elevator

was 13.3 miles from where we first noticed its top. We also observed a similar situation in Norfolk, East Anglia, England, in 1997. There the flat landscape is dotted with more than six hundred medieval churches, each with a tower. We could not ascertain our distance from them because the roads are not straight as they are in Kansas, but the rides were more interesting. Our driver, an expert on the churches of East Anglia, was Charles Frake. His wife, Joanne Coury, provided directions. I rode in the front with Chuck, my wife in the back with Joanne. For an illustration showing the Norfolk landscape see Charles O. Frake, "A Church Too Far Near a Bridge Oddly Placed: The Cultural Construction of the Norfolk Countryside," *Redefining Nature: Ecology, Culture, and Domestication,* ed. Roy Ellen and Katsuyoshi Fukui [Oxford: Berg, 1996], p. 90.

96. Wooley, *The Sumerians,* pp. 49–61. I believe the Standard of Ur can be dated to 3000 B.C.E. and the Stele of Vultures to 2500 B.C.E.

97. Postgate, *Early Mesopotamia,* pp. 146, 246.

98. The animal pulling the cart looks like a horse or donkey (domestic ass); experts now believe that the equid used was a sterile cross between a donkey and a wild onager (Postgate, *Early Mesopotamia,* pp. 165–66). The genus Equus is divided into several species: *E. asinus* (the wild ass and domestic donkey), *E. hemionus* (the onager), *E. ferus* (the wild horse), and *E. caballus* (the domestic horse) (Piggott, *Wagon, Chariot, and Carriage,* pp. 38, 43).

99. The socket ax is cast in bronze in such a manner that the nonblade side of the ax fits around a wooden handle. If the blade is narrow, it is referred to as a penetrating ax, since it is designed to pierce a copper helmet.

100. Richard Gabriel and Karen Metz believe the soldiers are "wearing leather cloaks on which are sewn a number of spined metal disks. The disks do not appear arranged in any particular order to protect the most vital areas of the body, and we do not know if the disks were made of bronze or copper" (*From Sumer to Rome,* p. 51). My wife, who has an expertise in textiles, has me convinced that the cloaks are likely to be made of felted wool. Wool fleece, as it is sheared from

sheep, has the unique property of forming a substantial fabric when it is pounded and rubbed when wet. This process does not require the steps of spinning threads and interweaving them. The felted wool can be a heavy fabric, and it can be shaped in the wet state without being stitched. Such shaping is, of course, demonstrated by modern felt hats.

101. See, for example, Yadin, *The Art of Warfare in Biblical Lands,* pp. 132–33.

102. Ferrill, *The Origins of War from the Stone Age to Alexander the Great,* p. 42.

103. Gabriel and Metz, *From Sumer to Rome,* p. 5. For the cuneiform translation see Pollock, *Ancient Mesopotamia,* p. 184; for the interpretation of the upper register as a victorious phalanx, see Yadin, *The Art of Warfare in Biblical Lands,* pp. 49–50.

104. See Yadin, *The Art of Warfare in Biblical Lands,* pp. 134–35, for a two-page color plate of the stele; O'Connell, *Ride of the Second Horseman,* pp. 98–99.

105. As I write (Labor Day weekend, 2000), the fiftieth anniversary of the Korean War is being celebrated in the small town where I live in the summer, and there was a "victory" parade honoring veterans. My first Ph.D. student, Alan G. LaFlamme, lives across the street from the American Legion Hall, so I had a front-row seat. Near the end of the parade, which lasted twenty minutes and thirteen seconds, was a tank. At night there were fireworks.

106. Postgate, *Early Mesopotamia,* p. 254.

107. Dawson, *The First Armies,* p. 89.

108. Gabriel and Metz, *From Sumer to Rome,* pp. 54, 56–58, 60–63.

109. Drews, *The End of the Bronze Age,* pp. 104, 204, 209–12; Adcock, *The Greek and Macedonian Art of War,* p. 47.

110. Drews, *The End of the Bronze Age,* p. 105.

111. H. Wright, "The Southern Margins of Sumer," p. 327.

112. Wooley, *Ur of the Chaldees,* pp. 63–67.

113. Wooley, *The Sumerians,* pp. 36–44.

114. M. Mann, *The Sources of Social Power,* 1:133–55; Postgate, *Early Mesopotamia,* pp. 38–41.

115. Pollock, *Ancient Mesopotamia,* pp. 10, 15.

116. Gabriel and Metz, *From Sumer to Rome*, pp. 67–69. A color plate in Yadin, *The Art of Warfare in Biblical Lands*, p. 150, shows the bow.

117. Here is an ethnographic analogy from my own experience. When I was a boy my father had a small, two-wheeled cart for pulling, by hand, tools and supplies on his farm. My father, who had driven both work horses and show horses, had shafts made to replace the cart's handles and a harness crafted for our "billy goat," a white domestic goat with horns and a beard. My father also put a seat across the cart. With reins in hand, I, at the age of twelve, drove my billy goat around the farm. There was room on the seat for my younger brother, but as I grew larger, I made him walk. The goat would run and I would pretend to be a charioteer. My brother did not like being an infantryman. A few years later, I "graduated" to a horse and became a cavalry commander.

118. Piggott, *Wagon, Chariot, and Carriage*, pp. 42–49.

119. The spellings of Chinese words are taken from Liu, "Settlement Patterns, Chiefdom Variability, and the Development of Early States in North China," p. 244; dates and stages on Figure 6.4 are from Chang, *Shang Civilization*, p. 354, with an adjustment for the Battle of Muye subsequently dated as 1045 B.C.E. (see Shaughnessy, "Historical Perspectives on the Introduction of the Chariot into China," p. 229). Any quoted material retains the spelling conventions followed by its author.

120. The term "defensive moat" is Robert Wenke's (*Patterns in Prehistory*, p. 519).

121. Chang, *Shang Civilization*, p. 338. Wenke suggests the chief's house or meeting hall (*Patterns in Prehistory*, p. 520).

122. Chang, *The Archaeology of Ancient China*, p. 261.

123. Ibid., pp. 248, 273.

124. Chang, *Shang Civilization*, pp. 245–48.

125. Chang, *The Archaeology of Ancient China*, p. 270. On the leagues of villages, see Chang, *Shang Civilization*, p. 361.

126. Chang, *Shang Civilization*, p. 339; *The Archaeology of Ancient China*, p. 270.

127. Liu, "Settlement Patterns, Chiefdom Variability, and the Development of Early States in North China," pp. 243–45.

128. For example, Claudio Cioffi-Revilla and David Lai state that "in China . . . the earliest evidence of pristine warfare and politics consists of the system of fortified Lung-Shan villages in northern Henan, dated at ca. 2600 B.C.E." ("War and Politics in Ancient China," p. 468). More recently, Cioffi-Revilla has recognized that Chinese villages at an earlier period were located on high ground to prevent the ravages of flooding: "This and other locational events on elevated grounds may have been motivated by ensuring against flooding, not necessarily against threats of aggression" ("Ancient Warfare," p. 81).

129. For Settlement cluster 6, see maps in Liu, "Settlement Patterns, Chiefdom Variability, and the Development of Early States in North China," pp. 249, 262; on the floods, see p. 263.

130. All quotes from Liu, "Settlement Patterns, Chiefdom Variability, and the Development of Early States in North China," p. 264.

131. O'Connell, *Ride of the Second Horseman*, p. 164.

132. Chang, "China on the Eve of the Historical Period", pp. 69, 71; Wu, *The Chinese Heritage*, p. 357; see Wu, *The Chinese Heritage*, pp. 69-117, for the detailed story of flood control in China.

133. Lattimore, *Inner Asian Frontiers of China*; McNeill, *The Rise of the West*; O'Connell, *Ride of the Second Horseman*.

134. O'Connell, *Ride of the Second Horseman*, p. 163. On the introduction of the horse-drawn chariot to the Shang see Bagley, "Shang Archaeology," pp. 202–208; Piggott, *Wagon, Chariot, and Carriage*, p. 63; Shaughnessy, "Historical Perspectives on the Introduction of the Chariot into China," p. 192.

135. See Chang, *The Archaeology of Ancient China*; Fried, "Tribe to State or State to Tribe in Ancient China?"; Liu, "Settlement Patterns, Chiefdom Variability, and the Development of Early States in North China."

136. Liu, "Settlement Patterns, Chiefdom Variability, and the Development of Early States in North China," p. 272.

137. Ibid., p. 269. The three-tier settlement hierarchies are in Liu's Clusters 1 to

4, while the two-tier settlement hierarchies are in Clusters 5 and 6.

138. McNeill, *A History of the Human Community,* 1:143–46.

139. Chang, *The Archaeology of Ancient China,* pp. 363, 414.

140. Chang, *Shang Civilization,* pp. 352–53.

141. Ibid., pp. 214–15; Creel, *The Birth of China,* pp. 72–74, 321; Creel, *The Origins of Statecraft in China,* 1:273–74; M. Lewis, *Sanctioned Violence in Early China,* pp. 17–18.

142. Haas, *The Evolution of the Prehistoric State,* pp. 105, 109–10, 122.

143. M. Lewis, *Sanctioned Violence in Early China,* pp. 36–42.

144. Ibid., pp. 17–27.

145. Keegan, *A History of Warfare,* p. 168; McNeill, *A History of the Human Community,* 1:146–47.

146. O'Connell, *Ride of the Second Horseman,* p. 166.

147. Bagley, "Shang Archaeology," pp. 202–208; Shaughnessy, "Historical Perspectives on the Introduction of the Chariot into China," pp. 190–210.

148. Bagley, "Shang Archaeology," p. 208; see also Piggott, *Wagon, Chariot, and Carriage,* pp. 63–68.

149. Chang, *Shang Civilization,* pp. 231, 232; Chang, *The Archaeology of Ancient China,* p. 282.

150. Keegan, *A History of Warfare,* pp. 155–78; McNeill, *A History of the Human Community,* 1:59–70.

151. Drews, *The End of the Bronze Age,* pp. 209–25; McNeill, *A History of the Human Community,* 1:87; M. Lewis, *Sanctioned Violence in Early China,* p. 60. The Assyrians had both chariots and cavalry but placed greater reliance on the former. Only after Assyria's defeat in 612 B.C.E. did cavalry supplant chariot forces on the field of battle (Ferrill, *The Origins of War from the Stone Age to Alexander the Great,* pp. 71–74, 83–85; Gabriel and Metz, *From Sumer to Rome,* p. 77). The Persians, however, continued to use chariots until their defeat by Alexander the Great, using light infantry, at the Battle of Gaugamela (331 B.C.E.) (Adcock, *The Greek and Macedonian Art of War,* p. 47; Ferrill, *The Origins of War from the Stone Age to Alexander the Great,* pp. 208–209).

152. Gabriel and Metz, *From Sumer to Rome,* p. 78.

153. Chang, *Shang Civilization,* pp. 5–7.

154. Ibid., p. 198. Chang's analysis was based upon seven Shang chariots, but as Robert Bagley reported in 1999, "The number of such burials excavated at Anyang has now reached about twenty" ("Shang Archaeology," p. 203).

155. Chang, *Shang Civilization,* p. 200. Photographs of the horse skeletons can be found in Chang's *Shang Civilization,* p. 199; and *The Archaeology of Ancient China,* p. 323; and in McNeill, *A History of the Human Community,* 1:147.

156. Chang, *Shang Civilization,* p. 196.

157. Gabriel and Metz, *From Sumer to Rome,* p. 70.

158. Creel, *The Birth of China,* p. 145; Gabriel and Boose, *The Great Battles of Antiquity,* p. 178. Measurements of weapons were taken by me from scale drawings in Chang, *Shang Civilization,* p. 197.

159. Gabriel and Boose, *The Great Battles of Antiquity,* p. 189.

160. Ibid., p. 179.

161. Creel, *The Birth of China,* p. 148.

162. Bagley, "Shang Archaeology," p. 206.

163. Piggott, *Wagon, Chariot, and Carriage,* p. 67. On archery, see Creel, *The Birth of China,* pp. 139, 321–23.

164. Shaughnessy, "Historical Perspectives on the Introduction of the Chariot into China," pp. 229, 231.

165. Shaughnessy, "Western Zhou History," p. 309.

166. Wu, *The Chinese Heritage,* p. 289.

167. I realize that if there were 25 chariots to each company, the total number would only be 250 chariots and their crews. But perhaps Chou chariot companies were larger than Shang chariot companies, or perhaps the figure of 300 chariots is inflated.

168. Shaughnessy, "Western Zhou History," p. 310.

169. Shaughnessy, "Historical Perspectives on the Introduction of the Chariot into China," p. 228.

170. On army size, see Hsu, *Ancient China in Transition,* p. 67; for other data, see pp. 56–57, 59, 66.

171. Kierman, "Phases and Modes of

Combat in Early China," pp. 29, 52, 53. I know how much fun it is to take a sketchy account of a battle and draw a series of battle maps showing the ebb and flow of combat. In my case it was a 1649 set of battles between two North American Indian nations, the Huron and Iroquois. A French Jesuit priest with the defeated Hurons left an account (Otterbein, "Huron vs. Iroquis," p. 146; *Feuding and Warfare,* p. 16).

172. Gabriel and Metz, *From Sumer to Rome,* 73.

173. Journalists John Barry and Evan Thomas note that "against military targets, high-altitude bombing is overrated" ("The Kosovo Cover-Up," p. 26).

174. M. Lewis, *Sanctioned Violence in Early China,* p. 59.

175. Hsu, *Ancient China in Transition,* p. 68.

176. M. Lewis, *Sanctioned Violence in Early China,* p. 60; Shaughnessy, "Historical Perspectives on the Introduction of the Chariot into China," p. 227.

177. Hsu, *Ancient China in Transition,* p. 73.

178. Ibid., pp. 69–71.

179. Mark Edward Lewis states that "armies never exceeded 100,000 . . . and were generally much smaller" ("Warring States: Political History," p. 627).

180. Cotterell, *The First Emperor of China;* Hoh, "China's Great Enigma," p. 37; Wenli, *The Qin Terracotta Army;* Hsu, *Ancient China in Transition,* p. 68. The terra-cotta army is the ultimate in toy soldiers—not to be confused with miniatures.

181. M. Lewis, "Warring States," p. 623; Hsu, *Ancient China in Transition,* p. 68.

182. Diamond, *Guns, Germs, and Steel,* pp. 218–22; Pollock, *Ancient Mesopotamia,* pp. 149–72; Postgate, *Early Mesopotamia,* pp. 51–70.

183. Chang, *Shang Civilization,* pp. 245, 247–48.

184. Creel, *The Birth of China,* p. 173; see pp. 161–63 for the other applications of early Chinese writing.

185. Diamond, *Guns, Germs, and Steel,* p. 222; Marcus, "Mesoamerican Writing," pp. 22–23.

Chapter 7

1. Claessen and Skalnik, eds., *The Early State,* p. 629.

2. Pollock, *Ancient Mesopotamia,* pp. 80, 94–96.

3. The military sophistication scale is a composite measure of the efficiency of a military organization; its derivation is described in Otterbein, *The Evolution of War,* pp. 70–76. Methodological aspects of the scale are discussed in an appendix to that study (C. S. Otterbein, "Appendix B: Methodological Aspects of the Military Sophistication Scale," in *The Evolution of War,* by Keith Otterbein).

4. Claessen and Skalnik, eds., *The Early State,* pp. 562–63, 587.

5. Otterbein, *The Evolution of War,* p. xxiv.

6. Fried, *The Notion of Tribe.*

7. I prefer to call combat personnel soldiers, not warriors, but sometimes for the sake of textual variety I use the terms interchangeably.

8. The numbers were thirteen out of forty-six societies for professional *and* nonprofessional military organizations, and nine of the same forty-six societies for professional military organizations. The remaining twenty-four societies had nonprofessional military organizations. Four societies had no military organization, which brought the sample size to fifty (Otterbein, *The Evolution of War,* pp. 144, 148).

9. See Otterbein, "Weapons Control, Warfare, and Warrior Aristocracy."

10. Weapons control can mean one of two things: (1) All able-bodied men must be proficient in the use of arms; (2) only personnel designated by political leaders may have arms. This double meaning of weapons control is highlighted by political humorist Mark Russell's definition of a conservative as a person who believes that gun control is a good, steady aim. (I do not have a citation to Russell; I heard—and remembered—the definition when I attended a live broadcast of the *Mark Russell Comedy Special,* which was at that time broadcast on PBS from a theater near my office at the University at Buffalo. The date was probably in the late 1970s.)

11. In a classic work on the relationship of aggression to frustration, the frustra-

tion-aggression hypothesis was applied to Ashanti warfare. The Ashanti were a west African state that engaged in offensive warfare against their neighbors (Dollard et al., *Frustration and Aggression*, pp. 172–90).

12. See Otterbein, "Socialization for War."

13. Perrin, *Giving Up the Gun*, pp. 45–67.

14. Ibid., p. 33.

15. Ibid., p. 35.

16. Hatch, *The Right to Keep and Bear Arms*, p. 1.

17. Fuller, *A Military History of the Western World*, p. 457.

18. Hatch, *The Right to Keep and Bear Arms*, p. 2.

19. Perrin, *Giving up the Gun*, pp. 59, 62.

20. Malone, *The Skulking Way of War*, p. 50.

21. See Otterbein, "The Dilemma of Disarming."

22. Edgerton, *Like Lions They Fought*, p. 34; see also Otterbein, "The Evolution of Zulu Warfare," on initiation into age-grade regiments.

23. Ferdon, *Early Tonga*, pp. 262–63.

24. Pollock, *Ancient Mesopotamia*, p. 137.

25. Claessen and Skalnik, eds., *The Early State*, pp. 562–63, 587.

26. Keegan, *The Mask of Command*, pp. 113–26.

27. Perlmutter, *Visions of War*, describes at length how early rulers portrayed themselves in stone as larger, better muscled, and better attired than other figures. They also usually placed themselves at the head of their soldiers.

28. Otterbein, *The Evolution of War*, pp. 81–84.

29. Hanson, *The Western Way of War*.

30. Pollock, *Ancient Mesopotamia*, p. 184.

31. Early conquerors erected stone monuments that depict siege warfare and the devices used in assaults. For the Near East many of these monuments are pictured in Yadin, *The Art of Warfare in Biblical Lands*.

32. Adcock, *The Greek and Macedonian Art of War*, pp. 56–61.

33. Otterbein, *The Evolution of War*, pp. 61–63.

34. My father had a picket gate that swung across the driveway of our urban home. When locked with a hook and eye, it blocked the only way I could leave the enclosed backyard. At a very young age, I learned to unlatch it. My escape was carefully planned. I obtained a cardboard box from the garage, unlatched the gate, got under the box, and proceeded to walk around the block. My mother, when she noted my absence, went looking for me, asking neighbors if they had seen me. One woman told Mother that she had seen a cardboard box go by with small feet under it. My disguise revealed, I was soon apprehended.

35. I am reminded of the Robert Frost poem with its famous line that "good fences make good neighbours" (Robert Frost, "Mending Wall," *New Enlarged Anthology of Robert Frost's Poems*, edited by Louis Untermeyer [New York: Washington Square Press, 1971], pp. 94–95). The fence in New England was made of stones; thus, it was a "stone fence" or stone wall.

36. For the Early Neolithic of central Europe (5400–4600 B.C.E.), Janusz Kruk and Sarunas Milisauskas argue that "probably many ditched enclosures were multifunctional: defense, habitation, keeping of domestic animals, and ceremonials" (*The Rise and Fall of Neolithic Societies*, p. 306).

37. An exception to this statement: The palisade walls of the Iroquoian-speaking peoples were constructed of poles, which could be destroyed by fire or ax.

38. Pollock, *Ancient Mesopotamia*, pp. 47, 175–81.

39. Readers may recognize that these data can be projected onto a 2 × 2 contingency table. If the four cells of the table are labeled A, B, C, and D, the cell numbers are 2 (A), 13 (B), 15 (C), and 10 (D). The correlation is a Phi coefficient of 0.46, and it is statistically significant at the .01 level (Otterbein, *The Evolution of War*, p. 60).

40. Otterbein, *The Evolution of War*, pp. 59, 148–49.

41. The analyses and statistical tests were not performed and reported upon in my 1970 study. The cell numbers are 15 (A), 3 (B), 10 (C), and 9 (D). The Phi coefficient of 0.33 is statistically significant at the .05 level.

42. I am using two different ways to consider the distribution of cases found in these cross-cultural studies. The first is to examine the strength of the association, using a measure of correlation; this is especially useful in comparing the strength of two relationships. For example, using my 1970 data, there is a higher correlation between village fortifications and political level (0.46) than between fortifications and internal warfare (0.32). A second way is to ask the question: If we know that a society has village fortifications, can we assume or predict that there was warfare? And the reverse: If we know a society has warfare, can we predict that it had fortifications?

43. The cell numbers are 12 (A), 3 (B), 10 (C), and 34 (D). The correlation is a Phi coefficient of 0.52, and it is statistically significant at the .01 level (Griffiths, "Village Fortifications," pp. 8, 12. This unpublished University at Buffalo master's thesis is in my manuscript collection.)

44. For Griffiths's model, see Griffiths, "Village Fortifications," pp. 19–20.

45. The cell numbers are 7 (A), 0 (B), 5 (C), and 10 (D). I have produced a 2 × 2 table based on Peregrine's 5 × 5 table. The correlation is a Phi coefficient of 0.62, and it is statistically significant at the .01 level. Peter Peregrine's 5 × 5 table yielded a regression coefficient of 0.62 (p < .002) (Peregrine, "Raoul Naroll's Contribution to Archaeology," pp. 358, 359).

46. Although each of these three studies was conducted independently of the others, there is some overlapping of societies in the samples. Hence, these results are not independent in the sense that they can be added together. However, they are independent estimates of the relationship between fortifications and warfare.

47. Keegan, *A History of Warfare,* p. 124. In addition to walls, towers, and moats, Cioffi-Revilla includes ramparts, baffled gates, and guard houses as structural evidence for early warfare ("Ancient Warfare," pp. 66–68).

48. Cioffi-Revilla, "Origins and Age of Deterrence," p. 249; Ehrenreich, *Blood Rites,* p. 121; Ferrill, *The Origins of War from the Stone Age to Alexander the Great,* p. 13; Keegan, *A History of Warfare,* pp. 124–25, 139–42; O'Connell, *Of Arms and Men,* p. 30; O'Connell, "The Origins of War," p. 15; O'Connell, *Ride of the Sec-*

ond Horseman, pp. 58–61; Wrangham and Peterson, *Demonic Males,* pp. 26, 47.

49. Roper, "Evidence of Warfare in the Near East from 10,000–4,300 B.C.," p. 306; Gabriel, *The Culture of War,* p. 30.

50. Bar-Yosef, "The Walls of Jericho," p. 161. In personal correspondence dated October 26, 1998, Bar-Yosef has informed me that for the walls at Jericho,

> the earliest dates are 8300 B.C. The walls as described in my 1986 paper went out of use within several centuries and therefore could not serve as a defense system against humans. . . . In my concluding remarks I stated and still feel that this is what the evidence shows, that real fortifications (against human aggression), appeared only from the 6th millennium onwards. . . . My paper was written in order to 'erase' the argument that Jericho walls had the same meaning as Bronze Age walls and that the tower, contrary to a defense tower[,] was built inside the walls and not outside. I also remarked that the changing thickness of the walls, which one does not see among Bronze–Iron Age walls, indicate[s] that the original PPNA [Pre-Pottery Neolithic A] walls in front of the tower had a different function.

51. Mellaart, *The Neolithic of the Near East,* p. 49.

52. Ibid., pp. 48–51.

53. Otterbein, *The Evolution of War,* p. 81.

54. The point biserial correlation is 0.48, significant at the .01 level (Otterbein, *The Evolution of War,* p. 83). Although this hypothesis pertains only to the casualty rates of the societies in the sample, it is in all probability correct to assume that the enemy's casualty rates are as high, if not higher.

55. Otterbein, "Killing of Captured Enemies," p. 439. Data were obtained from the Human Relations Area Files sixty-society probability sample.

56. Otterbein, "Killing of Captured Enemies," p. 441.

57. After publication of the study, I found an error in one of the categories under type of political system. Category 7, "tribe with no council, no feuding" should read "feuding." This error has led to seven societies in the Societies and

Codes appendix being mislabeled. Some of the societies with Category 7 include famous feuding societies such as the Ifugao, Kapauku, and Yanomami (Otterbein, "Killing of Captured Enemies," p. 443).

58. Otterbein, "Killing of Captured Enemies," p. 440–41.

59. See Otterbein and Otterbein, "An Eye for an Eye and a Tooth for a Tooth"; Otterbein, *Feuding and Warfare,* pp. 107, 125.

60. Shiels, "A Comparitive Study of Human Sacrifice," pp. 245, 252.

61. In my cross-cultural study of capital punishment, I discussed differences among forms of killing and pointed out the fine distinction:

> Human sacrifice is the most difficult of the related forms of killing to differentiate from capital punishment. Human sacrifice, like capital punishment, occurs within a political community and is deemed appropriate by political leaders. A . . . cross-cultural study of human sacrifice defined it simply as a way to "approach the spirit world" and as an "institutionalized religious practice" [Shiels, "A Comparative Study of Human Sacrifice," pp. 245, 252]. In other words, there is a culturally approved reason, supported by the political leaders and by the members of the political community, for killing the sacrificial victims. The persons who are offered to the deities have not necessarily committed crimes: they may be loyal subjects of a king or the wives and servants of a wealthy man. . . . Persons who have committed crimes or prisoners of war may also be used as sacrifices, however. When criminals and war captives . . . are used as sacrifices to the spirit world, the phenomenon can be classified as both capital punishment and human sacrifice. (Otterbein, *The Ultimate Coercive Sanction,* p. 12)

62. Otterbein, *The Ultimate Coercive Sanction,* p. 118. After the Nuremberg trials, Hermann Goering avoided hanging by obtaining poison from an unknown source and taking his own life (see chapter 5, n. 93).

63. Brackman, *The Other Nuremberg,* pp. 44, 412–13.

64. Shiels, "A Comparative Study of Human Sacrifice."

65. If societies in the "absent" column are contrasted with societies in the "sometimes" and "common" columns, Fisher's Exact Test can be calculated for each half of Figure 7.2. The relationships are statistically significant at the .05 and .01 levels, respectively.

66. The classic source for such an argument is A. R. Radcliffe-Brown's *The Andaman Islanders* (1922).

Chapter 8

1. Lawrence H. Keeley and Daniel Cahen argue that in northwestern Europe contact between bands and villages led to war ("Early Neolithic Forts and Villages in NE Belgium," p. 171). Fortifications were erected, probably as a defense against raids by foragers. Keeley and Cahen note that at one site the high proportion of burnt houses may indicate that hunters and gatherers raided the settlement before fortifications were erected (p. 168). Janusz Kruk and Sarunas Milisauskas review Keeley and Cahen's work and concur with their interpretations (*The Rise and Fall of Neolithic Societies,* p. 289).

2. The classic interpretation is to be found in George Peter Murdock's *Social Structure* (1949) and Elman R. Service's *Primitive Social Organization* (1962). I could write much more about the basics of kinship systems, and in the past I have. My small textbook in cultural anthropology (*Comparative Cultural Analysis*) provides a summary. Most anthropology textbooks adequately cover the subject of kinship. I have kept my discussion here brief and oversimplified; this book is about warfare, not kinship systems.

3. Divale, "The Causes of Matrilocal Residence"; and "Migration, External Warfare, and Matrilocal Residence."

4. "The military organization [of the Higi] has three types of personnel: warriors, *katsala,* and the war leader (*medala*). A young man becomes a *katsala* when he distinguishes himself through bravery and skill in archery. Each village has several *katsala;* since all able bodied men . . . go to war, every man has the opportunity to achieve this status. A *katsala* slain in battle is not buried until vengeance is

taken; an ordinary warrior will be buried first. A man who distinguishes himself as a *katsala* by killing many enemies is eligible to become war leader" (Otterbein, "Higi Armed Combat," p. 206).

5. Otterbein, "Internal War." In an earlier study my wife and I discovered that societies with fraternal interest groups were likely to have feuding, defined as blood revenge following a homicide that occurred within the polity (Otterbein and Otterbein, "An Eye for an Eye and a Tooth for a Tooth").

6. Otterbein, *The Evolution of War,* pp. 89, 95.

7. One scholar, political scientist Azar Gat, has made the point that "among hunter-gatherers and simple horticulturalists, as in intraspecific fighting among animals, most serious attempts at killing and most killings are done when the victims of the attack can be caught helpless, relatively defenseless, and above all, little capable of effectively harming the attackers" ("The Pattern of Fighting in Simple, Small-Scale, Prestate Societies," p. 564).

8. In my cross-cultural study of warfare, I found that one-third of the uncentralized political systems had a tactical system based on lines and ambushes. Out of thirty societies nine had both ambushes and lines, while the other twenty-one had either ambushes or lines (Otterbein, *The Evolution of War,* p. 42). Among those twenty-one societies are the Tiwi; we learned in chapter 4, in the section "Warfare," that the Tiwi had the basic pattern of ambushes and lines. My coding of ethnographic data for that study was done in 1965, prior to the publication in 1988 of data on Tiwi "sneak attacks" (Pilling, "Sneak Attacks"). The new information moves the Tiwi from one category to the other. I suspect that other uncentralized political systems in the ambush or the line category had both ambushes and lines.

9. Heider, *Grand Valley Dani,* pp. 85–120; Otterbein, *The Evolution of War,* 2nd ed., p. xxi.

10. Chagnon, *Yanomamo;* Otterbein, *The Evolution of War,* 2nd ed., p. xx. Napoleon Chagnon's fieldwork with the Yanomamo has made both the people and their ethnographer famous. I am citing Chagnon's second edition here because the third, fourth, and fifth editions have

omissions (e.g., female infanticide) and other changes that appear to be designed to make the book more politically correct. These changes have not stopped criticism; see Begley, "Into the Heart of Darkness."

11. The Aztec, originally a tribal people who entered the Valley of Mexico, are another possible candidate; by the thirteenth century numerous typical chiefdoms covered the valley floor. Elizabeth Brumfiel describes their evolution from the inchoate early state stage through the mature state stage ("Aztec State Making").

12. This case study is an expanded version of my research report, "More on the Nuer Expansion," published in *Current Anthropology* in 1995. Although much ethnographic information was removed from the longer version at that time, my review of sources on the Nuer has left me amazed at the paucity of data on warfare. This shortage is surprising because the Nuer are one of anthropology's famous warlike peoples. My treatment here provides more information on Nuer and Dinka warfare than is to be found in the two major books on the Nuer expansion: E. E. Evans-Pritchard's *The Nuer: A Description of the Modes of Livelihood and Political Institutions of a Nilotic People,* and Raymond Kelly's *The Nuer Conquest.*

13. Evans-Pritchard, *The Nuer,* p. 126; Kelly, *The Nuer Conquest.*

14. Otterbein, "The Anthropology of War," p. 740.

15. Evans-Pritchard, *The Nuer;* D. Johnson, *Nuer Prophets;* Kelly, *The Nuer Conquest.*

16. Petherick, *Travels in Central Africa.*

17. Kelly, *The Nuer Conquest,* p. 262.

18. Evans-Pritchard, *The Nuer,* pp. 126–27; D. Johnson, "The Fighting Nuer," p. 513. On the language issue, see Evans-Pritchard, *The Nuer,* pp. 3–4; and D. Johnson, *Nuer Prophets,* p. 36.

19. D. Johnson, "The Tribal Boundaries and Border Wars," p. 185; and *Nuer Prophets,* pp. 36–38, 44–55.

20. Sacks, "Causality and Chance on the Upper Nile," pp. 438–41.

21. On defense/revenge, see Otterbein, *The Evolution of War,* pp. 63–70. For a discussion of the "war system" concept, see Falk and Kim, eds., *The War System,* p. 2.

22. Kelly, "Reply to: 'On the Nuer Conquest' by Sharon Hutchinson," p. 650. An exchange between Hutchinson and Kelly assesses population size, population density, and cattle density (Hutchinson, "On the Nuer Conquest"; Kelly, "Reply to: 'On the Nuer Conquest' by Sharon Hutchinson"). Hutchinson rejects Kelly's "cattle population pressure" hypothesis without offering an explicit alternative hypothesis. Kelly attributes to Hutchinson a population pressure hypothesis, which he believes is drawn from Douglas Johnson's discussion of the influence of periodic floods. Another critique of Kelly's book, by Jan de Wolf, cited by neither Hutchinson nor Kelly, also does not focus on Nuer military efficiency (de Wolf, "Ecology and Conquest"). Expansion is attributed to the desire of some Nuer to become leaders of new communities. However, the need for land, whether it be for people or cattle, does not explain expansion. The missing intervening variable is military superiority. Increased numbers of people and/or cattle do not create that superiority.

23. Evans-Pritchard, *The Nuer*, p. 126.

24. Petherick, *Travels in Central Africa*, 1:319, 321.

25. Ibid., 1:119–20, 138–39.

26. Ibid., 1:131.

27. Ibid., 1:117, 2:11.

28. Seligman and Seligman, *Pagan Tribes of the Nilotic Sudan*, p. 137.

29. D. Johnson, *Nuer Prophets*, pp. 44–55.

30. Evans-Pritchard, *The Nuer*, pp. 253–54.

31. Ibid., pp. 126–28.

32. Quotation from Petherick, *Travels in Central Africa*, 1:319; Deng, *The Dinka of the Sudan*, p. 76.

33. Evans-Pritchard, *The Nuer*, p. 128; for "war companies," see p. 254.

34. Kelly, *The Nuer Conquest*, pp. 51–52, 158.

35. Deng, *The Dinka of the Sudan*, pp. 75–77.

36. Otterbein, *The Evolution of War*, pp. 39–49.

37. See, for example, Kelly, *The Nuer Conquest*, pp. 1–3.

38. In a cross-cultural study of war, I found that thirteen out of forty-three societies had expanding territory; ten of the thirteen expanding societies had a high level of military sophistication. The remaining three seemed to have had neighbors with lesser military ability (Otterbein, *The Evolution of War*, pp. 92–108).

39. Burton, review of *The Nuer Conquest*, by Raymond C. Kelly; de Wolf, "Ecology and Conquest"; Hutchinson, "On the Nuer Conquest."

40. This case study is based upon two articles I published in *Ethnohistory:* Otterbein, "Why the Iroquois Won," and "Huron vs. Iroquois."

41. Snow, "Migration in Prehistory."

42. The classic description of Iroquois sociopolitical organization is Lewis Henry Morgan's *The League of the Iroquois* (1851).

43. In cross-cultural research I have classified them as a "tribe with council, no feuding" because they did not have chiefs that performed economic redistribution (Otterbein, "Killing of Captured Enemies," p. 442), which is Elman Service's criterion for a chiefdom (Service, *Primitive Social Organization*, pp. 167–68).

44. Champlain is quoted in Russell, *Guns on the Early Frontiers*, pp. 2–3.

45. Colden, *The History of the Five Indian Nations*, pp. 7–9.

46. Wood, *Wood's New-England's Prospect, 1634*, pp. 65–67.

47. Much of this description is based on the eyewitness accounts of Jesuit missionaries to the Huron during this period (Thwaites, *The Jesuit Relations and Allied Documents*).

48. Colden, *The History of the Five Indian Nations*, p. 9; Hunt, *The Wars of the Iroquois*, pp. 174–75.

49. The priests probably died knowing that they were martyrs. At least their surviving colleagues left detailed descriptions of their prolonged torture and referred to their agony as martyrdom.

50. For a detailed military analysis of the Campaign of 1649, see my article "Huron vs. Iroquois" (reprinted in Otterbein, *Feuding and Warfare*), which describes the battles in detail. A schematic map showing the ebb and flow of combat over four days accompanies the article.

51. Explanations for why the Iroquois won may be found in Hunt, *The Wars of the Iroquois;* and Tooker, "The Iroquois Defeat of the Huron."

52. Otterbein, "The Evolution of Zulu Warfare," reprinted in Otterbein, *Feuding and Warfare.*

53. Gluckman, *Analysis of a Social Situation in Modern Zululand,* pp. 28–29.

54. Brian Ferguson pointed out to me on November 19, 1995, the importance of the Portuguese slave trade along the coast.

55. Bryant, *Olden Times in Zululand and Natal,* p. 98.

56. Gluckman, "The Individual in a Social Framework."

57. Ritter, *Shaka Zulu,* p. 10.

58. Gluckman, "The Rise of the Zulu Empire," p. 162.

59. Figure 8.1 is modified from a table that appeared in my original study, "The Evolution of Zulu Warfare," published in the *Kansas Journal of Sociology* in 1964.

60. Gluckman, "The Rise of the Zulu Empire," p. 162.

61. For Service's taxonomy, see Service, *Primitive Social Organization.*

Chapter 9

1. Thoden van Velzen and van Wetering, "Residence, Power Groups and Intrasocietal Aggression."

2. Otterbein and Otterbein, "An Eye for and Eye and a Tooth for a Tooth."

3. Otterbein, "Internal War"; and "Cross-Cultural Studies of Armed Combat" (reprinted in Otterbein, *Feuding and Warfare*).

4. W. S. Ferguson, "The Zulus and the Spartans," reviewed in Turney-High, *Primitive War,* p. 83; von Hagen, *Realm of the Incas,* pp. 213–15.

5. Keeley, *War before Civilization;* Otterbein, "The Origins of War"; and "A History of Research on Warfare in Anthropology."

6. Otterbein, "Socialization for War"; and Comment on "Violence and Sociality in Human Evolution," by Bruce Knauft.

7. Steward, *Theory of Culture Change,* p. 192.

8. Service, *Primitive Social Organization,* pp. 143–74; and *Origins of the State and Civilization,* pp. 270–73, 297–99.

9. Otterbein, "The Origins of War," p. 264.

10. Sponsel, "Response to Otterbein"; Whitehead, "A History of Research on Warfare in Anthropology—Reply to Otterbein"; Otterbein, "The Doves Have Been Heard from, Where Are the Hawks?"

11. Recently the doves have launched an all-out assault upon the work of ethnographer Napoleon Chagnon, denying that the people he studies—the Yanomamo—were a warlike people. Chagnon is accused of not only misdescribing them but also creating through misdeeds the Yanomamo violence that is depicted in his ethnographic films (see Begley, "Into the Heart of Darkness"). Fellow anthropologists have defended both Chagnon's ethnographic work as well as the films of the Yanomamo made by him and Timothy Asch (Biella, "Tierney and the Yanomamo Films of Asch and Chagnon"; Ruby, "Tierney's Claims about Tim Asch"; Tooby, "Witchcraft Accusations in Anthropology").

12. A. Mann, "The Humanity of Neanderthal," p. 10.

13. G. Clark, "Neanderthal Archaeology—Implications for Our Origins," p. 58.

14. Kelly, *Peaceful Societies and the Origin of War,* pp. 121–47.

15. Haas, *The Evolution of the Prehistoric State,* pp. 105–106, 192–208.

16. Keegan, *A History of Warfare,* pp. 387–89.

17. O'Connell, *Ride of the Second Horseman.*

18. Karatnycky, "The State of Democracy: 2000," pp. 24, 49.

19. Nietschmann, "Militarization and Indigenous Peoples."

20. Karatnycky, "The State of Democracy," p. 49. But the picture is not clear. I have seen a figure as high as sixty-eight conflicts for 2000 and one as low as thirteen for 1998. The CIA has thirty-one conflicts on its classified list (Associated Press, "Report: Wars on the Rise," p. 6-A). Much depends on definition.

21. Russett and Antholis, "Do Democracies Fight Each Other?"; Russett, *Grasping the Democratic Peace;* Russett and Starr, "Democracy and Conflict in the International System."

22. This view assumes that nondemocratic polities do not splinter into smaller and smaller nondemocratic polities.

23. Russett, *Grasping the Democratic Peace,* p. 4.

24. Bruce Russett attributes the "peace" to "normative restraints on conflicts between democracies" (ibid., p. 119); Amartya Sen stresses the importance of democracy (*Development as Freedom,* in particular chapter 6, pp. 146–59).

Bibliography

Adcock, F. E. *The Greek and Macedonian Art of War.* Berkeley: University of California Press, 1962.

Aldenderfer, Mark S. *Montane Foragers: Asana and the South- Central Andean Archaic.* Iowa City: University of Iowa Press, 1998.

Algaze, Guillermo. "Initial Social Complexity in Southwestern Asia: The Mesopotamian Advantage." *Current Anthropology* 42 (2001): 199-233.

———. "The Uruk Expansion: Cross-Cultural Exchange in Early Mesopotamian Civilization." *Current Anthropology* 30 (1989): 571-608.

Ardrey, Robert. *The Hunting Hypothesis: A Personal Conclusion Concerning the Evolutionary Nature of Man.* New York: Atheneum, 1976.

Associated Press. "Report: Wars on the Rise." *The Post and Courier* (Charleston, S.C.), December 30, 2000, 6-A.

Bachechi, L., P. F. Fabbri, and F. Mallegni. "An Arrow-Caused Lesion in a Late Upper Paleolithic Human Pelvis." *Current Anthropology* 38 (1997): 135-40.

Bacon, Margaret K., Irving L. Child, and Herbert Barry III. "A Cross-Cultural Study of Correlates of Crime." *Journal of Abnormal and Social Psychology* 66 (1963): 291-300.

Bagley, Robert. "Shang Archaeology." In *The Cambridge History of Ancient China: From the Origins of Civilization to 221 B.C.,* edited by Michael Loewe and Edward L. Shaughnessy. Cambridge: Cambridge University Press, 1999.

Baker, Joan Elisabeth. "No Golden Age of Peace: A Bioarchaeological Investigation of Interpersonal Violence on the West Gulf Coastal Plain." Ph.D. dissertation, Texas A&M University, 2001.

Balter, Michael. "In Search of the First Hominids." *Science* 295 (February 15, 2002): 1214-25.

Balter, Michael, and Ann Gibbons. "A Glimpse of Humans' First Journey Out of Africa." *Science* 288 (2000): 948-50.

Barry, John, and Evan Thomas. "The Kosovo Cover-Up." *Newsweek,* May 15, 2000, 22-26.

Bar-Yosef, Ofer. "The Walls of Jericho: An Alternative Interpretation." *Current Anthropology* 27 (1986): 157-62.

Bawden, Garth. *The Moche.* Cambridge, Mass.: Blackwell Publishers, 1996.

Beals, Ralph L., and Harry Hoijer. *An Introduction to Anthropology.* 2nd ed. New York: Macmillan, 1959.

Begley, Sharon. "Into the Heart of Darkness." *Newsweek,* November 27, 2000, 70-75.

Begley, Sharon, and Andrew Murr. "The First American." *Newsweek,* April 26, 1999, 50-57.

Biella, Peter. "Tierney and the Yanomamo Films of Asch and Chagnon." *Anthropology News* 41 (December 9, 2000): 5-6.

Bigelow, Robert. "The Role of Competition and Cooperation in Human Evolution." In *War: Its Causes and Correlates,* edited by Martin A. Nettleship, R. Dale Givens, and Anderson Nettleship. The Hague: Mouton, 1975.

Billman, Brian R., Patricia M. Lambert, and Banks L. Leonard. "Cannibalism, Warfare, and Drought in the Mesa Verde Region during the Twelfth Century A.D." *American Antiquity* 65 (2000): 145-78.

Bingham, Paul M. "Human Evolution and Human History: A Complete Theory." *Evolutionary Anthropology* 9 (2000): 248–57.

Biolsi, Thomas. "Ecological and Cultural Factors in Plains Indian Warfare." In *Warfare, Culture, and Environment,* edited by R. Brian Ferguson. Orlando, Fla.: Academic Press, 1984.

Blanchard, D. Caroline. "Applicability of Animal Models to Human Aggression." In *Biological Perspectives on Aggression,* edited by Kevin J. Flannelly, Robert J. Blanchard, and D. Caroline Blanchard. New York: Alan R. Liss, 1984.

Blanchard, D. Caroline, Mark Hebert, and Robert J. Blanchard. "Continuity vs. Political Correctness: Animal Models and Human Aggression." *The HFG Review: A Publication of the Harry Frank Guggenheim Foundation* 3, no. 1 (1999): 3–12.

Blanton, Richard E. "Beyond Centralization: Steps toward a Theory of Egalitarian Behavior in Archaic States." In *Archaic States,* edited by Gary M. Feinman and Joyce Marcus. Santa Fe, N.Mex.: School of American Research, 1998.

Blitz, John H. "Adoption of the Bow in Prehistoric North America." *North American Archaeologist* 9 (1988): 123–45.

Boehm, Christopher. "Egalitarian Behavior and Reverse Dominance Hierarchy." *Current Anthropology* 34 (1993): 227–54.

———. *Hierarchy in the Forest: The Evolution of Egalitarian Behavior.* Cambridge, Mass.: Harvard University Press, 1999.

Boesch, Christopher, and Michael Tomasello. "Chimpanzee and Human Cultures." *Current Anthropology* 39 (1998): 591–614.

Bohannan, Paul, ed. *Law and Warfare: Studies in the Anthropology of Conflict.* New York: Natural History Press, 1967.

Bower, Bruce. "Ultrasocial Darwinism: Cultural Groups May Call the Evolutionary Shots in Modern Societies." *Science News* 48 (1995): 366–67.

Brackman, Arnold C. *The Other Nuremberg: The Untold Story of the Tokyo War Crime Trials.* New York: William Morrow, 1987.

Bram, Joseph. *An Analysis of Inca Militarism.* American Ethnological Society monograph no. 4. New York: J. J. Augustin, 1941.

Breasted, James H. *Ancient Times, a History of the Early World: An Introduction to the Study of Ancient History and the Career of Early Man.* New York: Ginn and Company, 1916.

———. *The Conquest of Civilization.* Edited by Edith W. Ware. Rev. ed. New York: Literary Guild of America, 1938.

Brown, Barton M. "Population Estimation from Floor Area: A Restudy of 'Naroll's Constant.'" *Behavior Science Research* 21 (1987): 1–49.

Brown, Robert. *Explanation in Social Science.* London: Routledge and Kegan Paul, 1963.

Brumfiel, Elizabeth M. "Aztec State Making: Ecology, Structure, and the Origin of the State." *American Anthropologist* 85 (1983): 261–84.

———. "Factional Competition and Political Development in the New World: An Introduction." In *Factional Competition and Political Development in the New World,* edited by Elizabeth M. Brumfiel and John W. Fox. Cambridge: Cambridge University Press, 1994.

Bryant, Alfred T. *Olden Times in Zululand and Natal, Containing Earlier History of the Eastern-Nguni Clans.* London: Longmans, Green, 1929.

Bunge, Mario. *Causality: The Place of the Causal Principle in Modern Science.* Cambridge, Mass.: Harvard University Press, 1959.

Burenhult, Goran, ed. *People of the Stone Age: Hunter-Gatherers and Early Farmers.* Vol. 2 of *The Illustrated History of Humankind.* New York: Harper Collins, 1993.

Burger, Richard L. *Chavín and the Origins of Andean Civilization.* London: Thames and Hudson, 1992.

Burton, John W. Review of *The Nuer Conquest: The Structure and Development of an Expansionist System,* by Raymond C. Kelly. *American Ethnologist* 14 (1987): 396–97.

Carneiro, Robert. "The Chiefdom: Precursor of the State." In *The Transition to Statehood in the New World,* edited by Grant D. Jones and Robert R. Kautz. Cambridge and New York: Cambridge University Press, 1981.

——— *Evolutionism in Cultural Anthropology: A Critical History.* Boulder, Colo.: Westview Press, 2003.

———. Foreword to *The Evolution of War: A Cross-Cultural Study,* by Keith F. Otterbein. New Haven, Conn.: Human Relations Area Files Press, 1970.

Cartmill, Matt. *A View to a Death in the Morning: Hunting and Nature through History.* Cambridge, Mass.: Harvard University Press, 1993.

Cattelain, Pierre. "Hunting during the Upper Paleolithic: Bow, Spearthrower, or Both?" In *Projectile Technology,* edited by Heidi Knecht. New York: Plenum Press, 1997.

Cauvin, Jacques. *The Birth of the Gods and the Origins of Agriculture.* Translated by Trevor Watkins. Cambridge: Cambridge University Press, 2000.

Cavalli-Sforza, Luigi Luca, and Francesco Cavalli-Sforza. *The Great Human Diasporas: The History of Diversity and Evolution.* Reading, Mass.: Addison-Wesley, 1995.

"Celebrity-Skull Toumai Debated." *Anthropology News* 43, no. 9 (December, 2002): 24.

Chagnon, Napoleon. *Yanomamo: The Fierce People.* 2nd ed. New York: Holt, Rinehart, and Winston, 1977.

Chaliand, Gerard. "Warfare and Strategic Cultures in History." In *The Art of War in World History: From Antiquity to the Nuclear Age,* edited by Gerard Chaliand. Berkeley: University of California Press, 1994.

Chang, Kwang-chih. *The Archaeology of Ancient China.* 4th ed. New Haven: Yale University Press, 1986.

———. "China on the Eve of the Historical Period." In *The Cambridge History of Ancient China: From the Origins of Civilization to 221 B.C.,* edited by Michael Loewe and Edward L. Shaughnessy. Cambridge: Cambridge University Press, 1999.

———. *Shang Civilization.* New Haven: Yale University Press, 1980.

Chapple, Eliot, and Carleton S. Coon. *Principles of Anthropology.* New York: Henry Holt, 1942.

Chatters, James C. "The Recovery and First Analyses of an Early Holocene Human Skeleton from Kennewick, Washington." *American Antiquity* 65 (2000): 291–316.

Childe, V. Gordon. *Man Makes Himself.* Rev. ed. New York: New American Library, 1951.

———. *What Happened in History.* Rev. ed. Harmondsworth, England: Penguin Books, 1954.

Cioffi-Revilla, Claudio. "Ancient Warfare: Origins and Systems." In *Handbook of War Studies II,* edited by Manus I. Midlarsky. Ann Arbor: University of Michigan Press, 2000.

———. "Origins and Age of Deterrence: Comparative Research on Old World and New World Systems." *Cross-Cultural Research* 33 (1999): 239–64.

———. "Origins and Evolution of War and Politics." *International Studies Quarterly* 40 (1996): 1–22.

Cioffi-Revilla, Claudio, and David Lai. "War and Politics in Ancient China, 2700 B.C. to 722 B.C." *Journal of Conflict Resolution* 39 (1995): 467–95.

Claessen, Henri J. M., and Peter Skalnik, eds. *The Early State.* The Hague: Mouton, 1978.

Clark, G. A. "Neanderthal Archaeology—Implications for Our Origins." *American Anthropologist* 104 (2002): 50–67.

Clark, John E., and Michael Blake. "The Power of Prestige: Competitive Generosity and the Emergence of Rank Societies in Lowland Mesoamerica." In *Factional Competition and Political Development in the New World,* edited by Elizabeth M. Brumfiel and John W. Fox. Cambridge: Cambridge University Press, 1994.

Clark, Robert P. *The Global Imperative: An Interpretive History of the Spread of Mankind.* Boulder, Colo.: Westview Press, 1997.

Cohen, Ronald. "Warfare and State Formation: Wars Make States and States Make Wars." In *Warfare, Culture, and Environment,* edited by R. Brian Ferguson. Orlando, Fla.: Academic Press, 1984.

Cohen, Yehudi A. "Ends and Means in Political Control: State Organization and the Punishment of Adultery, Incest, and Violation of Celibacy." *American Anthropologist* 71 (1969): 658–87.

Colden, Cadwallader. *The History of the Five Indian Nations: Depending on the Province of New York in America.* Ithaca, N.Y.: Cornell University Press, 1958.

Corning, Peter A. "Synergy Goes to War: An Evolutionary Theory of Collective Violence." Paper presented at the annual meeting of the Human Behavior and Evolution Society, Rutgers, N.J., June 19–23, 2002.

Coser, Lewis A. *The Functions of Social Conflict.* Glencoe, Ill.: Free Press, 1956.

Cotterell, Arthur. *The First Emperor of China: The Greatest Archeological Find of Our Time.* New York: Holt, Rinehart, and Winston, 1981.

Cowley, Robert, ed. *What If ?: The World's Foremost Military Historians Imagine What Might Have Been.* New York: G. P. Putnam's Sons, 1999.

———. *What If ?* 2: *Eminent Historians Imagine What Might Have Been.* New York: G. P. Putnam's Sons, 2001.

Crawford, Michael H. *The Origins of Native Americans: Evidence from Anthropological Genetics.* Cambridge: Cambridge University Press, 1998.

Creel, Herrlee Glessner. *The Birth of China: A Study of the Formative Period of Chinese Civilization.* 1937. Reprint, New York: Frederick Ungar Publishing, 1954.

———. *The Origins of Statecraft in China,* vol. 1, *The Western Chou Empire.* Chicago: University of Chicago Press, 1970.

Culotta, Elizabeth. "Neanderthals Were Cannibals, Bones Show." *Science* 286 (October 1, 1999): 18–19.

Dart, Raymond A. "*Australopithecus africanus:* The Man-Ape of South Africa." *Nature* 115 (1924): 195–99.

Darwin, Charles. *The Descent of Man and Selection in Relation to Sex.* 1871. New York: P. F. Collier & Son, 1902.

Dawson, Doyne. *The First Armies.* London: Cassell, 2001.

———. *The Origins of Western Warfare: Militarism and Morality in the Ancient World.* Boulder, Colo.: Westview Press, 1996.

Defleur, Alban, Tim White, Patricia Valensi, Ludovic Slimak, and Évelyne Crégut-Bonnoure. "Neandertal Cannibalism at Moula-Guercy, Ardèche, France." *Science* 286 (October 1, 1999): 128–31.

Deng, Francis Mading. *The Dinka of the Sudan.* New York: Holt, Rinehart, and Winston, 1972.

Dentan, Robert K. "The Rise, Maintenance, and Destruction of Peaceable Polities: A Preliminary Essay in Political Ecology." In *Aggression and Peacefulness in Humans and Other Primates,* edited by James Silverberg and J. Patrick Gray. New York: Oxford University Press, 1992.

———. "Surrendered Men: Peaceable Enclaves in the Post-Enlightenment West." In *The Anthropology of Peace and Nonviolence,* edited by Leslie E. Sponsel and Thomas Gregor. Boulder, Colo.: Lynne Rienner, 1994.

de Waal, Frans B. M. *The Ape and the Sushi Master: Cultural Reflections of a Primatologist.* New York: Basic Books, 2001.

———. Comment on "The Social Behavior of Chimpanzees and Bonobos: Empirical Evidence and Shifting Assumptions," by Craig B. Stanford. *Current Anthropology* 39 (1998): 407–408.

de Waal, Frans, and Frans Lanting. *Bonobo: The Forgotten Ape.* Berkeley: University of California Press, 1997.

de Wolf, Jan J. "Ecology and Conquest: Critical Notes on Kelly's Model of Nuer Expansion." *Ethnology* 29 (1990): 341–63.

Diamond, Jared. *Guns, Germs, and Steel: The Fates of Human Societies.* New York: Norton, 1997.

Dickson, D. Bruce. "The Atlatl Assessed: A Review of Recent Anthropological Approaches to Prehistoric North American Weaponry." *Bulletin of the Texas Archaeological Society* 56 (1985): 1–38.

———. *The Dawn of Belief: Religion in the Upper Paleolithic of Southwestern Europe.* Tucson: University Press of Arizona, 1990.

Diesing, Paul. *How Does Social Science Work?* Pittsburgh: University of Pittsburgh Press, 1991.

Dillehay, Thomas D. *The Settlement of the Americas: A New Prehistory.* New York: Basic Books, 2000.

Divale, William T. "The Causes of Matrilocal Residence: A Cross-Ethnohistorical Survey." Ph.D. dissertation, State University of New York at Buffalo, 1974. Published as *Matrilocal Residence in Pre-Literate Society.* Ann Arbor, Mich.: UMI Research Press, 1984.

———. "Migration, External Warfare, and Matrilocal Residence." *Behavior Science Research* 9 (1974): 75–133.

———. *Warfare in Primitive Societies: A Bibliography.* Rev. ed. Santa Barbara, Calif.: ABC-Clio, 1973.

Dollard, John, et al. *Frustration and Aggression.* New Haven: Yale University Press, 1939.

Donnan, Christopher B. *Moche Art and Iconography.* Los Angeles: Latin American Center Publications, University of California, 1976.

Dray, William. *Perspectives on History.* London: Routledge and Kegan Paul, 1980.

Drews, Robert. *The End of the Bronze Age: Changes in Warfare and the Catastrophe ca. 1200 B.C.* Princeton: Princeton University Press, 1993.

Dyer, Gwynne. *War.* New York: Crown, 1985.

Edgerton, Robert B. *Like Lions They Fought: The Zulu War and the Last Black Empire in South Africa.* New York: Free Press, 1988.

———. *Warrior Women: The Amazons of Dahomey and the Nature of War.* Boulder, Colo.: Westview Press, 2000.

Ehrenreich, Barbara. *Blood Rites: Origins and History of the Passions of War.* New York: Metropolitan Books/Holt, 1997.

Ellis, Christopher J. "Factors Influencing the Use of Stone Projectile Tips: An Ethnographic Perspective." In *Projectile Technology,* edited by Heidi Knecht. New York: Plenum Press, 1997.

Ember, Carol R. "Myths about Hunter-Gatherers." *Ethnology* 17 (1978): 439–48.

———. "Residential Variation among Hunter-Gatherers." *Behavior Science Research* 10 (1975): 199–227.

Ember, Melvin, and Keith F. Otterbein. "Sampling in Cross-Cultural Research." *Behavior Science Research* 25 (1991): 217–33.

Engelbrecht, William. *Iroquoia: The Development of a Native World.* Syracuse, N.Y.: Syracuse University Press, 2003.

Engels, Friedrich. *The Origin of the Family, Private Property, and the State.* 1891. Edited by Eleanor Burke Leacock. New York: International Publishers, 1972.

Evans-Pritchard, E. E. *The Nuer: A Description of the Modes of Livelihood and Political Institutions of a Nilotic People.* New York: Oxford University Press, 1940.

Eysenck, H. J. *Crime and Personality.* 3rd ed. London: Routledge and Kegan Paul, 1977.

Fagan, Brian. *Floods, Famines, and Emperors: El Niño and the Fate of Civilizations.* New York: Basic Books, 1999.

Falk, Richard A., and Samuel S. Kim, eds. *The War System: An Interdisciplinary Approach.* Boulder, Colo.: Westview Press, 1980.

Farb, Peter. *Man's Rise to Civilization as Shown by the Indians of North America from Primeval Times to the Coming of the Industrial State.* New York: Dutton, 1968.

Farmer, Malcolm F. "The Origins of Weapon Systems." *Current Anthropology* 35 (1994): 679–81.

Feest, Christian. *The Art of War.* London: John Colmann and Cooper, 1980.

Feinman, Gary. "Scale and Social Organization: Perspectives on the Archaic State." In *Archaic States,* edited by Gary M. Feinman and Joyce Marcus. Santa Fe, N.Mex.: School of American Research, 1998.

Ferdon, Edwin N. *Early Tonga: As the Explorers Saw It, 1616–1810.* Tucson: University of Arizona Press, 1987.

Ferguson, R. Brian. "Violence and War in Prehistory." In *Troubled Times: Violence and Warfare in the Past,* edited by Debra L. Martin and David W. Frayer. Amsterdam: Gordon and Breach Publishers, 1997.

Ferguson, R. Brian, and Neil L. Whitehead, eds. *War in the Tribal Zone: Expanding States and Indigenous Warfare.* Seattle: University of Washington Press, 1992.

———. *War in the Tribal Zone: Expanding States and Indigenous Warfare.* 2nd ed. Santa Fe, N.Mex.: School of American Research, 1999.

Ferguson, W. S. "The Zulus and the Spartans: A Comparison of Their Military Systems." *Varia Africana II.* Harvard African Studies II. Cambridge, Mass.: Harvard University, 1918.

Ferrill, Arther. *The Origins of War from the Stone Age to Alexander the Great.* New York: Thames and Hudson, 1985. Reprint, Boulder, Colo.: Westview Press, 1997.

Firth, Raymond. *We, the Tikopia.* 2nd ed. Boston: Beacon Press, 1963.

Flannery, Kent V. Comment on "The Tortoise and the Hare: Small-Game Use, the Broad-Spectrum Revolution, and Paleolithic Demography," by Mary C. Stiner, Natalie D. Munro, and Todd A. Surovell. *Current Anthropology* 41 (2000): 64–65.

———. "The Ground Plans of Archaic States." In *Archaic States,* edited by Gary M. Feinman and Joyce Marcus. Santa Fe, N.Mex.: School of American Research, 1998.

———. "Zapotec Warfare: Archaeological Evidence for the Battles of Huitzo and Guiengola." In *The Cloud People: Divergent Evolution of the Zapotec and Mixtec Civilizations,* edited by Kent V. Flannery and Joyce Marcus. New York: Academic Press, 1983.

Flannery, Kent V., and Joyce Marcus. "The Origin of War: New ^{14}C Dates from Ancient Mexico." *Proceedings of the National Academy of Science* 100, no. 20 (September 30, 2003): 11801–11805.

Flannery, Tim. *The Eternal Frontier: An Ecological History of North America and Its Peoples.* New York: Atlantic Monthly Press, 2001.

Fortes, Meyer, and E. E. Evans-Pritchard. Introduction to *African Political Systems,* edited by Meyer Fortes and E. E. Evans-Pritchard. London: Oxford University Press, 1940.

Fratkin, Elliot, Eric Abella Roth, and Martha Nathan. "When Nomads Settle: The Effects of Commoditization, Nutrition, and Education on Rendille Pastoralists of Northern Kenya." *Current Anthropology* 40 (1999): 729–35.

Fried, Morton H. *The Evolution of Political Society: An Essay in Political Anthropology.* New York: Random House, 1967.

———. *The Notion of Tribe.* Menlo Park, Calif.: Cummings Publishing, 1975.

———. "Tribe to State or State to Tribe in Ancient China?" In *The Origins of Chinese Civilization,* edited by David N. Keightley. Berkeley: University of California Press, 1983.

Friedman, Meyer, and Ray H. Rosenman. *Type A Behavior and Your Heart.* New York: Fawcett Crest, 1974.

Fruth, Barbara, and G. Hohmann. "How Bonobos Handle Hunts and Harvests: Why Share Food?" In *Behavioral Diversity in Chimpanzees and Bonobos,* edited by C. Boesch, G. Hohmann, and L. F. Marchant. Cambridge: Cambridge University Press, 2002.

Fuller, J. F. C. *A Military History of the Western World: From the Earliest Times to the Battle of Lepanto.* New York: Funk & Wagnalls, 1954.

Gabriel, Richard A. *The Culture of War: Invention and Early Development.* New York: Greenwood Press, 1990.

Gabriel, Richard A., and Donald W. Boose, Jr. *The Great Battles of Antiquity: A Strategic and Tactical Guide to Great Battles That Shaped the Development of War.* Westport, Conn.: Greenwood Press, 1994.

Gabriel, Richard A., and Karen S. Metz. *From Sumer to Rome: The Military Capabilities of Ancient Armies.* New York: Greenwood Press, 1991.

Gabunia, Leo, et al. "Earliest Pleistocene Hominid Cranial Remains from Dmanisi, Republic of Georgia: Taxonomy, Geological Setting, and Age." *Science* 88 (2000): 1019–25.

Gat, Azar. "The Pattern of Fighting in Simple, Small-Scale, Prestate Societies." *Journal of Anthropological Research* 55 (1999): 563–83.

Gearing, Fred. *Priests and Warriors: Social Structures for Cherokee Politics in the 18th Century.* Memoirs of the American Anthropological Association no. 93. *American Anthropologist* 64, no. 5, part 2 (1962).

Gibbons, Ann. "In Search of the First Hominids." *Science* 295 (February 15, 2002): 1214–19.

Ginn, John L. *Sugamo Prison, Tokyo: An Account of the Trial and Sentencing of Japanese War Criminals in 1948, by a U.S. Participant.* Jefferson, N.C.: McFarland & Company, Publishers, 1992.

Gluckman, Max. *Analysis of a Social Situation in Modern Zululand.* Rhodes-Livingstone Papers 28. Manchester: Manchester University Press, 1958.

———. "The Individual in a Social Framework: The Rise of King Shaka of Zululand." *Journal of African Studies* 1, no. 2 (1974): 113–44.

———. "The Rise of the Zulu Empire." *Scientific American* 202 (April, 1960): 157–68.

Goldschmidt, Walter. "A Perspective on Anthropology." *American Anthropologist* 102 (2000): 789–807.

Goodall, Jane. *The Chimpanzees of Gombe: Patterns of Behavior.* Cambridge, Mass.: Belknap Press of Harvard University Press, 1986.

Gore, Rick. "New Find." *National Geographic Magazine* 202 (August, 2002): [frontal material, 10 pages preceding p. 2].

———. "People Like Us." *National Geographic Magazine* 198 (July, 2000): 90–117.

Gould, Stephen Jay. "Introduction: The Scales of Contingency and Punctuation in History." In *Structure and Contingency: Evolutionary Processes in Life and Human Society,* edited by John Bintliff. London: Leicester University Press, 1999.

Gowlett, John A. J. *Ascent to Civilization: The Archaeology of Early Man.* New York: Knopf, 1984.

Gregor, Thomas, ed. *A Natural History of Peace.* Nashville, Tenn.: Vanderbilt University Press, 1996.

Griffiths, Donald F. "Village Fortifications: A Cross-Cultural Validation." M.A. thesis, Department of Anthropology, State University of New York at Buffalo, 1973.

Gumplowicz, Ludwig. *The Outlines of Sociology.* Philadelphia: American Academy of Political and Social Science, 1899.

Guterl, Fred. "All in the Family." *Newsweek,* July 22, 2002, 46–49.

Haas, Jonathan. "The Archaeology of War." *Anthropology News* 44, no. 5 (2003): 7.

———. *The Evolution of the Prehistoric State.* New York: Columbia University Press, 1982.

———. "The Exercise of Power in Early Andean State Development." In *The Origins and Development of the Andean State,* edited by Jonathan Haas, Shelia Pozorski, and Thomas Pozorski. Cambridge: Cambridge University Press, 1987.

———. "War." In *Encyclopedia of Cultural Anthropology,* edited by David Levinson and Melvin Ember. New York: Henry Holt, 1996.

Hallpike, C. R. *The Principles of Social Evolution.* Oxford: Clarendon Press, 1987.

Hanson, Victor Davis. *Carnage and Culture: Landmark Battles in the Rise of Western Power.* New York: Doubleday, 2001.

———. *The Western Way of War: Infantry Battle in Classical Greece.* New York: Oxford University Press, 1989.

Harding, Thomas G. "Obituary: Elman Rogers Service (1921–1996)." *American Anthropologist* 101 (1999): 161–64.

Harris, David R., ed. *The Origins and Spread of Agriculture and Pastoralism in Eurasia.* Washington, D.C.: Smithsonian Institution Press, 1996.

Harris, David R., and G. C. Hillman, eds. *Foraging and Farming: The Evolution of Plant Exploitation*. London: Unwin Hyman, 1989.

Hart, C. W. M., and Arnold R. Pilling. *The Tiwi of North Australia*. New York: Holt, Rinehart, and Winston, 1960.

Hart, C. W. M., Arnold R. Pilling, and Jane C. Goodale. *The Tiwi of North Australia*. 3rd ed. New York: Holt, Rinehart, and Winston, 1988.

Haslip-Viera, Gabriel, Bernard Ortiz de Montellano, and Warren Barbour. "Robbing Native American Cultures: Van Sertima's Afrocentricity and the Olmecs." *Current Anthropology* 38 (1997): 419–41.

Hassig, Ross. *War and Society in Ancient Mesoamerica*. Berkeley: University of California Press, 1992.

Hatch, Orrin. *The Right to Keep and Bear Arms*. Report of the Subcommittee on the Constitution of the Senate Committee on the Judiciary, 97th Cong., 2nd sess., 1982.

Heider, Karl. *Grand Valley Dani: Peaceful Warriors*. 3rd ed. Fort Worth: Harcourt Brace College Publishers, 1997.

———. "The Rashomon Effect." *American Anthropologist* 90 (1988): 73–81.

Henry, Donald O. *From Foraging to Agriculture: The Levant at the End of the Ice Age*. Philadelphia: University of Pennsylvania Press, 1989.

———. "Preagricultural Sedentism: The Natufian Example." In *Prehistoric Hunter-Gatherers: The Emergence of Cultural Complexity,* edited by T. Douglas Price and James A. Brown. Orlando, Fla.: Academic Press, 1985.

Hobhouse, Leonard T., Gerald C. Wheeler, and Morris Ginsberg. *The Material Culture and Social Institutions of the Simpler Peoples*. London: Chapman and Hall, 1915.

Hoh, Erling. "China's Great Enigma: What's Inside the Unexcavated Tomb of Emperor Qin Shihuangdi?" *Archaeology* 54, no. 5 (2001): 34–37.

Holliday, Trenton W. "Evolution at the Crossroads: Modern Human Emergence in Western Asia." *American Anthropologist* 102 (2000): 54–68.

Holling, Holling C. *The Book of Indians*. New York: Platt & Munk, Publishers, 1935.

Homans, George C. *Social Behavior: Its Elementary Forms*. New York: Harcourt, Brace, and World, 1961.

Howard, Michael. *The Causes of Wars and Other Essays*. London: Temple Smith, 1983.

Hsu, Cho-yun. *Ancient China in Transition: An Analysis of Social Mobility, 722–222 B.C.* Stanford, Calif.: Stanford University Press, 1965.

Hublin, Jean-Jacques. "The Quest for Adam." *Archaeology* 52, no. 4 (July/August, 1999): 26–35.

Hunt, George T. *The Wars of the Iroquois*. Madison: University of Wisconsin Press, 1940.

Huntingford, George W. B. "The Political Organization of the Dorobo." *Anthropos* 49 (1954): 123–48.

Hutchinson, Sharon. "On the Nuer Conquest." *Current Anthropology* 35 (1994): 643–51.

Ibn Khaldun. *An Arab Philosophy of History: Selections from the Prolegomena of Ibn Khaldun of Tunis (1332–1406)*. Translated and arranged by Charles Issawi. London: John Murray, 1950.

Itani, Juniciro. "Inequality versus Equality for Coexistence in Primate Societies." In *Dominance, Aggression, and War,* edited by Diane McGuinness. New York: Paragon House, 1987.

Joffe, Alexander H. "Egypt and Syro-Mesopotamia in the 4th Millennium: Implications for the New Chronology." *Current Anthropology* 41 (2000): 113–23.

Johanson, Donald C., and Maitland A. Edey. *Lucy: The Beginnings of Humankind*. New York: Simon and Schuster, 1981.

Johanson, Donald C., and Blake Edgar. *From Lucy to Language*. New York: Simon and Schuster, 1996.

Johnson, Douglas H. "The Fighting Nuer: Primary Sources and the Origins of a Stereotype." *Africa* 51 (1981): 508–27.

———. *Nuer Prophets: A History of Prophecy from the Upper Nile in the Nineteenth and Twentieth Centuries*. Oxford: Clarendon Press, 1994.

———. "Tribal Boundaries and Border Wars: Nuer-Dinka Relations in the Sobat and Zerof Valleys, c. 1860–1976." *Journal of African History* 23 (1982): 183–203.

Johnson, Gregory Alan. "The Changing Organization of Uruk Administration on the Susiana Plain." In *The Archaeology of Western Iran,* edited by F. Hole. Washington, D.C.: Smithsonian Institution Press, 1987.

———. *Local Exchange and Early State Development in Southwestern Iran.* Anthropological Papers, Museum of Anthropology, University of Michigan, no. 51. Ann Arbor: University of Michigan, 1973.

Jones, David E. *Women Warriors: A History.* Washington, D.C.: Brassey's, 1997.

Kang, Bong W. "A Reconsideration of Population Pressure and Warfare: A Protohistoric Korean Case." *Current Anthropology* 41 (2000): 873–81.

Kano, Takayoshi. "Commentary: Social Regulation for Individual Coexistence in Pygmy Chimpanzees (*Pan paniscus*)." In *Dominance, Aggression, and War,* edited by Diane McGuinness. New York: Paragon House, 1987.

———. *The Last Ape: Pygmy Chimpanzee Behavior and Ecology.* Stanford, Calif: Stanford University Press, 1992.

Karatnycky, Adrian. "The State of Democracy: 2000." *American Educator: The Professional Journal of the American Federation of Teachers* 20, no. 2 (Summer, 2000): 23–29, 49–50.

Keegan, John. *A History of Warfare.* New York: Knopf, 1993.

———. *The Mask of Command.* New York: Viking, 1987.

Keeley, Lawrence H. "Giving War a Chance." In *Deadly Landscapes: Case Studies in Prehistoric Southwestern Warfare,* edited by Glen E. Rice and Steven A. LeBlanc. Salt Lake City: University of Utah Press, 2001.

———. *War before Civilization: The Myth of the Peaceful Savage.* New York: Oxford University Press, 1996.

Keeley, Lawrence H., and Daniel Cahen. "Early Neolithic Forts and Villages in NE Belgium: A Preliminary Report." *Journal of Field Archaeology* 16 (1989): 157–76.

Kelly, Raymond C. *The Nuer Conquest: The Structure and Development of an Expansionist System.* Ann Arbor: University of Michigan Press, 1985.

———. *Peaceful Societies and the Origin of War.* Ann Arbor: University of Michigan Press, 2000.

———. Reply to "On the Nuer Conquest" by Sharon Hutchinson. *Current Anthropology* 35 (1994): 647–51.

Kierman, Frank A., Jr. "Phases and Modes of Combat in Early China." In *Chinese Ways in Warfare,* edited by Frank A. Kierman, Jr., and John K. Fairbank. Cambridge, Mass.: Harvard University Press, 1974.

Kline, Richard G. *The Human Career: Human Biological and Cultural Origins.* 2nd ed. Chicago: University of Chicago Press, 1999.

Knauft, Bruce M. "Culture and Cooperation in Human Evolution." In *The Anthropology of Peace and Nonviolence,* edited by Leslie E. Sponsel and Thomas Gregor. Boulder, Colo.: Lynne Rienner, 1994.

———. "The Human Evolution of Cooperative Interest." In *A Natural History of Peace,* edited by Thomas Gregor. Nashville, Tenn.: Vanderbilt University Press, 1996.

Kortlandt, A. "Wild Chimpanzees Using Clubs in Fighting an Animated Stuffed Leopard." In *War: Its Causes and Correlates,* edited by Martin A. Nettleship, R. Dale Givens, and Anderson Nettleship. The Hague: Mouton, 1975.

Kramer, Samuel Noah. *History Begins at Sumer: Twenty-seven "Firsts" in Man's Recorded History.* Garden City, N.Y.: Doubleday, 1959.

Kroeber, Clifton B., and Bernard Fontana. *Massacre on the Gila: An Account of the Last Major Battle between American Indians, with Reflections on the Origin of War.* Tucson: University of Arizona Press, 1986.

Kruk, Janusz, and Sarunas Milisauskas. *The Rise and Fall of Neolithic Societies.* Krakow, Poland: Instytut Archeologii i Etnologii, Polskiej Akademii Nauk, 1999.

Kurtz, Donald V. "The Legitimation of the Aztec State." In *The Early State,* edited by Henri J. M. Claessen and Peter Skalnik. The Hague: Mouton, 1978.

———. *Political Anthropology: Paradigms and Power.* Boulder, Colo.: Westview Press, 2001.

———. "Strategies of Legitimation and the Aztec State." *Ethnology* 23 (1984): 301–14.

Lamb, Harold. *Alexander of Macedon: The Journey to World's End.* Garden City, N.Y.: Doubleday, 1946.

Lambert, Patricia M. "Patterns of Violence in Prehistoric Hunter-Gatherer Societies of Coastal Southern California." In *Troubled Times: Violence and Warfare in the Past,* edited by Debra Martin and Douglas Frayer. Toronto: Gordon and Breach, 1997.

Lathrop, Stacy. "Policy Monitor." *Anthropology News* 41 (November 8, 2000): 26.

Lattimore, Owen. *Inner Asian Frontiers of China.* 2nd ed. 1951. Reprint, Boston: Beacon Press, 1962.

Laughlin, W. S., and A. B. Harper. "Peopling the Continents: Australia and America." In *Biological Aspects of Human Migration,* edited by C. G. N. Mascie-Taylor and Gabriel Ward Lasker. Cambridge: Cambridge University Press, 1988.

Leakey, Richard. *The Origin of Humankind.* New York: Basic Books, 1994.

LeBlanc, Steven A. *Constant Battles: The Myth of the Peaceful, Noble Savage.* New York: St. Martin's Press, 2003.

Lee, Richard B. *The Dobe !Kung.* New York: Holt, Rinehart, and Winston, 1984.

Lee, Richard B., and Irven DeVore, eds. *Man the Hunter.* Chicago: Aldine, 1968.

Legge, A. J., and P. A. Rowley-Conway. "The Exploitation of Animals." In *Village on the Euphrates: From Foraging to Farming at Abu Hureyra,* edited by A. T. M. Moore, G. C. Hillman, and A. J. Legge. Oxford: Oxford University Press, 2000.

Lemonick, Michael D. "How Man Began." *Time,* 143, no. 11 (March 14, 1994): 80–87.

Lévi-Strauss, Claude. "The Social and Psychological Aspects of Chieftainship in a Primitive Tribe: The Nambikuara of Northwestern Mato Grosso." *Transactions of the New York Academy of Sciences* 7 (1944): 16–32. Reprinted in *Comparative Political Systems,* edited by Ronald Cohen and John Middleton. Garden City, N.Y.: Natural History Press, 1967.

Lewin, Roger. *In the Age of Mankind.* Washington, D.C.: Smithsonian Books, 1988.

Lewis, Herbert S. "The Galla State of Jimma Abba Jifar." In *The Early State,* edited by Henri J. M. Claessen and Peter Skalnik. The Hague: Mouton, 1978.

———. *Leaders and Followers: Some Anthropological Perspectives.* Reading, Mass.: Addison-Wesley, 1974.

———. "Warfare and the Origin of the State: Another Formulation." In *The Study of the State,* edited by Henri J. M. Claessen and Peter Skalnik. The Hague: Mouton, 1981.

Lewis, Herbert S., and Sidney M. Greenfield. "Anthropology and the Formation of the State: A Critical Review and an Alternate Formulation." *Anthropology* 7, no. 1 (1983): 1–16.

Lewis, Mark Edward. *Sanctioned Violence in Early China.* Albany: State University of New York Press, 1990.

———. "Warring States: Political History." In *The Cambridge History of Ancient China: From the Origins of Civilization to 221 B.C.,* edited by Michael Loewe and Edward L. Shaughnessy. Cambridge: Cambridge University Press, 1999.

Linton, Ralph. "Nomad Raids and Fortified Pueblos." *American Antiquity* 1 (1944): 28–32.

Liu, Li. "Settlement Patterns, Chiefdom Variability, and the Development of Early States in North China." *Journal of Anthropological Archaeology* 15 (1996): 237–88.

Livingstone, Frank B. "The Effects of Warfare on the Biology of the Human Species." In *War: The Anthropology of Armed Conflict and Aggression,* edited by Morton Fried, Marvin Harris, and Robert Murphy. Garden City, N.Y.: Natural History Press, 1968.

Lorenz, Konrad. *On Aggression.* New York: Harcourt, Brace, and World, 1966.

MacDonald, Douglas H., and Barry S. Hewlett. "Reproductive Interests and Forager Mobility." *Current Anthropology* 40 (1999): 501–23.

Mackey, Carol J. "The Middle Horizon as Viewed from the Moche Valley." In *Chan Chan: Andean Desert City,* edited by Michael E. Moseley and Kent C. Day. Albuquerque: University of New Mexico Press, 1982.

MacNeish, Richard S. *The Origins of Agriculture and Settled Life.* Norman: University of Oklahoma Press, 1992.

Malinowski, Bronislaw. "An Anthropological Analysis of War." *American Journal of Sociology* 46 (1941): 521–50.

————. *Argonauts of the Western Pacific.* London: George Routledge and Sons, 1922.

————. *A Scientific Theory of Culture and Other Essays.* Chapel Hill: University of North Carolina Press, 1944.

————. "War—Past, Present, and Future." In *War as a Social Institution: The Historian's Perspective,* edited by J. Clarkson and T. Cochran. New York: Columbia University Press, 1941.

Malone, Patrick M. *The Skulking Way of War: Technology and Tactics among the New England Indians.* Lanham, Mass.: Madison Books, 1991.

Mann, Alan. "The Humanity of Neanderthal. Listening for the Bones to Speak: Interview with Alan Mann." *Penn: Arts and Sciences,* Spring, 2000, pp. 4–5, 10.

Mann, Michael. *The Sources of Social Power,* vol. 1, *A History of Power from the Beginning to A.D. 1760.* Cambridge: Cambridge University Press, 1986.

Marcus, Joyce. "Aztec Military Campaigns against the Zapotecs: The Documentary Evidence." In *The Cloud People: Divergent Evolution of the Zapotec and Mixtec Civilizations,* edited by Kent V. Flannery and Joyce Marcus. New York: Academic Press, 1983.

————. "Mesoamerican Writing." In *New World and Pacific Civilizations: Cultures of America, Asia, and the Pacific,* edited by Goran Burenhult. New York: Harper Collins, 1994.

————. "The Peaks and Valleys of Ancient States: An Extension of the Dynamic Model." In *Archaic States,* edited by Gary M. Feinman and Joyce Marcus. Santa Fe, N.Mex.: School of American Research, 1998.

Marcus, Joyce, and Kent V. Flannery. *Zapotec Civilization: How Urban Society Evolved in Mexico's Oaxaca Valley.* London: Thames and Hudson, 1996.

Marzke, Mary W. "Joint Functions and Grips of the *Australopithecus afarensis* Hand with Special Reference to the Region of the Capitate." *Journal of Human Evolution* 12 (1983): 197–211.

Maschner, Herbert D. G. "The Evolution of Northwest Coast Warfare." In *Troubled Times: Violence and Warfare in the Past,* edited by Debra Martin and Douglas Frayer. Toronto: Gordon and Breach, 1997.

McGrew, William C. *Chimpanzee Material Culture: Implications for Human Evolution.* Cambridge: Cambridge University Press, 1992.

McManamon, Francis P. "K-Man Undergoes Complete Physical." *Anthropology News* 41 (May 5, 2000): 21–22.

McNeill, William H. *A History of the Human Community,* vol. 1, *Prehistory to 1500.* 5th ed. Upper Saddle River, N.J.: Prentice Hall, 1997.

————. *The Rise of the West.* Chicago: University of Chicago Press, 1963.

McRandle, James H. *The Antique Drums of War.* College Station: Texas A&M University Press, 1994.

Meggers, Betty. "The Transpacific Origin of Meso-American Civilization." *American Anthropologist* 77 (1975): 1–27.

Mellaart, James. *The Neolithic of the Near East.* New York: Charles Scribner's Sons, 1975.

Mercader, Julio, Melissa Panger, and Christopher Boesch. "Excavation of a Chimpanzee Stone Tool Site in the African Rainforest." *Science* 296 (May 24, 2002): 1452–55.

Millett, Allan R. "American Military History: Clio and Mars as 'Pards.'" In *Military History and the Military Profession,* edited by David A. Charters, Marc Milner, and J. Brent Wilson. Westport, Conn.: Praeger, 1992.

Millett, Allan R., and Peter Maslowski. *For the Common Defense: A Military History of the United States.* New York: Free Press, 1984.

Mitani, J. C., and D. P. Watts. "Demographic Influences on the Hunting Behavior of Chimpanzees." *American Journal of Physical Anthropology* 109 (1999): 439–54.

Moore, A. T. M., G. C. Hillman, and A. J. Legge, eds. *Village on the Euphrates: From Foraging to Farming at Abu Hureyra.* Oxford: Oxford University Press, 2000.

Morgan, Lewis Henry. *Ancient Society.* 1877. Reprint, Gloucester, Mass.: Peter Smith, 1963.

———. *League of the Iroquois.* 1851. Reprint, New York: Corinth Press, 1962.

Morris, Desmond. *Manwatching: A Field Guide to Human Behavior.* New York: Harry N. Abrams, 1977.

Morschauser, Joseph. *How to Play War Games in Miniature.* New York: Walker and Company, 1962.

Moseley, Michael E. *The Incas and Their Ancestors: The Archaeology of Peru.* Rev. ed. New York: Thames and Hudson, 2001.

Moseley, Michael E., and Kent C. Day, eds. *Chan Chan: Andean Desert City.* Albuquerque: University of New Mexico Press, 1982.

Murdock, George Peter. *Africa: Its Peoples and Their Culture History.* New York: McGraw-Hill, 1959.

———. *Atlas of World Cultures.* Pittsburgh: University of Pittsburgh Press, 1981.

———. *Social Structure.* New York: Macmillan, 1949.

Murdock, George Peter, and D. O. Morrow. "Subsistence Economy and Supportive Practices: Cross-Cultural Codes I." In *Cross-Cultural Samples and Codes,* edited by Herbert Barry III and Alice Schlegel. Pittsburgh: University of Pittsburgh Press, 1980.

Naroll, Raoul. "Does Military Deterrence Deter?" *Trans-Action* 3, no. 2 (1966): 14–20.

———. "Floor Area and Settlement Population." *American Antiquity* 27 (1962): 249–54.

Nemecek, Sasha. "Who Were the First Americans?" *Scientific American* 283, no. 3 (2000): 80–87.

Newcomb, William W., Jr. "Toward an Understanding of War." In *Essays in the Science of Culture,* edited by Gertrude Dole and Robert Carneiro. New York: Crowell, 1960.

Nietschmann, Bernard. "Militarization and Indigenous Peoples, Introduction: The Third World War." *Cultural Survival Quarterly* 11, no. 3 (1987): 1–16.

Oberg, Kalervo. "Types of Social Structure among the Lowland Tribes of South and Central America." *American Anthropologist* 57 (1955): 472–87.

O'Connell, Robert. *Of Arms and Men: A History of War, Weapons, and Aggression.* New York: Oxford University Press, 1989.

———. "The Origins of War." *MHQ: The Quarterly Journal of Military History* 1, no. 3 (1989): 9–15.

———. *Ride of the Second Horseman.* New York: Oxford University Press, 1995.

Oman, Charles W. C. *The Art of War in the Middle Ages, A.D. 378–1515.* Ithaca, N.Y.: Great Seal Books, 1960.

Oppenheimer, Franz. *The State: Its History and Development Viewed Sociologically.* 1907. Indianapolis: Bobbs-Merrill, 1914.

Otterbein, Charlotte Swanson. "Appendix B: Methodological Aspects of the Military Sophistication Scale." In *The Evolution of War,* by Keith F. Otterbein. New Haven, Conn.: Human Relations Area Files Press, 1970.

Otterbein, Keith F. *The Andros Islanders: A Study of Family Organization in the Bahamas.* Lawrence: University of Kansas Press, 1966.

———. "The Anthropology of War" In *Handbook of Social and Cultural Anthropology,* edited by John J. Honigmann. New York: Rand McNally, 1973.

———. "Basic Steps in Conducting a Cross-Cultural Study." *Behavior Science Notes* 4 (1969): 221–36.

———. "Clan and Tribal Conflict." In *Encyclopedia of Violence, Peace, and Conflict,* edited by Lester R. Kurtz. San Diego, Calif.: Academic Press, 1999.

———. Comment on "Egalitarian Behavior and Reverse Dominance Hierarchy," by Christopher Boehm. *Current Anthropology* 34 (1993): 244.

———. Comment on "The Human Community as a Primate Society," by Lars Rodseth, Richard W. Wrangham, Alisa M. Harrigan, and Barbara Smuts. *Current Anthropology* 32 (1991): 245–47.

———. Comment on "On Semai Homicide," by Robert K. Dentan. *Current Anthropology* 29 (1988): 633–36.

———. Comment on "Reconsidering Violence in Simple Human Societies," by Bruce M. Knauft. *Current Anthropology* 28 (1987): 484–85.

———. Comment on "Violence and Sociality in Human Evolution," by Bruce Knauft. *Current Anthropology* 32 (1991): 413–14.

———. *Comparative Cultural Analysis: An Introduction to Anthropology.* 2nd ed. New York: Holt, Rinehart, and Winston 1977.

———. "Crime." In *The Encyclopedia of Cultural Anthropology*, vol. 1, edited by David Levinson and Melvin Ember. New York: Henry Holt, 1996.

———. "Cross-Cultural Studies of Armed Combat." Studies in International Conflict, Research Monograph no. 1. *Buffalo Studies* 4, no. 1 (1968): 91–109.

———. "The Dilemma of Disarming." In *Cold War and Nuclear Madness: An Anthropological Analysis,* edited by Paul R. Turner, David Pitt, et al. South Hadley, Mass.: Bergin and Harvey Publishers, 1989. Reprinted in Keith F. Otterbein, ed., *Feuding and Warfare: Selected Works of Keith F. Otterbein.* Langhorne, Pa.: Gordon and Breach, 1994.

———. "The Doves Have Been Heard from, Where Are the Hawks?" *American Anthropologist* 102 (2000): 841–44.

———. "Dueling." In *The Encyclopedia of the Martial Arts,* edited by Thomas A. Green. Santa Barbara, Calif.: ABC-Clio Publishing, 2001.

———. *The Evolution of War: A Cross-Cultural Study.* New Haven, Conn.: Human Relations Area Files Press, 1970.

———. *The Evolution of War: A Cross-Cultural Study.* 2nd ed. New Haven, Conn.: Human Relations Area Files Press, 1985.

———. "The Evolution of Zulu Warfare." *Kansas Journal of Sociology* 1 (1964): 27–35.

———. "Feuding: Dispute Resolution or Dispute Continuation?" *Reviews in Anthropology* 5 (1985): 73–83.

———. "Five Feuds: An Analysis of Homicides in Eastern Kentucky in the Late Nineteenth Century." *American Anthropologist* 102 (2000): 231–43.

———. "Higi Armed Combat." *Southwestern Journal of Anthropology* 24 (1968): 195–213.

———. "A History of Research on Warfare in Anthropology." *American Anthropologist* 101 (1999): 794–805.

———. "Huron vs. Iroquois: A Case Study of Inter-Tribal Warfare." *Ethnohistory* 26 (1979): 141–52.

———. "Internal War: A Cross-Cultural Study." *American Anthropologist* 70 (1968): 277–89.

———. "Killing of Captured Enemies: A Cross-Cultural Study." *Current Anthropology* 41 (2000): 439–43.

———. "More on the Nuer Expansion." *Current Anthropology* 36 (1995): 821–23.

———. "Obituary: Raoul Naroll (1920–1985)." *American Anthropologist* 89 (1987): 136–42.

———. "The Origins of War." *Critical Review* 2 (1997): 251–77.

———. "Sampling and Samples—An Update." *Cultural Anthropology Methods Newsletter* 1, no. 2 (1989): 4–5.

———. "Sampling and Samples in Cross-Cultural Studies." *Behavior Science Research* 11 (1976): 107–21.

———. "Socialization for War." Appendix E in *The Evolution of War: A Cross-Cultural Study.* 3rd ed. New Haven, Conn.: Human Relations Area Files Press, 1989.

———. "Socialization for War: A Study of the Influence of Hunting on Warfare." Paper read at American Anthropological Association Annual Meeting, Washington, D.C., November 13, 1989.

———. "Two Styles in Cross-Cultural Research." *Cultural Anthropology Methods Newsletter* 2, no. 3 (1990): 6–7.

———. *The Ultimate Coercive Sanction: A Cross-Cultural Study of Capital Punishment.* New Haven, Conn.: Human Relations Area Files Press, 1986.

———. "Warfare: A Hitherto Unrecognized Critical Variable." *American Behavioral Scientist* 20 (1977): 693–710.

———. "Weapons Control, Warfare, and Warrior Aristocracy." Paper read at the American Anthropological Association Annual Meeting, Washington, D.C., November 20, 1993.

———. "Why the Iroquois Won: An Analysis of Iroquois Military Tactics." *Ethnohistory* 11 (1964): 56–63.

———, ed. *Feuding and Warfare: Selected Works of Keith F. Otterbein.* Langhorne, Pa.: Gordon and Breach, 1994.

Otterbein, Keith F., and Charlotte Swanson Otterbein. "An Eye for an Eye and a Tooth for a Tooth: A Cross-Cultural Study of Feuding." *American Anthropologist* 67 (1965): 1470–82.

Owsley, Douglas W., and Richard L. Jantz. "Biography in the Bones: Skeletons Tell the Story of Ancient Lives and Peoples." *Scientific American Discovering Archaeology,* January/February, 2000, 56–58.

Palmer, Craig T., and Scott A. Wright. "On Cultural-Selection Mechanics." *Current Anthropology* 38 (1997): 447–49.

Parfit, Michael. "Dawn of Humans." *National Geographic Magazine* 198 (December 6, 2000): 40–67.

Pauketat, Timothy R. *The Ascent of Chiefs: Cahokia and Mississippian Politics in Native North America.* Tuscaloosa: University of Alabama Press, 1994.

Peregrine, Peter N. "Cross-Cultural Comparative Approaches in Archaeology." *Annual Review of Anthropology* 30 (2001): 1–18.

———. "Ethnology versus Ethnographic Analogy: A Common Confusion in Archaeological Interpretation." *Cross-Cultural Research* 30 (1996): 316–29.

———. "Raoul Naroll's Contribution to Archaeology." *Cross-Cultural Research* 28 (1994): 351–63.

Perlmutter, David D. *Visions of War: Picturing Warfare from the Stone Age to the Cyber Age.* New York: St. Martin's Press, 1999.

Perrin, Noel. *Giving Up the Gun: Japan's Reversion to the Sword, 1543–1879.* Boston: David R. Godine, 1979.

Peters, Ralph. *Fighting for the Future: Will America Triumph?* Mechanicsburg, Pa.: Stackpole Books, 1999.

Petherick, John. *Travels in Central Africa and Explorations of the Western Nile Tributaries by Mr. and Mrs. Petherick.* 2 vols. London: Tinsley Brothers, 1869.

Piggott, Stuart. *Wagon, Chariot, and Carriage: Symbol and Status in the History of Transport.* New York: Thames and Hudson, 1992.

Pilling, Arnold R. "Discussion: Predation and Warfare." In *Man the Hunter,* edited by R. B. Lee and I. DeVore. Chicago: Aldine, 1968.

———. "Sneak Attacks." In *The Tiwi of North Australia,* C. W. M. Hart, Arnold R. Pilling, and Jane C. Goodale. 3rd ed. New York: Holt, Rinehart, and Winston, 1988.

Pollock, Susan. *Ancient Mesopotamia: The Eden That Never Was.* Cambridge: Cambridge University Press, 1999.

Possehl, Gregory L. "Sociocultural Complexity without the State: The Indus Civilization." In *Archaic States,* edited by Gary M. Feinman and Joyce Marcus. Santa Fe, N.Mex.: School of American Research, 1998.

Postgate, J. N. *Early Mesopotamia: Society and Economy at the Dawn of History.* London: Routledge, 1992.

Price, T. Douglas, and James A. Brown, eds. *Prehistoric Hunter-Gatherers: The Emergence of Cultural Complexity.* Orlando, Fla.: Academic Press, 1985.

Radcliffe-Brown, A. R. *The Andaman Islanders.* Cambridge: Cambridge University Press, 1922.

Redman, Charles L. *The Rise of Civilization: From Early Farmers to Urban Society in the Ancient Near East.* San Francisco: W. H. Freeman and Company, 1978.

Rice, Glen E., and Steven A. LeBlanc, eds. *Deadly Landscapes: Case Studies in Prehistoric Southwestern Warfare.* Salt Lake City: University of Utah Press, 2001.

Ritter, E. A. *Shaka Zulu: The Rise of the Zulu Empire.* New York: G. P. Putnam's Sons, 1957.

Rivers, William H. R. *The Todas.* London: Macmillan, 1906.

Roper, Marilyn Keyes. "Evidence of Warfare in the Near East from 10,000–4,300 B.C." In *War: Its Causes and Correlates,* edited by Martin A. Nettleship, R. Dale Givens, and Anderson Nettleship. The Hague: Mouton, 1975.

———. "A Survey of the Evidence for Intrahuman Killing in the Pleistocene." *Current Anthropology* 10 (1969): 427–59.

Ross, Marc Howard. "Social Structure, Psychocultural Dispositions, and Violent Conflict: Extensions from a Cross-Cultural Study." In *Aggression and Peacefulness in Humans and Other Primates,* edited by James Silverberg and J. Patrick Gray. New York: Oxford University Press, 1992.

Roth, Eric Abella. "On Pastoral Egalitarianism: Consequences of Primogeniture among the Rendille." *Current Anthropology* 41 (2000): 267–71.

Rowley-Conway, Peter. "Abu Hureyra: The World's First Farmers." In *People of the Stone Age: Hunter-Gatherers and Early Farmers.* Vol. 2 of *The Illustrated History of Humankind,* edited by Goran Burenhult. New York: Harper Collins, 1993.

Ruby, Jay. "Tierney's Claims about Tim Asch." *Anthropology News* 41 (December 9, 2000): 7.

Russell, Carl P. *Guns on the Early Frontiers.* Berkeley: University of California Press, 1957.

Russett, Bruce, and William Antholis. "Do Democracies Fight Each Other? Evidence from the Peloponnesian War." *Journal of Peace Research* 29 (1992): 415–34.

Russett, Bruce M., and Harvey Starr. "Democracy and Conflict in the International System." In *Handbook of War Studies II,* edited by Manus Midlarsky. Ann Arbor: University of Michigan Press, 2000.

Russett, Bruce, with contributions by William Antholis, Carol R. Ember, Melvin Ember, and Zeev Maoz. *Grasping the Democratic Peace: Principles for a Post–Cold War World.* Princeton: Princeton University Press, 1993.

Sacks, Karen. "Causality and Chance on the Upper Nile." *American Ethnologist* 6 (1979): 437–47.

Salzman, Philip Carl. "Toward a Balanced Approach to the Study of Equality." *Current Anthropology* 42 (2001): 281–84.

Sanders, Andrew. "Warriors, Anthropology of." In *Encyclopedia of Violence, Peace, and Conflict,* edited by Lester R. Kurtz. San Diego, Calif.: Academic Press, 1999.

Scott, John F. *The Danzantes of Monte Alban.* 2 vols. Studies in Pre-Columbian Art and Archaeology no. 19. Washington, D.C.: Trustees of Harvard University, Dumbarton Oaks Publishing Service, 1978.

Scupin, Raymond, and Christopher R. DeCorse. *Anthropology: A Global Perspective.* 3rd ed. Upper Saddle River, N.J.: Prentice Hall, 1998.

Seligman, C. G., and Brenda Z. Seligman. *Pagan Tribes of the Nilotic Sudan.* London: Routledge and Kegan Paul, 1932.

Sen, Amartya. *Development as Freedom.* New York: Knopf, 1999.

Service, Elman R. *Origins of the State and Civilization.* New York: Norton, 1975.

———. *Primitive Social Organization: An Evolutionary Perspective.* New York: Random House, 1962.

Shaughnessy, Edward L. "Historical Perspectives on the Introduction of the Chariot into China." *Harvard Journal of Asiatic Studies* 48 (1988): 189–237.

———. "Western Zhou History." In *The Cambridge History of Ancient China: From the Origins of Civilization to 221 B.C.,* edited by Michael Loewe and Edward L. Shaughnessy. Cambridge: Cambridge University Press, 1999.

Shea, John J. "Middle Paleolithic Spear Point Technology." In *Projectile Technology,* edited by Heidi Knecht. New York: Plenum Press, 1997.

———. "Neanderthals, Competition, and the Origin of Modern Human Behavior in the Levant." *Evolutionary Biology* 12 (2003): 173–88.

Shiels, Dean. "A Comparative Study of Human Sacrifice." *Behavior Science Research* 15 (1980): 245–62.

Shimada, Izumi. *Pampa Grande and the Mochica Culture.* Austin: University of Texas Press, 1994.

Siddle, D. A. T. "Electrodermal Activity and Psychopathy." In *Biosocial Bases of Criminal Behavior,* edited by Sarnoff A. Mednick and Karl O. Christianson. New York: Gardner Press, 1977.

Smith, Maria O. "Osteological Indications of Warfare in the Archaic Period of the Western Tennessee Valley." In *Troubled Times: Violence and Warfare in the Past,* edited by Debra Martin and Douglas Frayer. Toronto: Gordon and Breach, 1997.

Snow, Dean R. "Migration in Prehistory: The Northern Iroquoian Case." *American Antiquity* 60 (1995): 59–79.

Sociobiology Study Group of Science for the People. "Sociobiology—Another Biological Determinism." *Bioscience* 26, no. 3 (1976): 182, 184–86.

Spencer, Herbert. *The Principles of Sociology.* Vol. 2. New York: D. Appleton, 1896.

Spitzer, Steven. "Notes toward a Theory of Punishment and Social Change." *Research in Law and Sociology* 2 (1979): 207–29.

———. "Punishment and Social Organization: A Study of Durkheim's Theory of Penal Evolution." *Law and Society Review* 9 (1975): 613–37.

Sponsel, Leslie E. "The Natural History of Peace: A Positive View of Human Nature and Its Potential." In *A Natural History of Peace,* edited by Thomas Gregor. Nashville, Tenn.: Vanderbilt University Press, 1996.

———. "Response to Otterbein." *American Anthropologist* 102 (2000): 837–41.

Sponsel, Leslie E., and Thomas Gregor, eds. *The Anthropology of Peace and Non-violence.* Boulder, Colo.: Lynne Rienner, 1994.

Stanford, Craig B. *The Hunting Apes: Meat Eating and the Origins of Human Behavior.* Princeton: Princeton University Press, 1999.

———. *Significant Others: The Ape-Human Continuum and the Quest for Human Nature.* New York: Basic Books, 2001.

———. "The Social Behavior of Chimpanzees and Bonobos: Empirical Evidence and Shifting Assumptions." *Current Anthropology* 39 (1998): 399–420.

Stefánsson, Vilhjálmur. *My Life with the Eskimo.* New York: Macmillan, 1913.

Steward, Julian H. *Handbook of South American Indians,* vol. 4, *The Circum-Caribbean Tribes.* Bureau of American Ethnology Bulletin 143. Washington, D.C.: Smithsonian Institution, 1948.

———. *Theory of Culture Change.* Urbana: University of Illinois Press, 1955.

Steward, Julian H., and Louis C. Faron. *The Native Peoples of South America.* New York: McGraw-Hill, 1959.

Stiner, Mary C., Natalie D. Munro, and Todd A. Surovell. "The Tortoise and the Hare: Small-Game Use, the Broad-Spectrum Revolution, and Paleolithic Demography." *Current Anthropology* 41 (2000): 39–73.

Sussman, Robert W. "The Myth of Man the Hunter/Man the Killer and the Evolution of Human Morality." In *The Biological Basis of Human Behavior,* edited by Robert W. Sussman. Upper Saddle River, N.J.: Prentice Hall, 1999.

Tacon, Paul S., and Christopher Chippendale. "Australia's Ancient Warriors: Changing Depictions of Fighting in the Rock Art of Arnhem Land, N. T." *Cambridge Archaeological Journal* 4 (1994): 211–48.

Tattersall, Ian. *The Last Neanderthal: The Rise, Success, and Mysterious Extinction of Our Closest Human Relatives.* Rev. ed. Boulder, Colo.: Westview Press, 1999.

Tattersall, Ian, and Jeffrey H. Schwartz. *Extinct Humans.* Boulder, Colo.: Westview Press, 2000.

Teggart, Frederick J. *Rome and China: A Study of Correlations in Historical Events.* Berkeley: University of California Press, 1939.

Thieme, Harmut. "Lower Paleolithic Hunting Spears from Germany." *Nature* 385, no. 6619 (1999): 807–10.

Thoden van Velzen, H. U. E., and W. van Wetering. "Residence, Power Groups, and Intrasocietal Aggression." *International Archives of Ethnography* 49 (1960): 169–200.

Thomas, David Hurst. *Archaeology: Down to Earth.* 2nd ed. Fort Worth: Harcourt Brace College Publishers, 1999.

———. *Exploring Ancient North America: An Archaeological Guide.* New York: Macmillan, 1994.

Thwaites, Reuben G., ed. *The Jesuit Relations and Allied Documents . . . 1610–1791.* 73 vols. Cleveland: Burrows, 1896–1901.

Tiger, Lionel. *Men in Groups.* New York: Random House, 1969.

Tooby, John. "Witchcraft Accusations in Anthropology." *Anthropology News* 41 (December 9, 2000): 8.

Tooker, Elizabeth. "The Iroquois Defeat of the Huron: A Review of Causes." *Pennsylvania Archaeologist* 33 (1963): 115–23.

Topic, John, and Theresa Topic. "The Archaeological Investigation of Andean Militarism: Some Cautionary Observations." In *The Origins and Development of the Andean State,* edited by Jonathan Haas, Shelia Pozorski, and Thomas Pozorski. Cambridge: Cambridge University Press, 1987.

Turney-High, Harry H. *Primitive War: Its Practice and Concepts.* Columbia: University of South Carolina Press, 1994.

Tusa, Ann, and John Tusa. *The Nuremberg Trial.* London: Macmillan, 1995.

van der Dennen, Johan. *The Origin of War: The Evolution of a Male-Coalitional Reproductive Strategy.* Groningen, the Netherlands: Origin Press, 1995.

Vayda, Andrew P. "Expansion and Warfare among Swidden Agriculturalists." *American Anthropologist* 63 (1961): 346–58.

———. "Explaining Why Marings Fought." *Journal of Anthropological Research* 45 (1989): 159–77.

———. "Phases of the Process of War and Peace among the Marings of New Guinea." *Oceania* 44 (1971): 1–24.

Vencl, Slavomil. "Stone Age Warfare." In *Ancient Warfare: Archaeological Perspectives,* edited by John Carman and Anthony Harding. Phoenix Mill, England: Sutton Publishing, 1999.

Vogel, Gretchen. "Can Chimps Ape Ancient Hominid Toolmakers?" *Science* 296 (May 24, 2002): 1308.

von Hagen, Victor W. *Realm of the Incas.* New York: Mentor Books, 1957.

Walker, Alan, and Pat Shipman. *The Wisdom of the Bones: In Search of Human Origins.* New York: Knopf, 1996.

Walker, Phillip. "A Bioarchaeological Perspective on the History of Violence." *Annual Review of Anthropology* 30 (2001): 573–96.

Washburn, Sherwood L., ed. *The Social Life of Early Man.* Chicago: Aldine, 1961.

Washburn, Sherwood L., and C. S. Lancaster. "The Evolution of Hunting." In *Man the Hunter,* edited by R. B. Lee and I. DeVore. Chicago: Aldine, 1968.

Webb, Malcolm C. "The Flag Follows Trade: An Essay on the Necessary Interaction of Military and Commercial Factors in State Formation." In *Ancient Civilization and Trade,* edited by Jeremy A. Sabloff and C. C. Lamberg-Karlovsky. Albuquerque: University of New Mexico Press, 1975.

———. Review of *The Early State,* by Henri J. M. Claessen and Peter Skalnik. *Reviews in Anthropology* 11 (1984): 270–81.

Webster, David. "Warfare and the Evolution of the State: A Reconsideration." *American Antiquity* 40 (1975): 464–70.

———. "Warfare and Status Rivalry: Lowland Maya and Polynesian Comparisons." In *Archaic States,* edited by Gary M. Feinman and Joyce Marcus. Santa Fe, N.Mex.: School of American Research, 1998.

Weiss, Kenneth M. "In Search of Times Past: Gene Flow and Invasion in the Generation of Human Diversity." In *Biological Aspects of Human Migration,* edited by C. G. N. Mascie-Taylor and G. W. Lasker. Cambridge: Cambridge University Press, 1988.

Wells, H. G. *Little Wars.* 1913. Reprint, New York: Macmillan, 1970.

Wendorf, Fred, ed. *The Prehistory of Nubia.* Dallas: Southern Methodist University Press, 1968.

Wendorf, Fred, and Romuald Schild. "The Wadi Kubbaniya Skeleton: A Late Paleolithic Burial from Southern Egypt." In *The Prehistory of Wadi Kubbaniya,* edited by Angela Close. Dallas: Southern Methodist University Press, 1986.

Wenke, Robert J. *Patterns in Prehistory: Humankind's First Three Million Years.* 4th ed. New York: Oxford University Press, 1999.

Wenli, Zhang. *The Qin Terracotta Army: Treasures of Lintong.* London: Scala Books and Cultural Relics Publishing House, 1996.

White, Leslie A. *The Science of Culture.* New York: Grove Press, 1949.

Whitehead, Neil L. "A History of Research on Warfare in Anthropology—Reply to Otterbein." *American Anthropologist* 102 (2000): 834–37.

Whiten, A., J. Goodall, W. C. McGrew, T. Nishida, V. Reynolds, Y. Sugiyama, C. E. G. Tutin, R. W. Wrangham, and C. Boesch. "Cultures in Chimpanzees." *Nature* 399, no. 6737 (1999): 682–85.

Whittaker, John C., and Grant McCall. "Handaxe-Hurling Hominids: An Unlikely Story." *Current Anthropology* 42 (2001): 566–72.

Wilcox, David R., and Jonathan Haas. "The Scream of the Butterfly: Competition and Conflict in the Prehistoric Southwest." In *Themes in Southwest Prehistory,* edited by George J. Gumerman. Santa Fe, N.Mex.: School of American Research Press, 1994.

Willey, Gordon R. *Prehistoric Settlement Patterns in the Viru Valley, Peru.* Bulletin No. 155. Washington, D.C.: Bureau of American Ethnology, 1953.

Willey, Patrick S. *Prehistoric Warfare on the Great Plains: Skeletal Analysis of the Crow Creek Massacre Victims.* New York: Garland Publishing, 1990.

Wilson, David J. "Reconstructing Patterns of Early Warfare in the Lower Santa Valley: New Data on the Role of Conflict in the Origins of Complex North Coast Society." In *The Origins and Development of the Andean State,* edited by Jonathan Haas, Shelia Pozorski, and Thomas Pozorski. Cambridge: Cambridge University Press, 1987.

Wilson, Edward O. *On Human Nature.* Cambridge, Mass.: Harvard University Press, 1978.

———. *Sociobiology: The New Synthesis.* Cambridge, Mass.: Harvard University Press, 1975.

Wintringham, Tom. *The Story of Weapons and Tactics from Troy to Stalingrad.* Boston: Houghton Mifflin, 1943.

Wolf, Eric. *Europe and the People without History.* Berkeley: University of California Press, 1982.

Wood, William. *Wood's New-England's Prospect, 1634.* Boston: Publication of the Prince Society, 1865.

Woodburn, James. "Egalitarian Societies." *Man,* n.s., 17 (1982): 431–51.

Wooley, C. Leonard. *The Sumerians.* New York: Norton, 1965.

———. *Ur of the Chaldees.* Harmondsworth, England: Penguin Books, 1950.

Wrangham, Richard W., and Dale Peterson. *Demonic Males: Apes and the Origins of Human Violence.* Boston: Houghton Mifflin, 1996.

Wright, Henry T. "The Southern Margins of Sumer: Archaeological Survey of the Area of Eridu and Ur." Appendix to *Heartland of Cities: Surveys of Ancient Settlement and Land Use on the Central Floodplain of the Euphrates,* by Robert McC. Adams, Chicago: University of Chicago Press, 1981.

———. "Uruk States in Southwestern Iran." In *Archaic States,* edited by Gary M. Feinman and Joyce Marcus. Santa Fe, N.Mex.: School of American Research, 1998.

Wright, Quincy. *A Study of War.* Chicago: University of Chicago Press, 1942.

Wu, Kuo-Cheng. *The Chinese Heritage.* New York: Crown Publishers, 1982.

Yadin, Yigail. *The Art of Warfare in Biblical Lands: In the Light of Archaeological Study.* 2 vols. New York: McGraw-Hill, 1963.

Zubrow, Ezra. "The Demographic Modeling of Neanderthal Extinction." In *The Human Revolution: Behavioural and Biological Perspectives on the Origins of Modern Humans,* edited by P. Mellars and C. Stringer. Edinburgh: Edinburgh University Press, 1989.

Index

Abraham and Isaac, 198
Abu Hureyra, 70, 71, 222–23, 241 n.7
acculturation theory, 28
action theory, 20
Adcock, F. E., 155–56
Africa, 39, 50, 63, 64, 87, 114; Kenya, 40, 53; Nubia, 84, 237 n.32; Sudan, 73–74
agency (concept), 20–21
aggression, 5, 9; innate, 26–27; result of frustration, 252–53 n.11
agriculture and agriculturalists, 15, 199; and China, 164; and Mesoamerica, 123; and Mesopotamia, 142–43, 145–46; origin of, 3, 7, 11, 32, 70, 91, 92–96; peace in early period, 222–23; and Peru, 131, 134, 135; and rise of the state, 96–100; transition to, 220; and village life, 241 n.1. *See also* animals, domestic and domestication of; irrigation; plants, domestic and domestication of; village
Akkadians, 187, 236 n.9
Alda, Alan, 233 n.37
Alexander the Great, 154, 155–56, 188, 251 n.151
Alfred the Great, 184
alliances, 112, 116, 120
alpha male, 232 n.25
Alvard, Mike, xv
ambush, 10, 41, 48, 91; and early humans, 60, 61, 62; and hunter-gatherers, 73, 77, 83, 84, 86; and Iroquois, 211; and leader selection, 80; and Nuer, 207; and un-centralized political systems, 199, 202, 256 n.8
Anatolia, 98, 99
animals, domestic and domestication of, 15, 67–69, 94–96, 179, 190, 199, 241 n.12; alpaca, 135; cattle, 143, 146; cow, 95; dog, 123; goat, 95, 143, 146; guinea pig, 134; guanaco, 134; horse, 95, 157, 163, 166, 171, 205; llama, 95, 134–35, 142; pig, 95, 158; sheep, 95, 143, 146, 156; yak, 95; and warfare decline, 70
animals, prey, 36, 59, 68–70, 95, 122, 236 n.15; aquatic animals, 60, 65; and agri-

culture, 94; antelope, 122; baboon, 53; bison, 15, 60; camel, 59; carnivores not preferred, 66–67; and climate change, 67; collared peccarie, 122; deer, 60, 122, 134; extinction of birds, 67; extinction of large game, xiii, 12, 13, 66–68, 90, 221; fish, 60; gazelle, 95, 194, 241 n.13; giant baboon, 40, 66; giant ground sloth, 134; guanaco, 134; guinea pig, 134; horse, 40, 50, 54, 59, 62, 66, 67, 95, 122; hunting and warfare, 67–68, 89; kangaroo, 15; lion, 15; mammoth, 59, 66, 67, 121–22; marine life, 134; quail, 122; rat, 122; rabbit, 122; red colobus monkey, 49; reindeer, 67, 95; squirrel, 122; turtle, 122; and warfare decline and large game, 241 n.87, 241 n.88. *See also* nutrition
anthropology and anthropologists, 22, 27, 31, 33, 83, 236 n.15
Anuta, 81
Anyang, 168, 251 n.154
archaeology and archaeologists, 9–10, 16, 17, 56, 84, 93, 141, 173
Ardrey, Robert, 27, 85–86
Aristotle, 19, 105
archers, 171; in China, 168, 169; in Mesopotamia, 156–57, 158; rock art depiction of, 73. *See also* bows
armor, 117–18, 149, 154–55, 168, 210, 249 n.100. *See also* helmets; shields
Art of War, The (Sun Tzu), 172
Asch, Timothy, 258 n.11
Asia, 7, 39
assassination, 9, 72, 80, 117
Assize of Arms (1181), 184
Assyrians, 251 n.151
atlatl. *See* spear thrower
Australia, 58, 67, 71, 73, 235 n.85
Australopithecus, 26, 27, 39, 51, 53–54, 233 n.37, 233 n.50
Aztec: atlatl use, 65; a chiefdom, 256 n.11; and internal conflict theory, 244 n.70; not a pristine state, 244 n.65; and state legitmation, 108, 244 n.70; and Za-potec, 129

ISBN 1-58544-329-8

DATE DUE

Demco, Inc. 38-293